Managing Religious Diversity in the Workplace

Managing Religious Diversity in the Workplace

Examples from Around the World

Edited by

STEFAN GRÖSCHL
ESSEC Business School, Paris, France

REGINE BENDL
*Vienna University of Economics and Business
(WU Vienna), Austria*

Routledge
Taylor & Francis Group

LONDON AND NEW YORK

First published 2015 by Gower Publishing

2 Park Square, Milton Park, Abingdon, Oxfordshire OX14 4RN
52 Vanderbilt Avenue, New York, NY 10017

Routledge is an imprint of the Taylor & Francis Group, an informa business

First issued in paperback 2019

British Library Cataloguing in Publication Data
A catalogue record for this book is available from the British Library.

Library of Congress Cataloging-in-Publication Data
Gröschl, Stefan.
    Religious diversity in the workplace : lessons from around the world / by Stefan Gröschl and Regine Bendl.
        pages cm
    Includes bibliographical references and index.
    ISBN 978-1-4724-4106-5 (hardback : alk. paper) – ISBN 978-1-4724-4108-9 (ebook) – ISBN 978-1-4724-4107-2 (epub)
    1. Religion in the workplace. 2. Management – Religious aspects. 3. Work – Religious aspects. 4. Employees – Religious life. I. Bendl, Regine, 1963– II. Title.

BL65.W67G76 2015
331.5'8–dc23

2014044633

ISBN 13: 978-1-4724-4106-5 (hbk)
ISBN 13: 978-0-367-60612-1 (pbk)

Contents

List of Figures

List of Tables

Editors' Biographies

Stefan Gröschl is full Professor at the ESSEC Business School Paris/Singapore. He has published four books on diversity management, leadership and aspects of international human resources management. Stefan is widely known as a diversity management expert and has shared his expertise in a wide range of academic and public arenas. His research has also been published in numerous book chapters and articles in both the trade and academic press. Stefan is an editorial board member of several international journals within the area of diversity management and human resources management. His research has brought him to assignments in a wide range of academic institutions in Mexico, Taiwan, Spain, New Zealand, Germany, Bahrain and France.

Regine Bendl is Associate Professor, Institute for Gender and Diversity in Organizations at the Vienna University of Economics and Business. Regine carries out research on gender and diversity management, subtexts and queer perspectives in organization theory. An author and editor of numerous books, her writings have been published in *Gender Work and Organization*, *Journal of Management and Organization*, *British Journal of Management*, *Gender in Management – An International Journal*, *European Journal of International Management*, *Equality, Diversity and Inclusion – An International Journal*. She is Convenor of the EGOS Standing Working Group of Gender and Diversity (2010–2016). She has received a number of professional awards, including the Käthe Leichter Award for Women's and Gender Studies 2006, a Best Paper Award EURAM 2007 (stream gender equality and diversity in management) and an Emerald Highly Recommended Paper Award 2009 and 2013. She edits *Equality, Diversity and Inclusion – an International Journal* and *Diversitas – Zeitschrift für Managing Diversity und Diversity Studies* and is an editorial board member of *Gender in Management – An International Journal* and the *British Journal of Management* as well as associate editor of *Gender Work and Organization*.

About the Contributors

Tri Wulida Afrianty is a lecturer at the Department of Business Administration in the Faculty of Administrative Science at University of Brawijaya, Indonesia where she completed her Business Administration degree. She holds a Master of Science in Management certificate from Gadjah Mada University, Indonesia, and a Master in Human Resource Management certificate from Monash University, Australia. She received her PhD from the School of Management, Curtin University, Australia. Her research interests include international human resource management (IHRM) and human resource management (HRM) in Indonesia, and more recently mentoring in the workplace, and work and family issues. She has published her research in several major journals in Indonesia. She was also involved in several projects on human resource practices for Indonesian public organizations. She is actively developing research network with researchers from Indonesia and other countries.

Celia de Anca is currently the Director of the Saudi–Spanish Centre for Islamic Economics and Finance at IE Business School, and the Centre for Diversity in Global Management at IE Business School. She was previously the Director of Corporate Programmes at the Euro–Arab Management School (EAMS), Granada. She has also worked for the Fundación Cooperación Internacional y Promoción Ibero-América Europa. (CIPIE) and at the International Division of Banco de Santander. She has a master's degree from the Fletcher School of Law and Diplomacy (Boston), and from the Universidad Politécnica de Madrid. She holds a degree and a PhD from the Universidad Autónoma de Madrid, with a comparative thesis on Islamic, ethical/ecological investment funds and on the London Market. She is the author of *Beyond Tribalism*, 2012, and co-author of *Managing Diversity in the Global Organization*, 2007. She has had articles published in specialised journals, in addition to regular articles in the press. She was an external advisor of the Merrill Lynch's Diversity & Inclusion Council up to 2009. She is a member of the Ethics Committee of InverCaixa's Ethics Fund, Spain and a member of the International Scientific Committee of the University Euromed in Marseille, France. She is also member of the Executive Committee at IE Business School. She has received the Women Executive of the Year 2008 award from the Business Women Association of Madrid (ASEME). She is fluent in Spanish, English, French and Arabic. She is listed in the 2013 top 50 thinkers ranking of global management thinkers: http://www.thinkers50.com/biographies/celia-de-anca/.

Vincent Bagire is a senior lecturer and current Head of the Department of Business Administration at Makerere University Business School, Kampala Uganda. He has taught in universities for over 17 years. His teaching and research areas are corporate strategy, strategic management, general management, organizational theory and business administration. He has published in these areas both locally and internationally. For over ten years, he worked with various offices and projects of the Catholic Church where he shared many ideas on management principles and practices relevant to church leadership. For over 20 years he has run a series of periodical articles in *Leadership Magazine* – a local publication of the Comboni Missionaries in which he shares management insights for Christian Leaders. His contributions to this volume are based on his personal and professional exposure in working for a religious institution as well as religiously diverse organizations. He is currently focusing research attention on management theory and practices in the African context.

Desiderio Barungi Begumisa has been a lecturer for over 30 years handling secretarial professional programs. He has written textbooks, policy papers and study documents in this discipline. He has studied, practised and taught entrepreneurship development for the past few years at the Faculty of Entrepreneurship and Business Administration at Makerere University Business School, Kampala. He has served as a sports tutor for college students for over 20 years and is a national sports icon. During this successful teaching and professional career he has worked with people of all religious beliefs. He has observed that religious tolerance is key to the social fabric of Ugandan society. He has worked in religiously diverse institutions while practising his own faith but found this a rich organizational value when understood and handled well. He has read widely about the early years of the mainstream Christian institutions in Uganda and follows their current events to this day.

John Burgess is a Professor of HRM, School of Management, Curtin University, Perth, Australia. Research interests include gender and work; labour market policies; workplace participation; contingent employment arrangements; and job quality. Recent books include: *Resources and Competitive Advantage in Clusters* (2013); *Diversity Management in Australia: Theory and Practice* (2013); and *Method in Madness: Research Stories You Will Not Find in the Text Books* (2009).

Nasima Mohamed Hoosen Carrim is a Senior Lecturer in the Human Resource Department at the University of Pretoria, South Africa. She teaches diversity management at both the undergraduate and post-graduate levels. Her main academic interests include gender in management, identity, culture, religion and minorities in the workplace. Her PhD research focused on the identity work Indian women managers engage in during their upward mobility in corporate South Africa. She is currently researching the challenges South African Indian males experience in reaching senior and top managerial positions.

Frank J. Cavico is a Professor of Business Law and Ethics at the H. Wayne Huizenga School of Business and Entrepreneurship of Nova Southeastern University in Ft. Lauderdale, Florida. He has been involved in an array of teaching responsibilities, at the undergraduate, master's and doctoral levels, encompassing such subject matter areas as business law, government regulation of business, constitutional law, administrative law and ethics, labour law and labour relations, healthcare law and business ethics. In 2000, he was awarded the Excellence in Teaching Award by the Huizenga School; and in 2007 and 2012 he was awarded the Faculty Member of the Year Award by the Huizenga School of Business and Entrepreneurship. In 2014, he was named Professor of the Year by the Huizenga School. He holds a J.D. from the St Mary's University School of Law, an LL.M from the University of San Diego, School of Law, and is a member of the Florida and Texas Bar Associations. He is the author and co-author of several books and numerous law review and management journal articles.

Rana Haq is Assistant Professor at the School of Commerce and Administration in the Faculty of Management at Laurentian University in Sudbury, Ontario, Canada. She teaches undergraduate and graduate courses on campus and online in organizational behaviour and human resource management. Her research is primarily in the area of employment equity and managing diversity in the workplace, focusing particularly on Canada and India. Her work has been published in journals including the *International Journal of Human Resource Management, Gender in Management: An International Journal, European Journal of Industrial Relations, Journal of International Migration and Integration*, and *Entrepreneurial Practice Review*. She has also contributed to several international book chapters on equality and diversity in organizations.

Theordora Issa is multi-award winner, Senior Lecturer at Curtin University, Australia, and a visiting Professor at a European Business School, where she developed teaching material and continues to facilitate a Sustainable Development Business Strategies unit for students of the Master of

International Business (2010–to date). Currently, she is overseeing the final stages of publication of her two co-edited books *International Business Ethics and Growth Opportunities*, and *Empowering Organizations through Corporate Social Responsibility*. Further, she is conducting her research on ethical mindsets, spirituality and aesthetics working on a manuscript for a book on *Ethical Mindsets: A Comparative Study*. Her research is published in credible peer-reviewed journals in the areas of ethics, sustainability, teaching and learning. She is one of the webmasters of her community's website, http://soca.cjb.net (since 1995), and is one of the editors of the weekly bulletin since 1995 that is currently available online under from http://noohro.cjb.net. She is a member at the World Council of Churches (WCC) (a) appointed a delegate to WCC 10th Assembly (2012) held in South Korea, (b) elected member of the WCC Central Committee, Geneva, Switzerland (2013) and, (c) elected member of Education and Ecumenical Formation Commission of WCC, Geneva, Switzerland (2014).

Assya Khiat is a Professor at the University of Oran Es-Senia, where she is responsible for the PhD programmes in management and marketing, human resources, and the master's programme in HRM and communication. She is also a trainer for HRM-related skills and marketing competencies. She has led various audits within the human resources and corporate social responsibility area, and she holds research positions at REFEIRI (Economic Reformations for the Regional and International) and LAREEM (Research Laboratory on Savings (Economies) Euro-Mediterranean). She has published her research in textbooks, book chapters, international journals and conferences.

Koen Van Laer works as a Professor in the rank of lecturer at the Faculty of Business Economics at Hasselt University (Belgium), where he is a member of SEIN, a research group whose research focuses on identity, diversity and inequality. His main research interests are ethnicity, religion and sexual orientation at work, the way 'difference' is managed and constructed in organizations, and the way it influences workplace experiences and careers. He draws inspiration from a wide variety of theoretical traditions and perspectives, such as critical approaches to management, postcolonial theory, and discursive approaches focusing on power, resistance and identity. His work has appeared in books as well as in international journals such as *Human Relations* and *Scandinavian Journal of Management*.

Jasmin Mahadevan is a Professor of International Management with a special focus on Cross-Cultural Management at the School of Engineering, Pforzheim University, Germany. Trained in international business and in cultural anthropology, she works on how cultures and identities are constructed socially in international organizational and engineering fields and links this understanding to sociological theory and organization studies. This includes methodological contributions to understanding difference and otherness in organizational research, and to ethnographic writing and auto-ethnography. Her main research interests besides organizational ethnography are cross-cultural management theory and paradigms, intercultural engineering, and diversity, culture and identity. She has published in the *International Journal of Cross-Cultural Management, Journal of Organizational Change Management, Qualitative Research in Organizations and Management* and *Organizational Ethnography.*

Wolfgang Mayrhofer is Full Professor and Head of the Interdisciplinary Institute of Management and Organisational Behaviour, Department of Management, WU Vienna (Vienna University of Economics and Business), Austria. He previously has held full-time research and teaching positions at the University of Paderborn, Germany, and at Dresden University of Technology, Germany, after receiving his diploma and doctoral degrees in Business Administration from WU. He conducts research in comparative international HRM and leadership, work careers, and systems theory and management and has received several national and international rewards for outstanding research and service to the academic community. He has authored, co-authored and co-edited 27 books, more than 110 book chapters and 70 peer-reviewed articles. He is a member of the editorial board of several international journals and an associate at the Centre for Research into the Management of Expatriation (Cranfield, UK), a research fellow at the Simon Fraser University Centre for Global Workforce Strategy (Vancouver, Canada), and a member of the academic advisory board of AHRMIO, the Association of Human Resource Management in International Organisations. His teaching assignments both at the graduate and executive level and his role as visiting scholar have led him to many universities around the globe.

Nathalie Montargot is an Associate Professor in the Sup de Co La Rochelle, France, and a Member of the Chair of Change at the ESSEC Business, France. Her doctoral dissertation in Management Science was led by Professor Jean-Marie Peretti and focused on the integration of young people with low educational capital in the hospitality industry. Her key research interests focus on HRM, and in particular issues related to diversity, change, well-being, and organizational socialization and personal interactions in the workplace.

Farid Moukkes is a Maitre Assistant and doctoral student at the University of TiziOuzou, Algeria. Farid is also a trainer in the area of HRM, crisis management and organizational behaviour at the Higher International

Management Institute of TiziOuzou. His teaching assignments and research interests include HRM, humanism, research methods and organizational behaviour-related aspects.

Bahaudin G. Mujtaba is Professor of Management and Human Resources at the H. Wayne Huizenga School of Business and Entrepreneurship of Nova Southeastern University in Ft. Lauderdale, Florida. Bahaudin is the author and co-author of several professional and academic books dealing with diversity, ethics and business management, as well as numerous academic journal articles. During the past 25 years he has had the pleasure of working with human resource professionals in the United States, Brazil, Bahamas, Afghanistan, Pakistan, St. Lucia, Grenada, Malaysia, Japan, Vietnam, China, India, Thailand and Jamaica. This diverse exposure has provided him many insights in ethics, culture and management from the perspectives of different firms, groups of people and countries. Bahaudin can be reached at: mujtaba@nova.edu.

Rev. Gabriel Ezekia Nduye is a Tanzanian PhD candidate at the University of KwaZulu-Natal, College of Humanities, School of Religion Philosophy and Classics in South Africa. He has done intensive work around issues of ecology and theology, African eco-theological framework in the context of unjust economic order, ICTs and development, adverse impact of globalization, engendering climate change and the role of the church for social transformation. Based on the discipline of theology and development, his doctoral work pays attention to the interface between climate change, agriculture and Christian ethics with special reference in the African context in general and Tanzania in particular. On this basis, his research interest extends to public theology as expressed in the workplace and other public areas of African ethics of care as well as transformation theologies, exploring what contribution theology can make in the public realm.

Sylvie St-Onge, PhD, CHRP, ASC, holds a doctorate in organizational behaviour and industrial relations from the Schulich School of Business at York University in Toronto. Her areas of expertise encompass governance and HRM and, more specifically, compensation, performance, diversity, harassment and work–family balance. In addition to having written several scientific articles on these topics, she is the author or co-author of four books published by La Chenelière Education on compensation management, HRM, performance management and managerial skills. She is also editor or co-editor of four handbooks on performance management, career management and managing your career. She has been Director (Vice-Principal) for Research at HEC Montreal (2001–2004) and Editor and Publisher of *Gestion, revue internationale* *de gestion* (2007–13). Among her community involvements, she is currently Vice-Chair of College Ahuntsic (a community college).

Rupali Pardasani is a Research Scholar at Management Development Institute, Gurgaon, India (MDI). She is pursuing the Fellow Programme in Management in the area of Organizational Behaviour at MDI. Prior to this, she worked as Assistant Professor of HR/OB at an affiliate institute of Guru Gobind Singh Indraprastha University, Delhi. She holds a Master's and a Bachelors degree in Business Administration. Her research interests include leadership, positive-psychology, spirituality in the workplace and humanistic management.

Kathy Sanderson is a PhD Candidate in the Sobey School of Business at St Mary's University in Halifax, Nova Scotia, Canada. She works at Lakehead University in Thunder Bay, Ontario, Canada as a lecturer in prganizational behaviour, organizational change and strategic HRM. Her research interests include organizational culture and change, power, ethics and women in management. Her dissertation examines the impact of workplace ostracism on employees, from a gendered perspective. Kathy also works as the Program Coordinator for the Cross Cultural Care Program at Sioux Lookout Meno Ya Win Heath Centre and is the Executive Director of Crossroads Centre, an alcohol and drug recovery home in Thunder Bay.

Radha R. Sharma is ICCR Chair of Corporate Responsibility & Governance, HHL Leipzig Graduate School of Management, Germany, and Hero Honda Chair Professor & Professor, Organizational Behaviour and Human Resource Development at the Management Development Institute, (MDI), India. She has successfully completed research projects supported by the World Health Organization (WHO); UNESCO; McClelland Centre for Research and Innovation; IDRC, Canada, Government of India and Humanistic Management Network. She is recipient of AIMS International 'Outstanding Management Researcher Award' (2008) and 'Best Faculty Award: Excellence in Research' (2007 and 2006) at Management Development Institute, India and 'Outstanding Editor Award, 2007' *AIMS International Journal of Management* (USA); First Runners-up Research Paper 2008, World SME Conference co-author and Best Paper Award, IJTD (2013 and 2003). Her research interests include emotional intelligence, stress and burnout, humanistic management, spirituality in management, gender diversity, leadership and organizational transformation.

Martin A. Steinbereithner is research associate at the Department of Nonprofit Management at the WU Vienna (Vienna University of Economics and Business Administration). He received his diploma from WU, then joined a Christian missionary organization and worked as a youth and student worker for 15 years in England, the USA and Lebanon. From 2004 to 2013 he was responsible for organizational and mission development in his organization for Europe, the Middle East and Africa. In 2000 he returned to his alma mater and received his doctorate in organizational behaviour in 2004. His academic interests include management of not for profit organizations (NPOs), careers in not for profit organizations, managerialism, HRM in NPOs, and spirituality and management. Martin is an urban monk, part of an international, Christian religious order called 'The Servants of the Word'. Currently he works as novice master for this order in the training centre in Ann Arbor, Michigan.

Vivien T. Supangco is Professor at the University of the Philippines Virata School of Business. She handles courses in the undergraduate, MBA and PhD levels in such areas as organization theory, organizational behaviour, HRM, business research and general management. She is the contact person in the Philippines of two cross-cultural research networks: The Consortium for the Cross-Cultural Study of Contemporary Careers (5C), and Cranfield Network on Comparative Human Resource Management (CRANET). Her research interests are in career development and management, international HRM, corporate governance, organization diagnosis and design, gender and family issues in organizations, and corporate culture and organization development.

Shiva Taghavi is a doctoral candidate in the Department of Management and Human Resources at HEC Paris. Her research revolves around values, beliefs and identities, and their impact on attitudes and behaviours in the workplace. Growing up in Iran, working as a female engineer in a male-dominated industry, and later, working and studying as an immigrant in France, drew her attention to the importance of communication between multiple identities and its effects on attitudes and behaviour. In her dissertation she looks at the interaction between cultural and religious values and the way they influence work ethic. She has also worked in the area of multiple identities with a focus on gender-professional and bicultural identity integration/conflict.

Chapter 1

Introduction

REGINE BENDL AND STEFAN GRÖSCHL

This book provides a collection of texts dealing with religious and spiritual perspectives in organizations and societies, as there has been much debate about religious and spiritual diversity in the workplace in many countries around the world. From a secular perspective, religious and spiritual identity as a key characteristic of personal identity has moved into the centre of societal, political and organizational attention. Much of this debate has had negative connotations with the focus often being religious militantism, dogmatic prejudices, uncompromising and excluding attitudes, and religious worshipping practices and ceremonies disrupting organizational life and performance. Often, organizational contexts are considered as 'religious neutral' spaces without considering the fact that organizations operate in contexts shaped by religions in general, and often by unmarked and implicit religious norms in particular. Depending on the context, many (mostly secular) observers propose the exclusion of all religious- and spiritual-related aspects from organizational life, others promote a more tolerant approach to certain practices, symbols and ceremonies, and a few commentators highlight the benefits that the values, diverse religious beliefs and experiences of employees could bring to the organization. Arguments, conclusions and recommendations are often contradictive and inconclusive due to the complexity and dividing nature of religious and spiritual diversity and to the different cultural, political and legal contexts.

Our motivation for this book was to collect and present examples of how religious and spiritual diversity is managed in the workplace. In general, we wanted to understand how organizations address organizational and managerial challenges deriving from the religiously diverse backgrounds of their employees (believer/non-believer, spiritual or non-spiritual persons, different religions, and so on). As editors of this book who are working in the field of diversity in management and organizations, not only do we have a great scholarly interest in the topic but believe that scholarly interest goes far beyond the organizational boundaries and the workplace: it is the context and the relational perspective between the micro, meso and macro context (Syed and Özbilin, 2009; Tatli and Özbilgin, 2012; Tatli, Vassilopoulou, Al Ariss, and Özbilgin, 2012) which matters and influences the workplace and organizational practices of managing religion and spirituality. Thus, this collection on *Managing Religious Diversity at the Workplace: Examples from Around the World* addresses two levels: organizational practices as well as macro socio-political and/or legal perspectives. The chapters provide many organizational examples which address the different religious and spiritual beliefs of employees on the one hand and refer to cultural, socio-political and legal country perspectives on the other hand. The wide range of geographically different contexts covered in the book provide the reader with insights as to how organizational practices differ culturally when it comes to managing the religious and spiritual diversity of employees, and how religion and spirituality (re)produce workplace arrangements.

We have chosen regions as the structuring principle for the book, starting with the North American region, comprising chapters about Canada and the United States. Part II covers Africa, referring to South Africa, Uganda, Tanzania and Algeria. Part III represents the Middle East and Asia with chapters covering the United Arab Emirates, India, the Philippines and Indonesia. Last but not least, Part IV deals with European perspectives from Spain, Belgium and Germany. What all these texts have in common, despite their different cultural, political and legal contexts, is the fact that they show how religion and spirituality are deeply ingrained in organizational, societal and national values, cultures and laws and that they represent discursive elements which shape organizational, societal, legal and national as well as cultural discourse. In detail the chapters of this collection read as follows:

The first part of this book, the North American context, starts with religious and spiritual diversity in the Canadian context. In 'Accommodations in Religious Matters: Quebec and Canadian Perspectives', Sylvie St-Onge offers an overview of the state of law and practice in Canadian and Quebec organizations regarding accommodation based on religious grounds. Next, in 'Accommodating Religious Diversity in the Canadian Workplace: The Hijab Predicament in Quebec and Ontario', Rana Haq presents two stories of Hijabi women from two Canadian provinces. Haq demonstrates exemplarily why modern, educated, professional women are choosing to wear the hijab of their own free will despite facing challenges in Canadian society and the workplace. The third chapter within the Canadian context, 'Spirituality Meets Western Medicine: Sioux Lookout Meno Ya Win Health Centre', written by

Kathy Sanderson, covers spiritual aspects of aboriginal/indigenous people. She presents a case study on the Sioux Lookout Meno Ya Win Health Centre which serves as a model of best practice, in which all spiritual and religious beliefs are considered and encouraged in order to include traditional, cultural practices as complementary to mainstream Western medicine based upon the specific needs of the service community. Another North American, but USA-oriented, chapter is 'Islam in American Organizations: Legal Analysis and Recommendations' by Bahaudin G. Mujtaba and Frank J. Cavico. In the text, the authors analyse the US civil rights laws prohibiting religious and national origin discrimination, harassment and retaliation against employees in the context of Muslim, Arab and Arab American employees, and provide recommendations to employers on avoiding religious discrimination claims pursuant to US civil rights laws.

The second part of the book marks a shift to the African context and presents the role of spirituality and religion in four different African countries: Nassima Carrim describes how the changes in the socio-political landscape, namely from the Apartheid to the Post-Apartheid era, affected socio-religious developments in the South African context. In 'Managing Religious Diversity in the South African Workplace', Carrim focuses on the theoretical component of managing diverse religions, provides legal case studies and presents interview results with Muslim and Hindu female and male mangers. Next, Vincent Bagire and Desiderio Barungi Begumisa show how religious diversity is practised within different institutions in the Ugandian context. In their chapter on 'Practices of Managing Religious Diversity in Institutions: Lessons from Uganda', the authors highlight different institutions that have cemented harmony despite religious diversity among members. The next chapter within the African context focuses on Tanzania. In 'Rethinking Religious Diversity Management in Schools: Experience from Tanzania', Gabriel Ezekia Nduye explores actions which help to ensure the successful management of religious diversity in the workplace. In his chapter, Nduye uses a case study approach focusing on secondary schools in Tanzania. The last chapter of this part, written by Assya Khiat, Nathalie Montargot and Farid Moukkes, explores human resource (HR) practices and Ramadan in Algeria. In their chapter titled 'Are There Paths towards a New Social Pact during the Month of Ramadan? The Specific Case of Algerian Companies', the authors show how Ramadan influences HR practices in Algerian organizations.

In Part III of this collection, which refers to the Middle East and Asia, Celia de Anca explores the role of women in Islamic banking in the United Arab Emirates in her chapter 'Women in Islamic Banks in the United Arab Emirates: Tradition and Modernity'. For the Indian context, Radha R. Sharma and Rupali Pardasani present a chapter on 'Management of Religious Diversity by Organizations in India'. The authors discuss the concept of religious diversity in the workplace along with strategies for religious tolerance, and implications for human resources management (HRM) professionals for practising their religion/faith. In the chapter 'Managing Workplace Diversity of Religious Expressions in the Philippines', Vivien T. Supangco explores the ways by which organizations manage the diversity of religious expressions in the Philippines. She identifies the various forms of religious expressions in local and multinational companies and examines differences in policies and practices. Next, in the context of Indonesian higher education institutions, Tri Wulida Afrianty, Theodora Issa and John Burgess provide empirical evidence of the relationship between religiosity support usage and employees' work attitudes and behaviours. In their chapter 'Work-based Religiosity Support in Indonesia', the authors come to the conclusion that there is a negative correlation between religiosity support usage and employees' performance specific to the job requirement in the selected Indonesian higher education context.

Finally, the last part of the book brings the reader to the European context. In the their chapter 'Religion and Spirituality — the Blind Spot of Business Schools? Empirical Snapshots and Theoretical Reflections', Wolfgang Mayrhofer and Martin A. Steinbereithner proceed from the assumption that religion and spirituality represent a blind spot for the goals and values of business schools in their daily routines, infrastructure and in their leadership education curricula. In order to address this blind spot, the authors take an exploratory look at two top European Business schools. In the next the chapter on 'Managing Muslim Employees and Islamic Practices at Work: Exploring Elements Shaping Policies on Religious Practices in Belgian Organizations', Koen Van Laer aims to advance the understanding of the way organizations approach the management of Islam, Muslim employees and Islamic practices. Based on interviews in three Belgian organizations, this chapter explores how organizations deal with religions at work, especially with the different material and discursive elements that shape, influence or constrain the adoption of polices regarding Islamic practices. 'Performing Religious Diversity: Atheist, Christian, Muslim and Hindu Interactions in Two German R&D Companies' is the last chapter discussing the European context. In her text, Jasmin Mahadevan links multiple levels of analysis to reflect on imbalances of power, mainly the intersections between structure and agency. Mahadevan takes a performative stance and explores what people actually do when 'being religious' in the workplace, and links the meaning derived from these doings to larger structures, contexts and discourses on religion. The concluding chapter of this collective book focuses on 'Religious Stimuli in the Workplace and Individual

Performance: The Role of Abstract Mindset', written by Shiva Taghavi. In this conceptual chapter the author highlights the relationship between religious cues in the workplace and the individual's work behaviour.

This book is the first collection of texts on religious and spiritual organizational practices and the workplace. It contributes to the literature by providing an insight into how religious and spiritual diversity is managed in organizations and societies. As such, it complements the scholarly discourse in Management and Organization Studies on religion and spirituality (for example, Tracey, Phillips, Lounsbury 2014a, and texts published in the *Journal of Management, Spirituality and Religion*).

We believe that this book represents an important milestone in exploring and better understanding religious and spiritual diversity within organizational contexts across national borders. Like Tracey et al. (2014b, p. 5) we assume that the study of spirituality and religion in management and organizational contexts may 'generate significant novel insights on a range of topics and issues — such as identity, culture and motivation — with clear relevance for organizations of all kinds'. As such, this book represents another piece of moving religious and spiritual perspectives from the margin to the centre of Management and Organization Studies and of unveiling 'norm' and 'otherness' of spirituality and religion in organizational contexts and the workplace.

References

Tracey, P., Phillips, N. and Lounsbury, M. (2014a). *Religion and Organization Theory*. Emerald, Bingley.

Tracey, P., Phillips, N. and Lounsbury, M. (2014b). Taking Religion Seriously in the Study of Organizations. In Tracey, P., Phillips, N. and Lounsbury, M. (eds) *Religion and Organization Theory*. Emerald, Bingley: 3–21

Syed, J. and Özbilgin, M. (2009). 'A Relational Framework for International Transfer of Diversity Management Practices', *The International Journal of Human Resource Management*, 20(12): 2435–53.

Tatli, A. and Özbilgin, M.F. (2012). 'An Emic Approach to Intersectional Study of Diversity at Work: A Bourdieuan Framing', *International Journal of Management Reviews*, 14(2): 180–200.

Tatli, A., Vassilopoulou, J., Al Ariss, A. and Özbilgin, M. (2012). 'The Role of Regulatory and Temporal Context in the Construction of Diversity Discourses: The Case of the UK, France and Germany', *European Journal of Industrial Relations*, 18(4): 293–308.

PART I
North America

Chapter 2

Accommodations in Religious Matters: Quebec and Canadian Perspectives

SYLVIE ST-ONGE

Introduction

Over the past few decades, Canada has absorbed a considerable flow of immigrants relative to its population, in contrast to many other Western countries which have sharply curtailed immigration flows. As a result, in Toronto, Canada's largest metropolis, more than 50 per cent of the population is actually constituted of visible or linguistic 'minorities'. In Montreal, Canada's second largest city, more than 50 per cent of the pupils enrolled with the Montreal School Board have at least one parent who was born outside of Canada. One outcome of such large immigration flows is that Canadian society is now increasingly diverse.

This chapter offers an overview of the state of the law and practice in Canadian and Quebec organizations regarding accommodation based on religious grounds. We begin by presenting the exclusionary effect that accommodations are intended to mitigate. We then explain the debate on reasonable accommodations in light of the opposite perspectives that people may adopt. We also look at how Canadian courts define religious beliefs and we explain the State's obligation of neutrality and its duty to protect freedom of religion. We then illustrate the legal obligation of reasonable accommodation by citing various cases involving religion and the accommodations that have been imposed on or voluntarily adopted by employers. Finally, we explain and illustrate the concept of undue hardship justifying decisions to refuse accommodation.

Under Law, There is Injustice if There are Exclusionary Effects

History and experience have shown that people tend to value other individuals with customs and appearance which resemble their own and to reject, or at best tolerate, those who are perceived as different. The term for this is *ethnocentrism* or the tendency to prefer one's own group or culture and to perceive members of other groups or cultures in a less favourable light (Groupe Conseil Continuum, 2005). Ethnocentrism leads to *prejudice*, which is a preconceived positive or negative opinion about people or things based on certain characteristics. It also leads to *stereotypes*, whereby people attribute certain behaviours to a person on the grounds of their membership in a group; an example would be presuming an employee's reaction to a change solely on the basis of their ethnic origin, gender, age and so on. As Banon and Chanlat (2012) point out, 'the fact that a person has a North African sounding name does not necessarily mean that person is Muslim'. Indeed, many Muslim citizens act no differently than Catholics, Protestants, Jews or non-believers, and indeed even have common values.

All accommodation measures, but particularly those of a religious nature, are a source of social tension and debate in Canada. Such accommodations might be seen as 'privileges' that threaten the equality of citizens. However, as we will argue here, these accommodations are in fact a *natural consequence* of the right to equality; religious minorities have the right to preserve their differences from the majority by being granted accommodations in relation to uniformly applied standards that have an adverse effect on their freedom of religion. There remains a tendency within both workplaces and society at large to equate equality and justice with *formal*, uniform and equal or identical treatment, without regard for the differences, identities or specific realities of certain groups and their individual members. This occurs regularly, whether during hiring or in the course of employment, such as in the assignment of tasks, work schedules, vacation, disciplinary action, layoffs and so on. According to Brunelle (2008), the strong tendency of unions to negotiate the protection of seniority rights reflects this desire to counter 'employer arbitrariness' by urging the employer to treat all employees equally, based on a single, objective criterion that is common to all.

However, as Table 2.1 below shows, an apparently neutral condition of employment that is adopted in good faith for business reasons and that is applicable to all employees can be discriminatory (real injustice) if it has the effect of imposing a disadvantage or penalties on an individual or group that it does not impose on the other individuals (often members of the majority) to whom it may apply. This raises the issue of the distinction between equality and equity. While direct discrimination of the type 'We don't hire people belonging to group X' is clearly illegal, the principle of equity aims to correct indirect discrimination that arises when the uniform application of a rule that appears to be neutral and justified in practice excludes certain individuals because of a specific characteristic (unequal results or effects). For example, the requirement to work every other Saturday or scheduling an exam on a Saturday without offering the possibility of an alternative arrangement is more prejudicial to people who observe the Sabbath than to Christians.

Table 2.1   **Equality versus equity principles**

Equality Principle	Equity Principle
Declares that all individuals enjoy the rights and freedoms proclaimed and guaranteed by the charters.* It seeks the elimination of all forms of discrimination on the prohibited grounds covered by the charters.	Opposes the uniform and systematic application of standards or rules that leads to injustice or unequal treatment in terms of its effects or results. It advocates the diversity of means by taking into account the specific characteristics of individuals/groups in order to place them on an equal footing.

*   Quebec Charter of Human Rights and Freedoms [online], Retrieved on 26 January 2015 from http://www2.publicationsduquebec.gouv.qc.ca/dynamicSearch/telecharge. php?type=2&file=/C_12/C12_A.html; Canadian Charter of Rights and Freedoms [online], http://laws-lois.justice.gc.ca/eng/Const/index.html. Both retrieved 26 January 2015.

Discrimination in this context means 'practices or attitudes that have, whether by design or impact, the effect of limiting an individual's or a group's right to the opportunities generally available because of attributed rather than actual characteristics. What is impeding the full development of the potential is not the individual's capacity but an external barrier that artificially inhibits growth'.[1] Thus, for a practice to be considered a source of injustice, it is sufficient to have exclusionary effects that are deemed discriminatory.

To summarize, identical treatment of staff in a context of diversity can lead to oppressive and unfair consequences by failing to recognize the identity of members of minorities and forcing them to adopt the hegemonic model of the majority (Woehrling, 2007). As we will see below, the duty to accommodate does

---

1   Excerpt from the Report of the Commission on Equality of Employment (1984) (also known as the Abella Report), quoted by *Québec (Commission des droits de la personne et des droits de la jeunesse)* v. *Montréal (Ville)*; *Québec (Commission des droits de la personne et des droits de la jeunesse)* v. *Boisbriand (Ville)*, 2000 S.C.C. 27, [2000] 1 S.C.R. 665.

not require the withdrawal of a rule that is justified, but rather the mitigation of its effects on these individuals in the form of an exception, an exemption or a special adjustment to the rule that disadvantages or excludes them.

The Debate on Reasonable Accommodation

So far, many Canadian experts recognize that the debate on reasonable accommodation in Canada and Quebec is characterized by a clash between opposing perspectives, that is 'the unbridled Multiculturalism versus the "Fierce" Republicanism, or still, between "Open or Rigid Secularism"' (Bouchard and Taylor, 2008; Grey, 2007; Thériault, 2010).

UNBRIDLED MULTICULTURALISM VERSUS 'FIERCE' REPUBLICANISM

The debate on reasonable accommodation is characterized by a clash between two opposing perspectives. On the one hand, unbridled multiculturalism is deemed an asset for organizations and for society as it promotes complete relativism with respect to cultures. Such a view naturally translates into accommodations. On the other hand, 'fierce' republicanism promotes strict equality among citizens. Such a view is inspired by France's strict separation of State and Church and implies that immigrants must adapt to the host country without demanding concessions for their customs and ways of life because the laws have to apply equally or in the same way to everyone. According to Grey (2007), those who adopt the republican perspective tend to forget the following three facts: (1) The legal system operates by the constant creation of laws, their nuances and distinctions being reinterpreted on a continuous manner (inexorable rules system would quickly become unbearable for all); (2) The most fundamental equality within a society is economic in nature and it is difficult to think about applying the laws equally while the gap between rich and poor continues to widen. Also, a failure to accommodate differences can easily turn into a way to exclude immigrants, who suffer the most from this economic inequality, from certain jobs and professions; and 3) The refusal of any accommodation may favour the creation of walls that separate citizens of different origins, a result that is contrary to the initial intent underlying the imposition of secular institutions.

OPEN OR RIGID SECULARISM

In Quebec, 2008 was marked by the tabling of the report of the Consultation Commission on Accommodation Practices Related to Cultural Differences, the so-called Bouchard–Taylor Report. In their report, Charles Taylor and Gérard

Bouchard, two leading scholars, note the debate on reasonable accommodation is characterized by a continuum ranging from the most rigid, restrictive and severe positions, as typified by the French model, to flexible positions that are more accommodating of religious practice, similar to the current model in Quebec (which is not to claim that there is a social consensus on these positions in either France or Quebec).

Hence, an 'open' secularism is based on a more flexible and 'inclusive' approach that defends a model which focuses on the protection of freedom of conscience and religion and a more open concept of State neutrality. In contrast, rigid secularism places greater restrictions on the free exercise of religion in the name of a certain interpretation of State neutrality and the separation of political and religious powers seen as values and ends in themselves. For proponents of rigid secularism, the religious neutrality of the State is at odds with the duty of reasonable accommodation in public institutions and the latter are justified in limiting, if not refusing outright, accommodations for religion reasons (Vizkelety, 2012).

However, considering the case law dealing with religious matters based on the Canadian and Quebec charters of rights and freedoms, it is clear that the implementation of a rigid secularism would require not only legislative but also constitutional amendments. Indeed, under constitutional law, the duty of neutrality of the Canadian State has its foundation in freedom of religion and equality; the State must respect all religious positions, including that of not having a religion. Proponents of this more flexible conception of neutrality believe that it allows for the full recognition of accommodation (Vizkelety, 2012).

Religious Beliefs as a Prohibited Ground of Discrimination

As a corollary of the right to equality, the duty to accommodate aims to ensure that no person is placed at a disadvantage on grounds unrelated to their ability to perform work. These prohibited grounds, which are enumerated in section 10 of the Quebec Charter and section 15 of the Canadian Charter, include: 'race, colour, sex, pregnancy, sexual orientation, marital status, age (except as provided by law), religion, political beliefs, language, ethnic or national origin, social condition, disability or the use of any means to palliate a disability'. The duty to accommodate is also concomitant to Canada's Employment Equity Act, the purpose of which is to eliminate systemic discrimination against members of designated groups, including women, members of visible minorities, Aboriginal people and persons with disabilities, in order to achieve a representative workforce.

We can observe that the interpretation of *religion* as a prohibited ground of discrimination has taken on a more subjective and individual meaning over time (Woehrling, 2007). Today, a person requesting an accommodation based on religious belief must first prove the existence of this belief (objective criterion) and demonstrate that it was sincerely held (subjective criterion) at the time of the alleged infringement of freedom of religion. The situation becomes more complicated in cases that do not involve observance of the teachings of a recognized, traditional, religion but rather a new religion, individually held beliefs or the personal interpretation of a religion's teachings. In such cases, Canadian courts tend to place greater emphasis on the criterion of the 'sincerity' of the complainant's intention – that is, the credibility of their testimony and the seriousness of their desire to observe the basic tenets of their religion (Woehrling, 2007). Here, it is up to the complainant to prove that their individual beliefs or personal interpretations are not merely opinions, but rather serve bona fide spiritual values.

Duties of the State: Neutrality and Protection of Religious Freedom

The landmark case of *Big M Drug Mart*[2] marked the first time that the Supreme Court of Canada interpreted the notion of freedom of religion outlined in the Canadian Charter. The firm had challenged the constitutionality of the former Lord's Day Act, which forced stores to remain closed on Sunday for reasons of religious observance. The judge ruled in favour of the appellant firm, while specifying first that freedom of religion imposes a *duty of neutrality* on the State which precludes it from either favouring or disfavouring one religion over another.

This ruling suggests that the notion of religious freedom encompasses two obligations, one positive and the other negative. The positive element corresponds to *the right to hold religious beliefs*, to declare religious beliefs openly and to manifest religious beliefs by worship and practice or by teaching and dissemination. The negative component of freedom of religion relates to the absence of coercion or constraint; in other words, *the right not to be compelled*, either directly or indirectly, to adopt a religion or to act in a way contrary to one's beliefs or conscience.

However, Woehrling (2007) notes that the rulings show the Court moving away from the notion of a strict, *hostile neutrality* of the State under which

---

2   *R. v. Big M Drug Mart Ltd.*, 1985, 1 S.C.R. 295.

no form of assistance would be granted to any religion, in favour of a more *benevolent neutrality*, or an open and tolerant secularism, by which the State places the exercise or expression of different religions or religious beliefs on an equal footing. In doing so, it treats all religions equally and does not favour any one religion over others, nor does it favour religious conviction over atheist or agnostic positions.

In the context of public education, two decisions by the Ontario Court of Appeal found unconstitutional a regulation making the recitation of Christian prayers mandatory in schools[3] and another regulation requiring religious education of children in public schools.[4] Despite the fact that, in both cases, parents were able to obtain an exemption for their children, the Court ruled that these regulations subjected the parents and children to indirect pressure (pressure to conform and fear of social stigmatization) by coercing them to conform to the religious practices of the majority. According to the Court, while pluralist religious education in public schools is permitted under the Constitution, education favouring one religion for the purpose of indoctrination constitutes an infringement of freedom of religion. As pointed out by Woehrling (2007, p. 220), 'neutrality will subsist as long as the State treats all religions equally and does not give preference to or disfavour religious convictions over atheist or agnostic convictions' [translation]. Also according to this author, to prove that a condition or regulation infringes a person's religious freedom, 'the complainant must demonstrate that it forces him to go against his beliefs, prevents him from respecting or makes it difficult for him to respect an important principle of his moral code, or causes him to incur a financial disadvantage due to additional costs or the loss of an advantage' (p. 226, translation).

For example:

- In the *Chamberlain case*,[5] the Court found unreasonable a decision of a British Columbia school board to ban the use of books depicting families headed by same-sex couples as learning resources. The Court argued that no single conception of morality can be allowed to deny or exclude opposed points of view.

---

3   *Zylberberg* v. *Sudbury Board of Education* (1988) 65 O.R. (2d) (C.A. Ont.).
4   *Canadian Civil Liberties Association* v. *Ontario (Minister of Education)*, 1990, 71, O.R. (2d) 341; 65 D.L.R. (4th).
5   *Chamberlain* v. *Surrey School District* No. 36, 2002, 4 S.C.R. 710.

- *Commission des droits de la personne et des droits de la jeunesse* v. *Ville de Laval and Simoneau* v. *Tremblay pour la ville de Saguenay*: In these two cases, Quebec's human rights tribunal, the Commission des droits de la personne et des droits de la jeunesse (CDPDJ) (Human and Youth Rights Commission), confirmed that the recitation of a prayer at the opening of public sittings of city council infringed in a discriminatory manner upon the freedom of religion and conscience not only of religious minorities but also of non-believers. In the Ville de Saguenay case, in addition to the practice of reciting a prayer at the beginning of city council meetings, the Commission ruled that exhibiting a Sacred Heart statue and a crucifix at city hall violated the Quebec Charter by infringing on the plaintiff's right to freedom of conscience and religion.

However, in 1999, the CDPDJ concluded that the presence of religious symbols in public institutions does not necessarily constitute an infringement of freedom, provided that no constraint is imposed due to the context, such as the vulnerability of the persons exposed to them (for example, school children), or due to their conspicuous nature, as in a courtroom where the symbols could have the effect of undermining the perception of judicial impartiality. Similarly, the report by the Bouchard–Taylor Commission (2008) recommended that the crucifix be removed from above the Speaker's chair in the Québec's National Assembly (provincial parliament).

Burden of Proof in Demonstrating Infringement of Religious Freedom

While it is clear that the sincerity of a person's belief in the need to observe a religious practice is relevant to the issue of their right to religious freedom, the infringement of this right can only be established based on *objective proof* of the factors interfering with the observance of that practice. For example:

- *In the case of S.L.* v. *Commission scolaire des Chênes (17 February, 2012)*, the Supreme Court of Canada dismissed the appeal of parents who had claimed that the mandatory nature of the Ethics and Religious Culture (ERC) Education Program in Quebec schools infringed on their freedom of conscience and religion by advocating a relativist view of religion that could place children in a moral vacuum by requiring that they put aside their religious values. According to the Court, merely exposing children to a presentation of various religions (without forcing them to adhere to them) does not constitute proof of an indoctrination of students that would infringe on their freedom of religion and any suggestion to the contrary amounts to a rejection of the multicultural reality of Canadian society and ignores the Quebec Government's obligations with regard to public education. The judge held that State neutrality is assured when the State neither favours nor hinders any particular religious belief, that is, when it shows respect for all postures towards religion, including that of having no religious beliefs whatsoever, while taking into account the competing constitutional rights of the individuals affected.

- *In the Chamberlain case,*[6] Judge LeBel maintained that imparting information about different views of the world to schoolchildren cannot be equated with a violation of freedom of religion and does not constitute a violation of the Canadian and Quebec charters, nor is it incompatible with the State's attendant duty of neutrality.

Legal Duty of Reasonable Accommodation for Religious Reasons

Legally speaking, the duty to accommodate requires that employers make concrete adjustments or take measures to eliminate discriminatory situations in the workplace or to establish a workplace that is closer to the ideal of equality. It is also important to note that companies always grant accommodations on an *individual*, case-by-case basis; thus, we do not talk about collective accommodations.

REASONABLE ACCOMMODATION

The obligation of 'reasonable' accommodation refers to 'an effort at substantial compromise by adjusting to a person (or group) in order to eliminate or mitigate a direct or indirect discriminatory effect, without causing an undue hardship' (Groupe Conseil Continuum, 2005 [translation]). Thus, failure to respond to a request for accommodation can be interpreted, rightly or wrongly, as an unwillingness to rectify a situation that is discriminatory. When faced with a complaint, an organization must demonstrate that it has made every effort to find an alternative solution to accommodate the employee, short of causing undue hardship. It must also show that it has been vigilant and innovative

---

6   *Chamberlain* v. *Surrey School District*, no. 36, 2002 S.C.C. 86, 2002, 4 S.C.R. 710.

in investigating alternative accommodation approaches. If it fails to apply the measures identified, it must be able to prove that they were neither realistic nor reasonable. This demonstration must be based on concrete actions and substantiated by verifiable evidence.

ACCOMMODATION MEASURES AND DECISIONS RELATED TO RELIGIOUS PRACTICES AND THE WEARING OF RELIGIOUS SYMBOLS

In both Canada and Quebec, the religious rights of employees are protected by the employer's duty of reasonable accommodation, a legal principle set out by the Supreme Court in 1985, making it mandatory for employers to respect the religion of their employees, provided that this obligation does not create undue hardship for the organization, such as a substantial financial burden. Depending on the individual situation, reasonable accommodation can take many different forms.

First, it can involve *exempting people from the application of a rule*. For example, the CDPDJ recommended an accommodation in the case of a regulation in a public school, that bans the wearing of distinctive clothing by students by arguing that the regulation has a discriminatory effect on students, notably Muslim girls, whose religion requires that they wear the hijab (Woehrling, 2007). The following two specific cases were heard by the Supreme Court of Canada:

- *In the succah case:*[7] the Supreme Court of Canada ruled that the syndicate of co-owners should grant an exemption from the declaration of co-ownership of their property which prohibited the construction of a succah on an apartment balcony, despite the fact that the syndicate had proposed an accommodation in the form of permission to install a communal succah in the gardens. The Jews believed that the proposed accommodation would cause extreme hardship for their observance of their religion and would also be contrary to their religious beliefs. The judges gave decisive weight to the appellants' subjective beliefs and concluded that they should have the right to install their own succah on their balcony for the nine consecutive days of the annual festival of Succot, subject to restrictions concerning the size, precise location (for security reasons) and overall aesthetic aspect of these succahs (Woehrling, 2007).

7   *Syndicat Northcrest* v. *Amselem*, 2004, S.C.C. 47, 2004, 2 S.C.R. 551.

- *The Village de Lafontaine case*:[8] In this case, the municipality's zoning bylaws allowed places of worship to be built in a specific zone, but no owners in this zone were willing to sell a parcel of land to the Jehovah's Witnesses so that they could build their Kingdom Hall. The Supreme Court of Canada found that the municipality had not complied with its duty of procedural fairness and had acted arbitrarily by failing to justify its refusal to amend its zoning bylaw, and therefore had to revise its decision. Indeed, under the principle of religious neutrality, public authorities are required to adopt the necessary accommodations to remove obstacles to the exercise of religious freedoms.

The employer's duty to accommodate can also mean allowing employees to take *paid days of leave to observe a religious holiday*. Generally speaking, in the interest of fairness, employers tend to grant two paid holidays for religious observance, as with Christian holidays (Christmas and Good Friday) (Jézéquel and Houde, 2007). Note the following example:

- In the case of the *Commission scolaire de Chambly*:[9] Jewish teachers lost a day of salary (unpaid leave of absence) in order to practise their religion, while the religious holidays of the majority of their colleagues were recognized as paid holidays. In the absence of proof of undue financial hardship, the Court ordered that the employer could, in accordance with the provisions of the collective agreement, pay the Jewish teachers for their absence on holy days.

An accommodation can also be made by granting *different advantages or working conditions*. For example, a cafeteria in a public school that often offers pork as a standard menu item, having a discriminatory effect on the freedom of people belonging to the Jewish or Muslim religions, could propose a different menu for these people.

- *The case of the hijab for female prison guards*: In 2011, Montrealer Sondos Abdelatif won her appeal before the CDPDJ after being dismissed from her job as a prison guard for wearing her hijab to work, which at the time was prohibited by Quebec's Ministère de la Sécurité publique. According to the Commission, this regulation 'had a discriminatory effect' on the practice of religion and the

---

8   *Congrégation des témoins de Jéhovah St–Jérôme–Lafontaine* v. *Lafontaine (Village)*.
9   *Commission scolaire de Chambly* v. *Bergevin*, 1994, 2 S.C.R. 525.

right to equality guaranteed by the Charter of Human Rights and Freedoms. The Correctional Services Department consequently revised its regulations and decided to provide a headscarf to all Muslim correctional agents who so requested. The hijabs provided were to be equipped with Velcro strips so that they could be detached quickly in the case of an altercation with a prisoner (Thibault, 2011).

In Quebec, the *draft* 'Charter of Values' introduced by the Government in the summer of 2013 proposes to bar public sector employees from wearing 'ostentatious' religious symbols, but it appears destined to be challenged in the courts as abusive and anti-constitutional and will likely be struck down as it contravenes the Quebec and Canadian charters of rights and freedoms, especially since the provisions that place limitations on freedoms are not based on either actual and documented inconveniences, or sufficiently urgent or real objectives. At the most, the Charter will align itself with the recommendations of the Bouchard–Taylor Commission (2008) and the ban will be limited to positions that embody or represent the authority of the State, such as judges, Crown prosecutors, police officers, prison guards, teachers and so on, based on the positions and places where such a ban would eventually be deemed reasonable by the courts.

While most of the decisions in the examples cited above were imposed by a court or a commission, it should be noted that accommodations can also be recommended by the CDPDJ, negotiated by mutual agreement or made voluntarily, which is, in fact, preferable and much more common. Take the following examples:

- A *town in Quebec* decided to reserve the use of its pool for three hours each week for Muslim groups to permit members of the same sex to bathe together, as required by their religion.

- The *Royal Canadian Mounted Police* decided to hire Sikhs and to exempt them from the obligation of wearing the traditional RCMP Stetson; they were authorized to keep their turban, their beard and their ritual dagger (kirpan).

After reviewing the state of the law on this issue, Vizkelety (2012) concludes that there are many different types of religious accommodation that can be requested of any employer, whether in the private or public sphere. Possible accommodations include: providing specialized food services in establishments catering to religious minorities; authorizing paid or unpaid leaves of absence for religious holidays; adapting work or exam schedules that conflict with religious obligations; granting exemptions to zoning bylaws; postponing a driving test to a time when an examiner of the same sex is available and so on.

Undue and Unreasonable Hardship as Grounds for Refusing an Accommodation

Freedom of religion is not an absolute right and employees cannot make unreasonable demands in the name of their right to religious freedom. It is crucial to also take into account the rights of employers and co-workers and to avoid adversely affecting the rights of others or preventing others from exercising their rights, hence the obligation of the employer to find *reasonable* accommodations in attempting to satisfy their employees (Samson, 2011). In other words, a balance must be sought between the duty to accommodate, good governance of the organization and the pursuit of a collective interest. For example, the rights of one employee cannot infringe the rights of other employees. Accordingly, it would be unreasonable to force an employee to shift from the day shift to the night shift in order to accommodate a co-worker who is unavailable nights because of religious practices. Moreover, an individual cannot use the duty of reasonable accommodation as an entitlement to negotiate more advantageous working conditions.

On the other hand, an employer can only refuse to accommodate an employee if it can demonstrate that the accommodation would cause an undue or unreasonable hardship. An undue hardship is 'a legitimate point beyond which the requirement to make reasonable accommodations ceases to exist' (Groupe Conseil Continuum, 2005, [translation]). According to the Supreme Court of Canada, if norms or measures imposed by the employer have discriminatory effects on an employee that prevent him from following his religious beliefs, the employer can justify its decision by demonstrating that the desired objective (for example, safety or productivity) is important and that the means used are proportional to the desired objective. Thus, if an employer bans its employees from wearing clothing required by their religion for safety reasons, it must be able to show that this measure is essential to ensure the safety of all its employees and that there is no alternative way to ensure safety. If the employer is unable to meet this condition, then it must review its work regulations, as was done in the case of the hijab worn by female prison guards.

The following factors have been recognized in case law as leading to *undue hardship* for employers: unreasonable financial burden; major conflict with a collective agreement or with the rights of others; effect on staff morale; interchangeability of staff and facilities, and; *adverse effects on the health and safety of the parties* or on the organization's operations (Brunelle, 2007; Di Iorio and Lauzon, 2008). Unless the employer is able to demonstrate that the disputed accommodation measure would cause an undue hardship, the reluctance, fears, concerns, grievances and dissatisfaction of employees or clients in no way release employers (and unions) from their duty to accommodate (Di Iorio and Lauzon, 2007). The tensions that arise among staff or customers are often the result of ignorance and a lack of information regarding the obligations of the employer (and the union, where applicable) and the nature of the need for an accommodation.

At the same time, however, the person requesting an accommodation must keep an open mind, show tolerance and be willing to accept concessions or desirable accommodations. As Woehrling (2007) points out, accommodations should preferably take the form of dispensations, exemptions, or exceptions for members of minorities as opposed to structural changes to the system put in place by the majority. This is the principle upheld by the courts in their refusal to order the reorganization of the school calendar in favour of permitting leaves of absence on an individual basis;[10] this is an optimal solution considering that the structural reorganization of school calendars to take into account all religions would be unmanageable.

With regard to religion, then, *unreasonable accommodations that could be unsafe or too costly for society and institutions must be avoided*. For example, while a ban on carrying weapons – notably the kirpan that the Sikh religion requires be worn at all times – has been deemed to be justified in courthouses and airplanes, the Supreme Court of Canada and the tribunals have tended to consider that kirpans should be accepted in public schools under certain conditions that are reasonably verifiable by school staff, including that they be encased in a wooden (rather than metal) sheath and securely sealed and sewn up inside the pupil's clothing.[11] *Thus, when invoking respect for the rights of others, there must be objective proof of a conflict of rights*. In this case, the risks to public safety created by the wearing of the kirpan were not established.

In the construction sector, requests by Sikhs to keep their turban seem to conflict with another right protected by the Charter: *the right to safety*. In this case, wearing a hard hat is a professional requirement that justifies limiting the

---

10   *Islamic Schools Federation of Ontario,* (1997) 145 D.L.R. (4th) 659.

11   *Multani c. Commission scolaire Marguerite-Bourgeois,* 2006 S.C.C. 6.

right to freedom of religion, considering that *safety rules generally take priority over religious requirements*. An employee who cannot comply with workplace dress rules could be offered another position by the employer rather than being forced to quit his job (Jézéquel and Houde, 2007). On the other hand, in the case of an employee in a customer service job who can never work on Fridays, accommodation may be deemed unreasonable, given the impact of this employee's absences on the company's operations and performance.

- At *Cargill Foods*, a food processing plant in Chambly, most accommodation requests related to clothing are granted in the case of office employees. However, the requests of production employees who handle food and machinery and who seek the right to wear clothing related to a religious practice (for example, hijab, turban and diellaba) are treated differently. The company has the right to reject these requests because they represent an undue hardship requiring the company to lower the health, safety and hygiene standards regulating its production processes. However, in cases where a reasonable accommodation does not impose any such constraints, it is usually granted. Rooms inside the workplace have even been made available to certain employees to allow them to practise their religion during working hours (Groupe Conseil Continuum, 2005). Finally, according to some experts, considering that an accommodation becomes unreasonable if it prevents integration or socialization, allowing a full-face veil (tchador, nikab, burka) that hides the face of a Muslim woman can be seen as an unreasonable accommodation. Their conclusion rests on the premise that such clothing forcibly hinders a woman's real integration into schools or her relationships or communication with other students (a faceless person has no identity), which is contrary to the very mission of educational institutions in Quebec (Gaudreault-Desbiens, 2007; Grey, 2007). This perspective can be seen to inform the Quebec Government's introduction of Bill 94[12] on reasonable accommodations which has been widely debated in the National Assembly since 2010 and which stipulates that Government representatives must show their face while at work, which is the case for the hijab; thus, the bill would only ban the wearing of veils that cover the full face, such as the burka and niqab, by public service employees.

---

12 Retrieved on 13 October 2013 from http://www.assnat.qc.ca/fr/travaux-parlementaires/projets-loi/projet-loi-94-39-1.html.

Moreover, *an accommodation cannot have the effect of changing the nature of the job or service offered* by the employer or institution in fulfilling its mission. Here, we can take the example of requests for prayer rooms in universities. In one notable case, the complainant (a group acting on behalf of 113 Muslim students) had submitted a request to the École de technologie supérieure (ÉTS) for a safe, private space where they could pray in dignity. The institution invoked its secular nature to justify its refusal to provide a separate space for prayer. The Commission[13] pointed out that the secular nature of the institution does not remove its obligation to accommodate students, but stopped short of saying that the institution should offer a separate space for religious practice, which could be seen as creating an undue hardship. However, the Commission takes the view that the duty of accommodation incumbent on the ETS requires it to allow Muslim students to pray, on a regular basis, in conditions that respect their right to the safeguard of their dignity. This case illustrates the importance of the complainant's cooperation in seeking a solution and accepting reasonable accommodations even if they are not perfect. Universities thus have the option of making prayer rooms available for students, but are under no obligation to do so (Vizkelety, 2012).

According to Grey (2007), 'accommodations are limited by the fact that accommodations cannot be granted if they victimize innocent members of a group or take priority over the rights of others, such as their right to life, to security, to receive a service, etc.' For example:

- *In the judgement in the case of R. v. Jones,*[14] the Supreme Court refused to allow a group of fundamentalists to exempt their children from science classes based on the argument that society has an obligation to make the advantages and benefits of the majority culture accessible to all children. According to the author, 'membership in a religious or ethnic group must be a personal choice made by adults, not an obligation imposed by a group on their members with the help of the State' (p. 237 [translation]). In the case cited here, the Supreme Court recognized the right of parents not to send their children to public school and to provide them with religious instruction at a private school or at home, but it also ruled that the obligation for people who educate their children at home to have this instruction certified does not constitute a limitation on freedom

---

13 Commission des droits de la personne et des droits de la jeunesse, Resolution COM-510-5.2.1.

14 *R. v. Jones*, 1986, 2 S.C.R. 284.

of religion, since the legal requirements in this regard are a minimal intrusion on religion. In short, for an accommodation to be justified, the restrictive effect of the rule must be sufficiently important that it infringes freedom of religion or conscience.

- In the case of *B. (R.)* v. *Children's Aid Society of Metropolitan Toronto, (1995), S.C.R. 315*, the courts rejected an appeal alleging infringement of religious freedom by the parents of a child, who as Jehovah's Witnesses, were opposed to blood transfusions for their infant for religious reasons. The Children's Aid Society intervened in the case by seeking temporary wardship of the infant to authorize the blood transfusions against the parents' wishes.

Thus, situations such as a nurse who refuses to assist with abortions or a civil servant who refuses to officiate a civil wedding ceremony between two persons of the same sex for religious reasons can give rise to obligations of accommodation without, however, infringing the rights of mothers and same-sex couples to receive services without discrimination (see the review by Vizkelety, 2012).

Conclusion

In the current context of immigration and the globalization of business, accommodation must be seen as part of a larger issue that goes beyond simple constraints or fulfilment of legal obligations. In fact, accepting requests for accommodation can lead to many benefits, not only in terms of increasing loyalty among employees, but also improving staff mobilization and commitment, reducing absenteeism and taking better advantage of skills (St-Onge et al., 2013). Indeed, the accommodation process has a strong potential to foster intercultural and interreligious understanding and promote a sense of belonging among an organization's employees. And access to effective remedies in cases involving religious freedom and accommodation is considered a powerful tool for the integration of ethnoreligious minorities in both Quebec and Canadian society (CDPDJ, 2008).

> *No society has ever succeeded in implementing a system of multiculturalism without sooner or later seeing it deteriorate into hostility or conflict. Medieval Spain and the Balkans illustrate that it is impossible to preserve harmony if the different groups maintain their differences from one generation to the next. On the other hand,*

many societies have been able to integrate disparate groups and meld them into a new society. All modern nations, including France and England, are the product of such a mixing of cultures. Accommodations, where they have remained within the bounds of common sense, have not tended to hinder this process (Grey, 2007, pp. 237–8 [translation]).

Employers have much to gain by adopting a preventative and proactive (as opposed to corrective or reactive) approach and by meeting needs for accommodation at the organizational level and anticipating those needs based on the demographic evolution of their personnel. In fact, accommodation practices are an integral part of the best practices in diversity management. By accepting to play an active role in eliminating obstacles to integration in the workplace, employers demonstrate their accountability and commitment to equality, not only to their employees, but also to their clients. In other words, the organization as a whole stands to gain from offering adjustment measures for reasons that go beyond their legal obligations. In such cases, one can speak of the benefits of an 'inclusive' management culture, or one that is 'open to diversity' (Jézéquel, 2008).

Many people see religious accommodations as 'privileges' that threaten the equality of all citizens. However, as this chapter has demonstrated, such accommodations are a corollary of the right to equality: religious minorities have the right to maintain their differences from the majority by being granted accommodations in relation to neutral and uniformly applied norms that limit their freedom of religion.

In a republican society, it is good to recall the motto of the French Revolution: 'Liberté, égalité, fraternité' [liberty, equality, fraternity]. If individual liberty takes precedence in political and personal life, and if equality is essential in the economic sphere, then accommodating the reasonable requests of our fellow citizens appears to illustrate the value of fraternity, which allows everyone to feel sufficiently at ease in society to accept the common identity (Grey, 2007, p. 239 [translation]).

As this chapter has shown, the multicultural approach of Canadian liberal democracy does not lead to acceptance of any and all accommodations, given that a request for accommodation must be *reasonable* in its scope. People have always had the tendency to reasonably accommodate their neighbours; in today's context of increasing diversity, the challenge remains: to distinguish what is reasonable from what is unreasonable.

In this regard, we tend to agree with lawyer Julius Grey (2007), who observes shortcomings in Canadian multiculturalism and the policy of Aboriginal autonomy, which seek to protect the continuity of *groups*, whereas the charters of rights and freedoms seek to protect *individuals*. These limitations lead to ongoing debates among clinicians and health care employees. In January 2015, Makayla Sault, a 11-year-old girl who was a member of a First Nations tribe in Canada, died following her family's decision to stop chemotherapy treatment for her leukemia. The family's rationale for its decision was that chemotherapy was not consistent with traditional aboriginal medicine and poisoned the child's body. Her death came a few weeks after a decision, on a similar case, by judge Gethin B. Edward. Justice Edward ruled that the family of a girl with cancer would be allowed to pursue alternative treatment and stop chemotherapy because of their 'aboriginal right'. This Ontario judge concluded 'I cannot find that J.J. is a child in need of protection when her substitute decision-maker has chosen to exercise her constitutionally protected right to pursue their traditional medicine over the Applicant's stated course of treatment of chemotherapy.'[15] This controversial judgment leads many other experts to ask how, as a society, are we protecting the rights of a historically beleaguered community by sentencing one of its children to almost-certain death? (McLaren, 2015). As expressed by Blatchford (2015), in our days, child-welfare agencies and Courts are unwilling to investigate or put limits upon what is and isn't 'traditional medicine'. Hence, they are reluctant to force aboriginal children into life-saving treatment and to interject themselves into sad cases where genuinely loving parents make uninformed healthcare decisions.

To conclude, to the extent that constraint as a means of integration in a society that guarantees individual freedoms is impossible, reasonable accommodation is an important way to promote the constant integration of immigrant groups and to create a shared identity or social solidarity that is also constantly evolving. However, and as explained by Julius Grey (2007), accommodation, as a tool for integration, must necessarily be directed at individuals, not groups, since those who elect to live within a group exercise a legitimate choice protected by the right to freedom of association (religion), but this is an individual rather than a collective right and choice. In order to determine whether a practice ought to be accommodated, McKenna (2009) suggests to evaluate concrete cases in the light of abstract moral principles (such as liberty and equality) to insure that

---

15 *Hamilton Health Sciences Corp. v. D.H., P.L.J., Six Nations of the Grand River Child and Family Services Department and Brant Family and Children's Services*, 2014 ONCJ 603, C287/14E, 2014-11-14

political and human rights are protected and that there is consistent treatment of all citizens irregardless of cultural differences.

References[16]

Banon, P. and Chanlat, J.F. (2012). La diversité religieuse et culturelle dans les organisations contemporaines: principaux constats et proposition d'un modèle d'analyse et d'action pour le contexte français, *Equality, Diversity and Inclusion Conference,* Toulouse Business School, Toulouse, France, 25 July 2012.

Blatchford, C. (2015). Lest you imagine the death of Makayla Sault will galvanize someone, somewhere, give your head a shake, Full Comment, January 20, 2015. Retrieved on 26 January 2015 from http://news.nationalpost.com/2015/01/20/christie-blatchford-lest-you-imagine-the-death-of-makayla-sault-will-galvanize-someone-somewhere-give-your-head-a-shake/.

Bouchard, G. and Taylor, C. (2008). Fonder l'avenir: le temps de la conciliation, Gouvernement du Québec.

Brunelle, C. (2007). Le droit à l'accommodement raisonnable dans les milieux de travail syndiqués : une invasion barbare? In Jézéquel, M. (ed.), *Les accommodements raisonnables: quoi, comment, jusqu'où? Des outils pour tous,* Éditions Yvon Blais, Cowansville: 51–86.

Brunelle, C. (2008). 'L'accommodement and raisonnable dans les entreprises syndiquées: une valse à mille temps?', *Gestion,* 33(2): 59–65.

CDPDJ (Commission des droits de la personne et des droits de la jeunesse). (2008). La Charte et la prise en compte de la religion dans l'espace public, discussion paper.

Di Iorio, N. and Lauzon, M.C. (2007). À la recherche de l'égalité: de l'accommodement à l'acharnement. In Jézéquel, M. (ed.), *Les accommodements raisonnables: quoi, comment, jusqu'où? Des outils pour tous,* Éditions Yvon Blais, Cowansville: 113–64.

Di Iorio, N. and Lauzon, M.C. (2008). 'Aspects juridiques et pratiques de la gestion de l'accommodement', *Gestion,* 33(2): 53–8.

Gaudreault-Desbiens, J.F. (2007). Quelques angles morts du débat sur l'accommodement raisonnable à la lumière de la question du port de signes religieux à l'école publique: réflexions en forme de points d'interrogation. In Jézéquel, M. (ed.), *Les accommodements raisonnables: quoi, comment, jusqu'où? Des outils pour tous,* Éditions Yvon Blais, Cowansville: 241–86.

---

16 All previous court decisions are indicated as footnotes throughout the chapter.

Grey, J.H. (2007). L'accommodement raisonnable: multiculturalisme et vision républicaine. In Jézéquel, M. (ed.), *Les accommodements raisonnables: quoi, comment, jusqu'où? Des outils pour tous*, Éditions Yvon Blais, Cowansville: 235–9.

Groupe Conseil Continuum (2005). [online], Retrieved on January 5, 2015 from http://emploiquebec. net/publications/pdf/06_emp_guidediversite.pdf.

Jézéquel, M. and Houde, L. (2007). 'Accommodements religieux en milieu de travail: jusqu'où?', *Effectif*, 10(2): 32–5.

Jézéquel, M. (2008). 'Pour une gestion efficace, équitable et proactive des accommodements', *Gestion*, 33(2): 66–72.

McKenna, I. (2009). Equality and accommodation: A narrative approach to Canadian multiculturalism, Doctoral thesis, Ottawa University, Department of Philosophy.

McLaren, L. (2015). 'Makayla Sault: Whose right are served when a litttle girl dies?', The Globe and Mail, 21 January, Retrieved on 26 January 2015 fromhttp://www.theglobeandmail.com/life/parenting/whose-rights-are-served-when-a-little-girl-dies/article22562573/.

Samson, J. (2011). La liberté de religion dans les organisations, *VigieRT*, website of the Ordre des CRHA du Québec, November.

St-Onge, S., Guerrero, S., Haines, V. and Brun, J.P. (2013). *Relever les défis de la gestion des ressources humaines*, Chenelière Éducation/Gaëtan Morin Éditeur, Montreal.

Thériault, J.Y. (2010). Entre républicanisme et multiculturalisme: La Commission Bouchard-Taylor, une synthèse ratée. In *La Diversité québécoise en débat*, Montréal : Éditions Québec Amérique inc.: 143–55.

Thibault, É. (2011). Accommodement raisonnable: un hijab avec velcro pour les gardiennes de prison, on *Canoe.ca*, Actualités, 21 December 2011, [online]. Retrieved on 5 January 2015 from http://fr.canoe.ca/infos/quebeccanada/archives/2011/12/20111221-062502.html.

Vizkelety, B. (2012). Le Québec, la laïcité et le principe de la «*neutralité de l'État*», paper presented at the Canadian Bar Association Legal Conference, 12–14 August, Vancouver.

Woehrling, J. (2007). Les principes régissant la place de la religion dans les écoles publiques du Québec. In Jézéquel, M. (ed.), *Les accommodements raisonnables: quoi, comment, jusqu'où? Des outils pour tous*, Éditions Yvon Blais, Cowansville: 215–34.

Chapter 3

Accommodating Religious Diversity in the Canadian Workplace: The Hijab Predicament in Quebec and Ontario

RANA HAQ

Introduction

The debate on religious accommodation in the workplace has been on the increase in many countries receiving immigrants over the recent years as more immigrants are retaining their cultural values and customs as well as beginning to exercise their rights and freedoms in living and working in their adopted country of residence. As a country of immigrants, Canada is also adapting to this challenge. Although Canada has always welcomed immigrants, the earlier immigrants were predominantly white Anglo-Saxon people from Europe while the majority of the more recent immigrants are visible minorities. Canada has the highest proportion of foreign-born population amongst the G8 countries, at approximately 6,775,800 in 2011 representing 20.6 per cent of the population, living mainly in four provinces – Ontario, British Columbia, Quebec and Alberta (Statistics Canada, 2013). The 2011 National Household Survey (NHS) reports that, during the five-year period of 2006 to 2011, about 1,162,900 foreign-born people immigrated to Canada, primarily from Asia, Africa, Caribbean, Central and South America, making up 17.2 per cent of foreign born and 3.5 per cent of the total population (Statistics Canada, 2013).

As these immigrants move out into the rest of Canada in search of job opportunities, many Canadian provinces are becoming cognizant of the need for religious accommodation in the workplace in response to their assertion of maintaining their religious practices and cultural heritage. However, Quebec has traditionally taken a secular approach towards all aspects of religious symbolism and these assertions are often perceived as uncompromising, even militant and dogmatic, demands on existing historical organizational policies and procedures. Recently, the Government of Quebec reignited the sensitive debate over religious freedom and accommodation by claiming that, as a secular State, it is entitled to remove all religious aspects from the public sector workplaces. But is there any evidence that religious observance, particularly by wearing outward symbols such as the hijab, niqab, kirpan, kippa, cross and so on, is disruptive to organizational life, employee productivity and effectiveness? Are organizations really 'religion neutral' places or are there implicit religious norms in place? What values does religion bring into the workplace? Should the diversity of religious beliefs and practices be accommodated in the workplace?

In this chapter, we first introduce the Canadian demographic profile and protective anti-discrimination legislations, followed by the religious accommodation struggles in Quebec, and finally present some comparative experiences of hijabi women from Quebec and Ontario. Their perspective on these important questions may clarify misinformation about the hijab and have some implications for other countries also struggling with similar challenges.

Canada

Evidence that global changes are impacting the roots of our Canadian society and workplaces is indisputable given the increasing diversity of immigrants coming to Canada. Fortunately, Canada has been in the forefront of welcoming diversity and change in its population and society by presenting the first *Multiculturalism Act* in 1970 in Parliament, enacted in 1988, and a points-based immigration system to screen potential immigrants for their successful integration into Canadian society, consequently becoming well recognized around the world for its generous immigration levels and respectful anti-discrimination policies.

> *The government of Canada recognizes the diversity of Canadians as regards race, national or ethnic origin, colour and religion as a fundamental characteristic of Canadian society and is committed to a policy of multiculturalism designed to preserve and enhance the multicultural heritage of Canadians while working to achieve the equality of all Canadians in the economic, social, cultural and political life of Canada (CMA, 1988, Preamble).*

The Canadian Charter of Rights and Freedoms (CCRF) of the *Constitution Act* 1982 guarantees fundamental freedoms to all Canadians: 'Section 2. Everyone has the following fundamental freedoms: (a) freedom of conscience and religion; (b) freedom of thought, belief, opinion and expression, including freedom of the press and other media of communication; (c) freedom of peaceful assembly; and (d) freedom of association' (CCRF, 1982).

It protects equality rights and prohibits discrimination in 'Section 15 – (1) Every individual is equal before and under the law and has the right to the equal protection and equal benefit of the law without discrimination and, in particular, without discrimination based on race, national or ethnic origin, colour, religion, sex, age or mental or physical disability' (CCRF, 1982) and also supports Affirmative Action programmes in 'Section 15 (2) Subsection (1) does not preclude any law, program or activity that has as its object the amelioration of conditions of disadvantaged individuals or groups including those that are disadvantaged because of race, national or ethnic origin, colour, religion, sex, age or mental or physical disability' (CCRF, 1982).

The *Canadian Human Rights Act* prohibits discrimination on 11 grounds: race, national or ethnic origin, colour, religion, age, sex, sexual orientation, marital status, family status, disability or conviction for which a pardon has been granted (CHRA, 1977). In 1986, Canada also enacted the *Employment Equity Act* (EEA) which was revised and strengthened in 1995 and specifically emphasizes the need for employers to promote equality by the implementation of special measures and accommodation of differences:

> *The purpose of this Act is to achieve equality in the workplace so that no person shall be denied employment opportunities or benefits for reasons unrelated to ability and, in the fulfilment of that goal, to correct the conditions of disadvantage in employment experienced by women, aboriginal peoples, persons with disabilities and members of visible minorities by giving effect to the principle that employment equity means more than treating persons in the same way but* also requires special measures and the accommodation of differences *(EEA, 1995, c. 44, s. 2, emphasis added).*

It recognizes that failure to accommodate would have a negative impact on immigrants, their job opportunities and integration into Canadian society, increasing their discrimination and exclusion. Therefore, the law does not have to be applied in the same way for everyone. There is a legal obligation on employers to implement 'reasonable accommodation' and using the concept of 'undue hardship' for justifying why accommodation is refused by the employer (EEA, 1986). In addition, self-identification by individuals belonging to the protected groups balances the sharing of responsibility for accommodation between the employee and employer. See Chapter 2 by Sylvie St-Onge which further details the state of the law and practice in Canada and Quebec.

Canadian society and workplaces are changing too. It was not long ago, in 1985, that the ban on Sunday shopping was lifted in Canada, challenged under the CCRF of the *Constitution Act* 1982, after a lot of discussion and debate around the negative impact this would have on the personal lives and religious practices of Christian workers wanting to attend church on Sundays. The Supreme Court of Canada ruled:

> *The Lord's Day Act to the extent that it binds all to a sectarian Christian ideal, works a form of coercion inimical to the spirit of the Charter. The Act gives the appearance of discrimination against nonChristian Canadians. Religious values rooted in Christian morality are translated into a positive law binding on believers and nonbelievers alike. NonChristians are prohibited for religious reasons from carrying out otherwise lawful, moral and normal activities. Any law, purely religious in purpose, which denies nonChristians the right to work on Sunday denies them the right to practise their religion and infringes their religious freedom. The protection of one religion and the concomitant nonprotection of others imports a disparate impact destructive of the religious freedom of society. The power to compel, on religious grounds, the universal observance of the day of rest preferred by one religion is not consistent with the preservation and enhancement of the multicultural heritage of Canadians recognized in s. 27 of the Charter.[1]*

The decision also addressed the debate on the needs of other religious minorities, such as Jews and Muslims:

> *Whatever the origins of the division of belief, it is indisputable that there can now be seen among Canadians different deeply held beliefs of religion and conscience on this subject. One group, probably the majority, accepts Sunday as the Lord's Day. Another group consisting of those of the Jewish faith, and Sabbatarians whose religious beliefs do not accept Sunday as the Lord's Day distinct from Sabbath on the seventh day of the week, believe in Saturday as their holy day. Canadians of the Muslim religion observe Friday as their holy day. Some Canadians who*

---

1   (*R. v. Big M Drug Mart Ltd.*, [1985] 1 S.C.R. 295). Retrieved on 29 July 2013 from http://scc-csc. lexum.com/scc-csc/scc-csc/en/item/43/index.do.

have no theistic belief, while perhaps accepting the concept of a day for
rest and recreation, object to the enforcement of a Christian Sunday.[2]

However, in many Canadian schools, cities and municipalities there continue to be annual debates on the nativity scenes on display in public places during Christmas. Inevitably, change transforms our shared mental models of society, culture and work values and while this is largely a work-in-progress for many Canadian provinces that are adapting and moving towards workplace accommodations, the province of Quebec continues to experience difficulties in managing this change.

Quebec

The province of Quebec has historically claimed a special position in Canada as a result of its charter status, French language and distinct culture. The issue of Quebec's identity is a long-standing debate which is also recognized and protected in the Canadian Charter of Rights and Freedoms in the *Constitution Act* of 1982. However, as more and more francophone immigrants are moving into Quebec, especially from the former French colonies which are primarily Islamic countries or cultures, the province has been facing increasing requests for religious accommodations. Some of these have been very public debates over controversies such as the ban on the Islamic hijab (head cover) and niqab (face veil) (Stemp-Morlock, 2014; Golnaraghi and Mills, 2013; Choudhury, 2013; Bill 94, 2010; Bill 60, 2013).

In response to requests for religious accommodation by women wearing the niqab, Quebec introduced *Bill 94 – An Act to Establish Guidelines Governing Accommodation Requests within the Administration and Certain Institutions,* in 2010, which applies to institutions providing education, healthcare, social services and childcare services in Quebec. It would deny essential public services to women in niqabs due to public safety, communication and identification concerns. Choudhury (2012) argues that Bill 94, a recent legislation which requires all individuals to reveal their face when seeking Government services in Quebec, particularly targets Muslim women wearing the niqab and is related to Quebec's identity rather than its secularism.

---

2   (R. v. *Big M Drug Mart Ltd.,* [1985] 1 S.C.R. 295). Retrieved on 29 July 2013 from http://scc-csc. lexum.com/scc-csc/scc-csc/en/item/43/index.do.

The Sikh kirpan in schools and turbans on the soccer fields have also been controversial. In June 2013, the Quebec Soccer Federation banned the Sikh turban in the league's soccer pitches but had to repeal it under national condemnation, protests and pressure to lift the ban along with its suspension by the Canadian Soccer Association (CSA) and the Federation Internationale de Football Association (FIFA). Although, in 2011, FIFA had banned women from wearing Islamic headdresses on the grounds that it could potentially cause injury, such as choking, which was later revoked. The approval of the Parti Quebecois (PQ) Government for such a ban was based on Ms Marois's stand that the CSA had no authority to determine Quebec's rules. Other religions are also facing accommodation challenges in Quebec. For example, parking exemptions for the Jewish people during religious holidays in Montreal were condemned by Minister Drainville saying: 'We cannot start saying we are going to change the highway code and the parking signs according to different religions' (TGAM, 2013a).

Quebec politics have historically been based on issues about the Canadian identity and Quebec's place in the Canadian Confederation to the extent of persistent separatist ideology promoting an independent Quebec separate from Canada. After losing the 1980 Quebec referendum, Premiere Rene Levesque's statement was 'A la prochaine fois' (Until next time). Then, after losing the second referendum in 1995, Premiere Jacques Parizeau's infamous statement was 'It's true, it's true that we have been defeated, but basically by what? By money and some ethnic votes, essentially' (CBC Archives). Identity politics was also the PQ's winning strategy during the successful election campaign in 2012, albeit a minority Government, promising new secular rules on minority religious rights under the 'Charter of Quebec Values', removing religious symbols from public institutions and preventing public employees from wearing religious symbols of their faith in the workplace. However, 'the concept of secularism itself is deeply embedded in Christian worldview' argues Stemp-Morlock (2014) 'therefore, whenever a Canadian says that religion has no place in a secular institution, they are in fact giving primacy to a culturally Christian worldview, around which this country built its institutions.'

Charter of Quebec Values

In August 2013, Premiere Pauline Marois' PQ minority Government released its 'Charter of Quebec Values' (TGAM, 2013a; *National Post*, 2013), an extremely contentious legislation which would ban religious headgear, such as Islamic hijabs and niqabs, Sikh turbans, Jewish kippas and wearing big Christian crosses in the public sector and broader public sector workplaces such as all public servants in government jobs, police officers, judges, prison guards, childcare workers in daycares, staff and nurses in hospitals, school and university teachers. The Quebec Government released an official poster (see Figure 3.1) showing 'non-ostentatious' religious symbols that could be worn by public employees (top three images) and 'ostentatious' symbols that would be banned under the charter (bottom five images). Bernard Drainville, the Minister responsible for the values charter published in the *Journal de Quebec* and the *Journal de Montreal*, defended it as the Government's efforts to enshrine into law the secular character of the province.

> ### Bill 60 – Charter affirming the values of State secularism and religious neutrality and of equality between women and men, and providing a framework for accommodation requests.
> *Public bodies must, in the pursuit of their mission, remain neutral in religious matters and reflect the secular nature of the State. Accordingly, obligations are set out for personnel members of public bodies in the exercise of their functions, including a duty to remain neutral and exercise reserve in religious matters by, among other things, complying with the restriction on wearing religious objects that overtly indicate a religious affiliation. As well, personnel members of a public body must exercise their functions with their face uncovered, and persons to whom they provide services must also have their face uncovered when receiving such services (Bill 60 – Explanatory Note, 2013).*

'Banning hijabs won't halt honour killings' (Kay, 2013). Quebec's Status of Women Committee recently released a report addressing the disturbing phenomenon of honour killings of women. Since 1977, 17 such cases have occurred in Canada which are not exclusive to Muslim cultures but also include Hindus and Sikhs. The most recent being the Shafia family murders of three Quebec sisters and their mother orchestrated by their Afghan-born father, stepmother and brother, who were all sentenced to life imprisonment in January 2013, with no parole for 25 years. The Quebec Government immediately used it to support their proposed Charter with Bernard Drainville's statement, 'I wouldn't make a direct link between the two, but the symbolism of the Charter may help us prevent these kinds of crimes. The Charter sends a very strong signal that equality between women and men is an important value, a non-negotiable value in Quebec society' (Kay, 2013). Not surprisingly, there was an immediate backlash across Canada to Quebec's Charter which continues to be fiercely debated on both sides.

The Hijab

For the Western world, which has fought tirelessly for gender equality and the freedom of women's rights, understandably, the hijab provokes extremely strong negative reactions. Adorned in various forms, the hijab or headscarf; the niqab or the face veil; the chador or sheet which covers the whole body; the abaya which covers the clothes; the burqa which covers the whole body, face and clothes, are all perceived in the West as symbolic of female oppression and diminished women's rights. In fact, the Muslim woman's covering her body has long been a mystery to the West (Kingston, 2012). It is ironic that the mystery, fear and threat of the hijab which is intended to protect the Muslim woman from the eyes of others, has in fact become the very thing that bring all eyes upon her in the West. Unfortunately, the events of 11 September 2001 (or 9/11) have played a major role in transforming this mystery into suspicion and vicious targeting of the Muslim community, giving rise to anti-Islamic sentiment based upon a perceived threat of terrorist activities.

So why do some Muslim women continue to wear it, particularly in Canada? Notably, the first key point is that not all Muslim women wear the hijab. In fact, only a very small minority do so. And yes, there are some women who are forced to wear it by the men or women in their immediate or extended family, as is the case in honour killings. There are also some women who feel pressured by their 'madressa' (religious school) such as Irshad Manji (2004, p. 10) who describes the 'white polyester chador' as 'a condom over my head' intended to protect her from 'unsafe intellectual activity'.

But a legal ban on hijabs does nothing for protecting the rights and freedoms of the modern hijabi women. Haida Mubarak (2007) explains that 'it is ultimately each woman's prerogative to decide whether or not she will cover her hair. No one – not a father, husband or brother – can ever force a woman to cover against her will, for that in fact violates the Quranic spirit of "let there be no compulsion in religion"'. Meanwhile, there are some highly educated, independent, professional, empowered Muslim women, of right mind, who personally exercise their rights and choose to wear the hijab. Mubarak explains her decision to wear the hijab as 'the freedom the hijab gives me, the freedom from having my body exposed as a sex object or from being judged on a scale of 1–10 by strange men who have no right to know what my body or hair looks like' (Mubarak, 2007). She goes on to explain that the hijab is a form of modesty, security and protection, shifting the focus of attention from a woman's physical attraction, or lack thereof, to the personality that lies beneath. 'By forcing people to look beyond her physical realm, a woman is valued for her intellect, personality and merit' (Mubarak, 2007).

Understandably, the religious observers of the hijab in Quebec are livid: 'I will never take it off. I would choose another job first' said Hajder Ben Houla, who is from Tunisia and a childcare worker at the QwaQwaq Daycare in Montreal's multicultural Cote-des-Neiges district (TGAM, 2013b). She adds that she and women like her are feeling let down by the Quebec Government on the one hand encouraging immigrants from predominantly Muslim French-speaking north African countries such as Tunisia and Algeria but then changing the rules on their job prospects confirming that while Quebec wants French-speaking immigrants it does not want their cultural and religious values.

The Public Response

A public opinion poll, Leger with 1,000 respondents, reports that 65 per cent of francophone Quebeckers support the idea of a values charter as compared to only 25 per cent of anglophones and 33 per cent of allophones (TGAM, 2013c Interestingly, the poll shows highest support not in Montreal where immigration is highest but outside Montreal where immigration is lowest. Proponents agree that Quebec needs to protect and maintain its values despite, or in spite of, immigrant pressures for accommodation. The Coalition Avenir Quebec (CAQ) party supports the PQ on the Charter of Quebec Values.

In addition, the law would further inhibit immigrant integration by driving immigrants and minorities into religion-based private schools because the law exempts the private schools. However, it would apply to the private sector workplaces by amending the Quebec Charter of Human Rights under the principle of gender equality. Francoise David, Quebec Solidaire, says: 'A male Muslim teacher with a beard could teach, but his headscarf wearing wife could not' (TGAM, 2013). Nora Jaffary, Chair of Concordia University's History Department, is not a Muslim but she wore a hijab to work, protesting Bill 60 which would require professors and non-teaching staff at universities to remove their hijab. However, like any other Quebec citizen, university students would not be regulated under this ban, unless they were working on campus as lecturers, researchers or teaching assistants, in which case they would also have to comply with the Charter. Critics object, saying that the move is draconian and divisive. Human rights lawyer, Julius Grey, is convinced that this law is in contempt of the CCRF which includes strong freedom of religion provisions and would fail a Charter challenge. Meanwhile, the Charter of Quebec Values appears to be contradictory since the PQ has confirmed that the prominent crucifix in the National Assembly will remain as an artefact of Quebec's heritage.

Ontario

Ontario is not without controversy on the issue of religious accommodations for Muslims. The Human Rights Tribunal of Ontario recently ordered Human Rights Training to the owners of a Toronto restaurant and awarded damages of $100,000 to three Muslim employees working there who were forced to eat pork, work on religious holidays and break a religious fast to 'taste-test' a soup during Ramadan (HRMOnline, 2013). An article in University Affairs-Affaires Universitaires (UA/AU) on 8 January 2014, 'Women's rights or religious rights: which come first?' described a case where a professor in Ontario was outraged at his university administration's decision offering too much religious accommodation to a student who asked to be excused from participating in a required group assignment because he did not want to publicly interact with female students. The professor denied the request viewing it not as religious freedom but gender discrimination, which would be equally unacceptable if the case involved a student not wanting to interact with a group comprised of Blacks or homosexuals.

Stemp-Morlock (2014) explains that the argument 'gender rights take priority over religious rights' is not supported by the Canadian courts which have ruled that no right is absolute thus automatically trumping another and that each case claiming conflicting rights must be judged on its own merits. The law applies tests to determine to what extent accommodation may be allowed or may need to be limited. The onus is on the party limiting the religious freedom to prove that it is necessary. Some people support the 'slippery slope' argument fearing that starting to accommodate such oppressive religious rights will lead to further demands undermining women's constitutional rights, resulting in women becoming second-class citizens. This conflicts with the rights of women who request such religious accommodation based on their personal values and beliefs. How do we decide between protecting their right to gender equality or their inalienable right to freedom of religion and conscience?

Interestingly, a creative advertisement in Ontario has taken this Quebec controversy to promote their recruitment campaign for their organization in the healthcare industry vying for qualified professionals. See Figure 3.1 for the Quebec Charter of Values poster and Figure 3.2 for the Ontario advertisement. This clearly highlights the divergence in the extreme image and message being sent out to immigrants in Canada about their job prospects in the two provinces and will no doubt influence their decision over where to live, work and raise a family.

Figure 3.1   Non-ostentatious and ostentatious symbols

Source: © Gouvernement du Québec, 2013.

Stories of Two Hijabi Women

Interviews were conducted with two hijabi women to hear their perspective on the discussion. One participant, in her fifties, was from Quebec and had also lived in Ontario and the other participant, in her thirties, was from Ontario and had often visited Quebec. They shared their stories to compare their experiences in the two provinces. Both were professionally qualified working women who had travelled quite extensively internationally. Although the participants were fluent in French, both the interviews were conducted in English. Interviews, one and a half to two hours long, were audio-taped and transcribed for this chapter.

The first participant indicated that she was born and brought up in Quebec in a very traditional French–Canadian family. At the age of 25, she felt an inner spiritual awakening and decided to wear the hijab. At that time she was working as a hairdresser in a beauty salon and her co-workers were horrified at her decision. But she was determined, she said in her interview 'I felt that I was a Muslim from inside … At the time I started, I felt really destined for it but my friends did not like it.' Her family too was shocked and unsupportive of her decision to wear the hijab, 'My family was not happy when I started the hijab. I was 25 then, now I am 50! Twenty-five years of not wearing it then 25 years of wearing it,

WE DON'T CARE WHAT'S ON YOUR HEAD.

WE CARE WHAT'S IN IT.

We're Lakeridge Health, a leading hospital in the Greater Toronto Area.
Our focus is on safety and quality, and we're looking for people like you to join
our team of health professionals. Check us out: www.lakeridgehealth.on.ca

FOLLOW US: @LAKERIDGEHEALTH
LIKE US: FACEBOOK.COM/LAKERIDGEHEALTH

Lakeridge Health

Figure 3.2   An Ontario hospital's job advertisement
Source: Lakeridge Health, 2013.

I have passed every bad experience.' She started crying, 'The most difficult
thing is when they push every bad thing on Muslims but it is not in Islam! It is
not correct to force it. You need to feel it yourself. If not, you should take it off,'
she sobbed recounting the horrors of some hijabi women's recent experiences
in Quebec. 'The Charter opened all the bad things in Quebec. Some ladies are
asked to remove the hijab in public and some people spit at women wearing

the hijab, and one woman's hijab was pulled off her head in front of her son! You need to respect others. This is not correct!' Comparing her experiences in the two provinces she said:

> Most Quebecois people are not open to differences. They like to try the food but not more than that. Hijab was my own choice but after, I was treated differently. It is because of 9/11. It has changed everything. I work in the Catholic school and I am Catholic now still and also Muslim because many things between the two religions are very close, not much difference. I am married to a Muslim man. I became Muslim one year before I married him. I am very active with the mosque and Islamic center in Quebec and I was supported by them. Most of them were immigrants and students from French African colonies since they have the French language and not much English. I decided to have my kids and stayed at home with them. After ten years, I searched for a job and it was not easy! Then I moved to Ontario. I am Canadian but I had to start from zero, like most immigrants. I volunteered, retrained and went back to school for a two-year diploma and now I am a supervisor at two centres. It has been 14 years now and I still get 'the look' but I am confident in my job. All those who know me, know me for who I am not for my hijab. You are what you are and they accept me as I am because they did not know me before the hijab.

With respect to the accommodation of the hijab in the workplace she responded that, 'Every hijab shows the face for identification and can fit in with every workplace. Once the women start to wear the hijab then it is banned in the workplace, it is not fair to them in jobs. More women work in daycares, hospitals and schools. For sure it leads to discrimination, for sure, for sure!'

However, she was not supportive of extreme accommodation.

> I understand the point of the Charter. You need to leave your religion at home and the mosque. I am not in favour of the niqab because you cannot see the face. The hijab does not affect the workplace like Ramadan and five breaks for prayers during the day. I don't expect accommodations for that. I do that at home after work. If the company can accommodate, they should. If you have the time for a break and can get coverage then do it. I am flexible, but I do my best, I am not rigid.

Living in Ontario, she says that 'In Ontario, we do not experience any problems. That's correct! Come, we accept you as you are. In Ontario "We care what is IN your head, not ON it",' she happily quoted a popular advertisement (see Figure 3.2). Here, she lives a normal life. 'I swim, I have a long swimsuit. I go to the gym, they know me there. I do everything. I am a person. I live here and I do what I want. I can't give up the things I like. I like that people see me as who I am and not just the hijab.'

She expressed that immigrants are especially vulnerable but they have the right to protect their culture and values:

> Immigrants give respect to Canada but they don't get it back. Immigrants need to adapt and they do. Quebec already has a ban on hijabs in schools. If both parents are Arab, they have a right to keep their culture. There are too many mixed families. I am Canadian, my kids are Canadian but my husband is not. You need to respect differences. You need to educate people. Sometimes I see women coming to Canada wearing the hijab and she is shy and not confident. I want to look happy, confident, proud of my religion. If you are confident it makes a difference. Just like there are gay people in the workplace. I respect them and they respect me. I took a diversity course and you need to have it in the workplace because you can't judge people by how they look. Diversity is a good thing. We must respect it.

Her travel experiences in Muslim-majority countries have been very positive:

> Oh, it feels so good to travel to Muslim countries! I don't feel alienated. I feel so secure. I never feel judged. I can go everywhere alone without being afraid. There is no danger of harassment or uncomfortable looks. It will never be like that in Canada! Those who understand are those who travel. Others are very close-minded and stereotype everyone. If you want to know something, just ask questions, respectfully. 'Changez les idees' and bring awareness!

The second participant indicated that she came to Canada, from Algeria, seven years ago. Six years before arriving in Canada, she had started to wear the hijab at the age of 25 after completing two *Umra* (religious visits to Mecca) in her early twenties. After the first visit, at the age of 22, she was not even thinking of wearing the hijab. But by the second visit, three years later:

> In my mind the decision was already there. I was not influenced by anyone, it was from inside. I was thinking about it for a year and I was the first one in my family to wear it. My mother and sisters do not wear

it because it is not traditional in Algeria. But I have not changed, it is still me!

She explained a little bit about her Algerian background where, as a French colony:

Most families did not know much about their religion as the French did not allow it. My mother used to go secretly to learn Arabic. My father's French was better than his Arabic which he had learned from his mother. So that generation is good in French but not in classical Arabic which is the language of the Quran. After independence on July 5, 1962, we had access to international television channels and listened to preachers and started to learn more about our religion. In the 1990s, the ten dark years in Algerian history, some women started wearing hijab because they were afraid that they would be targeted by extremist Islamic groups if they did not!

She further detailed her Algerian heritage:

Before, the only ones who would cover were the old women. There is a tradition in Algeria, there is a dress that women wear, not a hijab, but a scarf and a long dress, when going outside the home to do groceries and so on. But some of my female cousins said that I should have waited until I got married! Now, I have no regrets. I have made the right decision. No, I cannot take it off now! There are some of women in Algeria who started wearing it but when they are invited out, they take it off. I cannot understand it! What is the point? In Algeria, it is very flexible. I went back after three years and I was surprised to see the new hijab styles. Some of them are not even hijab because sometimes they do not cover the hair and sleeves. A lot of women are wearing it because it's fashionable! It is a lot more acceptable there in the workplace also now.

She expressed frustration at the lack of awareness about the hijab in Canada and described her experiences in the two provinces:

To people who don't know much about this religion, most of the time I tell them that it is not my father, it is not my brother and it is not my husband because I am not married! For most women who wear the hijab in Canada, it is a challenge. In Ontario, I don't face anything here. I think in Ontario, there are very few wearing the hijab. Being in an Anglophone province makes a difference. They want to know before they start judging. I feel there is much more respect here than in Montreal, for example. When I go to Montreal, I don't feel that much at ease. I don't feel comfortable with the way people look at you. I have one example, like when I go to Montreal in the winter, I put my scarf in a different way. I put it like a French beret. All my hair is covered and I have a big sweater. In the summer, I can't. I can see the reaction of the people, it is completely different! When I wear the hijab or I'm wearing the beret style. I think that it is a judgement.

She does not support the Charter:

Sometimes I say, when I think about the people who are pushing the Charter in Quebec, there are so many things that are important to deal with in the world and they are making a big deal about this. Second thing is, they are saying Charter but they are targeting only one thing, the hijab! All the examples are about one thing, whenever there is a debate, the hijab. Is it really a Charter for religious symbols or is it just for the Muslims? I know a Canadian who is born and brought up here, her parents are from Lebanon, she is a professor and wears the hijab. Someone said to her 'You just go back home!' What does that mean? Canada is always asking for more immigrants but there is a big contradiction between what they say and what is reality.

She said that the media is biased against the Muslims in their reporting. Giving the example of the incident in Norway:

The guy went to the school and killed kids. What was his religion? Say it? What was his religion and origin? I think we should learn from what happened in France. This hatred and racism has spread everywhere. People are saying 'Go back to your country.' Before, we did not have this, now we are insulted on the streets. Ontario, as a reaction to Quebec said to the Muslim community 'We don't judge you by what is on your head but what is in it!' The whole Muslim community should leave Quebec, it will collapse. When immigrants come from Africa they go to Quebec because of the language. I know some of my friends who go to Montreal because there is a network who will help them. This time when I was traveling back from Algeria, I met a family in the airport migrating to Canada. I told them, don't stay in Quebec, go somewhere else in Canada. They are coming here for a better life for their family but they (Quebec) don't want immigrants to bring their culture? What is the culture of this country? You want people to follow the Canadian culture, but what is it? Is it French? With the immigration criteria the minimum they have is a bachelor's, master's, PhD and experience. They have to invest so much time and money. Then you come and tell me 'Ah, you wear the hijab, you cannot have the job!'

She believes that wearing the hijab is clearly her decision and freedom of choice which does not affect her performance on the job, yet there is clear discrimination:

'I really would like to see the face of the people without the hijab.' This is what they think. So, if I come with the hijab, I will be treated differently. Without the hijab I am a person, with the hijab I am nothing! I see it as a contradiction. Free the women? It's my choice to wear it. It's my freedom! My decision for wearing the hijab will never change. In France, women are obliged to remove it when they go to work or school. For me, it is 'No way!' For me that is not acceptable. If it is a place where there are only women, okay. If I go to work and take off my scarf and there are men, I am wearing it because I don't want people to see those parts of my body. I wear it so it will be for life. I can start my work without the hijab. The next day I convert and decide to wear it. Now can you give my job to someone else? We don't judge a book from its cover! The RCMP allow the Sikh turban. Wearing it does not affect the job. Those women when they are with the kids in the daycare they are not obliged to wear it, only when the parents come. How can that child know about religion? They will grow up hating others. Everyday going out for women in Quebec is a challenge. With this Charter, those who were not saying anything before is happening now. This kind of thing has been happening in France but they did not learn from it. They are just following the French way of doing it. If they could only tell me one good thing but I don't see anything good about it.

When asked if she would do things differently in hindsight, her response was: 'I would do the same thing. It was my decision. It took a year to do it. I have no regrets at all. Maybe the regret is that I did not do it sooner!'

Discussion

In the increasingly multicultural and multi-faith population of Canada, employers need to be sensitive to requests for religious accommodation just as they would be sensitive to accommodating disabilities, sexual orientation, age and other kinds of diversity in the workplace. Well-educated, professional, modern hijabi women who choose to wear the hijab based on their own strength of religious values and conviction are demanding workplace accommodations using their agency and voice to challenge the widely prevalent negative and oppressive stereotypes of Muslim women, enriching the debate on equality, individual rights and freedoms in Canada.

These two hijabi women's stories indicate that there are modern, educated, professional hijabi women who are choosing to wear the hijab of their own free will despite facing challenges in Canadian society and the workplace. They are convinced there is no evidence that religious observance by wearing outward symbols, such as the hijab, is disruptive to organizational life, employee productivity or effectiveness. Arguing that the value that the hijab, as a religious symbol, brings into the workplace is that of modesty and such diversity of religious beliefs and practices should be accommodated in the Canadian workplace.

A critical update, since writing this chapter, occurred on Monday 7 April 2014 when Phillipe Couillard, a former neurosurgeon, led the Quebec Liberal Party to a resounding majority victory in the provincial elections with 41 per cent, the PQ 25 per cent, the CAQ 23 per cent and Quebec Solidaire 8 per cent of the popular vote (*National Post*, 2014).

Pauline Marois, who had campaigned for these provincial elections on the promise to rid the public sector of employees wearing the hijab, had inadvertently misjudged the will of the people of Quebec who promptly voted her out of office with the lowest share of the vote since its first election in 1970 (*National Post*, 2014). In his victory speech, Premier Couillard reached out to the minorities who felt targeted by the Party Quebecois policies:

> *Dear friends, the time of inflicting wounds is over. We are all Quebeckers. We should focus on what brings us together. Division is over. Reconciliation begins. We share the values of generosity, compassion, solidarity and equality of men and women with our anglophone fellow citizens who also built Quebec and with our fellow citizens who came from all over the world to write the next chapter in our history with us. I want to tell them that the time of injury is over. Welcome, you are home here* (National Post, 2014).

Conclusion

This chapter has contributed to the debate on religious accommodation in the Canadian workplace which has been on the increase in recent years as diverse immigrants are beginning to exercise their rights in living and working in Canada as their adopted country. These results are from the perspective of hijabi women giving a point of view of those central to the issue of religious accommodation in the two Canadian provinces of Ontario and Quebec. The Charter of Values had resulted in targeting niqabi Muslim women and increasing hostility towards them in Quebec but the election results clearly did not support it. Canadians can indeed be proud of the Canadian Charter of Rights and Freedoms (CCRF, 1982) and our laws should uphold the CCRF, interpreting it in a manner consistent with the preservation and enhancement of the multicultural heritage of Canadians, as demonstrated in the 1985 Supreme Court decision on the *R. v. Big M Drug Mart Ltd.* on the *Lords Day Act* defining religious freedom as:

> *Freedom can primarily be characterized by the absence of coercion or constraint. If a person is compelled by the state or the will of another to a course of action or inaction which he would not otherwise have chosen, he is not acting of his own volition and he cannot be said to be truly free. One of the major purposes of the Charter is to protect, within reason, from compulsion or restraint. Coercion includes not only such blatant forms of compulsion as direct commands to act or refrain from acting on pain of sanction, coercion includes indirect forms of control which determine or limit alternative courses of conduct available to others. Freedom in a broad sense embraces both the absence of coercion and constraint, and the right to manifest beliefs and practices. Freedom means that, subject to such limitations as are necessary to protect public safety, order, health, or morals or the fundamental rights and freedoms of others, no one is to be forced to act in a way contrary to his beliefs or his conscience. What may appear good and true to a majoritarian religious group, or to the state acting at their behest, may not, for religious reasons, be imposed upon citizens who take a contrary view. The Charter safeguards religious minorities from the threat of 'the tyranny of the majority.*[3]

There may be other stories and experiences, undoubtedly, but the ones presented here are with the hope of other voices joining in on future research

---

3   Retrieved on 29 July 2013 from http://scc-csc.lexum.com/scc-csc/scc-csc/en/item/43/index.do.

projects. The theoretical and practical implications are pertinent to cultural values, political policies and societal change with important HRM strategies for practical and successful implementation of religious accommodation in organizations. The issue is not just Canadian but has worldwide implications and practical applications.

Acknowledgement

The author is grateful to the interviewees for participating in this research.

References

Bill 60 (2013). 'Charter Affirming the Values of State Secularism and Religious Neutrality and of Equality between Women and Men, and Providing a Framework for Accommodation Requests'. Retrieved on 4 February 2014, from Assemble Nationale Quebec at http://www.assnat.qc.ca/en/travaux-parlementaires/projets-loi/projet-loi-60-40-1.html.

Bill 94 (2010). 'An Act to Establish Guidelines Governing Accommodation Requests within the Administration and Certain Institutions'. Retrieved on 4 February 2014, from Assemble Nationale Quebec at http://ww.assnat.qc.ca/en/travaux-parlementaires/projects-loi/project-94-39-1.html.

Canadian Broadcasting Corporation (CBC) Archives. Retrieved on 14 February 2014, from http://www.cbc.ca/archives/categories/politics/federal-politics/separation-anxiety-the-1995-quebec-referendum/money-and-the-ethnic-vote.html.

Canadian Charter of Rights and Freedoms (CCRF, 1982). Canadian Constitution Act (1982). Retrieved on 29 July 2013 from http://laws-lois.justice.gc.ca/eng/const/page-15.html.

Canadian Human Rights Act (CHRA) (R.S., 1985, c. H- 6). Retrieved on 29 July 2013 from: http://laws-lois.justice.gc.ca/eng/acts/h-6/.

Canadian Multiculturalism Act (1988). Retrieved on 29 July 2013 from http://laws-lois.justice.gc.ca/eng/acts/C-18.7/page-1.html.

Choudhury, N. (2012). 'Niqab vs. Quebec: Negotiating Minority Rights within Quebec Identity', 1:1 *University of Western Ontario Journal of Legal Studies* 2. Retrieved 20 December 2013 from http://ir.lib.uwo.ca/uwojls/vol1/iss1/2.

Employment Equity Act (1986; Revised, 1995). Retrieved on 29 July 2013 from http://laws-lois.justice.gc.ca/eng/acts/E-5.401/page-1.html.

Golnaraghi, G. and Mills, A.J. (2013). 'Unveiling the Myth of the Muslim Woman: A Postcolonial Critique', *Equality Diversity and Inclusion: An International Journal*, 32(2): 157–72.

HRMOnline (2013). '$100,000 Fine for "Intolerable" Workplace Religious Discrimination', 18 December 2013. Retrieved on 13 January 2013 from http://www.hrmonline.ca/hr-news/100k-fine-for-intolerable-workplace-religious-discrimination-175902.aspx?keyword=$100k fine.

Kay, B. (2013). 'Banning Hijabs Won't Halt Honour Killings,' 4 November 2013. *National Post*. Retrieved on 10 February 2015 from http://news.nationalpost.com/2013/11/04/barbara-kay-banning-hijabs-wont-halt-honour-killings/.

Kingston, A. (2012). 'Veils: Who Are We to Judge?', Retrieved on 28 January 2014 from http://fullcomment.nationalpost.com/2013/11/04/barbara-kay-banning-hijabs-wont-halt-honour-killings/.

Manji, I. (2004). *The Trouble with Islam: A Muslim's Call for Reform in Her Faith*. St Martin's, New York.

Mubarak, H. (2007). 'My Hijab is for Me and for God'. Retrieved on 30 July 2013 from http://newsweek.washingtonpost.com/onfaith/panelists/haida_mubarak/2007/07/women_are_more_than_just_mens.html?.

National Post (2013). 'Quebec Releases Controversial Values Charter'. Retrieved on 28 December 2013 from http://news.nationalpost.com/2013/09/10/quebec-releases-controversial-values-charter-says-anyone-giving-receiving-public-services-needs-face-uncovered/.

National Post (2014). 'Quebec Releases Controversial Values Charter'. Retrieved on 27 April 2014 from http://news.nationalpost.com/2014/04/07/pauline-marois-loses-riding-then-resigns-as-quebec-liberals-hand-parti-quebecois-a-stunning-defeat/.

Statistics Canada (2013). Immigration and Ethnocultural Diversity in Canada. National Household Survey, 2011. Catalogue no. 99-010-X2011001.

Stemp-Morlock, L. (2014). 'Religion is a Human Right: This is a Matter of Reconciling Competing Rights'. University Affairs, 22 January 2014. Retrieved on 14 February 2014 from: http://www.universityaffairs.ca/religion-is-a-human-right.aspx.

The Globe and Mail (TGAM). (2013a). 'In Quebec, a Secular Charter Set to Clash with Religious Freedom'. Wednesday 21 August 2013: A4.

The Globe and Mail (TGAM). (2013b). 'Trudeau Criticizes Quebec's Proposed Charter of Values'. Thursday 22 August 2013: A4.

The Globe and Mail (TGAM). (2013c). 'Religious Freedom: PQ Gains Opposition Support for Limited Secular Charter'. Monday 26 August 2013: A4.

Chapter 4

Spirituality Meets Western Medicine: Sioux Lookout Meno Ya Win Health Centre

KATHY SANDERSON

Introduction

The Sioux Lookout Meno Ya Win Health Centre (Meno Ya Win) is located in Northwestern Ontario, Canada. 'The town of Sioux Lookout is situated in the traditional territory of the Ojibways of Lac Seul First Nation' (Sioux Lookout Meno Ya Win Health Centre, February 2013, p. 4). Aboriginal people are the first people of Canada. 'The term "First Nations" refers to one of three distinct groups recognized as "Aboriginal" in the *Constitution Act* of 1982. The other two distinct groups characterized as "Aboriginal" are the Métis and the Inuit' (Assembly of First Nations). 'These are three distinct peoples with unique histories, languages, cultural practices and spiritual beliefs. More than one million people in Canada identify themselves as Aboriginal persons, according to the 2006 Census' (Aboriginal Affairs and Northern Development Canada).

Sioux Lookout is a small community of approximately 5,300 people. The Health Centre provides service to the residents of Sioux Lookout, as well as the surrounding remote First Nation communities of Nishnawbe–Aski Nation. There are 32 communities serviced by the Health Centre, 28 of which are First Nations, with a total population of approximately 30,000. As a result of this massive geographic area, Meno Ya Win is in the unique situation of providing service to a largely First Nations population. Over 85 per cent of the patients of Meno Ya Win are Aboriginal, while over 85 per cent of the staff are non-Aboriginal (Sioux Lookout Meno Ya Win Health Centre, February 2013).

The name, Meno Ya Win is derived 'from the Oji–Cree term "miinoyawin", which means health, wellness, well-being and the wholeness of the individual'

(Sioux Lookout Meno Ya Win Health Centre, 2012). This word refers to a holistic view of health, in which the whole being is included. This definition of health goes beyond the medically focused, and includes the physical, spiritual, emotional and mental aspects of the person.

As a result of this diverse and unique service area, Meno Ya Win recognized over ten years ago that they needed to incorporate culture, in particular Aboriginal culture, into their practice and facility if they wanted to meet the needs of the population. When designing the new hospital, the cultural and spiritual needs of the patients were considered. As a result, a comprehensive in-house programme for patients was developed, as well as ongoing multi-faceted training for staff. Some of these programmes include language interpretation, spiritual guidance, Aboriginal healers and traditional foods.

The Aboriginal Health Policy for Ontario provides guidelines for organizations that work with Aboriginal populations. This policy presents a framework that can be utilized when designing programmes and services for Aboriginal people, regardless of where they live. Meno Ya Win utilized the recommendations from this policy when designing the new Health Centre, and conducted extensive consultations with the communities to ensure that the new facility would indeed address the cultural and spiritual needs of the people being served. As a result, the Health Centre has numerous programmes, training initiatives, physical features and ongoing community involvement to ensure this occurs.

A large part of these activities involves incorporating the spiritual beliefs of the First Nations into the Health Centre. The needs of this population are diverse, as there is the need to accommodate and recognize both the traditional and Christian belief systems. For this population, it has been found that the people find traditionally-based services to be extremely effective. From research conducted by the Aboriginal Healing Foundation (2006), the greatest portion of survey respondents stated that they prefer to participate in healing and talking circles, ceremonies, discussions with Elders and traditional medicines, over Western therapies. Within healthcare, it is largely recognized that including religious and spiritual practices and care within the Western medical care model is not only a best practice in terms of quality outcomes (College of Nurses of Ontario, 2009), it also assists in overcoming the healthcare disparities that exist for minority groups, including improving access to care, increasing justice and equity, preserving identity and respect (Denier and Gastmans, 2013).

It is also known that the dominant group within a society, systemically, imposes its own views, values and beliefs onto the less dominant, or minority groups (Allen, 2010; Mcauliffe et al., 2012). When ethnocentrism, discrimination or cultural bias occurs in healthcare, the results have significant impacts on patient outcomes, including lower quality of care, lower satisfaction with care, negative attitudes, higher stress levels and overall lower health outcomes (Allen, 2010; Denier and Gastmans, 2013). For these reasons, Meno Ya Win has embraced a comprehensive view of cultural and spirituality within the Health Centre.

The Sioux Lookout Meno Ya Win Health Centre case study is presented as a model of best practice, in which all spiritual and religious beliefs are considered and encouraged in order to include traditional, cultural practices as complementary to mainstream Western medicine, based upon the specific needs of the service community.

First, the health disparities associated with Northwestern Ontario are presented. This section discusses the significant differences in health between Aboriginal and non-Aboriginal populations. Next, the physical components of the hospital property and its relation to Aboriginal spirituality and holistic health are presented. This section includes how the grounds and interior design relate to both the geographic features of the region as well as the religious and spiritual practices of the people. Also, this section has descriptions and pictures of the Ceremonial Room, which is used for traditional Aboriginal ceremonies. The spiritual practices and artefacts section describes the ways in which Aboriginal culture and spirituality are represented throughout the hospital. The programmes of the hospital are outlined, describing how religion and spirituality is incorporated into departments and practices. This includes a detailed account of the Traditional Healing, Medicines, Foods and Supports Programme. The final section describes two ongoing staff training components: Bimaadiziwin and Cross-cultural Care. Both of these programmes were designed specifically for Meno Ya Win in order to ensure that all staff can be responsive to a culturally diverse population by including religious and spiritual needs with Western medicine.

Health Disparities

Significant health disparities exist within certain populations in Northwestern Ontario. Of particular interest for Meno Ya Win are the disparities that affect the majority of the population within the service area.

'The health of Canadian Aboriginal people is poorer than their non-Aboriginal counterparts on most measureable health indicators: life expectancy, infant mortality, unintentional injuries; chronic disease (for example, diabetes, asthma, heart disease, HIV/AIDS); infectious disease (tuberculosis, pneumonia); and hospitalizations' (Northwest Local Health Integration Network, April 2010). Aboriginal people across the country suffer a disproportionate burden of disease and ill-health than their non-Aboriginal counterparts. Their health is influenced by an interconnected confluence of historic and contemporary factors including poverty, unemployment, limited educational attainment, discrimination, marginalization and loss of cultural way of life. This is true for the communities that the Health Centre services.

Poor health status in Aboriginal communities in Northwestern Ontario is thought to be associated with factors such as: poor nutrition/diet; poverty/lack of employment; poor familial relationships (due primarily to intergenerational residential school impacts); inadequate housing conditions (for example, mould, crowding); lack of exercise, lack of health promotion and disease prevention activities as well as poor access to programmes and services; and loss of traditional lifestyles (Sioux Lookout First Nations Health Authority, 31 July 2006).

The complex interaction between factors such as sub-standard housing, overcrowding, isolation, low income, cultural genocide and the residential school experience has led many Aboriginal people to suffer from much poorer physical and mental health. For example (Northwest Local Health Integration Network, April, 2010):

- the cause of death due to alcohol use is 43.7 per 100,000 in the Aboriginal population, almost twice the rate of the general population (23.6 per 100,000);

- death due to illicit drugs is approximately three times the rate of the general population;

- overall, rates of spousal homicide among Aboriginal women are more than eight times higher than for non-Aboriginal women;

- diabetes rates for First Nations people are 1.5 per 100, almost three times the rate for non-First Nations (0.6 per 100);

- suicide and self-injury accounted for 38 per cent of deaths among youth and 23 per cent among adults aged 20 to 44.

These issues are a significant concern for healthcare providers. These disparities clearly highlight the need to look for new ways to include spirituality and culture into the Health Centre if the most effective type of service is to be provided (Northwest Local Health Integration Network, 7 September 2011).

The Physical Environment

In designing the new hospital, architect Douglas Cardinal of Stantec Architecture, consulted with the people of the northern First Nations. He asked people what they wanted to see in their health centre; they asked him to respect the land and elements and construct something that looks inviting. The result is a single storey building in his signature style of harmonious curvilinear forms. His buildings are designed with a soul (Sioux Lookout Meno Ya Win Health Centre, 2012).

Figure 4.1   Exterior view

There are many physical indicators at Meno Ya Win which speak to the holistic approach of the hospital. For example, as you approach our main entrance, you are welcomed by our Grandfather Rocks sitting in the four cardinal directions. One of the First Nation beliefs is that life begins in the East and ends in the North. Our palliative care room is on the North side of the building (Sioux Lookout Meno Ya Win Health Centre, 2012).

Figure 4.2   Grandfather Rocks

'An Elder teaching is to regard rocks and earth as very powerful spirits which are millions of years old. Their spirits and ours, flow together as one. These symbols connect our spirit with these ancient Grandfathers.... In the centre of the Grandfather Rocks is a fire place that can be used for special and sacred ceremonies, such as a sunrise service or blessing ceremony' (Sioux Lookout Meno Ya Win Health Centre, 2012, p. 7).

One of the largest and most prominent features of the health centre is called the 'Canoe Hallway'. This area is home to the registration area, as well as diagnostic services.

> *This area is lit from above by a clerestory skylight shaped like an upturned canoe. (The) definition of clerestory – pronounced 'clear story' is a wall that has a band of windows along the very top. The clerestory wall usually rises above adjoining roofs. The clerestory wall has often been used in architecture in Roman and Greek churches. In large buildings they were important objects, both for their beauty and their utility.... The floor pattern in this area also outlines the design of a canoe and the Douglas Fir columns support the canoe (Sioux Lookout Meno Ya Win Health Centre, 2012, p. 34).*

Figure 4.3   Canoe Hallway

This is one of many examples of ways in which the religious/spiritual beliefs of clients of Meno Ya Win have been incorporated into the physical structure. The physical structure is a direct representation of the philosophy of the Health Centre, in which the whole person is considered. The unique design of Meno Ya Win is that the spiritual considerations have been physically accommodated and honoured within the design of the space.

Figure 4.4   Main entrance lobby

Figure 4.5   Main entrance fire

The most prominent of these in terms of spiritual representations is the Chief Sakatcheway Healing Room, also known as the Ceremonial Room.

Figure 4.6   Ceremonial Room

Figure 4.7   Fire within the Ceremonial Room

This room was designed to ensure that First Nations patients and staff would be able to practice their traditional spiritual beliefs within the facility. The communities that Meno Ya Win services are mostly fly-in air-only with no road access, which means that when patients come to the hospital, they leave behind all that is familiar to them, including family. The Ceremonial Room allows for First Nations people to participate in their spiritual practices, such as smudging, while receiving medical care and treatment. This room was designed to allow for these practices and traditions within the hospital, as it was recognized that the health outcomes of patients is largely impacted by the ability of the facility to incorporate culture into care.

Meno Ya Win also recognizes that a Ceremonial Room does not meet the religious/spiritual needs of all patients and staff. That is why there is also a Multidenominational Meditation Room, located down the hall from the Ceremonial Room. 'This room is used as a quiet room for staff, patients and visitors. It can also be used for church services, education and counselling. The room has cedar lining, the same as the ceremonial room … (and) is open to all faiths and beliefs' (Sioux Lookout Meno Ya Win Health Centre, 2012).

Spiritual Practices and Artefacts

An important part of including spirituality and cultural within the workplace are the practices that can be enjoyed and the visual representations of acceptance. Meno Ya Win has included many different options for patients and staff.

Within Aboriginal practices, it would be difficult, if not impossible, to separate the cultural from the spiritual. The teachings related to culture are largely based upon the relationship between the land, the elements and the Creator. Therefore the inclusion of culture into the hospital represents an inclusion of spirituality.

'The four elements of antiquity and life are: Earth, Air, and Fire, Water, which have dominated natural philosophy for thousands of years … Many consider the four elements of nature as building blocks of the universe' (Sioux Lookout Meno Ya Win Health Centre, 2012, p. 21).

One of the most visible artefacts is the logo of the Health Centre. There are many different representations within the logo. As described in the Points of Interest and Stories and Traditions:

1.   Four people 'reach out' with open arms in a caring fashion to all directions across the region.

2.   Four parties come together to form the universal symbol of a healthcare facility.

3.   The circle represents a rising sun over the horizon, uniting all peoples.

4.   Blue and green waves represent a healthy natural environment.

5.   Colours reflect the medicine wheel and all people.

6.   The circle/slope resembles a 'Q' for continuous quest for Quality (Sioux Lookout Meno Ya Win Health Centre, 2012).

Figure 4.8   Health Centre logo

The logo also refers to the Medicine Wheel:

The Medicine Wheel is brought to healing practices as one way to address cultural diversity of the clients. Because it is so widely incorporated in healing treatments at Aboriginal and non Aboriginal institutions across Canada, many clients are familiar with it … The Medicine Wheel offers a clear visual representation of the perception of balance and harmony necessary to living a healthy life … is holistic; not only does it depict the balance of the physical, mental, spiritual, and cultural as represented in the Four Directions, but it also demonstrates foundations of healthy living within healthy relations between women and men, between individuals and community, and between the social and the spiritual. The Four Directions – north, south, east, and west – are represented by four colours, which also represent the world's people (Waldram, 2008).

Anishinabeg Medicine Wheel

Keewatinong - Spirit Keeper of the North
Colour: White
Direction: North
Time of Day: Night
Season: Winter
Stage of Life: Elder
Animal: Deer
Plant Medicine: Sweet Grass
Place: Mind

Sha'ngabi'hanong - Spirit Keeper of the West
Colour: Black
Direction: West
Time of Day: Evening
Season: Autumn
Stage of Life: Adult
Animal: Bear
Plant Medicine: Cedar
Place: Physical

Wabanong - Spirit Keeper of the East
Colour: Yellow
Direction: East
Time of Day: Morning
Season: Spring
Stage of Life: Baby
Animal: Eagle
Plant Medicine: Tobacco
Place: Spirit

Shawanong - Spirit Keeper of the South
Colour: Red
Direction: South
Time of Day: Afternoon
Season: Summer
Stage of Life: Youth
Animal: Coyote
Plant Medicine: Sage
Place: Emotion

Figure 4.9   Anishinabeg Medicine Wheel

The Medicine Wheel is symbolized by a cross within a circle which represents the power of the four cardinal directions: North, South, East and West. The Wheel is a ceremonial tool and the basis for all teaching. This is implied whenever a wheel or circle is drawn. Since traditional Native American cultures view life as a continuous cycle, life mirrors the cycling of the seasons, the daily rising of the sun and the phases of the moon. They also hold the view that all things are interrelated. The Sacred Mystery, the source of all the creation, reveals itself as powers of the four cardinal directions and these four powers provide the organizing principle for everything that exists in the world. The Anishnaabe often refer to the Medicine Wheel as 'The Circle of Life'. The Seasons, The Races, The Elements of the Universe, The Stages of Life and The Emotions and aspects of Human Behaviour are represented within the Medicine Wheel (Sioux Lookout Meno Ya Win Health Centre, 2012).

One of the more common ceremonies that take place in the Ceremonial Room is a Smudging Ceremony. Smudging is a traditional practice which uses the medicines and sacred plants of sweet grass, cedar, sage and tobacco.

The burning of various medicine plants to make a smudge or cleansing smoke is used by the majority of Native North American peoples. It is a ritual cleansing. As the smoke rises, our prayers rise to the Spirit World where the Grandfathers and our Creator reside. Negative energy, feelings, and emotions are lifted away. It is also used for healing of mind, body and spirit, as well as balancing energies. Our Elders teach us that all ceremonies must be entered into or begun with good intent. So many of us use the smudge as a symbolic or ritual cleansing of mind, body, spirit and emotion. The smell of the burning medicines stimulates our brains to produce beta-endorphins, which are part of the normal healing process of our bodies. Smudging may also be used to cleanse, purify and bless the part of our Mother, the Earth which we utilize in seeking after the spiritual, for example, around the area used for sweatlodge or powwow (KiiskeeNtum, 1998).

Hospital-based Programmes

As culture and spirituality are so closely linked, the hospital offers a comprehensive Traditional Healing, Medicine, Foods and Support Programme. As described in the Sioux Lookout Meno Ya Win poster series, this programme focuses on five main areas:

7.   Odabiidamageg – Governance and Leadership.

8.   Wiichi'iwenin – Patient and Client Supports.

9.   Andaaw'inewinand – Traditional Healing Practices.

10.   Mashkiki – Traditional Medicines.

11.   Miichim – Traditional Foods.

This model of care focuses on the integration of the cultural and spiritual needs of the Aboriginal population with the traditionally Western, scientific medicines. Also included in these programmes is the participation of Aboriginal people as leaders, experts, guides and employees. The goal is to have a holistic and diverse programme that improves access, patient outcomes and safety while building cultural competence.

Governance and Leadership ensures First Nations participation based upon a proportional representation; two-thirds of the Board of Directors of the Health Centre are Aboriginal. Additionally, there is an Elders Council which reviews and oversees programme development and is consulted on key aspects of administration.

Patient and Client Supports is one of the most important aspects of the Traditional Programme as it provides interpreter services. The interpreters provide translation in one of three languages: Ojibway, Cree or Oji–Cree.

This service is vital as so many patients speak a native language. In addition to translation, the interpreters act as advocates, cultural clarifiers and patient navigators. This programme continues to grow and provides support 24 hours a day, 365 days a year.

Another vital support is the Elders in Residence programme. There are two Elders employed by the hospital to provide support and comfort to patients, including visiting, counselling and prayer.

The Traditional Healing Practices and Medicines ensures that there are choices offered for healing. In addition to Western medicine, the Health Centre offers space and supports for ceremonial practices, traditional healing spaces, traditional healers (often called medicine men/women) and traditional medicines. These aspects allow for including spiritual and cultural practices to complement or augment the usual hospital-based services.

Traditional Foods, such as bannock (a type of bread), teas, wild rice, berries, wild game and fowl (moose, caribou, beaver, geese, ducks) and fish, are provided as an alternative to the standard hospital diet. Not only is the type of food important, allowing people to continue to eat the way they are used to at home and find to be the most comforting is part of the benefit, it also allows for the 'recognition of the gift of the Creator in the form of the animal or plant that is being sacrificed so that one can eat' (Sioux Lookout Meno Ya Win Health Centre, January 2009).

Staff Training

Meno Ya Win also recognized that the staff would need extensive training in order to know how to ensure that culture and care were well matched. First Nation culture has some beliefs which can conflict with the Western medicine culture of a hospital. As a collectivist culture, First Nations practices do not appear to fit with the very individualistic policies and methods of a hospital. In order to ensure that a fit could be established, Meno Ya Win developed extensive training programmes for staff.

The historical perspective is key to understanding the importance of respecting First Nations spirituality and religion. Over the course of many years, First Nations traditional practices were severely compromised, if not destroyed, by the introduction of residential schools run by churches and what is known as the '60s scoop', in which many children were removed from families and communities, and the language/culture/spirituality of the population was vilified by those in power. This extreme colonization and acculturation continues to plague First Nation communities in Canada. Therefore it was vital that Meno Ya Win would be able to show these communities that they would not continue to perpetuate these discriminatory and oppressive practices. Educating the staff is a key activity to ensure these patterns are not repeated.

BIMAADIZIWIN

The Bimaadiziwin programme focuses on recognizing the differences and diversities that exist amongst the patients of Meno Ya Win. One important difference that the staff members are educated on is historic: the ways in which the colonization of First Nations has resulted in cultural genocide. The training programme offers staff first-hand knowledge of the history of the population, including residential schools, acculturation and life realities in isolated and remote communities.

Bimaadiziwin is an Anishnabe term which means 'living in a good way'. Bimaadiziwin is about 'life' teachings, how one can achieve peace and harmony with one's self, and with the world around them.

> The teachings are about how to live a life that is in balance, and in doing so helps a person reach a state of menoyawin (health and wellness) … (The) Bimaadiziwin programme is rooted in difference and diversity, and hence based on awareness, understanding, acceptance, respect and empowerment of individuals within their personal cultural context (Sioux Lookout Meno Ya Win Health Centre, (nd) Bimaadiziwin, 1–2).

CROSS CULTURAL CARE

The 'Crosscultural Care' programme was developed specifically for Meno Ya Win, using a scientifically based process, including research informed practices. Research was conducted on best practices for cross-cultural care, largely from nursing journals. However, the intention of the hospital was to ensure that the programme would meet the specific and diverse needs of the First Nations populations. Consultations were held with the Elders Council and other groups which represented different cultural and spiritual/religious communities. The result is a comprehensive training project which focuses on self-awareness and understanding how the culture of service providers impacts how they view and deliver care. This mandatory training programme has been running for approximately five years and recently a review of the results was conducted, with very positive feedback. 'For both personal and professional relevance, respondents rank the training highly, with clusters around 8 to 10, with 10 indicating the highest score' (Florence Woolner and Associates, 2013). In 2013–2014, a modified version of the programme was provided to 11 small hospitals within Northwestern Ontario, recognizing Meno Ya Win's programme as a standard for excellence.

Nursing was used as the basis for cultural care direction for the programme for a number of reasons. First, nursing research in the area of culture has exceeded that of other health professions. The initial work in the area of transcultural nursing began in the 1950s and remains the primary theory connecting care practices to patient culture (Xu et al., 2006). Second, 'care is the essence of nursing and the central, dominant, and unifying feature of nursing. Care is viewed as a powerful means to help clients recover from illnesses or unfavourable human life conditions' (Leininger, 1988).

It is also recognized that 'nurses spend more time with the patients ... Greater involvement with patients gives nurses more opportunities to provide spiritual care ... there is a close relationship between the nature of spirituality and healthcare professions, particularly among nurses' (Kazemipour and Amin, 2012).

The care that is provided by an individual to an individual is one of the foundations of nursing. Not surprisingly, including care with cultural sensitivity results in better outcomes for patients, both physically and mentally. It has also been found that patients cope better and have improved feelings of well-being when culture and spirituality are included as part of care. Additionally, care at this level builds feelings of acceptance and belongingness (College of Nurses of Ontario, 2009; Misra-Hebert and Isaacson, 2012; Pawar, 2009; Sioux Lookout Meno Ya Win Health Centre, April 2005; Sprung et al., 2012).

These factors, however, have not resulted in a 'one best solution' type of approach for providing culturally safe care. There is not a packaged programme which can be implemented for educating on cultural and spirituality (Allen, 2010). This is why Meno Ya Win utilized a research-informed methodology, while balancing the scientific with the local (Registered Nurses' Association of Ontario, 2007). The inclusion of First Nations perspectives and other local consumers ensured that the programme met the specific needs and wishes of the Health Centre population. Also, all staff within Meno Ya Win are invited to the training, not just those who provide direct patient care. It is important that all staff are aware of ways in which cultural and spirituality impact patients, as these assumptions impact service in multiple ways.

One of the key messages in the 'Cross-cultural Care' training is related to welcoming and greeting. When there are visible cultural differences within populations, the minority group or the group that is disadvantaged in terms of power often doesn't feel as though they fit in or belong. The 'Crosscultural Care' training repeatedly reinforces the value of acknowledging people, all people, regardless of the context in which you meet or pass them, the importance of being welcoming and providing a greeting. These practices are things that all employees can do to ensure that everyone is feeling comfortable within what can be a very intimidating environment. Further, this practice also encourages additional acceptance and positive interactions between staff. 'Crosscultural Care' not only has impacts on patients, it also promotes understanding between staff members (Sanderson, 2009).

The training focuses on how to incorporate culture and spiritual/religious beliefs into healthcare, with an end goal of impacting health outcomes. There is much evidence that culture is a key aspect of healing (College of Nurses of Ontario, 2009; Registered Nurses' Association of Ontario, 2007). For Meno Ya Win, this meant the development of specific culturally based programmes that would ensure that all patients would be able to practice their culture within the hospital. Education for staff includes sensitivity training, so that staff members understand the historical perspectives which contribute to First Nations population health, as well as culturally safe care training which ensures that staff are comfortable asking questions about religion and spirituality.

The training that staff receives continues to evolve. The Health Centre has adopted a continuum to identify the stages of development when working towards culturally safe care.

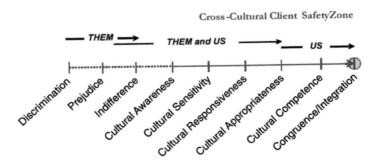

Figure 4.10   Cross-cultural client safety zone

As the continuum indicates, moving towards culturally safe care is a process, and it doesn't simply involve one aspect of care. Individuals, groups, communities, policies, practices and commitment all need to be congruent if progress is to be made.

Conclusion

This case study provides an example of a comprehensive model by which religion and spirituality have been built into a Western, medical service. By ensuring a holistic approach in all areas of hospital and programme design, Meno Ya Win has addressed one of the fundamental necessities for healing and recovery; feeling welcomed within a culturally representative care model. It has long been recognized that people heal faster and feel better when their religious and spiritual needs are met. Meno Ya Win has been hugely successful in ensuring this is communicated to patients and staff, not only by offering specific programmes and services, but by fully designing a structure which represents the population that it serves. Meno Ya Win represents a Centre of Excellence and model for providing access and acceptance for incorporating cultural and spirituality into care and the workplace.

References

Aboriginal Affairs and Northern Development Canada. (nd). Aboriginal Peoples and Communities. Retrieved on 2 March 2014, from http://www.aadnc-aandc.gc.ca/eng/1100100013785/1304467449155.

Aboriginal Healing Foundation. (2006). A Healing Journey: Final Report Summary Points. Aboriginal Healing Foundation, Ottawa, Ontario.

Allen, J. (2010). 'Improving Cross-cultural Care and Antiracism in Nursing Education: A Literature Review', *Nurse Education Today*, 30(4): 314–20.

Assembly of First Nations. (nd). Description of the Assembly of First Nations. Retrieved on 2 March 2014, from http://www.afn.ca/index.php/en/about-afn/description-of-the-afn014.

College of Nurses of Ontario. (2009). Culturally Sensitive Care. College of Nurses of Ontario: Toronto, ON. Retrieved on 6 February 2014, from www.cno.org.

Denier, Y. and Gastmans, C. (2013). 'Realizing Good Care within a Context of Cross-cultural Diversity: An Ethical Guideline for Healthcare Organizations in Flanders, Belgium', *Social Sciences & Medicine*, 93: 38–46.

Florence Woolner & Associates. (2013). Draft: Project Evaluation of Bimaadiziwin and Cross Cultural Care Training for Sioux Lookout Meno Ya Win Health Centre. Ontario, Sioux Lookout.

Kazemipour, F. and Amin, S.M. (2012). 'The Impact of Workplace Spirituality Dimensions on Organisational Citizenship Behaviour among Nurses with the Mediating Effect of Affective Organisational Commitment', *Journal of Nursing Management*, 20(8): 1039–48.

KiiskeeNtum. (1998). 'Gifts from the Creator for Man's Use…The Smudging Ceremony', *Windspeaker*, 16(2).

Leininger, M.M. (1988). 'Leininger's Theory of Nursing: Cultural Care Diversity and Universality', *Nursing Science Quarterly*, 1(4): 152–60.

Mcauliffe, G.J., Grothaus, T., Jensen, M. and Michel, R. (2012). 'Assessing and Promoting Cultural Relativism in Students of Counseling', *International Journal of Advanced Counselling*, 34(2): 118–35.

Misra-Hebert, A.D. and Isaacson, J.H. (2012). 'Overcoming Healthcare Disparities via Better Cross–cultural Communication and Health Literacy', *Cleveland Clinic Journal of Medicine*, 79(2): 127–33.

Northwest Local Health Integration Network. (2010). Aboriginal Programs and Service Analysis Strategies Report. Retrieved on 6 February 2014, from http://www.northwestlhin.on.ca/uploadedFiles/Home_Page/Report_and_Publications/NW%20LHIN%20Aboriginal%20Health%20Programs%20and%20Services%20Analysis%20and%20Strategy.pdf.

Northwest Local Health Integration Network. (2011). Diversity Session: A Value Added Dimension to our Health System. Retrieved on 6 February 2014, from http://www.northwestlhin.on.ca/uploadedFiles/Home_Page/Be_Informed/Summary%20Report%20from%20Diversity%20Sessions%20v2.pdf.

Pawar, B.S. (2009). 'Workplace Spirituality Facilitation: A Comprehensive Model', *Journal of Business Ethics*, 90(3): 375–86.

Registered Nurses' Association of Ontario. (2007). Embracing Cultural Diversity in Healthcare: Developing Cultural Competence. Nursing Best Practice Guidelines Program. Toronto, Canada. Retrieved on 6 February 2014, from www.rnao.ca.

Sanderson, K. (2009). *Cross Cultural Care Training, Day One. Sioux Lookout Meno Ya Win Health Centre*. Ontario, Sioux Lookout.

Sioux Lookout First Nations Health Authority. (2006). The Anishinabe Health Plan. Retrieved on 2 March 2014, from http://www.slfnha.com/wp-content/uploads/2011/12/AHP-FINAL-REPORT.pdf.

Sioux Lookout Meno Ya Win Health Centre. (nd). *Achieving Cultural Integration in Health Services: Linking Concept, Structure and Practice to Lead Organizational and Personal Congruency*. Ontario, Sioux Lookout.

Sioux Lookout Meno Ya Win Health Centre. (nd). Bimaadiziwin: A Menoyawin Program for Building Cross–Cultural Competency and Client Safety. Retrieved on 6 February 2014, from http://www.slmhc.on.ca/assets/files/traditional-healing/bimaadiziwin.pdf.

Sioux Lookout Meno–Ya–Win Health Centre. (2005). *Bii maa di zi win and Meno–Ya–Win: A Study of Development of Traditional Approaches to Healthcare at Sioux Lookout Meno–Ya–Win Health Centre*. Ontario, Sioux Lookout.

Sioux Lookout Meno Ya Win Health Centre. (2009). *An Introduction to Sioux Lookout Meno Ya Win Health Centre*. Ontario, Sioux Lookout.

Sioux Lookout Meno Ya Win Health Centre. (2012). *Points of Interest and Stories and Traditions*. Ontario, Sioux Lookout.

Sioux Lookout Meno Ya Win Health Centre. (2013). *Cultural Orientation to the Sioux Lookout Meno Ya Win Health Centre*. Ontario, Sioux Lookout.

Sprung, J.M., Sliter, M.T. and Jex, S.M. (2012). 'Spirituality as a Moderator of the Relationship between Workplace Aggression and Employee Outcomes', *Personality and Individual Differences*, 53(7): 930–34.

The Silent Canoe (nd). Anishinaabe Medicine Wheel. Retrieved on 2 March 2014, from http://www.thesilentcanoe.com/anishinaabe-medicine-wheel.html.

Waldram, J.B. (ed.) (2008). *Aboriginal Healing in Canada: Studies in Therapeutic Meaning and Practice*. Ottawa, Aboriginal Healing Foundation.

Xu, Y., Shelton, D., Polifroni, E.C. and Anderson, E. (2006). 'Advances in Conceptualization of Cultural Care and Cultural Competence in Nursing: An Initial Assessment', *Home Healthcare Management & Practice*, 18(5): 386–93.

Chapter 5

Islam in American Organizations: Legal Analysis and Recommendations

BAHAUDIN G. MUJTABA AND FRANK J. CAVICO

Introduction

The workplace is an arena where the private life of an employee, encompassing his or her religious beliefs, and his or her work life, can collide, thereby raising important as well as contentious issues of the role of religion in the workplace. The presence of religiously observant Muslim employees in the workplace, as well as employees of other religious beliefs, of course, can create conflicts between workplace policies and rules and religious observances and practices. These conflicts can become acute when the religious beliefs are held by, and the religious practices observed by, employees who are members of minority or non-traditional religions. Tension can also arise among employees when a particular employee's religious practices are perceived to impinge on another employee's work life. Examples of such conflicts and tensions are dress and grooming requirements, religious observances, prayer breaks, ritual washings, religious calendars and quotations, and prohibitions with certain medical examinations, testing and procedures.

This chapter provides a legal analysis of the role of Islam in American organizations, focusing primarily on the employment context, and also provides recommendations to employers on avoiding religious discrimination claims pursuant to US civil rights laws. The chapter first provides basic information as to the religion of Islam and a brief history of Muslims in America. The chapter then examines the most common challenges that American Muslims face in the workplace. Next, the authors analyse the laws that employers and managers must be aware of and abide by, principally Title VII of the *Civil Rights Act*, as well as the US federal government agency empowered to enforce Title VII –

the Equal Employment Opportunity Commission. The prohibitions against discrimination, harassment and retaliation based on religion are examined. Moreover, the employer's legal duty to accommodate the religious beliefs and practices of its employees is examined. The chapter then offers pertinent recommendations to organizational leaders so they not only can fulfil their legal duties, but also attract and retain the most qualified workers regardless of their religious affiliations, beliefs, observances and practices. Accordingly, the chapter also provides recommendations for ethics, diversity and sensitivity training as well as suggestions for future research.

Overview

Religion is a central component to culture and is thus tied closely to cultural identity. The religion of Islam, like other religions, has certain beliefs, observances and practices that may result in legal, ethical and practical ramifications for believers who are employees in the modern day workplace (Mujtaba, 2010, 2007). For example, appearance and grooming practices are regarded by many people as integral elements to their religious affiliation, beliefs and practices. For example, some Muslim men may choose to have a beard, and Muslim women may insist on wearing headscarves or head coverings both on and off the job, called hijabs, or refuse to wear certain trousers that are not loose-fitting because of their religious beliefs. An employer's appearance and grooming rules, therefore, may conflict with its employees' religious beliefs, thereby raising important civil rights issues. Religious beliefs can also form the essence of one's personal identity (Cavico and Mujtaba, 2012, 2011a, b, c). Ruan (2008) explains that:

> *Religious expression in particular can communicate many deeply held views. What people wear (such as a head scarf or prayer beads), what and whether they choose to eat (including strict dietary guidelines such as no pork or no meat on certain days or abstaining from all meals for certain periods), and what holidays they find important (such as Rosh Hashanah, Eid-al-Adha, or Good Friday) are expressions communicating both religious identity and the level of commitment that person holds. In many instances, these expressions cannot be changed, at least without altering the core of one's identity (pp. 6–7).*

MUSLIMS IN AMERICA

Ruan (2008) points out that 'as American workplaces become more diverse, it is inevitable that a growing number of workers will desire to express themselves in religious ways in the workplace' (p. 22). Zaheer (2007) adds that the Islamic religion will present 'unique problems' for employers in seeking to fairly allow religious expression in the workplace due to the 'practice intensive nature' of the faith (p. 497). Solieman (2009) points to a report by the Council on American–Islamic Relations (CAIR) concerning the state of Muslim–American civil liberties in the US, and which includes information on Muslim–Americans in the US workforce. In its 2008 report, the Council reported that discrimination in the workplace increased by 18 per cent from the previous year; and furthermore that in 2003 only 196 cases of employment discrimination were related to the Council, but by 2007 the number increased to 452 (Solieman, 2009, p. 1072).

The USA is a very pluralistic and heterogeneous country that has traditionally welcomed immigrants from around the work; and thus is a country that contains many different religions. Accordingly, all the world's principal religions are now observed and practiced in the US. Gandara (2006) depicts Arab–Americans as 'fast-growing minority' and notes that in the last two decades the Arab–American population has increased by at least 40 per cent (p. 171). Gandara also relates that as of 1 September 2004, there were approximately three million Arab–Americans and seven million Muslim–Americans residing in the US (p. 171). Zaheer (2007) notes that Islam will soon surpass Judaism as the largest minority religion in the US, thus 'marking the first time in recent American history that a non-Judeo-Christian religion is the most practiced minority faith in the United States' (p. 498).

American Muslims are comprised of a diverse group of professionals from different backgrounds and industries. These Muslims work and live amongst us throughout various cities and states in the country. To achieve the American dream, these Muslims have worked hard to be model citizens in hopes of creating better communities for themselves and their neighbors. Due to the Islamic emphasis on knowledge and education, a large proportion of Muslims in America hold advanced degrees and work in prominent fields such information technology, medicine, engineering, education, etc. Yet deeply-rooted stereotypes remain present, and many Muslims have become victims of prejudice and misinformation over the past few decades (Cavico and Mujtaba, 2011a).

Abdullah Antpeli, the Muslim chaplain at Duke University, also relates the challenges confronting Muslims in the United States:

> *Although it is the most recent face of discrimination, Islamophobia is nothing new. Islamophobia is very similar to anti-Semitism,*

homophobia, and racism, with which society has dealt with in the past. To view discrimination against Muslims as a unique issue pertaining only to Muslims would ignore the lessons of history. We must discuss Islamophobia as a human problem that has shown itself in different forms and shapes in other times and in different communities. Unfortunately, we human beings often seek a common enemy. And creating a common enemy is not without its benefits. Defaming and dehumanizing certain groups of people is often the best way to seize or hold power. It justifies certain foreign, domestic, and economic policies and unifies disharmonious factions ... Even though it should be understood as a persistent human problem, Islamophobia has become a growing concern since 9/11 ... why are things worse after 9/11? After the attacks, people were upset, people were confused, and they were questioning the nature of Islam ... So, since 9/11, Islam has been decried as evil and a religion of terrorists. Muslims have been branded as primitive, vengeful, and angry people who oppress women, who are anti-gay, and who possess values that are irreconcilable with the Western Judeo–Christian civilization. This message has been repeated so many times that it is no longer just an idea or an unfounded claim. It has started sinking into the hearts and minds of many people as a reality (Antepli, 2010, pp. 1–2).

Another challenge facing Muslims in the US today is their stereotyped portrayal by Hollywood in movies and television shows. Yin (2010, p. 103) recounts that:

Long before the 11 September, 2001 terrorist attacks, Muslims – especially Arab Muslims – had been a stock set of characters in American television shows and movies ... Hollywood has long stereotyped Arabs as blonde-lusting sheikhs or uncivilized terrorists. Unsurprising, since 9/11 there has been an explosion of thriller programs focusing on terrorism, often with Arab and/or Muslim villains.

In reviewing the new programming by the entertainment industry, Yin (2010) concludes:

The results are mixed. On the one hand, while Arabs and Muslims are still frequently depicted as terrorists, television and movie producers have made greater efforts to show Arab–Americans actively participating in counterterrorism. On the other hand, those 'good' Arab roles are still secondary characters whose contributions, though important on-screen, do not do justice to their real life counterparts.

In addition, many of the new programs introduce a sinister new type of terrorist: the 'sleeper.' The new archetype is a seemingly normal Arab–American who insidiously plots to carry out terrorist attacks from inside the country. Television shows and movies are, of course, stylized fiction, and their stereotyped depictions are not the same thing as actual discrimination against Arabs and Muslims. However, as one defender of movies with Arab villains notes: 'Hollywood reflects the perceptions and anxieties of the times.' It may be that Hollywood produces movies and television shows with Arab villains because that is what the audience expects (p. 104).

Aziz (2012) believes that as a result of the 11 September terrorist attacks, Islam has been recast as a hostile political ideology as opposed to a bona fide religion. As a result, Aziz (2012) explains:

Anything overtly Muslim becomes an indicia of terrorism. To some, the assertion is an exaggeration calling into question the speaker's impartiality. To others, this conclusion is becoming an alarmingly accurate appraisal of current events nationwide. Take for instance the furore in the fall of 2010 arising out of the approved plans to build a mosque two blocks from Ground Zero. What should have been a fringe right-wing effort to stop a lawful project exposed the entrenched animosity and distrust held against Muslims by a significant number of Americans are not patriotic. Indeed, nine years after 11 September, 2001, twenty-five percent of Americans believe that Muslims are not patriotic. Similarly, sixty-eight percent of Americans opposed the building of the mosque primarily because they associated a mosque with the terrorists of 11 September. While some commentators and political leaders reminded the public of American's cherished principle of freedom of religion, many doubted its applicability to the 'Ground Zero Mosque' (pp. 202–3).

Consequently, Aziz (2012) declares that actions that would normally constitute religious discrimination now have become 'legitimate safeguards to protect the homeland' (p. 202) and 'in the midst of a suspicious public, Islam's perceived status as a hostile political ideology as opposed to a religion exempts Muslim's religious practices from constitutional or statutory protections' (p. 203). Such antagonism and discrimination against Muslims will be most keenly felt in the workplace.

MUSLIMS IN THE WORKPLACE

The workplace is an arena where the private life of an employee, encompassing his or her religious beliefs and his or her work life, can collide, thereby raising important as well as contentious issues of the role of religion in the US workplace. The presence of religiously observant Muslim employees in the workplace, as well as employees of other religious beliefs, of course, can create conflicts between workplace policies and rules and religious observances and practices. These conflicts can become acute when the religious beliefs are held by, and the religious practices observed by, employees who are members of minority or non-traditional religions. Tension can also arise among employees when a particular employee's religious practices are perceived to impinge on another employee's work life. Examples of such conflicts and tensions are dress and grooming requirements, religious observances, prayer breaks, ritual washings, religious calendars and quotations, and prohibitions with certain medical examinations, testing and procedures. Ruan (2008) points out that 'as American workplaces become more diverse, it is inevitable that a growing number of workers will desire to express themselves in religious ways in the workplace' (p. 22). Zaheer (2007) adds that the Islamic religion will present 'unique problems' for employers in seeking to fairly allow religious expression in the workplace due to the 'practice intensive nature' of the Islamic religion (p. 497).

Regarding the prevalence of religious discrimination generally, the Equal Employment Opportunity Commission (EEOC) reports that for 2011 there were 4,151 religion-based charges filed (up from 2,127 in 2001) and specifically that 21.3 per cent were predicated on the Muslim religion (EEOC, 2013a). Furthermore, of the 11,833 national origin charges filed in 2011 (up from 8,025 in 2001), 8.9 per cent were parties who identified themselves as Middle Eastern or Muslim (up from 1.7 per cent in 2001 (EEOC, 2013a). Solieman (2009) points to a report by the CAIR concerning the state of Muslim–American civil liberties in the US, and which includes information on Muslim–Americans in the US workforce. In its 2008 report, the Council reported that discrimination in the workplace increased by 18 per cent from the previous year; and furthermore that in 2003 only 196 cases of employment discrimination were related to the Council, but by 2007 the number increased to 452 (Solieman, 2009, p. 1072). The EEOC reported that in the initial months after the 9/11 attacks, the agency saw a 250 per cent increase in the number of religion-based discrimination claims involving Muslims (EEOC, 2013d). Aziz (2012, p. 242), reporting on EEOC statistics, indicates that the complaints of illegal discrimination against Muslim employees more than doubled from 2004 to 2009, rising from 697 to 1,490, and that 425 complaints in 2009 were instituted by Muslim women. Furthermore, in 2009, the EEOC filed 803 formal charges on behalf of Muslim employees, 25 per cent of whom alleged religious discrimination (Aziz, 2012, p. 242). Bader (2011, p. 274) thus concludes that '...Muslims have faced great difficulty protecting their right to practice their faith in the workplace. This is particularly true because of the general American antipathy towards Muslims in recent history, especially since the terrorist attacks of September 11, 2011'.

Religion and Title VII of the *Civil Rights Act*

TITLE VII OF THE *CIVIL RIGHTS ACT*

The *Civil Rights Act* of 1964 is the most important civil rights law in the US. This statute prohibits discrimination by employers, labour organizations and employment agencies on the basis of race, colour, sex, religion and national origin (*Civil Rights Act*, 42 U.S.C. Section 2000-e-2(a)(1)). Regarding employment, found in Title VII of the statute, the scope of the statute is very broad, encompassing hiring, apprenticeships, promotion, training, transfer, compensation and discharge, as well as any other 'terms or conditions' and 'privileges' of employment. The act applies to both the private and public sectors, including State and local governments and their subdivisions, agencies and departments. An employer subject to this act is one who has 15 or more employees for each working day in each of 20 or more calendar weeks in the current or preceding calendar year. (42 U.S.C. Section 2000e(b)). One of the principal purposes of the act is to eliminate job discrimination in employment (Cavico and Mujtaba, 2014. The focal point of this work is Title VII of the *Civil Rights Act*, which deals with employment discrimination.

Religion, like race, colour, sex and natural origin, is a protected category pursuant to Title VII of the *Civil Rights Act* of 1964. Consequently, employers are forbidden from discriminating against employees due to the employees' religious beliefs, observances and practices when carrying out those beliefs (*Civil Rights Act* of 1964, 42 U.S.C. Section 2000e). Discrimination is forbidden regarding any aspect of employment, including hiring and discharge, layoffs, pay, job assignments, promotions, training, benefits, as well as any other terms or conditions of employment (EEOC, 2010d). The *Civil Rights Act* of 1964 in Title VII, as amended in 1972, broadly defines 'religion' to include 'all aspects of religious observance and practice, as well as belief' (*Civil Rights Act* of 1964, Title VII, 42 U.S.C. Section 2000e(j)).

RELIGIOUS DISCRIMINATION

The US Supreme Court defined religion as a 'sincere and meaningful belief which occupies in the life of its possessor a place parallel to that filled by the God' (*United States* v. *Seeger*, 1965). The Supreme Court also required that the beliefs professed by a person be sincerely held (Welsh, 1970). Religious beliefs, however, include any religious beliefs, regardless of the religion being a 'traditional' or 'mainstream' one; religion also encompasses any set of ethical or moral beliefs as well as agnosticism and atheism or the right not to believe (*Tiano* v. *Dillard Department Stores*, 1998; *Young* v. *Southwest Savings & Loan Association*, 1975). The EEOC also notes that the protections against discrimination based on religion extend to people who hold sincere ethical or moral beliefs (EEOC, 2010d). There are certain exemptions to the religious discrimination provisions in Title VII. Religious corporations, associations and educational institutions are allowed to discriminate based on religion if they choose to limit employment to persons of a particular religion (*Civil Rights Act*, 42 U.S.C. Section 2000e-1(a)). Also, colleges and schools that are run by religious organizations or whose curriculum is designed to propagate a particular religion have a similar exemption (*Civil Rights Act*, 42 U.S.C. Section 2000e-2(c)).

The EEOC is the federal agency in the US that is charged with enforcing civil rights laws. The EEOC also has the power to promulgate 'guidelines' as to what the agency considers to be legal employment practices as well as illegal discrimination. The agency's guidelines are treated as law by some courts (though not all). Regardless, the agency can sue to seek redress for private parties whom the agency believes were subject to illegal discrimination. The agency has asserted that after the terrorist attacks of 11 September 2001, it determined that 'special measures' were necessary to combat a backlash of employment discrimination against Muslims and people perceived to be Muslim or of Middle Eastern national origin; and furthermore that the agency would be 'vigilant' in preventing and remedying religious and national origin discrimination against Muslims and people of Middle Eastern national origin (EEOC, 2013d).

To sustain a case of discrimination – religious or otherwise – the plaintiff must establish an initial or *prima facie* case is. Basically, *prima facie* means the presentment of evidence which if left unexplained or not contradicted would establish the facts alleged. Generally, in the context of discrimination, the plaintiff employee must show that: 1) he or she is in a class protected by the statute; 2) the plaintiff applied for and was qualified for a position or promotion for which the employer was seeking applicants; 3) the plaintiff suffered an adverse employment action, for example, the plaintiff was rejected or demoted despite being qualified, or despite the fact that the plaintiff was performing his or her job at a level that met the employer's legitimate expectations; 4) after the plaintiff's rejection or discharge or demotion, the position remained open and the employer continued to seek applicants from people with the plaintiff's qualifications. These elements if present give rise to an inference of discrimination. The burden of proof and persuasion is on the plaintiff employee to establish the *prima facie* case of discrimination by a preponderance of the evidence (*Equal Employment Opportunity Commission* v. *The GEO Group, Inc.*, 2010; *Gul-E-Rana Mirza* v. *The Neiman Marcus Group, Inc.*, 2009; Grisham, 2006). In the case of *Imtiaz* v. *City of Miramar* (2009), the plaintiff, a Muslim employee of Indian origin, alleged in his initial complaint that he was subject to 'numerous discriminatory remarks and harassment' and was assigned 'undesirable tasks' that were not assigned to other similarly situated non-Indian and non-Muslim employees (p. 3). He sued for religious, national origin and racial discrimination and harassment; but the Federal District Court dismissed the lawsuit for the failure to establish a *prima facie* case due to the 'vagueness' and factual inadequacy of the allegations in his complaint (*Imtiaz* v. *City of Miramar,* 2009, pp. 3–4). To compare, in the Federal District Court case of *Talibah Safiyah Abdul Haqq* v. *Pennsylvania Department of Public Welfare* (2010), the plaintiff employee, a Muslim woman who practised a form of veiling that required her to cover her whole body with the exception of her hands and face, was a probationary income maintenance employee, who was not hired for a permanent position due to negative performance evaluations. She claimed religious discrimination; and sustained a *prima facie* case by showing that non-Muslim trainees received better training, more attention from their training supervisor and were granted more latitude to make mistakes without suffering repercussions (*Talibah Safiyah Abdul Haqq* v. *Pennsylvania Department of Public Welfare*, 2010, p. 18).

DISPARATE TREATMENT

'Disparate treatment', as noted, in essence means intentional discrimination. That is, the employer simply treats some employees less favourably than others because of their protected characteristics. The EEOC provides an example of disparate treatment of religious expression in the workplace, to wit: an employer allowing one secretary to display a Bible on her desk at work, while telling another secretary in the same workplace to put the Quran on his desk out of sight 'because co-workers will think you are making a political statement, and with everything going on in the world right now, we don't need that around here' (EEOC, 2010e, p. 3). Proof of a discriminatory intent on the part of the employer is critical to a disparate treatment case. The plaintiff employee can demonstrate this intent by means of direct or circumstantial evidence; but the employer's liability hinges on the presence of evidence that discrimination actually motivated the employer's decision. A disparate treatment case will not succeed unless the employee's protected characteristic actually formed a part to the decision-making process and had a determining affect on the outcome. The Federal District Court case of *Mohammed Karim* v. *The Department of Education of the City of New York* (2010) will serve as an example. In that case, a Muslim teacher, teaching English as a second language, was discharged, purportedly for a sufficient and non-discriminatory reason of unsatisfactory teaching based on performance reports. However, the evidence indicated that the school's principal made a number of discriminatory comments about the plaintiff teacher, for example, stating that Muslim men treated women badly, and that during Ramadan the plaintiff's breath was 'foul'. Moreover, the evidence indicated that the principal purposefully delayed the plaintiff's performance report in order to give it to him on a Muslim holiday so as to cause him distress. The Court ruled that these comments and actions raised an inference of a discriminatory animus against the plaintiff teacher (*Mohammed Karim* v. *The Department of Education of New York*, 2010, p. 25).

Of course, if the motivating factor in the employer's decision was some criterion other than the employee's protected characteristic, then there is no disparate treatment liability. For example, in the Federal District Court case of *Jaqueline Durden* v. *Ohio Bell Telephone Company* (2013), the plaintiff employee contended that she was fired from her position as a customer service representative in the phone company's call centre because she began studying and converting to the religion of Islam; but the evidence indicated that the company had a legitimate non-discriminatory reason for the discharge, to wit: the results of a company investigation which concluded that she had been dishonest in requesting leave pursuant to the *Family Medical Leave Act* as well as paid sick time and thus she had abused company benefits. Also, in the Federal District Court case of *M. Moin Masoodi* v. *Lockheed Martin Corporation* (2011), an engineer, a Muslim who was born in India but moved shortly after birth to Pakistan, claimed he was discriminated against when he was denied a promotion. However, the evidence indicated that there was a 'better' candidate for the position, one who had more education, including an MBA degree, which the plaintiff did not have, and who interviewed better. The case is important for the recitation by the Court of a legal principle from the Fifth Circuit Court of Appeals: '…Choosing some other candidate because he is the best-qualified individual for a job is generally a legitimate, non-discriminatory reason for an adverse employment decision' (p. 49). Similarly, in the case *Equal Employment*

Opportunity Commission v. *Kelly Services, Incorporated* (2010), a Muslim woman claimed disparate treatment discrimination when an employment service did not refer her to a job as a temporary worker for a commercial printing company. However, the evidence indicated the woman wore the Muslim headscarf and was not willing to take it off and that the employer had a dress policy, facially neutral and neutrally enforced, of prohibiting headwear and loose-fitting clothing for safety reasons due to the fact that the employees would be working on an assembly line with rolling and moving parts and chains; and thus the Court denied her discrimination claim since there was a legitimate and non-discriminatory reason not to hire her (*Equal Employment Opportunity Commission* v. *Kelly Services, Incorporated*, 2010).

DIRECT VERSUS CIRCUMSTANTIAL EVIDENCE

Direct evidence is evidence that clearly and directly indicates the employer's intent to discriminate; that is, such evidence is the motivating factor, and thus the proverbial 'smoking gun' that directly discloses the employer's discriminatory intent (*Nazeeh Younis* v. *Pinacle Airlines, Inc.*, 2010; *Gul-E-Rana Mirza* v. *The Neiman Marcus Group, Inc.*, 2009). To illustrate, in the case of *Yussef Johnson* v. *Comer Holding LLC and CL Automotive LLC* (2010), a Muslim employee, an operations manager at an automotive facility, was discharged for certain performance issues. He claimed discrimination and claimed as direct evidence of discrimination three instances: 1) the company's director of HR forwarded to the plaintiff employee along with nine other employees, and knowing that plaintiff was a Muslim, a 'chain-letter' with a Christian religious theme and a Biblical verse; 2) the director of HR saying in the context of another employee who was complaining of a malady and contemplating taking medication that he would take the medication if 'Man, I'm hurting like a Muslim'; and 3) the plant manager saying to plaintiff that he wanted to have a 'Come to Jesus meeting' with him to discuss performance issues (pp. 17–19). The Court, however, found that the three aforementioned incidents did not constitute sufficient evidence of a discriminatory animus to the plaintiff employee. The Court explained that the 'chain-letter' did have a Christian context, and could be construed as 'impolite and insensitive' but was not demeaning or derogatory towards Muslims or non-Christians; that the term 'come to Jesus' in the context of a meeting had a neutral meaning; and that term 'hurting like a Muslim', though 'peculiar', was not derogatory towards Muslims (*Yussef Johnson* v. *Comer Holding LLC and CL Automotive LLC*, 2010, pp. 19–21).

Yet as emphasized by Solieman (2009): 'Of course, clear proof of an employer's intent simplifies a Title VII case. For the most part however, cases with proof are few and far between' (p. 1093). Accordingly, as one Court noted, the evidentiary term, 'direct method' is a bit 'misleading' since it encompasses not only 'direct' evidence, such as admissions of discriminatory motive, but also indirect circumstantial evidence that suggests or raises an inference of discriminatory motive (*Abuelyaman* v. *Illinois State University*, 2011, pp. 809–10). To illustrate, in the case of *Abuelyaman* v. *Illinois State University* (2011) an Arab–Muslim professor claimed that he was not granted tenure due to religious discrimination; he offered as evidence the fact that the tenure determination was based in part on student evaluations of his teaching, which he felt were unduly prejudicial due to his religion and nationality. However, the university rebutted any inference of discrimination by showing that three other non-tenured assistant professors, who were not in a protected class, were also denied tenure due to average or below-average marks on evaluations (*Abuelyaman* v. *Illinois State University*, 2011). To illustrate, in the Federal District Court case of *Leila Diab v. Chicago Board of Education* (2012), it was found that there was a sufficient inference of discriminatory motive to support a disparate treatment claim by a Muslim female language teacher of Palestinian national origin, who asserted she was sanctioned more harshly, based on student complaints and accusations as well as performance evaluations, than other non-Muslim and non-Arab teachers when facing similar allegations of misconduct and poor performance. Key to the case was a statement by the school board administrator decision-maker, in a pre-disciplinary hearing, that the plaintiff employee 'intimidates students' when she tells them she was educated in the Middle East. That comment, which the plaintiff found 'demeaning', combined with the 'uneven' discipline raised the inference of religious and national origin discrimination (*Leila Diab* v. *Chicago Board of Education*, 2012, p. 920). To compare, in the Federal District Court case of *Yassim Mohamed v. Public Health Trust of Miami Dade County* (2010, pp. 21–2), the following statement by a supervisor made to a Muslim employee of Indian descent who requested and received a religious accommodation to attend Friday worship services was not construed by the Court as sufficient evidence of direct discrimination, to wit: 'So you went over my head … This is a Christian country. If I give you time off to go to the mosque, I have to give everybody time off to go to church. We don't kill people here. Your religion is your problem.' The employee who was a probationary employee was ultimately terminated for performance reasons.

Circumstantial evidence can also be used in a discrimination case. Illegal discrimination is an intentional legal wrong. Since proof of this wrongful intent – discriminatory or otherwise – is notoriously difficult for a plaintiff to obtain, the courts at times permit discriminatory motive to be inferred from the facts of the case (*Gul-E-Rana Mirza* v. *The Neiman Marcus Group, Inc.*, 2009).

For example, in the federal appeals case of *Kamal Aly* v. *Mohegan Council, Boy Scouts of America* (2013), the Court held that an inference of discrimination was present due to a 'correlation' between the plaintiff employee's expanded recruitment efforts in the Muslim community and the negative job evaluations he received which precluded his further training and a promotion opportunity; and that inference, said the Court, 'goes directly to (his) discrimination claim' (p. 37). Also, in the Federal District Court case of *Pervais Kaiser* v. *Colorado Department of Corrections* (2012), a probationary corrections officer of Pakistani national origin and a Muslim was terminated. He claimed he was the subject of religious and national origin discrimination based principally on the statement by a supervisor asking him if he was a Muslim and from Pakistan, and when he answered in the affirmative, the supervisor stated 'So you are the guy' (*Pervais Kaiser* v. *Colorado Department of Corrections*, 2012, p. 27). The Court, underscoring that the burden of establishing a *prima facie* case of inferential discrimination was 'light' and 'not onerous' ruled that his termination was sufficiently discriminatory to establish an initial case (*Pervais Kaiser* v. *Colorado Department of Corrections*, 2012). However, the evidence also indicated that the employer department of corrections possessed a legitimate, non-discriminatory reason for the discharge because the employee demonstrated unacceptable performance, particularly his chronic tardiness and unreliable attendance, being late for meetings and briefings and from returning from lunch, as well as not being available for duty without telling anyone that he was leaving and when he would return, even after he had been counselled on his unacceptable performance, which did not improve (*Pervais Kaiser* v. *Colorado Department of Corrections*, 2012).

Problematical discriminatory situations would arise from suspicious timing of or even from the fact of differences in treatment, such as better treatment of similarly situated employees not in the protected class (*Nazeeh Younis* v. *Pinacle Airlines, Inc.*, 2010; *Gul-E-Rana Mirza* v. *The Neiman Marcus Group, Inc.*, 2009). To illustrate, in the Federal District Court case of *Equal Employment Opportunity Commission* v. *Abercrombie & Fitch Stores* (2013), the plaintiff was a Muslim teenager, raised in a Muslim family, who wore a headscarf and who applied for a part-time sales associate position. She received a passing score on the exam; but she was not hired because she did not have the 'Abercrombie Look'. The defendant company also asserted as a legitimate non-discriminatory reason for not hiring her the fact that it was 'low season' in the retail industry and that she could only work three days a week. She claimed that the asserted reasons were merely a pretext masking religious discrimination. The Court agreed, stating:

The Court finds that the EEOC has supplied sufficient evidence to show a genuine question of material fact as to the validity of Abercrombie's justification. A reasonable jury considering the evidence suggesting that availability was not typically a hiring consideration and showing that three candidates with lower scores were hired over (plaintiff) could conclude that Abercrombie's 'availability' justification is a thinly veiled excuse cloaking the true motivation behind its decision not to hire (her). Taken in consideration with the evidence that (her) religion and her wearing of the hijab were addressed during the interview, a reasonable jury may further infer that Abercrombie's motivation was a discriminatory one (Equal Employment Opportunity Commission v. Abercrombie & Fitch Stores, 2013, p. 24).

THE PRETEXT DOCTRINE

In a circumstantial evidence case, when the defendant employer does contend that its rationale was an appropriate, legitimate and non-discriminatory business one, the plaintiff employee is allowed to show that the proffered reason was really a pretext for discrimination. Pretext means that the employer's stated reason was fake, phony, a sham, a lie; and not that the employer made a mistake or error in judgment or made a 'bad' decision (*Zahra Mowafy* v. *Noramco of Delaware, Inc.,* 2009; *Gul-E-Rana Mirza* v. *The Neiman Marcus Group, Inc.,* 2009; *Mansoor Alam* v. *HSBC Bank,* 2009). To illustrate, in the Federal District Court case of *Campbell* v. *Avis Rent A Car System* (2006), an employee, a recent convert to Islam who decided to wear a Muslim headscarf to work, was fired supposedly for failing to file in a timely manner a personal injury accident report when luggage fell on her. However, the evidence indicated that she was subject to numerous incidents of religious harassment, including being called a 'disgrace' and a 'symbol of 9/11 to customers'; and thus the purported reason for her discharge was deemed to be a pretext (*Campbell* v. *Avis Rent A Car System,* 2006, p. 6). To compare, in the Federal District Court case of *Lavotte Saunders* v. *Apothaker Associates, Inc.* (2012), the plaintiff, a Muslim African–American male, applied for a position as a debt collector. In the interview, the plaintiff wore traditional Muslim attire, which consisted of a one-piece garment called a 'thobe' and a headpiece called a 'Keffiyeh'. The plaintiff was hired for the position, subject to the passing of a required criminal background check. Soon after hiring, the plaintiff met one of the principal owners of the firm during a lunch break; and the plaintiff reported that the owner appeared 'visibly taken aback' by the plaintiff's traditional Muslim attire (*Lavotte Saunders* v. *Apothaker Associates, Inc.,* 2012, p. 2). The plaintiff was soon fired allegedly due to the fact that the background check indicated that the plaintiff was convicted of felony retail theft five years previously and also that he had not yet paid any of the $12,000 court-ordered restitution. The defendant company claimed that the criminal record was the legitimate, job-related, non-discriminatory reason for the discharge. However, the plaintiff pointed out that the company had hired several non-Muslim employees who also had criminal records and thus the asserted reason was a mere pretext. The Court, however, disagreed, explaining that the plaintiff's conviction was more severe than the other employees' records and that he had failed to make restitution, and thus the comparison to the other employees was not appropriate; and therefore there was no pretext and the reason for the termination was legitimate and non-discriminatory (*Lavotte Saunders* v. *Apothaker Associates, Inc.*, 2012, p. 9).

A pretexual reason thus is one designed to hide the employer's true motive, which is an unlawful act of discrimination. The employer's explanation can be foolish, trivial or even baseless, so long as the employer honestly believed it. The genuineness of the reason, not its reasonableness, is the key (Solieman, 2009). The plaintiff employee bears the burden of showing that the employer's proffered reason was merely a pretext. The plaintiff employee, however, need not show the pretext beyond all doubt; he or she need not totally discredit the employer's reasons for acting; rather, he or she must provide sufficient evidence to call into question and to cast doubt on the legitimacy of the employer's purported reasons for acting. Providing such evidence of pretext allows the plaintiff employee to contend that the reason given by the employer for the discharge or demotion or negative action was something other than the reason given by the employer (Solieman, 2009). An example of insufficient evidence of pretext is the Federal District Court case of *Ahmad Jajeh* v. *County of Cook* (2011), where the plaintiff, a Muslim doctor of Syrian national origin, was terminated from his position at the county hospital. The reason given for the termination was budgetary short-falls; and in fact hundreds of employees were discharged. The doctor claimed that the hospital's reason was a pretext and the true reason for his discharge was his religion and national origin. However, the only evidence that the doctor produced for pretext was an unsworn Declaration in which he asserted that he was treated poorly and discriminated against due to his religion and national origin. The Court ruled that the hospital's reason was a legitimate one and that the Declaration was insufficient evidence for a jury to infer pretext and thus dismissed the case (*Ahmad Jajeh* v. *County of Cook*, 2011, pp. 22–3). To further illustrate the pretext doctrine, in the Federal District Court case of *Salah Shakir* v. *Board of Trustees of Rend Lake College* (2010), the plaintiff employee, a Muslim of Iraqi national origin, was dismissed as the Vice-President of Student services after an investigation prompted by an anonymous letter alleging improper conduct. The defendant college cited poor performance as the reason for the dismissal. The plaintiff employee, however, claimed that the stated reason was a pretext, and pointed to the fact that other high-level administrators in the college, and not in a protected class, were not similarly sanctioned. Yet the Court found that the college's reason for the dismissal was a legitimate and justifiable one, and not a pretext. The Court pointed to certain key facts brought out by the investigation, to wit: certain college employees complained of fearing the plaintiff, the plaintiff improperly registered an international student, the plaintiff admitted international students to the college who did not meet admission requirements, a female employee stated that the plaintiff put her in an 'uncomfortable position' when he rubbed her shoulders at a college event, and that the plaintiff was monitoring the emails of college employees to try to ascertain the author of the anonymous letter that promoted the investigation (*Salah Shakir* v. *Board of Trustees of Rend Lake College*, 2010, pp. 30–31).

However, there are limits as to what a court will accept as evidence of pretext. The time between the allegedly discriminatory actions making a supposed work-related reason a pretext is also a factor. For example, in the Federal District Court case of *Nafis Zahir* v. *Patrick R. Donahoe* (2012), the plaintiff employee, a Muslim and a maintenance worker at a postal facility, was discharged for being absent from work without permission, using his facility access badge in an improper manner and lack of candour during an official postal investigation. The plaintiff employee contended that these reasons were merely pretextual; and rather he was discharged due to a discriminatory animus. The plaintiff employee cited as evidence the fact that a supervisor controlled the location for him and other Muslim employees to engage in prayers, and thus made it difficult for him to pray at work at a management-approved location, and also by the actions of the supervisor in changing rooms permissible for prayers (*Nafis Zahir* v. *Patrick R. Donahoe*, 2012, pp. 25–6). However, the Court noted that these actions occurred 15 years before the current controversy, and there was no evidence, not even a suggestion, of discrimination against the plaintiff employee in the intervening 15-year period. Accordingly, the Court ruled that no reasonable jury could conclude that the reasons given for the plaintiff's termination were pretextual. As the Court explained, 'there is a point in time at which a prior or subsequent act becomes so remote in time from the alleged discriminatory act at issue that the former cannot, as a matter of law, be relevant in intent' (*Nafis Zahir* v. *Patrick R. Donahoe*, 2012, p. 26).

Once sufficient evidence of pretext is shown, a judge may allow a jury, as finder of fact, to infer that the true reason for the action was improper discrimination. The Federal District Court case of *Mohammed Zakaria Memon* v.

Deloitte Consulting (2011) is an illustration. The plaintiff worked for a consulting firm as a lead consultant. He was Muslim, a naturalized US citizen and of Pakistani national origin. He wore a beard as part of his religious practice and engaged in regular religious observance, including praying five times a day and also performing a ritual cleansing, called Wazu, where he must wash his face, hands and arms up to his elbows, and wash his feet up to his ankles (but not remove his clothing). He was terminated, purportedly for legitimate non-discriminatory reasons, such as performance problems, work absences and dishonesty about his attendance at the office and work sites. However, the plaintiff provided certain evidence of pretext, to wit: though his performance was not outstanding he did have some adequate reviews; a supervisor said the plaintiff was the first Muslim he had encountered in the workplace; the supervisor did not investigate a complaint made about the plaintiff that he was in a 'state of undress' in the bathroom at a work site; the supervisor refused to let the plaintiff explain his religious practices; comments by the supervisor that the Court described 'at best as expressing discomfort' with the plaintiff's religion; and the presence of conflicting evidence that the plaintiff could work at home instead of coming to the office or work sites. Accordingly, overall, the Court ruled that a jury was needed to determine if pretext was present, especially since credibility determinations had to be made (*Mohammed Zakaria Memon* v. *Deloitte Consulting*, 2011, pp. 55–6).

HARASSMENT

A claim of religious discrimination, in addition, can be premised on harassment, that is, the presence of a hostile, offensive, or abusive work environment. The EEOC defines a hostile environment as constituting behaviour that '… has the purpose or effect of unreasonably interfering with an individual's work performance or creating an intimidating, hostile, or offensive working environment' (29 Code of Federal Regulations Section 1604.11(a)(3)). Harassment can include offensive remarks about a person's religion (EEOC, 2010d). The EEOC notes, however, that the law does not prohibit simple teasing, off-hand comments or isolated occurrences that are not very serious (EEOC, 2010d). To illustrate, in the Federal District Court case of *Zidan* v. *State of Maryland Department of Public Safety and Correctional Services* (2012), a motorcycle officer made the following comment to a Correctional Dietary Officer, an employee at a detention centre, who was a Muslim woman who wears a hair cover as part of her religious practice: 'What the hell is that on your head?' referring to the employee's head cover (p. 22). Other comments were made by other employees, such as, 'What are you doing?' What's wrong with you?' as well as a comment about the plaintiff employee getting paid for sitting around and doing nothing and crying (*Zidan* v. *State of Maryland Department of Public Safety and Correctional Services*, 2012, p. 21). The plaintiff employee asserted that these comments were evidence of a hostile religious environment. However, the Court ruled that 'this isolated query about her religious garb is by itself certainly not enough to establish a hostile work environment and certainly does not infect the other comments with a religious overtone' (*Zidan* v. *State of Maryland Department of Public Safety and Correctional Services*, 2012, p. 22). Similarly, in the Federal District Court case of *Mohamad* v. *Dallas County Community College District* (2012), a comment by the captain of security to a security officer who was Muslim and of Arab national origin that a student wearing a burka was 'dressed up like those terrorists' and implying that the security officer was familiar with the Taliban and terrorists due to his religion and national origin, was regarded as 'certainly offensive' but not legally actionable as religious harassment since the comment 'was not repeated with frequency and was not physically threatening' (pp. 36–7).

However, verbal epithets combined with a threat of physical violence can create a hostile work environment. The case of *Elwakin* v. *Target Media Partners Operating Company, LLC* (2012) is instructive. In the aforementioned Federal District Court case, a Muslim woman of Egyptian national origin complained that she was subject to a hostile work environment because on a few occasions she was told, including at staff meetings, that Arabs and Muslims were 'crazy', that they should not be in the US, and should leave. The Court first stated that such expressions would 'clearly offend common decency'; but that utterances that produce offensive feelings normally would not be enough to qualify as a hostile work environment (*Elwakin* v. *Target Media Partners Operating Company, LLC*, 2012, p. 56). However, at one staff meeting a manager told the employee to shut up and that he would physically strike her if she did not stop talking. Consequently, the Court ruled that offensive comments combined with actual, threatened or insinuated violence, can, and did in the case herein, create sufficient evidence of a hostile work environment (*Elwakin* v. *Target Media Partners Operating Company, LLC*, 2012, pp. 60–61).

The courts use a 'totality of the circumstances' test to determine whether a work environment is hostile, offensive or abusive based on religion (*Rami Awad* v. *National City Bank*, 2010; Grisham, 2006). This test 'includes the frequency of the discriminatory conduct; its severity; whether it is physically threatening or humiliating, or a mere offensive utterance; and whether it unreasonably interferes with an employee's work performance' (Grisham, 2006, p. 16). Furthermore, 'the effect on the employee's psychological well-being is relevant in determining whether the (employee) actually found the environment abusive' (Grisham, 2006, p. 16). To compare and contrast, two recent Federal District Court cases will nicely illustrate the foregoing rules. In one, *Spence v. Honorable Ray Lahood* (2013), the plaintiff, an African–American Muslim woman, who wears a traditional head covering in public at all times in accordance with her religious beliefs, was terminated at her job as a programme analyst with the Federal Aviation Administration. She claimed religious discrimination harassment based on a hostile work environment pursuant to Title VII. Her evidence consisted of the following: when she met with her new supervisor, who was neither an African–American or a Muslim, he allegedly told her that 'I bought you a Quran so I can understand you who are'; her supervisor then began to berate her and criticize her work for no apparent reason; several of plaintiff's co-workers made negative comments about her head covering; and that someone allegedly told another Muslim woman who wore a head covering that 'if you take that rag off your head, you will get somewhere in the FAA' (*Spence v. Honorable Ray Lahood*, 2013, pp. 4–5). The Court, however, ruled that the plaintiff did not produce enough evidence to support a *prima facie* case for a hostile work environment. The Court explained:

> … *The factual content of the complaint does not suggest that the discrimination was pervasive and regular, or that it was sufficiently severe, extreme, or abusive, or that it unreasonably interfered with work performance. The statements made … were offensive, insensitive, and, no doubt, hurtful to plaintiff. But the language of those comments was not particularly severe, and a handful of offensive remarks directed at plaintiff over the year that she was employed by the FAA does not indicate that the discrimination was pervasive or regular … Such conduct in the workplace toes not rise to the severity, regularity or pervasiveness required by Title VII (Spence v. Honorable Ray Lahood, 2013, pp. 11–12).*

In the other case, *Alzuraqi v. Group 1 Automotive, Inc.* (2013), the Court did find that a genuine dispute of material fact did exist as to a hostile work environment based on religious harassment to send the case to a jury. The plaintiff was a Muslim American of Palestinian descent who worked for an automotive dealership for approximately six months before he was terminated, but without being given any reason why he was terminated. The evidence indicated the following: the manager of the dealership, about three or four times a week, called plaintiff a 'towelhead', 'raghead', 'rock thrower', and 'terrorist', along with other very offensive names; on one occasion the manager told him that he was glad that the plaintiff was not going to have any more children as that meant 'fewer Palestinian kids in the world'; and on another occasion stated that the Persian food purchased by a co-worker of the plaintiff smelled like camel dung. The plaintiff was also cursed at by the manager, who also made inappropriate comments about his age (*Alzuraqi* v. *Group 1 Automotive, Inc.*, 2013, p. 4). The Court, as noted, ruled for the plaintiff, explaining:

> *Applying the totality of circumstances test, the court concludes that Alzuraqi has presented sufficient evidence to raise a genuine dispute of material fact as to whether the harassment that he suffered was sufficiently severe or pervasive as to create a hostile work environment. While none of the incidents alone is likely enough to establish server or pervasive harassment, when considered together and viewed in the light most favourable to Alzuraqi, the evidence demonstrates a frequent and continuous pattern of harassment over a period of six months that is sufficient for a reasonable jury to conclude that Alzuraqi established a claim of discrimination under Title VII based on religion and national origin (Alzuraqi v. Group 1 Automotive, 2013, pp. 20–21).*

Similarly, in the aforementioned Federal District Court case of *Leila Diab* v. *Chicago Board of Education* (2012, pp. 38–9), the Court ruled that the desecration of the Muslim teacher's Quran, as well as a note given to her after fighting in Gaza between Israel and the Palestinians stating that 'Israel is OK', although regarded as 'clearly evinc(ing) bigotry', as well as 'reprehensible', nonetheless did not create a hostile work environment because there was no physical contact or verbal abuse, no direct or implied threats to the plaintiff's safety of job, no evidence that these actions were committed or condoned by management and supervisors, and thus the actions were not sufficiently severe or pervasive.

To compare, in the recent case of *Mustafa Rehmani* v. *The Superior Court of Santa Clara County* (2012), the Court ruled that the 'larger picture' presented by the plaintiff employee, a Muslim born in Pakistan and an engineer, amounted to 'in the aggregate' enough evidence of harassment by Indian non-Muslim engineers to send the case to the jury based on a hostile work environment claim (p. 28, p. 959). Certain of the harassing acts complained of were as follows: his supervisor took no remedial action when he claimed of the harassment; his supervisor failed to curtail the verbal abuse of co-workers; a co-worker asked the plaintiff employee why he was going to Pakistan and Afghanistan; a co-worker told him that Afghanistan needed to be bombed and wiped out because of all the terrorist activity there which was spreading to India; when he asked a co-worker for assistance, the co-worker said, 'You are not going to blow me up, right?'; a co-worker said the Pakistan was a 'messed up' country and that the 'mess' was spreading to India; a co-worker said that there was lots of terrorism in Pakistan, and 'why don't you people do something about it?'; a co-worker said that the plaintiff employee was not in the break room because he was 'out celebrating 9/11 and planning terrorist attacks'; and that the plaintiff employee had told his fellow workers not to make jokes or comments about his religion and national origin anymore (*Mustafa Rehmani* v. *The Superior Court of Santa Clara County*, 2012, pp. 14–15, pp. 953–4). Moreover, in the Federal District Court case of *Ali Yedes* v. *Oberlin College* (2012), the plaintiff employee, a college professor in the French department, who was Muslim, of Arab descent, and of Tunisian national origin, and who was also the advisor for the college Muslim Student Association who regularly delivered prayers and sermons, established a initial case of a hostile work environment. Some of the evidence in the case consisted of offensive remarks and comments made at the school, including at faculty meetings, by fellow faculty members as well as school administrators, such as: 'I would not persecute you like this if you were an American'; 'So, you are a Holy man, what do you do when you lead the prayer?'; 'Oh, you are a Holy man, what do you say … in your preaching?'; 'You are a terrorist'; 'I know how to deal with you North Africans'; 'You should change your Friday prayer to Saturday or Sunday'; and 'Who is your prophet: Is it Muhammad or Ali?' The plaintiff employee, in addition, stated that he was excluded from certain department meetings and events, removed from the email distribution list, as well as similar 'cuts' to remove him from the department. Also important to the finding of an initial case of a hostile work environment was the fact that the school had notice of the discriminatory and harassing conduct but did not undertake any investigation (*Ali Yedes* v. *Oberlin College*, 2012, pp. 33–7).

The concept of a constructive discharge, that is, when working conditions are so intolerable that an employee is compelled to resign, can arise in a religious harassment context. The Federal District Court case of *Sofiene Romdhani, Michelle Maloney and Bobbi Joe Zeller* v. *Exxon Mobil Corporation* (2011) is an example. In the preceding case, the Court described the environment at the facility as so harassing and hostile to Arabs and Muslims and thus '… so intolerable that a reasonable person would have felt compelled to resign, as required to maintain a claim for constructive discharge' (*Sofiene Romdhani, Michelle Maloney and Bobbi Joe Zeller* v. *Exxon Mobil Corporation*, 2011, p. 30). The plaintiffs in the case were a man of Tunisian national origin and a Muslim as well as two Caucasian women who recently converted to Islam and commenced wearing the Muslim headscarf. Some of the many acts resulting in religious harassment and discrimination committed by manager and supervisors were: mocking the women for changing faiths; refusing to investigate anti-Muslim graffiti and comments by co-workers; refusing to prevent or stop other employees from making derogatory comments such as 'towel heads' and 'rag heads'; making threatening remarks such as 'getting each and every one of you out of here'; requiring the Muslim employees to clean bathrooms toilets, including the men's bathroom, but not requiring non-Muslim employees to do so; falsely accusing one Muslim employee of stealing cigarettes; and mocking the Tunisian employee's Arab accent (*Sofiene Romdhani, Michelle Maloney and Bobbi Joe Zeller* v. *Exxon Mobil Corporation*, 2011, pp. 9–14). As a practical matter, the EEOC, regarding religious harassment, advises that the employer should have a well-publicized and uniformly applied anti-harassment policy that 1) treats religious harassment, 2) clearly states prohibited behaviour; 3) explains the procedures for bringing harassment to the attention of management; and 4) includes an assurance that employees who complain will be protected from retaliation (EEOC, 2010a).

RETALIATION

Retaliation against an employee who seeks to vindicate rights pursuant to the *Civil Rights Act* is also a civil rights violation (*Farick Ali* v. *District of Columbia Government and District of Columbia Fire and Emergency Medical Service*, 2010). The Federal District Court case of *Mohamed Arafi* v. *Mandarin Oriental* (2012) is a very instructive retaliation case. The case stands for a very important legal principle, to wit: the plaintiff employee is not required to prove that the discriminatory activity complained of was in fact actual actionable discrimination, but rather only establish that he or she complained of unlawful discrimination. That is, there is no requirement that the plaintiff employee actually prove the underlying discrimination claim; the retaliation claim is a separate and distinct lawsuit (pp. 23–4). So, in the aforementioned case, the plaintiff employee, a Muslim born in Morocco and a US citizen, complained of disparate treatment discrimination because he was not allowed to provide valet laundry services to hotel guests on the eight and ninth floors for two days because they were Israelis from an Israeli delegation and his supervisor was concerned about the reaction of the Israelis. The Court did say that the plaintiff employee was treated differently because of his religion and national origin, but that he did not have an actionable discrimination claim because he did not suffer 'an adverse employment action' since the loss of potential tips was speculative, not serious and not material (*Mohamed Arafi* v. *Mandarin Oriental*, 2012, pp. 16–17). However, the plaintiff employee also sued for retaliation, claiming that when he complained of the aforementioned discriminatory treatment his supervisor retaliated by reducing his work hours to one day during the month that followed the complaint whereas before he had worked five to seven days a week. The Court ruled that although the underlying discrimination claim was trivial, the retaliation was a non-trivial reduction-in-pay and thus constituted a 'material adverse action' sustaining the Title VII retaliation claim (*Mohamed Arafi* v. *Mandarin Oriental*, 2012, p. 24). Similarly, in the Federal District Court case of *Najmah Rashad* v. *Metropolitan Area Transit Authority* (2013), the plaintiff employee was granted an accommodation to attend Friday prayers, but not the full accommodation she wanted due to an assertion by the employer of undue hardship because of staffing concerns. When she left work for prayers beyond the accommodation, she received an 'AWOL warning letter'. She sued for retaliation but the Court said that the warning letter was not a sufficient 'adverse action' to constitute a retaliation claim.

Another recent example of a retaliation case is the aforementioned Federal District Court case of *Sofiene Romdhani, Michelle Maloney and Bobbi Joe Zeller* v. *Exxon Mobil Corporation* (2011), where the plaintiff employees made several complaints of the religious discrimination and harassment to the company's management, including the Human Resources Department, and then were treated differently than other employees, and also the words of the facility's manager and supervisors became even more antagonistic, hostile, intimidating and threatening, such as 'I'm going to get you, one way or another' (p. 47). The male Muslim employee was fired, supposedly for tardiness though no employee had ever been fired for being late, and the two female employees who recently converted to Islam were, as noted, constructively discharged.

The EEOC relates that it is illegal to retaliate against a person for opposing employment policies or practices that discriminate based on religion or for filing a discrimination charge, or testifying or participating in any way in an investigation, proceeding, or litigation pursuant to Title VII of the *Civil Rights Act* (EEOC, 2010c). Furthermore, the EEOC states that requesting a religious accommodation is also a protected activity (EEOC, 2010e).

THE EMPLOYER'S DUTY TO REASONABLY ACCOMMODATE

There is a major distinction that the *Civil Rights Act* makes between religion and the other protected classes and other forms of discrimination. That is, regarding religion, based on a 1972 amendment to Title VII of the *Civil Rights Act*, the employer is under an affirmative obligation 'to reasonably accommodate an employee's or prospective employee's religious observance or practices' (*Civil Rights Act* 42 U.S.C. Section 2000e(j); EEOC, 2010d; Zaheer, 2007). Congress, however, did not define the term 'reasonable accommodation'. However, Ruan (2008) examined the law's legislative history which '... suggests that the lawmakers' intent was to protect employees from losing their jobs solely because their religious beliefs required them to do certain things, such as observe particular holidays, that the rules of the workplace otherwise might not allow' (p. 15).

As a result of the law, in addition to a disparate treatment and a disparate claim and a hostile work environment claim, an employee can also bring for religious discrimination a cause of action based on the employer's failure to reasonably accommodate the employee's religious practices and observances. The EEOC has provided some 'best practices' for employers regarding accommodation, to wit: employers should inform employees that they will make reasonable efforts to accommodate the employees' religious beliefs and practices, employers should train managers and supervisors how to recognize and deal with religious accommodation requests by employees, and employers should consider an employee's proposed method of accommodation, but if it is denied, the employer should explain to the employee why his or her proposed method of accommodation was not granted (EEOC, 2010a). The EEOC, moreover, has provided examples of some common religious accommodations: flexible scheduling and leave policies, alternative work schedules, 'floating' days off, voluntary shift substitutions or swaps, job reassignments, modifications or exceptions to workplace policies and practices, as well as providing mechanisms, such as a central file, bulletin board, group email and other means, to effectuate such accommodations (EEOC, 2010a; 2010d). Lateral transfers are another example of an accommodation suggested by the EEOC (2010a; 2010c). Other examples of typical reasonable religious accommodation include providing times as well as unused or private places to pray, leave for religious observances, job reassignments and the permission to wear religious clothing and coverings (EEOC, 2010a; Grisham, 2006). The EEOC even advises that if the employer is concerned about uniform appearance to the public, it would be appropriate for the employer to consider allowing the employee to wear religious garb in the company's uniform colours (EEOC, 2010a). This legal obligation to afford the employee a reasonable religious accommodation applies at the application stage and continues throughout the employment relationship (Grisham, 2006). An example of a case in which the employer afforded the employee a reasonable accommodation is the Federal District Court case of *Abdul-Raoof Mustafa* v. *Syracuse City School District* (2010). In that case, the plaintiff was an African–American and practising Muslim who taught special needs children at a magnet school. While at the school he was allowed to attend traditional Islamic prayers held at a mosque by using his lunch time. Furthermore, the plaintiff was allowed to use any personal time for religious observances; and also if he ran out of personal time, he would have been granted unpaid leave for religious observances. Moreover, if no students were in the building on a Friday afternoon, the plaintiff was released to attend services. Finally, the plaintiff did not show that he was subject to any discipline or unfavourable employment treatment as a result of his desire and request to attend religious services on Friday. Accordingly, the Court ruled that the 'Plaintiff was not forced to choose between his religion and his employment' and the accommodation made by the school was reasonable (*Abdul-Raoof Mustafa* v. *Syracuse City School District*, 2010, p. 32).

The employer, however, is not obligated to accommodate an employee's personal preference or mere convenience (*Tiano* v. *Dillard Department Stores,* 1998; *Heller* v. *EBB Auto Co.,* 1993). Furthermore, as noted by one Court, the defendant employer's legal duty is to offer a reasonable accommodation and 'not necessarily the accommodation plaintiff (employee) would have preferred' (*David C. Ross* v. *Colorado Department of Transportation*, 2012, p. 32). To illustrate a mere personal preference compared to a religious observance or practice that must be accommodated is the Federal District Court case of *Mohammed Hussein* v. *UPMC Mercy Hospital* (2011). In that case, the plaintiff employee, a nuclear medicine technologist and a Muslim of Pakistani national origin, requested vacation time to make a pilgrimage to Mecca as required by the religion of Islam. The Court first noted that making such a pilgrimage is a protected religious observance which is entitled to accommodation, since members of the Islamic faith are required as a principal tenet of their religion to go to Mecca if they are able to do so. However, in this case, the plaintiff had made two prior pilgrimages, and wanted to go again at a particular time to travel with a group and to obtain less expensive group travel rates. Moreover, the evidence indicated that the plaintiff put in his request for vacation time after the vacation schedule had been determined and set. The defendant hospital denied his request. The Court thus ruled that 'taken together the plaintiff has failed to present a prima facie case of Defendant's failure to accommodate his religious belief. His desire to travel … was a matter of personal preference, as opposed to a religious observance entitled to constitutional or statutory protection' (*Mohammed Hussein* v. *UPMC Mercy Hospital*, 2011, p. 23).

Another accommodation example in the Federal District Court case of *Kenneth Wallace* v. *City of Philadelphia* (2010), a police officer who became a practising Muslim wanted to wear a beard in contravention of the police department's policy of no facial hair. The police officer stressed the importance of a beard to the religion of Islam, in particular: 'The number one reason is that it was a command by the Prophet Mohammad to grow the beard and to trim the moustache and to be different and to be easily recognized by your brethren that's in your religion' (*Kenneth Wallace* v. *City of Philadelphia*, 2010, p. 10). The police department, however, offered an accommodation, that is, the police officer could wear a beard but only to the length of the 'medical exemption', which was a quarter inch. The police officer nevertheless wanted to wear his beard beyond the length permitted by the city's police department for religious reasons. The city claimed it would be an undue hardship to allow the officer to go beyond the medial exemption. The Court agreed with the city, saying that it had made a good faith effort to accommodate, and that to go beyond the medical exception 'would indeed impose the undue hardship of sacrificing the Department's commitment to a neutral appearance policy' (*Kenneth Wallace* v. *City of Philadelphia*, 2010, p. 25). The Court further indicated that 'this Circuit has made it very clear that to permit employees to mark themselves uniquely in the name of religious accommodation, at the cost of maintaining an employer's neutrality and uniformity, may ask too much' (*Kenneth Wallace* v. *City of Philadelphia*, 2010, p. 27).

To illustrate the position of the EEOC is the case of *Equal Employment Opportunity Commission* v. *Abercrombie & Fitch Stores, Inc.* (2011). In that case, the defendant company denied a job as a model to a 17-year-Muslim woman because she wore a black headscarf as part of her religious beliefs. The defendant store had a 'Look Policy' which required models to wear clothing similar to what the store sold, and the store did not sell any black clothing, though they did sell scarves (but not headscarves). The defendant store thus claimed undue hardship because its executives believed that if the store made an exception to its policy it would negatively impact the brand and sales. The Court noted, however, that the store had not conducted any studies or provided any examples to support this assertion of negative impact. The store, however, did rely on an expert who gave an expert opinion as to negative impact on marketing and strategy; but the Court rejected the expert's opinion because the expert did not collect or analyse any data to corroborate his opinion. Also important to the Court was the fact that in the past the defendant store had made other exceptions to its 'Look Policy'. Therefore, the Court agreed with the EEOC that the defendant store failed to meet its burden that granting an exception to the plaintiff would have caused undue hardship (*Equal Employment Opportunity Commission* v. *Abercrombie & Fitch Stores, Inc.*, 2011, pp. 37–8).

Finally, regarding religious accommodation law in the US, it should be noted that there is a proposed law in Congress, first introduced in 1994, and most recently re-introduced in the House of Representatives in 2007 and the Senate in 2008 respectively, which redefines the undue hardship limitation (Bader, 2011). The law, called *Workplace Religious Freedom Act* (WRFA), states that instead of a proposed accommodation being deemed an 'undue hardship' even if it involves some minimal cost or expense to the employer, as per the case law, the WRFA maintains that in order to qualify as a hardship the accommodation most involve 'significant difficulty or expense' (Bader, 2011, p. 273). The law has not been enacted; and as of the writing of this chapter in 2014, with the current political party 'split' in Congress, there is very little realistic possibility of the WRFA being passed into law.

THE UNDUE HARDSHIP LIMITATION ON THE DUTY TO ACCOMMODATE

There is a significant limitation in the *Civil Rights Act* regarding the employer's duty to accommodate the religious practices and observances of its employees. That is, the employer does not have to accommodate if to do so would place an 'undue hardship' on the conduct of the employer's business (*Civil Rights Act* of 1964, as amended, 42 U.S.C. Section 2000e(j)). An accommodation would create such a hardship if it is unduly burdensome or unreasonable or would produce significant expense for the employer. If it creates only a minor or minimal burden on the employer's business, the accommodation is reasonable and thus must be made. The US Supreme Court has ruled that an accommodation would cause an 'undue hardship' whenever it would result in 'more than a de minimis cost' to the employer (*Trans World Airlines, Inc.* v. *Hardison*, p. 84). Similarly, any accommodation that gave preferential treatment to the employee(s) would be deemed unreasonable (*Trans World Airlines, Inc.* v. *Hardison*, p. 81). The EEOC lists the following as factors relevant to undue hardship: the type of workplace, the nature of the employee's duties, the identifiable cost of the accommodation in relation to the size and operating costs of the employer, the number of employees who will need an accommodation (EEOC, 2010e). Furthermore, in making an accommodation the employer need not choose any particular accommodation; and any reasonable accommodation by the employer will be sufficient to comply with the law (Ansonia Board of Education, p. 68). To illustrate, in the Federal District Court case of *Haliye* v. *Celestica Corp.* (2010), the defendant employer was denied a summary judgment, disposing of the case, based on the employees' claim that the employer failed to accommodate the employees' religious practices by allowing prayer breaks. Critical to the employees' lawsuit was the fact that that the employer generally permitted employees to take unscheduled bathroom breaks, but nevertheless forbid the employees from taking unscheduled Muslim daily prayer breaks (*Haliye* v. *Celestica Corp.*, 2010). To compare, in the Federal District Court case of *Skwikar Ali Abdelkader* v. *Sears, Roebuck & Company* (2011), a voluntary swap-shift to allow a Muslim employee, an assistant store manager, to be excused from work to celebrate the holiday of Id al-Adha, was deemed to be a reasonable accommodation. Similarly, in *McLaughlin* v. *New York City Board of Education* (2008), the Federal District Court ruled that a Muslim teacher was afforded a reasonable accommodation when he was allowed to leave work early on Friday for Friday prayers except for the second Friday of each month when faculty conferences were held. Similarly, in the Federal District Court case of *Elmenayer* v. *ABF Freight Systems* (2001), the employee asked that 15 minutes be added to his hour-long lunch in order to attend Friday prayers, but the Court denied this requested accommodation, and instead held that having the employee bid for evening and night shifts was a reasonable accommodation.

In a truly hardship situation, of course, the accommodation would no longer be required by the *Civil Rights Act*. The EEOC advises that an accommodation would create an undue hardship for the employer if it is costly, endangers the safety of the workplace, decreases the efficiency of the workplace, infringes on the rights of other employees, or requires other employees to do more than their share of potentially hazardous or burdensome work (EEOC, 2010d). Moreover, the EEOC states that involuntarily requiring employees to substitute for one another or to swap shifts would pose an undue hardship (EEOC, 2010e). Similarly, if substitutions or swaps would result in the employer having to pay premium or overtime pay, there might be an undue hardship depending on the 'frequency of the arrangement' (EEOC, 2010e, p. 6). Yet the EEOC also takes the position that it 'will presume that the infrequent payment of premium wages for a substitute or the payment of premium wages while a more permanent accommodation is being sought are costs which an employer can be required to bear as means of providing reasonable accommodation' (EEOC, 2010b, p. 30). Moreover, the EEOC warns employers that 'a mere assumption that many more people with the same religious practices as the individual being accommodated may also seek accommodation is not evidence of undue hardship' (EEOC, 2010e, p. 5). The EEOC also counsels that an accommodation would present an undue hardship if it would conflict with another law or regulation or would contravene the terms of a collective bargaining agreement or job rights established through a seniority system (EEOC, 2010c). Nonetheless, the EEOC also counsels the employer not to assume that an accommodation would conflict with the terms of a collective bargaining agreement or a seniority system; rather, the employer should check to see if there are any exceptions for religious accommodation as well as check to see if there are other ways to accommodate the employee consistent with the collective bargaining agreement or the seniority system (EEOC, 2010a).

If an accommodation would compromise safety, security and health at the workplace, or would create a legal risk for the employer, it is unreasonable and thus not required (Bandsuch, 2009; Grisham, 2006). To illustrate, in one Federal Appeals Court case, the Court ruled that due to safety and security issues it would be an undue hardship for a prison to allow its Muslim female employees to wear a khimar, or head covering, because, like a hat, it could be used to smuggle contraband into and around the prison, conceal the identity of the wearer and could be used as a means to attack prison employees (*Equal Employment Opportunity Commission* v. *The GEO Group, Inc.*, 2010). A good illustration of a safety case is the Federal District Court case of *Mohamed-Sheik* v. *Golden Foods/Golden Brands LLC* (2006), where the employees, Muslim women, told their employer that they could not wear form-fitting, tucked-in shirts because their religious beliefs did not allow them to dress like a man or reveal their female shape. The employer cited a safety risk since the extra-long and untucked clothing could become entangled in moving machinery. The Court found the hardship to the employer to be 'undue', and thus no accommodation was required.

Recommendations for Employers and Managers

A multi-religious workplace in the 'best of times' presents legal, ethical and practical challenges to employers and managers, especially regarding how to prevent conflict, avoid discrimination, accommodate religion and yet maintain a profitable business. However, the terrorist attacks on 11 September 2001 surely have contributed to a culture of bias and discrimination against Muslim and Arab–American employees in the workplace. Focusing on religious garb, Aziz (2012) describes the challenges for Muslims, especially women in the workplace, and thus the concomitant challenges for employers:

> As national security prerogatives filter perceptions of Muslims through the prism of terrorism, the Muslim 'veil' has become a symbol of terror. The critical shift in perception results in palpable adverse consequences to a Muslim woman's freedom of religion, freedom of individual expression and physical safety ... The shift in meaning of the Muslim headscarf is due in large part to a recasting of Islam as a political ideology as opposed to a religion. Once this definitional shift occurs, acts that would otherwise qualify as actionable religious discrimination are accepted as legitimate, facially neutral national security law enforcement measures or protected political activity by private actors. Recasting thus serves as the basis for calls to deny Muslims rights otherwise protected under the law. Moreover, mundane religious accommodation cases become evidence of stealth, imperialistic designs of hostile ideology. Contrary to America's traditional deference to religious precepts in personal affairs, opponents of mosque construction

and Muslim religious accommodation dismiss religious freedom for Muslims as inapplicable by focusing on extremist Muslims to shift the debate to Islam's alleged pathological violence (pp. 193–4).

Nonetheless, Civil Rights laws exist to protect the rights of all employees in the workplace. The EEOC and the courts have been enforcing such laws to prevent discrimination against Muslim and Arab–American employees. Accordingly, employers must comprehend the importance of educating and training employees, including and especially managers and supervisors, to act in a legal manner as well as the consequences for not acting legally. Employers also must instruct their employees to be culturally competent, that is, to be cognizant of and sensitive to their employees' religious beliefs, observations and practices as well as their cultures, heritages and ethnic backgrounds. Regarding the employer's duty to make a reasonable accommodation to an employee's religious observations and practices, it must emphasized that when the employer makes no effort to accommodate the employee the employer places itself in a very precarious legal position. As noted, the courts in such a case will be very sceptical of any subsequent undue hardship claim. The employer must at the least attempt to accommodate the employee in a reasonable and good faith manner. Bader (2011) sets forth the religious context:

Failure to accommodate prayer is the one of the most common complaints by Muslim employees. Muslims pray five times a day, for a few minutes each time. Muslim men also participate in special prayers held each Friday at a mosque. Islamic grooming and dress standards also cause friction between employer and employee. Men are encouraged to wear beards as a show of piety. Some interpretations of Islam hold that women should dress in body-covering clothing that hides their female form, including khimars, which cover head and neck. Some Muslims ... believe this dress style to be mandatory to protect women's modesty (pp. 274–5).

Accordingly, accommodation suggestions would be whenever possible and practical to allow Muslim women to wear headscarves, to wear shirts untucked to accommodate a desire for modesty in appearance, for men to wear beards and to allow Muslim employees to pray during their breaks (Aziz, 2012; Bader, 2011).

Employers, therefore, need to be aware of their legal and ethical responsibilities and thus to be vigilant in ensuring that the workplace is free from discrimination. Employers must recognize, and must make the employees aware of the fact, that the US is an increasingly diverse and pluralistic country regarding religion and religious practices and observances. Accordingly, employers and employees must learn to be aware of, respect and be more tolerant of different religions and employees who wish to express their religious identity in the workplace. The objective is to create a workplace that is balanced and equitable in the sense that employees are free to express their religious identities without unduly burdening the employee or other employees, that is free from hostility and abuse based on religion, and that is a workplace where all the employees are treated with respect and respect others. Such a workplace, the authors submit, will also be an efficient, effective and productive one for the employer. Zaheer (2007) agrees, stating that 'because satisfied employees foster a productive work environment, it behooves employers to learn how best to accommodate the religious practices of their employees, particularly when those employees practice a religion with which the employer is likely unfamiliar, such as Islam' (p. 529).

Grisham (2006) advises that regarding religious discrimination and harassment, the employer's anti-discrimination policies and procedures must specifically address religious discrimination and harassment, and must clearly state that religious discrimination and harassment will not be tolerated in the workplace. Ruan (2008) advises that the prudent employer should create and promote a set of 'best practices' guidelines for managers, supervisors and employees that incorporate the values of diversity, respect, inclusion and non-discrimination (p. 30). Grisham (2006) also notes that the employer's defence to a religious discrimination claim frequently depends on the sufficiency and consistency in the application, investigation and enforcement of the employer's anti-discrimination and anti-harassment policies. Regarding the employer's duty to accommodate the religious beliefs and practices of its employees, the EEOC emphasizes that:

> *Employer–employee cooperation and flexibility are key to the search for a reasonable accommodation. If the accommodation request is not immediately apparent, the employer should discuss the request with the employee to determine what accommodation might be effective … Moreover, even if the employer does not grant the employee's preferred accommodation, but instead provides an alternative accommodation, the employee must cooperate by attempting to meet his religious needs through the employer's proposed accommodation, of possible' (EEOC, 2010e, p. 4).*

Grisham (2006) further counsels that the employer should not summarily reject the employee's accommodation request even if the employer considers it to be unduly burdensome; rather, the employer should consider the offered accommodation, explain to the employee why the employer believes it is unreasonable, and then work with the employee to devise a less burdensome alternative accommodation. The proper process thus should be a good faith effort between the employer and employee to resolve the conflict between the employee's religious beliefs, observances and practices and the legitimate business needs of the employer. Ruan (2008) emphasizes that employers should note that a 'proactive approach for employers to create a respectful place for religious diversity is arguably good for business, as well as good for employees' (p. 30).

The authors of this chapter strongly suggest to employers who seek and strive to reasonably accommodate the religious needs of their employees that they devise policies, procedures and standards in the following areas in order to seek to accommodate the religious beliefs, observances and practices of their Muslim employees:

- attending worship services;

- praying and ritual washings (times and locations);

- fasting and dietary rules;

- Ramadan obligations;

- attending Hajj;

- wearing religious garb, such as headscarves and clothing;

- wearing religious symbols;

- displaying religious objects;

- proselytizing and other forms of religious expression;

- alcohol prohibitions.

The authors hope that the analysis of the law, legal commentary and management commentary provided in this chapter will provide some guidance to employers in promulgating policies, procedures and standards in the effort to reasonably accommodate the religious beliefs, observances and practices of their Muslim employees. Furthermore, it must be emphasized that educating the workforce is a critical element to legally, morally and practically solving religious issues and potential conflicts in the workplace. Accordingly, awareness of, tolerance to and respect for other religions and their observances and practices should be included by the employer in the employees' diversity, sensitivity and cultural competency education and training. The goal should be for the employees to embrace religious diversity, as they are inculcated to do, and hopefully will do, with other forms of diversity.

Conclusion

Muslim–Americans face many challenges in the US today, particularly after the attacks of 11 September, America's ongoing commitment to Iraq, and the continuing war in Afghanistan. One of these challenges will be religious and national origin discrimination in the workplace. Furthermore, the number of Americans practising the religion of Islam has increased substantially, and will continue to increase. Consequently, employers too very likely will find themselves confronted with the contentious issue – legally, morally and practically – on how to deal with Muslim employees in the workforce and especially how to accommodate the religious needs of their Muslim employees in an equitable and efficacious manner.

This chapter examined important aspects of the laws against employment discrimination in the US. The chapter, therefore, provided an overview of the US *Civil Rights Act* and also briefly discussed the nature and role of the EEOC in implementing and enforcing discrimination law. This chapter also provided some basic material regarding the religion of Islam and the presence of Muslims in the US workforce. One purpose of the chapter, of course, was to analyse the laws prohibiting religious and national origin discrimination, harassment and retaliation against employees in the context herein of Muslim, Arab and Arab–American employees. The employer's duty to reasonably accommodate the religious needs of its Muslim employees was explicated in detail, along with the concomitant undue hardship limitation on the accommodation duty.

One 'theme' to this chapter is surely that the prudent and wise managers are well-advised to be cognizant of important civil rights anti-discrimination statutes. Accordingly, an objective of this chapter was to provide to managers practical suggestions and recommendations on how to solve the accommodation versus burden dilemma; and thus to help managers accommodate in a reasonable manner the religious beliefs, observances and practices of their Muslim employees without undergoing any undue hardship. The authors hope that the information, examples and insights they provided will be helpful to managers who seek to attain a legal and ethical, fair and equitable, efficient and effective, and value-maximizing workplace.

References

Abdul-Raoof Mustafa v. *Syracuse City School District*, 2010 U.S. Dist. LEXIS 11567 (Northern Dist. N.Y. 2010).

Abuelyeman v. *Illinois State University*, 667 F.3d 800 (7th Circuit 2011).

Ahmad Jajer v. *County of Cook*, 2011 U.S. Dist. LEXIS 52241 (Northern Dist. Il.2011).

Ali Yedes v. *Oberlin College*, 2012. U.S. Dist. LEXIS 39761 (Northern Dist. Ohio).

Alzuraqi v. *Group 1 Automotive, Inc.*, 2013. U.S. Dist. LEXIS 13743 (N. District of Texas).

Ansonia Board of Education v. Philbrook, 479 U.S. 60 (1986).

Antpeli, A. (2010). 'Introductory Remarks at the Duke Forum for Law & Social Change Symposium – The New Face of Discrimination: "Muslim" in America', *Duke Forum for Law & Social Change*, 2: 1–2.

Aziz, S.F. (2012). 'From the Oppressed to the Terrorist: Muslim American Women in the Crosshairs of Intersectionality', *Hastings Race & Poverty Law Journal*, 9: 191–248.

Bader, N.K. (2011). 'Hats Off To Them: Muslim Women Stand against Workplace Religious Discrimination in GEO Group', *Saint Louis University Law Journal*, 56: 261–305.

Bandsuch, Mark (2009). The Troubles with Title Seven and Trait Discrimination Plus One Solution. Capital University *Law Review*, Vol. 37, pp. 965–1084.

Campbell v. *Avis Rent A Car System, Inc.*, 2006 WL 2865169 (E. Dist. Michigan).

Cavico, F. J. and Mujtaba, B. G. (2014*). Legal Challenges for the Global Manager and Entrepreneur* (Second Edition). Dubuque, Iowa: Kendall Hunt Publishing Company.

Cavico, F.J. and Mujtaba, B.G. (2011a). 'Employment Discrimination and Muslims in America', *Journal for Global Business Advancement*, 4(3): 279–97.

Cavico, F.J. and Mujtaba, B.G. (2011b). 'Managers Be Warned: Third-party Retaliation Lawsuits and the United States Supreme', *International Journal of Business and Social Sciences*, 2(5): 8–17.

Cavico, F.J. and Mujtaba, B.G. (2011c). 'Reasonable Accommodation Dilemmas for Muslim–American Employees' Religious Beliefs', *Proficient: An International Journal of Management*, 3(9): 7–33.

Cavico, F.J. and Mujtaba, B.G. (2012). 'Discriminatory Practices against Muslims in the American Workplace', *Journal of Leadership, Accountability and Ethics*, 9(1): 98–117.

Civil Rights Act of 1964. 42 United States Code Sections 2000e *et seq*. Thomson/West Publishing Company.

Civil Rights Act of 1991. 105 US Statutes, Sections 1071 and 2000. Thomson/West Publishing Company.

David C. Ross v. *Colorado Department of Transportation*, 2012 U.S. Dist. LEXIS 162591 (District of Colorado).

EEOC Compliance Manual 1993. EEOC Enforcement Guidance on Application of Title VII to Conduct Overseas and to Foreign Employers Discriminating in the U.S., Notice 915.002, p. 2169.

Elmenayer v. ABF Freight Systems, 2001 U.S. District LEXIS 15357 (Eastern District of New York 2001).

Elwakin v. *Target Media Partners Operating Company, LLC.*, 2012. U.S. Dist. LEXIS 145137 (Eastern District of Louisiana).

Equal Employment Opportunity Commission (EEOC). (2010a). Best Practices for Eradicating Religious Discrimination in the Workplace. Retrieved on 7 July 2010 from http://www.eeoc.gov./policy/docs/best_practices_religion.html.

Equal Employment Opportunity Commission (EEOC). (2010b). Compliance Manual, Section 12: Religious Discrimination. Retrieved on 7 July 2010 from http://www.eeoc.gov/policy/docs/religion.html.

Equal Employment Opportunity Commission (EEOC). (2010c). Facts About Religious Discrimination. Retrieved on 7 July 2010 from http://www.1.eeoc//eeoc/publicatons/fs-religion.

Equal Employment Opportunity Commission (EEOC). (2010d). Religious Discrimination. Retrieved on 7 July 2010 from http://www1.eeoc.gov//laws/types/religion.

Equal Employment Opportunity Commission (EEOC). (2010e). Questions and Answers: Religion Discrimination in the Workplace 2010. Retrieved on 7 July 2010 from http://www.eeoc.gov/policy/docs/quanda_religion.html.

Equal Employment Opportunity Commission (EEOC). (2013a). National Origin-Based Charges Filed from 10/01/200 thru 09/30/2011. Retrieved on 18 January 2013 from: http://www1.eeoc.gov//eeoc/events/9-11-11_natl_origin_charges.cfm.

Equal Employment Opportunity Commission (EEOC). (2013d). What You Should Know about the EEOC and Religious and National Origin Discrimination. Retrieved on 18 January 2013 from: http://www1.eeoc.gov//eeoc/newsroom/wysk/religion_national_origin_9-11.cfm.

Equal Employment Opportunity Commission v. *Abercrombie & Fitch Stores, Inc.*, 2012. 798 F. Supp. 2nd 1272 (Northern Dist. Oklahoma).

Equal Employment Opportunity Commission v. *Abercrombie & Fitch Stores, Inc.*, 2013. U.S. Dist. LEXIS 51905 (Northern District of California).

Equal Employment Opportunity Commission v. *Kelly Services, Incorporated.*, 2010. 598 F.3d 1022 (8th Circuit).

Equal Employment Opportunity Commission v. *The GEO Group, Inc.*, 2010. 2010 U.S. App. LEXIS 15973.

Equal Opportunity Employment Act of 1972, Public Law No. 92-261, 86 Statutes 103, codified as 42 U.S.C. Section 2000e(j).

Farick Ali v. *District of Columbia Government and District of Columbia Fire and Emergency Medical Service*, 697 F. Supp2d 88 (District Court for the District of Columbia 2010).

Gandara, C. (2006). 'Post-9/11 Backlash Discrimination in the Workplace: Employers Beware of Potential Double Recovery', *Houston Business and Tax Law Journal*, 7: 169–205.

Grisham, J.G. (2006). 'Religion at Work: Balancing the Rights of Employees and Employers', *Tennessee Bar Journal*, 14: 14–23.

Gul-E-Rana Mirza v. *The Neiman Marcus Group, Inc.*, 2009. 649 F. Supp.2d 837; 2009 U.S. Dist. LEXIS 38102.

Haliye v. *Celestica Corp.*, 2010. 717 F. Supp.2d 873 (D. Minnesota).

Heller v. *EBB Auto Co.*, 8 F.3d 1433 (9th Circuit Court of Appeals 1993).

Imitiaz Izakh v. *City of Miramar*, 2009. U.S. Dist. LEXIS 51109.

Jacqueline Durden v. *Ohio Bell Telephone Company*, 2013 U.S. District LEXIS 4757 (2013).

Kamal Aly v. *Mohegan Council, Boy Scouts of America*, 2013. U.S App. LEXIS 5804 (1st Circuit).

Kenneth Wallace v. *City of Philadelphia*, 2010 U.S. District LEXIS 42437 (Eastern District of Pennsylvania (2010).

Lavotte Saunders v. *Apthaker Associates*, Inc., 2012. U.S. LEXIS 53848 (Dist. N.J.).

Leila Diab v. *Chicago Board of Education*, 2012. 850 F. Supp. 2nd 899 (Northern District of Illinois).

M. Moin Masoodi v. *Lockheed Martin Corporation*, 2011. U.S. Dist. LEXIS 21245 (Eastern Dist. La.).

Mansoor Alam v. *HSBC Bank*, 2009 U.S. District LEXIS 89438, affirmed 2010 U.S. App. LEXIS 13158.

McLaughlin v. *New York City Board of Education*, 2008 LEXIS 4794 (District Court for the Southern District of New York 2008).

Mohamed Arafi v. *Mandarin Oriental*, 2012. U.S. Dist. LEXIS 78286 (D.C. Dist.).

Mohamed v. *Dallas County Community College District*, 2012. U.S. Dist. LEXIS 141578 (Northern District of Texas).

Mohamed-Sheik v. *Golden Foods/Golden Brands LLC.*, 2006. WL 709573 (W.D. Kentucky).

Mohammed Hussein v. *UPMC Mercy Hospital*, 2011. U.S. Dist. LEXIS 396 (Western Dist. Pa.).

Mohammed Karim v. *The Department of Education of the City of New York*, 2010. U.S. Dist. LEXIS 14156 (Eastern Dist. N.Y.).

Mohammed Zakaria Memon v. *Deloitte Consulting Consulting*, 2011. LLP, 779 F. Supp. 2d 619 (Southern District of Texas).

Mujtaba, B.G. (2007). *Cross Cultural Management and Negotiation Practices*. ILEAD Academy Publications; Florida.

Mujtaba, B.G. (2010). *Workforce Diversity Management: Challenges, Competencies and Strategies* (2nd edition). ILEAD Academy Publications, Florida.

Mustafa Rehmani v. *The Superior Court of Santa Clara County*, 2012. 204 Cal. App. 4th 945, 139 Cal Rptr. 3d 464.

Nafis Zahir v. *Patrick R. Donahoe*, 2012. U.S. Dist. LEXIS 178406 (Eastern District of Pennsylvania).

Najmah Rashad v. *Metropolitan Area Transit Authority*, 945 F. Supp2d 152 (District Court for the District of Columbia 2013).

Nazeeh Younis v. *Pinnacle Airlines, Inc.*, 2010. 610 F.d 359; 2010 U.S. App. LEXIS 13325.

Pervaiz Kaiser v. *Colorado Department of Corrections*, 2012. U.S. Dist. LEXIS 30343 (District of Colorado).

Rami Awad v. *National City Bank*, 2010 U.S. District LEXIS 37576 (2010).

Ruan, N. (2008). 'Accommodating Respectful Religious Expression in the Workplace', *Marquette Law Review*, 92: 1–27.

S. Shamin v. *Siemens Industry, Inc.*, 854 F. Supp. 2d 496 (Northern District of Illinois).

Salah Shakir v. *Board of Trustees of Rend Lake College*, 2010 U.S. District LEXIS 8119 and 10682.

Skwikar Ali Abdelkader v. *Sears, Roebuck & Company*, 2011. 780 F. Supp. 2d 389 (District of Maryland).

Sofiene Romdhani, Michelle Maloney and Bobbi Joe Zeller v. *Exxon Mobil Corporation*, 2011. U.S. Dist. LEXIS 18070 (District of Delaware).

Solieman, I. (2009). 'Born Osama: Muslim American Employment Discrimination', *Arizona Law Review*, 51: 1069–104.

Spence v. *Honorable Ray Lahood*, 2013. U.S. Dist. LEXIS 11409 (District of New Jersey).

Talibah Safiyah Abdul Haqq v. *Pennsylvania Department of Public Welfare*, 2010. U.S. Dist. LEXIS 27207 (Eastern District of Pennsylvania).

Tiano v. *Dillard Department Stores*, 1998. 139 F.3d 679 (9th Cir.).

Trans World Airline, Inc. v. *Hardison*, 1977. 432 U.S. 63.

United States v. *Seeger*, 1970. 398 U.S. 333.

Yassim Mohamed v. *Public Health Trust of Miami Dade County*, 2010 U.S. District LEXIS 72385 (2010).

Yin, T. (2010). 'Through a Screen Darkly: Hollywood as a Measure of Discrimination against Arabs and Moslems', *Duke Forum for Law & Social Change*, 2: 103–30.

Young v. Southwest Savings & Loan Association, 509 F.2d 140 (5th Circuit 1975).

Yussef Johnson v. *Comer Holding LLC.,* 2010. Mich. App. LEXIS 459 (Court of Appeals of Michigan).

Zafar Arain v. *Double R. Remodeling, Inc.,* 2010. U.S. Dist. LEXIS 29496 (Middle Dist. Fl.).

Zaheer, B. (2007). 'Accommodating Minority Religions Under Title VII: How Muslims Make the Case for a New Interpretation of Section 701(j)', *University of Illinois Law Review,* 497–534.

Zahra Mowafy v. *Noramoc of Delaware, Inc.,* 2009. 620 F. Supp.2d 603; 2009 U.S. Dist. LEXIS 46387.*Welsh v. U.S,* 380 U.S. 163 (1965).

Zidan v. State of Maryland Department of Public Safety and Correctional Services, 2012 U.S. App. LEXIS 24366 (2012).

PART II
Africa

Chapter 6

Managing Religious Diversity in the South African Workplace

NASIMA MOHAMED HOOSEN CARRIM

Introduction

Religion plays a pivotal role in the lives of the majority of South Africans. During the apartheid era, religious freedom and accommodation within the workplace was restricted. Religious diversity was not present as the workplace consisted of fairly homogeneous individuals who shared similar views of religious practices and observances. In 1994, with the election of a democratic government, South Africa witnessed an increase in number of Muslims, Hindus, Jews, followers of the African indigenous religions (AIR) and other minority religious groups entering the workplace (Coertzen, 2008). For the first time in South African history, religious freedom was guaranteed by the constitution. However, government's support of religious freedom in the form of legislation does not guarantee that religious accommodation is respected in the workplace. Nor does it guarantee that it is a simple managerial task to fulfil within organizations. 2014 marks the twentieth anniversary of democracy in South Africa and the question remains, how far did organizations come in accommodating and managing their diverse religious employees?

Like all other societies, South African organizations have to manage their diverse religious groups in terms of what constitutes permissible levels of religious discussions, whether religious days warrant legitimate absence, whether religious identities are to be disclosed and whether religious dress are to be tolerated (Bouma et al., 2003). With a strong presence of diverse religious groups in organizations, managers these days are faced with the challenges of divesting themselves of their own prejudices and accommodating a multitude of varying beliefs and customs. Religious diversity within South African organizations is not an ephemeral phenomenon but it is a reality which is here to stay and is a key element to successful management in today's workplace (Coertzen, 2008).

This chapter highlights the changes in the socio-political landscape namely from the apartheid to the post-apartheid era that affected socio-religious developments within the South African context. It also focuses on the theoretical component of managing diverse religions in South Africa organizations. Thereafter, case studies and data from interviews conducted with Muslim and Hindu women and male managers regarding religious accommodation and tolerance in the workplace will be provided. A conclusion will end this text.

Religion as a Concept

The concept of religion is conceptualized in various ways by different scholars and there is therefore not a unified understanding of the term (Day, 2005). From the multitude of understandings of the concept religion, in this chapter we will opt for a general view of the term by providing two perspectives of the term. According to Day (2005, p. 109) religion serves the following purposes:

- an experiential dimension that provides a religious experience;

- a belief system where certain beliefs are adopted in adherence to a specific faith;

- a ritual dimension where adherents perform certain rites;

- a devotional dimension where one can in private practice certain acts;

- an intellectual dimension that allows one to understand the religion's teachings.

Bouma et al. (2003, p. 52) point out that the main characteristics of religion are:

- beliefs about the ultimate nature of reality, including hope, destiny, purpose and the relationship of the now to the eternal, the changing to the persistent, the human to the more than human;

- practices, rights and rituals through which religion is expressed, related to life and the beliefs inculcated, celebrated and put into practice.

The main idea behind these understandings of religion is that the concept consists of various practices which are performed in terms of devotional rituals and consist of one's understanding of the teachings of a particular faith.

South Africa's Religious Diversity

South Africa is a religiously diverse country. Approximately 80 per cent of the population is Christian and is divided into various denominations (Kuperus, 2011; Malherbe, 2011; Ryan, 2010). The white Afrikaner community belong to the Dutch Reform Church which is sub-divided into three other groups. The second dominant Christian group Afrikaners belong to the Apostolic Faith Group. White English-speaking people belong to the Methodist, Roman Catholic or Anglican Churches (Goodsell, 2007). Almost 25 per cent of people from mixed groups (that is people who have an admixture of ancestors from slaves brought into South Africa from Central and East Africa, Malay, Javanese and Indian slaves as well as British and Dutch settlers) belong to the Roman Catholic or Anglican Churches (Ryan, 2010). Nearly 10 per cent of Asians are Christians (van der Walt et al., 2010). Almost 25 per cent of black Africans belong to one of 6,000 denominations of black separatists or indigenous Christian movements, frequently described as 'syncretistic' churches combining Christianity with African traditions such as worshipping spirits and revering ancestors (Goodsell, 2007, p.115; van der Walt et al., 2010).

AIR refers to the native religion of black Africans which has been orally transmitted across generations (Mutugi Gathogo, 2008, p. 577) and which has no founder (Adamo, 2011). Black Africans are extremely religious and each of the nine ethnic groups[1] within South Africa has its own customs and practices which are rooted in African traditional religion (Mbiti, 1990). About 15 per cent of the South African population, that is black Africans, belong to the AIR and constitute the second largest religious group (Goodsell, 2007).

Hindus, Muslims and Jews comprise the next three largest religious denominations. Although they are minority religious groups (Hindus are 1.75 per cent of the total population, Muslims consist of 1.09 per cent of adherents and Jews who are mainly orthodox constitute 0.41 per cent of followers) they have established a lasting presence in South African history and society (Goodsell, 2007, p. 116). Each of these three religions has had to endure discrimination legislation and anti-alien restrictions during British colonialism and thereafter apartheid.

---

1   Basotho, Batswana, Bapedi, Zulu, Xhosa, Venda, Ndebele, Tsonga and Shangaan.

For example, from 1913, Hindu and Muslim marriages were not recognized and only received recognition in post-apartheid South Africa (Goodsell, 2007). Other religious groups such as Rastafarians, Jainism, Buddhism and Baha'i constitute a minute proportion of the population (Goodsell, 2007).

Given the religious diversity in South African organizations and the possibility of even greater diversity in the future, managers need to ensure that they accommodate all these groups and to avoid interreligious conflicts.

A true understanding of the management of diverse religions within the South African workplace and the current legislation cannot be fully appreciated and understood without insight into the country's past history related to religion. Equally important is an understanding of the role current legislation plays in terms of encouraging employers to embrace and advance religious eclecticism in the workplace.

Religion in the Apartheid and Post-Apartheid Eras

LACK OF RELIGIOUS FREEDOM DURING THE APARTHEID ERA

Scholars criticize the view that South Africa was a Christian country during the apartheid years. The main critique is that the Government had constructed skewed statistical data in order to enhance the idea that the majority of people in South Africa were Christians (Dreyer et al., 1999; Kumar, 2006). Nevertheless, under the apartheid regime, South Africa was proclaimed a Christian country and other religions and faiths, especially AIR, were not tolerated and respected (Chidester, 2003) although some concessions were given to Islam, Hinduism and Judaism (Loubser, 2004). For example, black Africans practised their religion in secret as it was regarded as barbaric and superstitious by white South Africans (Adamo, 2011). Missionaries believed that Africans were not human and they therefore prohibited polygamy, initiation ceremonies, ancestor worship and other ethnic practices (Mercado, 2005).

During this period the Dutch Reformed Church (DRC) was involved in politics and supported the moral and philosophical beliefs of the apartheid system by providing theological and biblical sanctions for certain laws and making statements which backed Government actions (Chidester, 2006; Hale 2006; Kuperus, 1996). In 1948, the official proclaimer for the DRC stated that '... as a church we have as a rule ... always deliberately aimed at separation of white and non-white groups. In this respect, apartheid can rightfully be called the "church policy"' (Goodsell, 2007, p. 119). In return the DRC received favoured treatment from the State by protecting Christian customs and traditions (Blake and Litchfield, 1998; Goodsell, 2007; Kuperus, 1996). For example, Sunday observance laws required that businesses be closed on Christian holy days and on the Sunday Sabbath. Religious education in schools had a Christian preference. Only Christian oaths were accepted in criminal cases (Van der Vyver, 1991). The apartheid Government's constitution accorded Christianity a privileged position in terms of values, education, public and holidays. Apartheid's political philosophy was thus rooted in the teachings of the DRC which biblically justified racial segregation (Haron, 2006). In this way the apartheid era established a strong Christian bias in the macro environment. The DRC adopted an attitude of dominating and controlling all non-white groups and regarding these groups as racially and intellectually inferior. They interpreted their scriptures in a prejudicial manner and believed that only they were following the true path which was chronicled for them through a divine plan (Du Toit, 2006; Haron, 2006). Today, however, this Church does not have a voice in relation to the ruling party (Kuperus, 2011).

Some churches, for example the Anglican, Methodist and Presbyterian Churches, which operated under the South African Council of Churches (SACC) banner condemned apartheid (Kuperus, 2011). Other white Christian denominations, such as the Lutheran and Catholic Churches, while not sanctioning apartheid, still consented to the State's injustices (Goodsell, 2007). For example, they supported the *Immorality Act* of 1950 which prohibited marriages between people of different race groups. Religion was therefore used to 'reinforce racist legislation and segregation on the basis of racial, ethnic, cultural, linguistic and religious signs of difference' (Chidester, 2006, p. 65).

Ultimately, constitutional matters were governed by Parliament who had the authority to impinge religious freedom in order to promote apartheid policies (Blake and Litchfield, 1998). The apartheid Government adopted a draconian and repressive attitude towards religious institutions. During this period blacks' religious freedom was curbed. For example, the 'Church Clause' in the *Natives (Urban Areas) Consolidation Act* of 1957 allowed the Minister of Co-operation and Development to restrict black Africans from attending church service outside their residential area (Van der Vyver, 1999). In addition, black African churches and leaders were banned under the *Internal Security Act* when they supported organizations that were opposed to the Government. Another act that was used to control the activities of religious groups was the *Affected Organisations Act* which prohibited foreign financial assistance to organizations that were under the influence of individuals and organizations from abroad (Goodsell, 2007, p. 120). Religious leaders and groups that opposed the apartheid Government were persecuted and therefore most religious groups would only mildly criticize apartheid when they were dissatisfied. Religious intolerance and non-accommodation translated into the workplace where no other religions beside Christianity were accepted. 'Religious marginalization was therefore closely linked to racial discrimination, social exclusion and political disempowerment' (Goodsell, 2007, p. 120).

An exception was the Kairos document that was signed by many theologians and lay persons in 1985. The document requested Christians to work towards a just society and church leaders to further the cause of an equitable populace by standing up to the apartheid Government. In due course, the number of religious activism cases against apartheid far outstripped religious acceptance of the apartheid system. Religion therefore played a significant role in the fight against apartheid (Goodsell, 2007).

RELIGIOUS AUTONOMY IN THE POST-APARTHEID ERA

Since the democratic elections of 1994, when South Africa surfaced from the repressive and racist period of apartheid to become a united democratic nation, religion has become a pivotal element in nation building (Van der Vyver, 1999). The most important role of the secular democratic Government was to steer South Africa from a mono-cultural society by passing legislation and policies, to one based on a multicultural and multi-religious ethos (Kuperus, 2011). In a break with the past, religion plays an important role in the democratic South Africa's highly religious civil society (Goodsell, 2007, p. 121). Religion has been included in the public sphere by the new constitutional order adopting a 'cooperative model' for relations between religion and the State. This has been achieved by Government drawing upon the resources of diverse religions in the welfare and civil society sectors (Chidester, 2006). Religious leaders also played a role in South Africa's Truth and Reconciliation Commission (a commission which brought to justice individuals who had perpetrated injustices during the apartheid era) (Goodsell, 2007).

In the post-apartheid era the general public still believes that the Christian religion is the chief religion in South Africa although it is no longer a State religion nor does it enjoy any special privileges (Dreyer et al., 1999). However, the media, government bureaucracy and private organizations are dominated by white Christians (Kumar, 2006) and the country's statutory and common law reveals a Christian bias (Du Toit, 2006).

Constitutional Framework of South Africa

Given the role religion played during and after the apartheid era it is easy to understand the emphasis of religious freedom in the Constitution and the prohibition of favouritism and discrimination of any religious group (Goodsell, 2007). Religion forms an integral part of South African communities and is enshrined in the South African Constitution which is regarded by scholars as 'one of the best and most liberal constitutions in the world' (Du Toit, 2006 p. 677; Goodsell, 2007, p.109). Hence, the South African constitution has accorded religious freedom, respect and accommodation as a human rights as well as a moral issue (Kumar, 2006).

Government has, through various pieces of legislation, protected religious freedom which is addressed in the Constitution specifically in Chapter 2 which is the Bill of Rights, *The Promotion of Equality and Prevention of Unfair Discrimination Act* and through The Commission for the Promotion and Protection of the Rights of Cultural, Religious and Linguistic Communities. These pieces of legislation focus on religious freedom from a general perspective and address all South African communities. A charter called The South African Charter of Religious Rights and Freedoms was also endorsed by religious leaders from all major religions in South Africa (Malherbe, 2011). Within the workplace, religious freedom is addressed through labour legislation referred to as the *Employment Equity Act*.

For the purpose of this chapter it is important to understand the various pieces of legislation relating to religious autonomy and protection as they highlight the importance of the role of religion in all spheres within the South African context.

SOUTH AFRICAN CONSTITUTION, 1996

The Constitution which is the supreme law in South Africa was promulgated in 1996 and consists of the principles and main elements of the new democratic constitutional order. All laws and behaviour that is not in accordance to the Constitution are considered invalid (Malherbe, 2011). One of the founding principles of the South African Constitution is based on non-racism and non-sexism. Considering the history of apartheid, a key focus and objective in a democratic South Africa is the protection of human rights. This is another founding principle in the Constitution, which explicitly states that its purpose is to eradicate inequality, discrimination and injustices perpetrated in the past (Malherbe, 2011). This extends to religion as well as individuals not being discriminated against and persecuted on religious grounds. The Constitution has also been designed to instil religious tolerance and plurality. The right to religious freedom and equality forms part of the idea of promoting tolerance and supports religious activities such as preaching, proselytizing, congregating and witnessing (Du Plessis, 2001).

BILL OF RIGHTS

The Bill of Rights forms a part of the South African Constitution and is a human rights charter which protects the socio-economic, political and civil rights of all South Africans. The Bill of Rights protects religious freedom through various clauses, as indicated in section 15(1) which states that 'Every person shall have the right to freedom of conscience, *religion,* thought, belief and opinion, which shall include academic freedom in institutions of higher learning' (South Africa, 1996). Other clauses incorporating a general freedom of religion clause in the Bill of Rights section 9(3) state that 'No person shall be unfairly discriminated against, directly or indirectly, and, without derogating from the generality of this provision, on one or more of the following grounds in particular: race, gender, sex, ethnic or social origin, colour, sexual orientation, age, disability, *religion,* conscience, belief, culture or language and birth' (South Africa, 1996). Under the Freedom of Expression clause 16(2c), the Bill of Rights prohibits 'advocacy of hatred that is based on race, ethnicity, gender or religion and that causes incitement to cause harm' (South Africa, 1996). The Bill of Rights also includes a clause in section 15(2) regarding religious observances at State institutions and schools which assert that 'religious observances may be conducted at state or state-aided institutions under rules established by an appropriate authority for that purpose provided that such religious observances are conducted on an equitable basis and attendance at them is free and voluntary' (South Africa, 1996).

Other provisions relating to religion and religious freedom are also stated in the Bill of Rights. For example, sections 185 and 186 stipulate for the establishment of a commission to promote and protect the rights of religious, cultural and linguistic communities. Clauses relating to human dignity, the right to freedom of expression and association in the Bill of Rights also relate to religious freedom (South Africa, 1996). However, the right to religious freedom is not supreme as it is limited by a law of general application and the constitution (South Africa, 1996). Therefore tolerance of diverse religions according to the Bill of Rights implies the equal treatment of plural religions and religious groups within workplace limits.

THE EMPLOYMENT EQUITY ACT, 55 OF 1998

The Employment Equity Act, 55 of 1998 is a piece of labour legislation that promotes equal opportunity and fair treatment in employment through the elimination of unfair discrimination. Chapter 2 of the *Employment Equity Act* redresses unfair discrimination through clause 2.1 which states that:

> *no person may unfairly discriminate, directly or indirectly, against an employee in any employment policy or practice, on one or more grounds including race, gender, pregnancy, marital status, family responsibility, ethnic or social origin, colour, sexual orientation, age disability, religion, HIV status, conscience, belief, political opinion, culture, language, and birth (South Africa, 1998).*

Additionally, the *Employment Equity Act* states that religious observances should be accommodated as long as they do not interfere with the operational requirements of the employer.

THE COMMISSION FOR THE PROMOTION AND PROTECTION OF THE RIGHTS OF CULTURAL, RELIGIOUS AND LINGUISTICS COMMUNITIES (CRL RIGHTS COMMISSION)

The South African Constitution had established a group of organizations which are referred to as 'Chapter nine institutions' in order to guard democracy. The Commission for the Promotion and Protection of the Rights of Cultural, Religious and Linguistics Communities (CRL Rights Commission) is one of these organizations (South Africa, 1996). The objective of the CLR Rights Commission in terms of the South African Constitution Chapter 9 section 185(1) is:

> *to promote respect for and further the protection of the rights of cultural, religious and linguistic communities; promote and develop peace, friendship, humility, tolerance, national unity among and within cultural, religious and linguistic communities on the basis of equality, non-discrimination and free association; to promote the right of communities, to develop their historically diminished heritage and to recognise community councils (South Africa, 2002).*

This Commission is therefore tasked to take care of people's religious freedom on a macro level.

THE SOUTH AFRICAN CHARTER OF RELIGIOUS RIGHTS AND FREEDOMS

Chapter 14 section 234 of the South African Constitution makes provisions for the establishment of charters of rights (South Africa, 1996). One of the charters was established in accordance with the constitution was The South African Charter of Religious Rights and Freedoms (SACRRF) which was endorsed on 21 October 2010 (Malherbe, 2011). The SACRRF was established to define the religious freedom, rights and responsibilities of South African communities and organizations. The SACRRF deals with the legal and civil rights to freedom of religion for individuals, groups and organizations. This includes the right to congregate to observe religious beliefs, freely expressing one's religious convictions, making choices according to one's convictions, the freedom to change one's faith, the right to obtain religious education, the right of parents to educate children in accordance with their religious beliefs and convictions and to refuse to perform duties and assist in activities that contravene their religious principles (Malherbe, 2011).

PROMOTION OF EQUALITY AND PREVENTION OF UNFAIR DISCRIMINATION ACT, 2000

The Promotion of Equality and Prevention of Unfair Discrimination Act 2000, also referred to as *the Equality Act* No. 4 of 2000, is an all-inclusive, anti-discrimination South African law. It forbids unfair discrimination by government and private workplaces and individuals and prevents harassment and hate speech (South Africa, 2000). This Act clearly states that race, gender, sex, pregnancy, marital status, ethnic or social origin, colour, sexual orientation, age, disability, religion, conscience, belief, culture, language and birth are forbidden bases for discrimination (South Africa, 2000).

In this section, the various pieces of legislation that deal with religion freedom and rights in the South Africa context have been highlighted. Religious observances, that is, the practice of religious beliefs and rituals both in the public and private domains, and the promotion of religions form the crux of these pieces of legislation.

The next section focuses on accommodating diverse religions in the workplace from a theoretical perspective. Practical examples of religious issues within South African workplaces through case studies and interviews conducted with Indian women managers will be provided.

Religious Accommodation in the Workplace

For most people work dominates a large part of their lives and it is therefore difficult to separate their religious beliefs from the workplace. Therefore religious diversity is emerging as a workplace issue since it is propelled by demographic trends (Day, 2005). In addition to religious freedom, accommodation and respect, South African organizations also face issues of nationality, ethnicity, race and citizenship as foreign employees enter the workplace in increasing numbers (Kumar, 2006). It is therefore important that attention be paid to how managers deal with religious accommodation and the disagreements that follow when a compromise cannot be reached (Borstroff and Arlington, 2010). While the concept of religious pluralism is not a new issue as it can be traced to colonialism, the managing of religious diversity in South African organizations is certainly a new idea.

SECULARISM IN THE WORKPLACE

There is a growing tendency of South Africans becoming secular (Kumar, 2006). Secularism is on the increase as more people are moving from rural to urban areas where traditional customs are giving way to more modern ways. Increasingly, people are driven more by non-religious goals as they are no longer diligent attendees of mosques, churches and temples but are finding their own diverse ways of combining beliefs from new age religious and non-religious origins (Kumar, 2006). Not all employees have adopted secular ways and the majority of South Africans are still very religious. However, adhering to their religious practices has become a problem as most South African organizations are secular. When organizational secularism is not an issue, the problem arises as many individuals do not adhere to the majority religion in the organization. Black African managers are calling for an Afrocentric organizational culture, but workplaces still remain Eurocentric in their religious approach (Horwitz et al., 1996) as white Christians still dominate South African organizations. White managers do tolerate unconventional religions practices up to a point until they feel that they are inconvenienced (Beckley and Burstein, 1991) as illustrated in the case studies that follow.

RELIGIOUS DISCRIMINATION IN THE WORKPLACE

Religious discrimination is practiced to a lesser degree in South African workplaces than in the past but it has not disappeared entirely. There are two perspectives of what constitutes fair treatment and non-discrimination of diverse religious groups in the workplace. The *assimilationist perspective* implies that employers are not to distinguish among employees based on religious beliefs. Thus, if employees from a certain religious group want a day off for a religious celebration the employer is not obliged to accommodate them if it interferes with standard business operations. The *cultural pluralist view* on the other hand states that employers should accommodate religious practices and beliefs and that these employees should be given the day off (Beckley and Burstein, 1991). The onus lies on employers to accommodate individuals' practices from diverse religious backgrounds. For example, not forcing a Hindu male to work on Diwali day. Diverse religions may be protected in the South African workplace through legislation but accommodation and freedom may be minimal as it is dependent on the operational requirements of the workplace.

The challenge facing South African organizations in the post-apartheid era is overcoming deeply ingrained discriminatory practices and social divisions relating to diverse religions. Within South African organizations, HR development and diversity management are treated as separate spheres although they are intertwined concepts (Horwitz et al., 1996). Since these spheres are regarded as separate processes they follow a hard or soft approach. The *soft approach* focuses on raising awareness and understanding among employees. The idea is to change people's attitudes and values relating to religious diversity through, for example, training sessions, workshops and discussions. The *hard approach* focuses on changing company policies relating to religious accommodation and tolerance (Horwitz et al., 1996). These approaches do not form part of the overall strategic and HRM processes and therefore managing a diverse religious workforce presents a challenge (Human, 1996). The latter two interventions only pay lip service to diversity management but still lack institutional adaptation in managing religious diversity, especially since many HR managers believe that religious discrimination and conflict is not a workplace issue. Therefore, the majority of employees do not report religious discrimination, as they feel no positive action will be taken against the perpetrators (Day, 2005).

South African managers are also not familiar with the growing variety of religions within the workplace. There are various ways in which religious discrimination by managers takes place. For example, employees may not be promoted due to their religious beliefs or workers are harassed because they don religious garb. Due to religious discrimination, organizations are losing their competitive advantage as top talent work for the competition (Huang and Kleiner, 2001). Huang and Kleiner (2001, p. 129) point out various ways in which religious discrimination can take place:

- when individuals with weak religious beliefs criticize those with strong religious beliefs;

- when individuals indulge in offensive religious jokes;

- when religious services such as memorial services are made compulsory;

- when a public prayer is closed off by taking the name of Jesus;

- when one does not associate with people from other religious beliefs;

- when the organization fails to provide alternative services to accommodate all religious beliefs;

- when people of diverse religious groups are overlooked when arranging work schedules.

PRACTISING RELIGION IN THE WORKPLACE

Religion may directly impact employees' work. For example, Muslim employees may refuse to work in a brewery. Catholic nurses may refuse to assist in abortions. Workplaces are also places where workers decide religious obligation (Bouma et al., 2003). For example, Muslim employees may leave the job site when a family member dies, as burials are conducted on the day the individual dies. Within the South African context managers are increasingly confronted with these issues as religious diversity rises and the workforce consists of employees who want to openly practice their religious beliefs and practices (Day, 2005). These practices and observances become especially difficult to follow when managers keep religion and work separate. Workers then have to choose whether they want to follow their religion and rebel against management or they want to move to other organizations that are more accommodating. In some cases, when managers are not willing to accommodate employees' religious beliefs, these cases end up in court (Estreicher and Gray, 2006).

Many South African organizations promote an awareness of religious diversity by discussing religious stereotypes, conducting training in religious discrimination and accommodation as managers believed that religious tenets and beliefs were an important part of the overall organizational culture (Cash and Gray, 2000). However, since the main objective of organizations is to achieve profitability, productivity and produce quality products and services, religious accommodation can be a barrier to achieving these objectives if management does not take into account customer service, delivery and scheduling. Organizations have to first determine their parameters of flexibility before they can accommodate religious observances as these may conflict with processes and productivity (Day, 2005).

Practical Examples of Managing Diverse Religions in South African Organizations

South African managers are confronted with having to accommodate various religious expressions that conflict with established work schedules, rules and conditions (Spognardi and Ketay, 2000). Globalization, technological advancement, reengineering and downsizing has brought a South African diverse workforce that practices religion not only in their homes but in the workplace as well (Cash and Gray, 2000) as religious beliefs and rituals are a pivotal part of their identities (Christian, 1997). For example, traditional religions like Islam integrate their religious practices in the social, political, legal and work environments (Cash and Gray, 2000). Therefore, greater religious management, tolerance and accommodation have become a basis for workers achieving a sense of self-worth in the workplace.

This has led the number of court cases dealing with religious discrimination, lack of religious freedom and accommodation within South African workplaces to increase. A few recent examples brought before the courts illustrate this point as indicated next.

DAGGA USED FOR RELIGIOUS PURPOSES

One of the most difficult cases that the South African Labour Court was faced with was that of Gareth Price. As a Rastafarian, Price consumed *cannabis sativa* (dagga) for ceremonial, medicinal, culinary and spiritual reasons as an important part of his religion. After successfully completing his legal studies, he was eligible to register as a candidate attorney doing community service. After being arrested twice for using dagga the question was whether he was fit to register as a candidate attorney considering he intended continuing to use dagga. The Law Society of the Cape of Good Hope refused his candidature and he challenged their decision in the Cape High Court. The Court held that dagga was prohibited by statutory law in order to protect public safety, health, morals and order and these concerns outweigh Rastafarian's religious expressions of using dagga. The Court accepted the law society's decision (Du Plessis, 2001).

REFUSAL TO COMPLY WITH DRESS CODE

Employers expect employees to adhere to the organization's dress code as this creates brand awareness, image and reputation, professionalism, uniformity and avoids inappropriate dressing (Rycroft, 2011). For example, in August 2013, after numerous complaints from customers, a sangoma initiate who worked at Auto Tyres in the Eastern Cape was asked by management to take time off to sort out his image when he came to work dressed in traditional beads, white head gear and painted his face white (Sowetan, 2013).

South African Muslim women are demanding that they be allowed to wear the headscarf although there is a ruling forbidding this practice in some workplaces. In the 'Worchester Prison' case a Muslim social worker was dismissed from the Worchester Prison for violating the 'corporate identity' of the Department of Correctional Services by wearing a headscarf and refusing to tuck in her shirt into her skirt which contravened the official uniform of the organization (Lenta, 2007). She maintained that it is obligatory in Islam that she cover her head and she did not tuck in her shirt as she was expected to hide the contours of her body as Muslim women are expected to be modest. In South Africa, Muslim women who are religiously obliged to wear the headscarf are denied employment in positions where religiously symbolic clothing is banned although the Constitutional Court indicates that individuals should be accommodated and allowed religious freedom within reason. The Court is prepared to protect individuals' right to religious freedom by allowing exemptions to laws that apply generally and where there is scope to do so. As long as it does not violate the basic rights of others, there is no reason to refuse the exemption and it is a religious obligation and not customary (Lenta, 2007).

- *Dlamini and Others* v. *Green Four Security* ([2006] 11 BLLR 1074 (LC)) Security guards belonging to the Nazarene Church refused to shave their beards because it was against their religious persuasion. They claimed that their dismissal was unfair. The employer claimed that it was part of their contract to be clean shaven and that they were beardless when they commenced employment (Rycroft, 2011). The security guards could not prove that trimming their beards was against their Church. They in fact worked on Sundays which was prohibited by their Church. They therefore selectively applied religious practices in the workplace. The Court ruled that the employees were not unfairly dismissed (Rycroft, 2011).

- *Popcru and Others* v. *Department of Correctional Services and Another* ([2010] 10 BLLR 1067 (LC))
  Five male officers working for the Department of Correctional Services received a written instruction to comply with the Department's dress code and to remove their dreadlocks. They refused to remove their dreadlocks due to religious reasons. They were accordingly dismissed. The case was referred to the Labour Court. The Department mentioned during the case hearing that Rastafarians were associated with drug use and dreadlocks could be grabbed in physical involvement with prisoners which could be a life threatening situation. The Court ruled in favour of the Department and mentioned there was no indirect discrimination. However, since women officers were allowed to wear dreadlocks, the Court ruled the Department directly discriminated against male officers (Rycroft, 2011).

RESPECTING RELIGIOUS DAYS

- *Fawu and Others* v. *Rainbow Chickens* ((2000) 21 ILJ 615 (LC))
  Muslim butchers who slaughtered chickens according to Muslim rites that is the halaal way, were dismissed by Rainbow Chickens because they took the day off on Eidul Fitar which is their religious holiday. The collective agreement between the union and management was that employees could only take off on gazetted holidays. Since Eid was not a gazetted holiday, when the butchers took off all operations came to a standstill, implying that even employees who were not Muslims would be paid for not doing any work on that day. Although the employees alleged that their dismissal was unfair, the Court refuted this claim. The reasoning was that if the operations of the organizations are halted due to some employees' religious days, then discrimination is not unfair. The Court in this case ruled that the operational requirements of the company take precedence over employees' religious days, which is in accordance with the *Employment Equity Act* 66 of 1995. Had the religious day not had an impact on the operations of the organization then their dismissal would have been regarded as discriminatory (Rycroft, 2011).

- *Lewis* v. *Media 24 Ltd* ((2010) 31 Ilj 2416 (LC))
  In another court case, Lewis claimed that his employer Media 24 channel required him to work on a Saturday his Sabbath although

he is a Jew. The Court ruling was that since Media 24 management was not aware of Lewis' religious affiliation as he did not disclose it to them they were not guilty of religious discrimination (Rycroft, 2011).

TRADITIONAL HEALERS CALLING AND CERTIFICATES

- *Kieviets Kroon Country Estate (Pty) Ltd* v. *CCMA and Others* (unreported, LC, 1 Oct 2010, case no JR1856/2008)
  The post-apartheid era has also witnessed an increase in the practice of AIR in South Africa which was curbed during the apartheid era. This religion has become an important part of public life where Parliament and health workers recognize African traditional healers (Adamo, 2011). This case involves an employee who worked as a chef de partie, handling conferences and leisure in a multi-million rand company for eight years. The employee started getting visions and consulted a sangoma (traditional healer) who advised her to become a sangoma as she had to appease her ancestors (Rycroft, 2011). She discussed the matter with her manager who requested her to work during the mornings and to attend sangoma training sessions during the afternoons. She requested a month's unpaid leave to complete her training as a sangoma but her manager was prepared to allow her one week's unpaid leave only. The company was short staffed as some employees were on leave and it was also a busy period. The company could therefore not dispense of her services. She however decided to attend the training course although she was not granted the unpaid leave. Before she went on unpaid leave, she handed her manager a traditional healer's certificate stating she had premonitions (Rycroft, 2011). The employer refused to accept a certificate and wanted a doctor's certificate stating that she was sick. Had she handed a doctor's sick note, she would not have been dismissed from employment. The employee referred the case to the Commission for Conciliation Mediation and Arbitration (CCMA) Commissioner which handles labour disputes before they are submitted to the labour courts for further judgement (Rycroft, 2011). The Commissioner ruled in her favour and passed the verdict that she was unfairly dismissed. In this case she had to heed the calling of the ancestors as her life was in danger had she ignored their request. The Commissioner found her decision was beyond her control and she had to disregard her employer's request as her life was in danger. This case is an

exception and not the rule as employees have to obtain permission from their employers and conduct their religious obligations during the weekends (Rycroft, 2011).

- *Ppwawu* v. *Nampak Corrugated Containers* ((1998) 3 LLD 48 (CCMA)) The *Traditional Health Practitioners Act* 22 of 2007 makes provisions for people in the taxi industry, domestic workers; contract cleaners and in the clothing and knitting sector to use the services of traditional healers and to obtain their certificate (Rycroft, 2011). A worker at Nampak was dismissed after he disappeared for 14 days without notifying his employer of his whereabouts. The employee stated that he had gone to a traditional healer in a rural area and only intended to stay for a week. The traditional healer however requested he stay longer. He had no means of contacting his employer during the 14 days. His drinking problem had since been resolved. The Commissioner found that in a country like South Africa one cannot rely solely on Western medicine and could not deny the employee's need to seek alternate medical assistance and therefore asked the employer to reinstate him (Rycroft, 2011).

Findings from Interviews with Hindu and Muslim Women and Men

As part of my data collection, I interviewed 20 Muslim and Hindu women managers and seven Muslim and Hindu men from diverse organizations in various positions.[2] Muslim men pointed out that they could not wear their traditional clothes to work as their managers disapproved of such garb. The reasoning would be that it was against corporate dress code.

The participants indicated that organizational meetings were scheduled on their religious holidays. Even when they brought it to their managers' notice their requests were not heeded and no alternate scheduling arrangements were conducted with them or their colleagues. As a result, the participants

---

2   Purposive and snowball sampling was used. Participants were provided with the aim of the study and told that all identities would be kept confidential. Interviewees signed consent forms and agreed to be part of the study. Semi-structured interviews lasting 60 minutes each were conducted with every participant. Content analysis was used to analyse transcribed data. To enhance the credibility of the data obtained, a trained observer was provided with the transcripts of the interviews and independently coded the themes. Face-to-face sessions with the trained observer and compared themes were held. The trained observer also obtained similar themes, which enhanced the credibility of the study. Participants were also provided with a copy of the final themes. They agreed that their narratives had been captured accurately.

had to attend these meetings and could not celebrate their festival days. The participants complained that precedence was given to Christianity as businesses did not operate on Christmas and New Year's days and even during Easter.

Muslim participants mentioned that they were not comfortable shaking hands with members of the opposite sex. Yet, due to organizational protocol they were expected to do so and could not refuse on religious grounds.

One major problem the participants encountered was that their dietary requirements were not met during organizational meetings and functions. Bringing such arrangements to the notice of organizers also did not guarantee that their dietary requirements would be met. Where organizations had cafeterias, these would also not cater to their dietary needs. Although the participants complained about this issue to their managers, their requests were ignored and were not raised with the catering service department and organizers of events.

Both Muslim and Hindu participants pointed out that meetings were deliberately scheduled during the Muslim prayer times on Friday so that Muslim males could not attend prayers during this time. Although Muslim men complained about organizational meetings being held during these times, they were ignored and the trend to have meetings scheduled during their prayer times still persists. Muslim women on the other hand prayed in their offices as they have more flexibility around prayer times.

The participants mentioned that Christian colleagues would during lunch breaks approach them to try and convert them to Christianity. Participants noted with some resentment that only their Christian colleagues were allowed the privilege by management to preach their religion in the workplace. Cash and Gray (2000) point out that proselytizing to colleagues during work breaks but not taking leave to conduct missionary work is a common occurrence in organizations (Cash and Gray, 2000). Spognardi and Ketay (2000) and Day (2005) point out this could be regarded as offensive by members of other religious groups, cause friction among executives and employees and leads to a hostile work environment, especially when managers only allow Christians to practice their religion and even make evangelism part of their mission statement.

None of the participants filed for religious discrimination against their colleagues and managers. Most are afraid of being dismissed and opted to work around these issues. However, they unanimously agreed that South African workplaces need to accommodate religious diversity.

Conclusion

Religious restrictions were explicated in terms of the apartheid era but democracy had led to religious freedom albeit only in terms of legislation. The reality is that religious discrimination still exists in South African organizations despite legislation granting employees religious freedom. Most South African organizations already have established workplace cultures that do not recognize employees' diverse religious affiliations. These workplace cultures do not place emphasis on religious diversity being a strategic issue. Hence, managers do not have the skill to deal with religious accommodation and freedom due to a lack of diversity training and education within the workplace. Also South African organizations accommodate Christian festivities thus excluding employees from other religious denominations. The result is that there is an increase in lawsuits against managers in corporate South Africa and an unhappy workforce.

Labour courts also hand down dichotomous judgements which contradict current legislation. This is evident where labour law states that religious accommodation should take place as long as it does not interfere with the operational requirements of the employer. Yet, in the case where the chef was training as a sangoma, her dismissal was regarded as unfair due to religious convictions although it infringed on the operational requirements of the employer. On the other hand, the Court regarded the Muslim butchers' dismissal as being fair and non-discriminatory.

South African organizations thus have a long road to tread in terms of accommodating and managing diverse religions. Failing which, discriminatory law suits in terms of religious freedom will increase and organizations are bound to lose their most valued employees to rival companies. Managing religious diversity should therefore become a priority for managers at all levels and should be inculcated in the organizational culture if employers want a productive and happy workforce.

References

Adamo, D.T. (2011). 'Christianity and the African Traditional Religion(s): The Postcolonial Round of Engagement', *Verbum et Ecclesia*, 32(1): 1–10.
Beckley, G.T. and Burstein, P. (1991). 'Religious Pluralism, Equal Opportunity and the State', *The Western Political Quarterly*, 44(1): 185–208.

Blake, R.C. and Litchfield, L. (1998). 'Religious Freedom in Southern Africa: The Developing Jurisprudence', *BYU Law Review*, 1998(2): 515–62.

Borstroff, P. and Arlington, K. 2010. The perils of religious accommodation: employees' perceptions. Paper presented at the Allied Academies International Conference, New Orleans, USA, April.

Bouma, G., Haidar, A., Nyland, C. and Smith, W. (2003). 'Work, Religious Diversity and Islam', *Asia Pacific Journal of Human Resources*, 41(1): 51–61.

Cash, K.C. and Gray, G.R. (2000). 'A Framework for Accommodating Religion and Spirituality in the Workplace', *The Academy of Management Executive*, 14(3): 124–33.

Chidester, D. (2003). 'Religion Education in South Africa: Teaching and Learning about Religion, Religions, and Religious Diversity', *British Journal of Religious Education*, 25(4): 261–78.

Chidester, D. (2006). 'Religion Education and the Transformational State in South Africa', *Social Analysis*, 50(3): 61–83.

Christian, E.N.I. (1997). 'Facing the Truth Commission', *Century*, 114(35): 1149–51.

Coertzen, P. (2008). 'Grappling with Religious Differences in South Africa: A Draft for a Charter of Religious Rights', *BYU Law Review*, 2008(3): 779.

Day, N.E. (2005). 'Religion in the Workplace: Correlates and Consequences of Individual Behavior', *Journal of Management, Spirituality and Religion*, 2(1): 104–35.

Dreyer, J.S., Peterse, H.J.C., and van der Ven, J.A. (1999). 'Interreligious Orientation among South African Youth', *Religion and Theology*, 6(2): 194–220.

Du Plessis, L. (2001). 'Freedom of or Freedom from Religion: An Overview of Issues Pertinent to the Constitutional Protection of Religious Rights and Freedom in the New South Africa', *BYU Law Review*, 2001(2): 439–66.

Du Toit, C.W. (2006). 'Religious Freedom and Human Rights in South Africa after 1996: Responses and Challenges', *BYU Law Review*, 2006(2): 677–700.

Estreicher, S. and Gray, M.J. (2006). 'Religion and the US Workplace', *Human Rights*, 33: 17–20.

Goodsell, E.E. (2007). 'Constitution, Custom, and Creed: Balancing Human Rights Concerns with Cultural and Religious Freedom in Today's South Africa', *BYU Journal of Public Law*, 2007(1): 109–52.

Hale, F. (2006). 'The Baptist Union of Southern Africa and Apartheid', *Journal of Church and State*, 48(4): 753–77.

Haron, M. (2006). 'The Dynamics of Christian-Muslim Relations in South Africa (circa 1960–2000): From Exclusivism to Pluralism', *The Muslim World*, 96(3): 423–68.

Horwitz, F.M., Bowmaker–Falconer, A. and Searll, P. (1996). 'Human Resource Development and Managing Diversity in South Africa', *International Journal of Manpower*, 17(4/5): 134–51.

Huang, C.C., and Kleiner, B.H. (2001). 'New Developments Concerning Religious Discrimination in the Workplace', *International Journal of Sociology and Social Policy*, 21(8/9/10): 128–36.

Human, L. (1996). 'Managing Workforce Diversity: A Critique and Example from South Africa', *International Journal of Manpower*, 17(4/5): 46–64.

Kumar, P.P. (2006). 'Religious Pluralism and Religion Education in South Africa', *Method and Theory in the study of Religion*, 18(3): 273–92.

Kuperus, T. (1996). 'Resisting or Embracing Reform? South Africa's Democratic Transition and NGK-State Relations', *Journal of Church and State*, 38(4): 841–73.

Kuperus, T. (2011). 'The Political Role and Democratic Contribution of Churches in Post-apartheid South Africa', *Journal of Church and State*, 53(2): 278–306.

Lenta, P. (2007). 'Muslim Headscarves in the Workplace and in Schools', *South African Law Journal*, 124(1): 296–319.

Loubser, J.A. (2004). 'Religious Diversity and the Formation of Closed Cultural Systems, or When Does Religion Turn Bad?' *Religion and Theology*, 11(3/4): 3–4.

Malherbe, R. (2011). 'The Background and Contents of the Proposed South African Charter of Religious Rights and Freedoms', 2011(3): *BYU Law Review*, 613–35.

Mbiti, J.S. (1990). *African Religions and Philosophy*. Heinneman, Nairobi, Kenya.

Mercado, L.N. (2005). 'The Change in Catholic Attitudes towards Traditional Religion', *Dialogue and Alliance*, 18(2): 93.

Mutugi Gathogo, J. (2008). 'The Challenge and Reconstructive Impact of African Religion in South Africa Today', *Journal of Ecumenical Studies*, 43(4): 577–95.

Ryan, C.P. (2010). 'Church and State in the 'New' South Africa', *Political Theology*, 11(6): 894–908.

Rycroft, A. (2011). Accommodating Religious or Cultural Beliefs in the Workplace: *Kieviets Kroon Country Estate* v. *CCMA*; *Dlamini* v. *Green Four Security*; *POPCRU* v. *Department of Correctional Services*: case notes. Retrieved on 6 January 2014 from www.sabinet.co.za.

South Africa. (1996). Constitution of the Republic of South Africa, No 108 of 1996. Retrieved 5 January 2014 from www.info.gov.za/documents/constitution/1996/a108-96.pdf.

South Africa. (2000). *Promotion of Equality and Prevention of Unfair Discrimination Act. Government Gazette, 416(20876)*. Retrieved on 19 January 2015 http://www.info.gov.za/view/DownloadFileAction?id=68207.

Sowetan. (2013). Sangoma Initiate in Trouble at Work. Retrieved on 5 January 2014 from http://www.sowetanlive.co.za/news/2013/08/05/sangoma-initiate-in-trouble-at-work?.

Spognardi, M.A., and Ketay, S.L. (2000). 'In the Lion's Den: Religious Accommodation and Harassment in the Workplace', *Employee Relations Law Journal*, 25(4): 7–28.

Van der Walt, J.L., Potgieter, F.J., and Wolhuter, C.C. (2010). 'The Road to Religious Tolerance in Education in South Africa (and Elsewhere): A Possible 'Martian Perspective', *Religion, State and Society*, 38(1): 29–52.

Van der Vyver, J.D. (1991). 'Constitutional Options for Post-Apartheid South Africa', *Emory Law Journal*, 40(3): 745–822.

Van der Vyver, J.D. (1999). 'Constitutional Perspective of Church–State Relations in South Africa', *BYU Law Review*, 1999(3): 635–72.

Chapter 7

Practices of Managing Religious Diversity in Institutions: Lessons from Uganda

VINCENT BAGIRE AND DESIDERIO BARUNGI BEGUMISA

Introduction

Religious identity is a key prominent personal characteristic in Ugandan society. However, there have not been uncompromising and excluding attitudes; religious worshipping practices and ceremonies have not disrupted organizational life and performance. Rooted in the early adoption of different religious affiliations by the local chiefs in the pre-colonial era, living and working together despite differences is soft. Religious observance does not disrupt organizational life, but rather complements it. Many observers and commentators highlight the values, diverse religious beliefs and experiences of employees as being shaped by the inclusion of religious practices in organizations. The complexity and dividing nature of religious diversity is well documented in various parts of Africa. Nkurunzinza (2002, p. 137) defined religion as 'a force both creative and destructive'. Gatera (2002) reports the shortfall of religious bodies to play their prophetic role in Burundi and instead cultivated nepotism, favouritism and materialism that have bred conflict and intolerance. Adenyi (2002) studied the Nigerian situation where Islam, Christianity and Traditional religious groups have been engaged in direct confrontation manifesting into bloodshed. In Uganda, however, mild confrontations were recorded between 1879 and 1888 and thereafter religion has been a uniting factor among certain groupings of society (Ndyabahika, 2002; Nkurunzinza, 2002).

The Ugandan Constitution guarantees freedom of worship. Chapter 2 (7) stipulates non-adoption of a state religion; Chapter 4 (21, 29) provides for freedom of belief and non-discrimination on the basis of religion (Uganda 1995 Constitution). The national motto, stated as 'For God and my country', is entwined in religious belief. This is possibly the foundation of religious inclusion as a country that has institutions embracing religious diversity of employees without difficulty. There are traditionally two widely embraced religions – Islam and Christianity. In these main religions there are several denominations but it is uncommon to detect any differences or discrimination on the basis of faith among employees in organizations.

This chapter will highlight practices in different organizations that have cemented harmony despite religious diversity among members. A historical background of Christianity and Islam is given, underlining key national aspects that characterize how organizations view the religious factor among workers. Cases of how firms address organizational and managerial challenges deriving from the religious diverse backgrounds of their employees will be illustrated. It is noted that there are few established differences between local firms and multinational companies regarding policies and practices that address the different religious beliefs of the members at the workplace. The discussion recognizes certain implicit religious norms that latently or directly influence the way religious issues in organizations are handled. Finally, this chapter dwells on the benefits of a religiously diverse workforce in the Ugandan context.

The Coming of Islam and Christianity into Uganda

The Muslim and Christian faiths were introduced to Uganda in pre-colonial times. The first Islamic preachers entered in 1877, followed by the Anglican missionaries in 1878 and finally the Catholics in 1879. Uganda was initially composed of a host of strong kingdoms with different systems of governance. These included Buganda, Bunyoro, Tooro, Busoga and Ankole. There were also smaller chiefdoms. The rulers were powerful and recognized the source of their influence to cultural and religious beliefs. When Asian traders and European explorers entered the region, local leaders sought alliances as a way of gaining advantage over the others. The coming of the missionaries was by a request from the King (Kabaka) of Buganda. The Kabaka wanted the missionaries to train and teach his subjects. However, successive kings did not find peace with the missionaries as the converts begun to question some traditional practices. There were also rivalries and skirmishes among the Muslims, Anglicans and Catholics, which puzzled the Kabaka (Mbiti 1996; Faupel, 1984; Mereui, 1986).

According to Mbiti (1996), it is known that when the first Catholic missionaries, Father Simeon Lourdel and Brother Amans Delmas, arrived in February 1879, they were kept under house arrest for two weeks on the orders of Kabaka Mutesa I. Thereafter, they were allowed to have an audience with him in the presence of Alexander Mackay, the Church Missionary Society member who had arrived earlier. It was not surprising therefore, that Alexander Mackay expressed very negative attitudes towards the Catholic Church, in the presence of the King. These great disagreements between Catholics and Anglicans by foreign white men seemed to confuse the Kabaka. However, it turned out that he was more interested in safeguarding his kingdom from being taken over by Europeans, and the religious factors were of no significance at all.

Gradually, the Kabaka allowed the missionaries to set up camp at different hills not far from the palace. At some point, Kabaka Mutesa I became excited with the Catholic faith and eventually requested to be baptized. Inadvertently, Father Lourdel refused to baptize him because of the King's polygamous lifestyle. This did not go down well with the King. Instead, the missionaries got many young converts, some of whom were the pages in the palace (Faupel, 1984).

Historic events involving the murder of religious men and women on the orders of those with authority were pivotal in the growth of religion in Uganda. The first and oldest recorded murder was the execution of Bishop James Huntington of the Church Missionary Society on his entry into the Uganda Protectorate on 29 October 1885. This was done on instruction of the Kabaka after the advice of his henchmen who predicted a foreigner entering from the East as being a bad omen. The second and most significant event was the martyrdom of over 70 Muslim, Anglican and Catholic converts on the orders of Kabaka Mwanga of Buganda. Another politically driven high-level religious execution was during the regime of President Idi Amin who ruled Uganda between 1971 and 1979. When the head of the Anglican Church in Uganda expressed some misgivings in the way the country was being run, it is recorded that President Amin was depressed and directed his elimination. Archbishop Janani Luwum was murdered in 1977 by Government functionaries.

Traditional Beliefs

Prior to the advent of the white missionaries, there were many traditional cults and healers. The fate of those traditional healers was doomed when they failed to cure Kabaka Mutesa I of dysentery as they had always claimed competent. Instead, it was Father Simeon Lourdel who treated it successfully in May 1881. After his recovery, the Kabaka tried to turn to the Islamic faith after being convinced by Masudi – the Islamic leader of the time. The Islamic clerics were also focused on trade and this appealed to the Kabaka for his economic gains. It was the intention of the Kabaka that his subjects should observe the teachings and practices of the Islamic faith. Traditional beliefs continued to thrive among those who did not want to be quick to adopt the ways of the white men. Even today, some practices thrive despite over a century of religion in present-day Uganda. Despite expressing his allegiance to one faith after another and by order, his subjects, the Kabaka accepted and tolerated all other religions at any time (Stark et al., 1981, Fapaul, 1984, Mbiti, 1996).

Religion in Uganda Today

Religion continued to be embraced by many Ugandans through independence up to today. As noted already, freedom of belief is enshrined in the national Constitution. Religion is therefore a way of life in Ugandan organizations and communities. The Ugandan Constitution guarantees freedom of worship. The national motto, stated as 'For God and My Country', is entwined in religious belief. The Country's National Anthem also has connotations of religion by singing 'Oh Uganda, May God Uphold Thee, We Lay Our Future in thy Hand'. In Uganda, religion has been used as a uniting factor, despite the different religious groups that exist (Nkurunzinza, 2002). Many times, people have been reminded that Uganda is a God-fearing country which requires them to embrace tolerance despite religious diversity. Religious bodies have been key players in enhancing dialogue where conflicts have surfaced due to various driving forces. This is possibly the foundation of religious inclusion as a country that has institutions embracing religious diversity of employees without difficulty. The Uganda National Population and Housing census of 2002 put the following statistics to the religious affiliations (Table 7.1).

Table 7.1   Religious distribution in Uganda by percentage

Catholics	41.8%	Anglicans (Protestants)	35.9%
Pentecostals	4.6%	Seventh Day Adventists	1.5%
Muslims	12.1%	Other Non-Christians	3.2%
No Religion	0.9%		

Source: Uganda Bureau of Statistics (2008).

Cases from Institutions of Higher Learning

Tertiary institutions are a significant context for studies on the phenomenon of religious diversity because such institutions are host to very large numbers of students and staff of diverse religious backgrounds. Religious identity in tertiary institutions is a key personal characteristic and a matter of individual choice. Right from the days of adoption of religion as a national identity in early stages of statehood, the Government recognized tertiary institutions as collections of various people and did not institute internal policies on matters of faith. Many religious denominations have sprung up in the last 20 years. While we read from other country contexts of religion as the source of tribal wars, mass killings and property destruction, in Uganda religion has not had a negative connotation like dogmatic prejudices, uncompromising and excluding attitudes.

Tertiary institutions that are collections of many relatively learned people with diverse religious affiliations have been calm. There is smooth integration and tolerance. In many cases, religious practices and ceremonies do not disrupt organizational life and performance but rather complement them. The values, diverse religious beliefs and experiences of students and staff are shaped by the inclusion of religious groups into the recognized structures of the institutions. While the complexity and dividing nature of religious diversity is documented elsewhere, no cases of adversity have been documented in Ugandan tertiary institutions (Makerere University 2012, 2013).

Religious diversity has been used as a tool for enhancing growth and maturity space in all institutions of higher learning. There are formally appointed Catholic and Anglican chaplains along with Muslim Mullahs at each national educational institution. Key religious festivals and feasts are fully supported and organized by managements of the institutions. During the Muslims' period of fasting for example, the universities make special provisions for all Muslim followers to observe their fasts and attend their prayers. Despite that, students are encouraged to put their studies first, as it is supposed to be their primary objective. According to the university almanac, classes, course work and examinations are conducted on any day of the week, despite some differences in the observance of religious practices. Institutions only observe national religious holidays that are marked countrywide (Makerere University Business School, 2013).

Students have both secular and religious leaders in their midst. In the student guilds, which are the union bodies for all students, the regulations provide for non-discrimination based on religion in elective posts. In many cases, the same students who are leaders in their specific religious groups are elected as guild leaders; however, they are not allowed to use their religions to seek or foster the union leadership. This is clearly documented in the constitutions of the guilds to avoid biter rivalries that could come with religious diversity.

A brief look at religious diversity in secondary schools will help explain the situation in tertiary institutions. In the majority of the secondary schools, many of which were founded by religious bodies or individuals inclined to a given faith, there are strict rules on religion activities. Students are expected to follow a given routine like prayers, payment of tithe, alms-giving among others. When they enter university and colleges, the students find a big difference; there are no institutional rules and regulations on matters of faith. It is upon the leaders of the various religious groups to mobilize and orient the new students into their communities. Some students go through secondary school abiding by the rules but without any strong commitment. Many such students commit to religions instructions at tertiary level and are initiated into denominations of their choice. This situation is common among students who come from disintegrated family units.

The learning point here is that secondary schools seek to bring up God-fearing and morally upright young men and women. They emphasize general religious practices without discrimination. Moore (1994) and Cimino and Lattin (1998) have related this to a business-like approach of marketing and economics. It has not, however, fostered rivalries of a commercial nature in Uganda. Most schools are founded by the mainstream religious groups hence students enrolled in such institutions are expected to participate in major religious activities without question. This Ugandan experience of harmony despite religious diversity in schools is diverse from the Nigerian experience, where, as reported by Adenyi (2002), schools are run on the basis of religion and used to propagate tenets of Christianity to students, whether Muslim or Traditionalist, which has been grounds for intolerance.

In addition to the public colleges and universities, there are several private universities, colleges and institutions founded and run by religious bodies. As much as such institutions demonstrate their identities, they do not foster religious differences in teaching and administration; the exception is those purely for religious formation like seminaries. The majority of private institutions observe basic religious rites that embrace the general life of the institutions. For instance, The Seventh Day Adventist Church runs a university in which students or employees do not perform any tasks on Saturdays in observance of their

Sabbath. Uganda hosts a regional Islamic University which conducts secular education programmes but keeps the traditions of the founders. The Anglican and Catholic Churches also own and run universities. The arrangement of integrating religions only where necessary is accommodated by other students and staff who do not profess the faith of the founders.

The religious institutions also use their structures to promote generally acceptable values among students and staff. It is known that dress codes for ladies at the Islamic university must be in line with expected decency as such as they do not dictate putting on full Islamic dress. At one Anglican-founded university, employees are expected to be wedded in their respective faiths in a way of promoting basic family values. At a private university with Muslim owners and top management, the structure also provides for chaplains for other denominations. Across from Uganda, at the University of Nairobi, in Kenya, the Catholic chaplain in the recent past was also the Dean of students, and this has had no effect on the integration of students outside his chaplaincy. Prayer in institutions is not only respected as a private matter, but also observed by managements at meetings. In many organizations, the first agenda at all meetings is institutionally prayer; this is also common in many public ceremonies.

One landmark legal case is worthy to mention here. In 2003, the Seventh Day Adventist (SDA) students filed a court suit arguing against the policy by Makerere University to schedule lectures and tests on Saturdays in the case of *Sharon and Others* v. *Makerere University* (Wamimbi, 2010). They contended that Saturday being their Sabbath, and the University being a national public institution, it infringed on their freedom of worship. In their faith, Saturday is a day for no work and only prayer. The University management argued for religious diversity, that no single group could be given preference. The appeal was dismissed by the High Court. The students then appealed to the Supreme Court. In August 2006, the Supreme Court upheld the earlier ruling that the prayer could not be entertained as it could make the running of the University very difficult. As a public institution, its policy of running academic programmes throughout the week without partiality did not infringe on the constitutional right of freedom of worship (Supreme Court of Uganda, Constitutional Appeal No.2 of 2004, Wamimbi, 2010).

Notably, religious tolerance is the choice of top management in the institutions of higher learning. In the public educational institutions, at no time has it been an issue that the top managers are from one religion and not the other. Appointments by Government have purely been competence based;

latently it could be possible that some balance among the various institutions may be done in the nomination and approval stages. For the private religious institutions, the top management is necessarily from the founding body and no one has any objection to such choice. Private secular institutions have no leaning at all.

Cases in the Government Departments

In the political realm, religious affiliations have been used to enhance national perspectives. The Government attempts to balance equally the focus on development and the sharing of national resources with religious bodies. Religion is a political issue whenever new cabinets, central government representatives or permanent secretaries are appointed. Although basically such appointees do not have direct religious agendas to promote, as a secular but religious nation, groups take pride whenever one of their own is in such a position. A renowned but unwritten practice has prevailed for the past number of years in the appointment of a Vice President; the current President, being Anglican, has to balance the other big group by appointing a Catholic second-in-command. Even among senior cabinet ministers, this balance on religious lines is maintained. The President in person, however, embraces the functions of all religious groups. He even attends end of the year night prayers organized by the Pentecostals, commonly known as *Abalokole* (The New Vision, 2012a, 2012b).

For the balance in management of national affairs, religious diversity is recognized and appreciated. The Uganda Government has made it simple for all believers to adhere to their practices unhindered so long as they do not infringe on freedom and basic human rights of others. Several big events of the religious groups are recognized at national level (The New Vision, 2012c). The Government observes up to eight public holidays annually which we can attach to religious life. These are Christmas and Boxing Day, Good Friday, Easter and Easter Monday and the Uganda Martyrs Day; these are Christian oriented but have never been contested by Ugandans of other beliefs. The national public holidays based on the Islamic faith are Eid el-Fitri and Eid el-Adha. In addition to these holidays, all Sundays are official days of rest; there is no open complaint from Muslims whose day of prayer is Friday wanting it to be a public holiday (Ministry of Public Service, 2014).

To enhance religious diversity in the harmonious way possible in public institutions, all other Government institutions such as the army, police and prisons have gazetted places of worship. By strict legal provisions the armed forces institutionally must promote national harmony above the individual beliefs. Across the country, religious groups have set up churches or other places of worship without requirement to report to public offices for clearance. The Government only moved recently to regulate activities where some people were using the cover of religion to undertake criminal activities like child trafficking, financial extortion and tax evasion (Wamimbi, 2010). The Government required the upcoming religious groups to register and declare their missions. Although this policy direction was resisted at first, they have gradually complied. There was at first a legal hitch. The mainstream religious bodies were recognized under the *Trustees Act* but the new sects were required to register under the *Non-Governmental Organizations (NGOs) Act* which, among others, imposes the duty to file financial statements and annual reports. This did not go down well with the pastors of the Pentecostal Churches who feared such information being made public.

There are several other practices of religious tolerance which may not be written but are widely recognized and practised. For instance, all public abattoirs must have Muslim clerics to slaughter animals whose meat is to be sold and prepared in all public eating places, a ban on the preparation of pork in public eating places including educational institutions, and so on.

In all national ceremonies, prayer is recognized. As noted earlier, the national motto and first words of the National Anthem entrust the nation into the hands of God. The National Anthem itself is like a national prayer, with words like, 'Oh Uganda, may God uphold thee, we lay our future in thy hands…'. Despite these wordings, specific prayers are recited after the Anthem. To recognize religious diversity as a nation, senior clerics from the main faiths are usually invited to say prayers, separately or one of them on behalf of the rest. This has cemented religious tolerance at all workplaces.

Cases of Religion in Ugandan Sports

One context where religion has possibly not been mentioned at all is that of sports. There has not been any issue of whether the coach or choice of players should balance religious faith. Some people have called sports 'the religion of unity'. There has been absolute religious indifference among the fans and managers of the various sports. No public case has ever been reported where religious differences have come up during national and local sporting events. There have not been known teams, whether local or national, founded on religious grounds. A practical example is from Makerere University Business School, where the current Chaplain of the Catholics is also the sports tutor; other than being referred to as 'Monsignor' – his priestly title, and possibly emphasizing an ecumenical prayer before activities, he remains a sports leader embraced by all according to internal management reports at the University. In Uganda, as elsewhere in the world, there have been cases of bitter confrontations among sports fans on other grounds like funding, players, victory and playgrounds but not religious grounds. Commentators have alluded to a reciprocal relationship between sports and religion across all regions of the world (Jason, 2014).

Religion at Workplaces of Business Firms

Religion has not featured much as a segregating factor in business as a whole. There are shops and business malls that stock religious items, with employees from different religions. Their major concern is in gaining customers, and this does not infringe on the freedoms of others. Recently, many entrepreneurs have set up radio and television stations as businesses. Religious bodies have not been left behind, establishing similar stations either as business ventures in (where they run secular programmes) or religious outlets (which they use for evangelization). At such workplaces, they have clear rules and regulations on religion. In the public-owned stations, there are programmes specifically for different mainstream religions. Since the selection of radio or TV is a decision of taste and independent choice, Ugandans have embraced religious stations with indifference. This has been observed by the authors through their interactions at work and in the community.

Religious organizations in Uganda do not directly run business enterprises. However, they own radio and television stations, banks, agro-businesses, hotels, educational institutions and medical facilities. In all these business ventures, the purpose is first to provide a service and create employment, and then to get surpluses to fund their activities. Miller (2002) has indicated that resources are a basis of both collaboration and rivalry among religious groups. According to Wuthnow (1994), regardless of their origin and nature of their beliefs, survival and growth of religious groups depends on resources they access externally. In the early years of religion in Uganda between 1879 and 1918, there was direct confrontation among the groups over resources. But this has long been consigned to the dustbin of history.

Churches today do not provide for their members' livelihoods. They are thus accommodative of their members' mainstream lifestyles. The faithful have to work to fend for themselves and they find opportunity for employment in various secular organizations. Other than grants and donations that religious groups receive from foreign donors, they greatly depend on local contributions from their members, who in turn work in various secular organizations alongside colleagues of other faiths. Religious diversity in the workplace is thus obligating to normal work life.

Uganda has recently had a big inflow of multinationals through foreign direct investment and joint ventures. These are in the sectors of telecommunication, manufacturing, power generation, agriculture and general trading. However, there is hardly a scholarly study that has been made on their cultural integration. From general perspectives of their businesses, there has been religious tolerance between foreign managers and the local employees. These firms have provided basic respect to the religious affiliations of their staff, and respect the practices congruent to operating in a God-fearing country.

Religious bodies also seek collaboration and financial support from business firms, especially multinationals. Local newspapers have reported variously on managers encouraging workers to adhere to basic organizational rules and minimize religious differences. Organizations have also publicized their contributions to religious events; whether such support is treated as corporate social responsiveness is not clearly documented. It may be latent that religious groups will be closer to those business enterprises where the top manager(s) professes their own faith. Some business enterprises have a religious foundation although autonomous in operations. This kind of religious diversity in normal organizational life has built a society of people who embrace religion as a personal choice. It has therefore had several benefits for institutions and the Ugandan population as a whole.

The Uganda Martyrs – the Making of a National Symbol of Unity

Possibly the most outstanding religious symbol of unity is that of the Uganda Martyrs. The story of the making of the Martyrs is long and in this chapter we can only provide highlights. The three mainstream religions, Muslim, Catholic and Anglican, share this symbol. The first religious group to arrive in Uganda were the Muslim clerics in 1877, followed by Anglican missionaries in 1878 and Catholics in 1879. All these were welcome into the Kingdom of Buganda as earlier mentioned. In his wisdom to benefit from all groups, the King allowed them the freedom to preach their faith. It is said that even the Kabaka himself kept changing from one faith to another. Kabaka Mwanga, who reigned in the late 1880s, became concerned that religious converts were beginning to challenge his authority. In 1886 he expressed indignation over their activities and ordered all converts who were pages or officials in the palace to revert. This was met with resistance to his annoyance. He consequently asked the missionaries and their converts to stop or be punished. When the converts did not pay heed, he ordered their execution. They were marched over 20 miles along the dangerous routes known to be inhabited by criminals while being tortured and asked if they had relented. Some were killed on the way as symbol of the trouble ahead. Many did not relent, instead they claimed stronger faith; they reached the execution site called Namugongo. Here they were bound into dry grass and set on fire. They numbered over 72 young men of Muslim, Catholic and Anglican faith. The 22 Catholic Martyrs were eventually canonized in 1964. It is important to note that those martyred were not Baganda only. They comprised young men from other parts who had been captured and brought into the service of the Kabaka. The Catholic and Anglican shrines built at Namugongo have since become national symbols of faith and attract many tourists. The Catholic shrine was elevated to a Basillica by the Holy See. To date, the 3 June every year, which was the climax of the killing, is marked as a national holiday by Catholics and Anglicans. It is the day when the single biggest congregation is witnessed in Uganda made up of pilgrims from all over the world. A detailed account of the Uganda Martyrs can be found in Faupel (1984).

The Government is working with the religious groups to enhance the tourism potential of these religious sites. There are various places where the first missionaries landed, shrines and churches they built and the artefacts that they used. There are sacred places where the pages were marched through on their way to martyrdom. Thousands of pilgrims come from all over the world to celebrate this occasion. The local businesses are boosted by many foreign and local tourists during the weeks around the celebration and even after that. The key mark is that the first visit by a Pope to Africa was made as a pilgrimage to Namugongo in 1969, and it is the single place where two different Popes have paid homage in Africa including another visit in 1993. Annually, among the Catholics and Anglicans, celebrations are led on a rotational basis by different dioceses which enhances the cultural inclusion. The facts surrounding the Uganda Martyrs have led to a strong national cohesion around the religious diversity of the country. The Government has designated a special commission on tourism and this is one of the areas of focus (Nabagesera, 2012; The New Vision, 2012c).

The Teaching of Religion – The Early Making of Tolerant Employees

The teaching of religion as part of the curriculum in early primary schools is a foundation to the management of religious diversity in workplaces. The future workers, in their very early formative stage, appreciate religious differences. In the lower primary school classes, basics in Islam and Christianity are taught and tested equally. In the upper primary school classes, the pupils are guided to learn both. However, the section on religion in the tests has two questions for each number, one on Islam, the other on Christianity. The pupil is expected to answer consistently one of the questions in the options provided.

In the Ordinary Certificate of Education (Senior One to Senior Four) level, Christian Religious Education and Islamic studies are taught. In some schools, they are compulsory while other schools treat them as electives. They are both tested in the national examinations. The two courses become absolute options at the Advanced Certificate of Education (Senior Five and Senior Six) level. Those students who passed either of them very well at the end of the Ordinary Certificate are free to include them in their three-subject combinations allowed at this level. In universities and colleges, the two courses are principal considerations for those choosing to undertake their undergraduate degrees in Religious Studies. The scores obtained at the advanced level are, however, considered in raising entry points for the relevant degree course selected. The teaching of religion at the different education levels provides a strong foundation in managing religious diversity at workplaces when the graduates take up formal employment (Balyage, 1998).

The Joint Christian and Inter-Religious Councils of Uganda

The Uganda Joint Christian Council (UJCC) recently celebrated 50 years of existence. It brings together the main denominations – the Catholic, Anglican and Orthodox Churches. At its inauguration, the UJCC Mission was to have a 'Peaceful and Prospectus Uganda with Happy People'. Among the Council's goals are the recognition of the struggle against the forces of repression, exploitation, corruption, inequality, moral degeneration and low levels of civic consciousness that were expected to threaten the very existence of Uganda as a new nation after gaining independence in 1962. The members of UJCC closely collaborate with other religions and Pentecostal groups under the Inter-religious Council of Uganda (IRCU), established about ten years ago. UJCC and IRCU are both strong voices on national issues of common interest including advocating for workers rights, in a way influencing how religious diversity is managed in workplaces. These bodies collaborate with and monitor Government programmes.

They maintain national structures with no branches or chapters in regions or organizations. However, the religious organizations are big employers through institutions directly founded by them or those with close affiliation. In this regard, although there may not be written rules, religious diversity is taken as a serious matter. The secular institutions employ people of all backgrounds but with bias to the founding religion. Religious diversity in workplaces is thus managed in a latent manner through tradition and practices espoused in individual's beliefs.

An illustration – The Seventh Day Adventist Church is a founding body to 296 primary schools, 98 secondary schools, nine vocational institutions, one university, one hospital and 19 dispensaries. The Church of Uganda (Anglican) has founded 5,118 primary schools, 460 secondary schools, 50 post-secondary institutions, six oriented universities, 28 hospitals and 203 dispensaries and health centres. In addition it has one guesthouse, one bookshop and one Holiday Inn. The Uganda Muslim Supreme Council has 1,114 primary schools, 150 secondary schools, six post-secondary institutions, one university, five hospitals, 56 dispensaries and health centres. The Orthodox Church has 26 primary schools, 16 secondary schools, eight post-secondary institutions, one hospital and 18 dispensaries and health centres. The Catholic Church has 4,781 primary schools, 582 secondary schools, 148 technical/vocational institutions, four universities and university colleges, 36 hospitals, 286 dispensaries and health centres and one bank (Ministry of Education and Sports, 2009; Ministry of Health, 2010).

From these data, we recognize how religious diversity in Uganda is deeply rooted in various institutions. As noted earlier in this chapter, the country is widely religious without confrontation of the various faithful. Religious diversity is managed across the organizational levels in a quite subtle manner.

The smooth relationship of the top religious leaders in the country under UJCC and IRCU has a definite indirect influence on how the managers respond to issues of faith among the employees. UJCC and IRCU collaborate on HIV/AIDS programmes, poverty eradication and democratic/human rights initiatives (for example, monitoring elections) (Inter-Religious Council of Uganda, 2008, 2012). Berger (1963), an economist, stated that the rationale for ecumenism was marketing economies, operations and reducing competitive rivalry. In the Ugandan case, these cannot directly be attached to the ecumenical principles of UJCC. Possibly the 'scared canopy' principle (Miller, 2002) may apply where the religious leaders wish to show that wherever their believers are, their religious diversity should not be a dividing factor. Nkurunzinza (2002) contends that the presence of religious leaders manifests divine presence in a world torn apart by conflict and violence. They have advocated for various matters without bias to their own doctrine which in essence promotes religious diversity in the community and in workplaces.

UJCC joined the call to review the poor or low salaries for teachers throughout the country. At the same time, there were constructive recommendations to the Government about the implementation of Universal Primary Education (UPE) and the Universal Secondary Education (USE) programmes in the country. Furthermore, there were stern issues with regard to teacher recruitments, deployments and their eventual access to the Government payroll.

Another important reproach to the Government was about the meals for the primary school pupils that attended the UPE schools throughout the country. While the Government was not in view of parents paying for those meals, UJCC strongly supported the payments for the meals by all the pupils for their own better learning environment. As stated earlier, a large number of the schools in the country are founded by religious bodies. This puts them in a better and proper position to speak about critical issues within the schools that fall under their jurisdiction. In this respect, the UJCC is regarded by the Government as a development partner, and not as an opponent or a competitor. Generally speaking, all good schools in Uganda today are owned or founded by churches or mosques. It has already been noted that employees of different religious denominations are found and are working together smoothly in these schools.

Benefits from Religious Diversity

Benefits accruing from religious diversity have made the people of Uganda live harmoniously irrespective of their differences in faith. Socially, there have been inter-marriages between spouses of different beliefs, with their children being a blend of national identities who take up a religion of one of the parents but with understanding and appreciation of the other religion.

Religious organizations are on record as having been the pioneers in championing education and health in Uganda, right from the early days of statehood. The religious bodies have set up much infrastructure, on which the Government still depends to provide services to its citizenry. These are schools, hospitals, social centres, agricultural farms and radio stations among others. Some of the best institutions, which are the pride of the country, were founded by religious bodies (Vision 2025, 1999). The examples include religious founded hospitals such as Nsambya for Catholics, Mengo for Anglicans and Kibuli for Muslims. The three best-performing Girls schools in the country, founded by the religious groups as mentioned above, are Mt. St. Mary's Namagunga, Gayaza High and Nabisunsa. All these institutions provide employment to thousands of people regardless of their faith. Religious choice that began as a competition eventually yielded into national cohesion. Each religious group, with its foreign partners, continue to set up developmental community projects that benefit all citizens regardless of their beliefs. Across the country, the places where religious groups concentrated their early activities are more developed. These are the centres where previous governments expeditiously extended power, water and telephone lines. Along the routes to such institutions and in the neighbourhood, trading centres sprung up. According to the Vision 2025 (1999), 'different religious groups in Uganda have mobilized funds and individuals for development work mainly in the education and health sectors' (p. 26). Such projects (water and sanitation, micro finance, sustainable agriculture, HIV/ AIDS, mass media campaigns among a host of many others) are not reserved for only their faithful. Since the various religious groups have their international affiliations with different wealthy nations, it is a way for Uganda to tap into the rich resources of such countries. For instance, in the early years of nationhood, the Catholic groups were sponsored by French, Irish and German charities; those in Britain benefitted the Anglicans while the rich nations of the Middle East supported Muslim projects; later, American Evangelicals extended huge support to the Pentecostal Churches. The religious hospitals in the country employ people of all faiths and provide services to patients regardless of their background. The same applies to the best schools. These have in many ways made people in Uganda respect and honour religious diversity as in the end it benefits all human kind. The working papers for establishing the National Vision 2025 noted that religion had also sustained Ugandans through the bad times, spiritually, materially, morally and psychologically (Vision 2025, 1999).

Wamimbi (2010) reported that the Government of Uganda:

> was fully cognizant and appreciative of the substantial contribution made by religious organizations to communities. The efforts of a number of such organizations towards among others, poverty alleviation, are commendable and admirable. The above considerations, among others, form the basis upon which the Government of Uganda has ensured the

existence of a conducive environment within which religious freedom and tolerance are able to flourish (p. 5).

Religious diversity in its backdrop of the various denominations is becoming a potential for tourism in Uganda. It has been noted above that the Government is working with religious organizations to enhance the Uganda Martyrs as an attraction to thousands of international pilgrims and tourists. The relics of the early missionaries, their journeys and other works are attractive to the tourism industry alongside other natural treasures like Uganda's flora and fauna.

There are many cultural groupings. Uganda as a nation was founded from various chiefdoms that the colonial masters fought hard to bring together under one leadership. Uganda got her independence in October 1962 and was declared a republic in 1967, with the first national Constitution. The traditional cultural groups are not anchored in religion; although most of the monarchies embraced Anglicanism, they did not force it on their subjects. Cultural differences are forgotten because of religion. It is notable that when the missionaries arrived in the seventeenth century, the cultural leaders sought to benefit from the different groups, so they allowed all of them to seek converts as long as they paid allegiance to the kingship.

Generally, the moral uprightness of many Ugandans can be attributed to religious diversity. As emphasized in this chapter, it has created an inbuilt mode of tolerance on compensators; these are postulations of non-temporal rewards. Many Ugandans reach the level of a working life aware that religion is not a dividing factor. Even recently, when Uganda was listed among the most corrupt nations in the world, many calls were made for the religious leaders to re-emphasize morality and evangelization of their members. This was hoped to revitalize ethical values in managing public resources with high levels of integrity and stewardship.

Performance and effectiveness of many organizations in Uganda can be attributed to harmony and co-existence. Religious tolerance and appreciation of the teachings of various religious denominations has definitely contributed to this organizational culture. Wherever workplace factors are not favourable for employees, they have embraced industrial action as a body and without lines of division. Even elections of employee unions have not been rumoured to be based on religious affiliation in any organization. Religious diversity has not been an issue for managers to worry about while allocating resources.

Religion has played a very big part towards good governance since most politicians have to do the right thing as dictated by their relevant religious beliefs. This also applies to Ugandan lawmakers in Parliament, where religion is highly recognized. Instead of being a line of difference, religious arguments have at times cemented cohesion on the floor of Parliament.

Although the country has been through military coups and guerrilla warfare, the religious factor has never become a dividing tool. Even the notorious dictatorial regime of Idi Amin (a Muslim) did not ban other religious groups; in his rule, between 1971 and 1979, Friday was declared a public holiday in addition to Sunday. When Amin's Government fell and Friday reverted to being a normal working day, there was no uproar about it. Thus, Uganda as a nation in good and bad times has learned from and taken religion as a unifying factor benefitting every citizen in their individual and group rights.

Conclusion

This chapter illustrates the religious diversity among the Ugandan workforce. We have shown that in different organizations, workers profess different religious affiliations. This diversity has, however, not had negative effect on the operations and performance of the organizations. Picking from the national constitution that provides for freedom of worship and guarantees no discrimination on religious grounds, some organizations have written guidelines of how individuals conduct themselves on religious basis. Generally, many organizations respect individual or group choices as long as this does not interfere with laid out staff policies. Organizations have therefore managed religious diversity through both express guidelines and, more widely, on the basis of practices and unwritten rules. The respect for individual religious rights and the unity among national religious leaders have cultivated a climate of religious tolerance in various firms. Organizations only focus on enhancing these values to ensure smooth relationships among the workforce. The values, diverse religious beliefs and experiences of employees have contributed to the good performance of many organizations.

References

Adenyi, M.O. (2002). 'A Case Study of Conflicts and Accommodations in the Nigerian Islam', *African Journal of Leadership and Conflict Management*, 1(1): 127–34.

Balyage, Y. (1998). The Christian Education Syllabi for Secondary Schools: An Adventist assessment proposal. Paper for the 23rd Faith and Learning seminar, University of Eastern Africa Kenya, 22 November–4 December 1998.

Berger, P.L. (1963). 'A Market Model for the Analysis of Ecumenicity', *Social Research*, 30: 77–93.

Cimino, R. and Lattin, D. (1998).*Shopping for Faith: American Religion in the New Millennium*. Jossey-Bass, San Francisco, CA.

Faupel, J.F. (1984). *Africa Holocaust*. St. Paul's Publications, Africa, Nairobi, Kenya.

Gatera, E. (2002). 'The Role of the Christian Church in Resolving Conflicts in Burundi (1902–1997). *African Journal of Leadership and Conflict Management*, 1(1): 97–126.

Government of Uganda (1965).*The Public Holidays Act*, Chapter 255, Statute 9/1992.

Inter-Religious Council of Uganda (2008).Complementarities between religious and traditional mechanisms for conflict resolution, Research Report, 2008.

Inter-Religious Council of Uganda (2012). Report of URCU National HIV/AIDS Conference on Harnessing Inter-religious Action and Collaboration for Accelerated HIV/ADS Response – 'Different Religions – One Action'.

Jason, W.L. (2014). 'An Overview of the Reciprocating Role between Sport and Religion', *Smart on Line Journal*, 1(1): 26–30.

Makerere University (2012, 2013). Information Policy and Procedures; Fresher's Joining Instructions 2012/2013, 2013/2014.

Makerere University Business School (2013). University Almanac 2013/2014 Academic Year.

Mbiti, S.J (1996). *African Religions and Philosophy*, Heinneman, London, Ibadan, Nairobi.

Mereui, J. (1986). *L'Ouganda – La Mission Catholique et les Agents de La Compagnie*, Anglaise, Paris.

Miller, K.D. (2002). 'Competitive Strategies of Religious Organizations', *Strategic Management Journal*, 23: 435–56.

Ministry of Education and Sports (2009).Uganda Education Statistical Abstract, Education Planning and Policy Analysis Department, Ministry of Education and Sports – Republic of Uganda.

Ministry of Health (2010). Health Sector Strategic and Investment Plan, 2010/11–2014/15, Republic of Uganda.

Ministry of Public Service (2010). The Uganda Public Service Standing Orders. Republic of Uganda, January 2010, p. 66.

Moore, R.L. (1994). *Selling God: American Religion in the Marketplace of Culture*. Oxford University Press, New York.

Nabagesera, N. (2012). Presidential Initiative on Sustainable Tourism (PRESTO) Jubilee Martyrs Day Report, 2012, President's Office, Government of Uganda.

Ndyabahika, J. (2002). 'Religious Strategies for Managing Religio-Political Conflicts in Uganda', *African Journal of Leadership and Conflict Management*, 1(1): 157–74.

Nkurunzinza, R.K.D (2002). 'Religion – Conflict and Violence', *African Journal of Leadership and Conflict Management*, 1(1): 135–56.

Republic of Uganda (1995). *The 1995 Constitution of the Republic of Uganda*. Uganda Publishing Corporation, Kampala, Uganda.

Stark, R., Bainbridge, W.S. and Kent, L. (1981).'Cult Membership in the Roaring Twenties: Assessing Local Receptivity', *Sociological Analysis*, 42(2): 137–62.

The New Vision (2012a). President Museveni Prays for Uganda at the Jubilee Prayer Night, Tuesday 9 October 2012.

The New Vision (2012b). For the Sins of Uganda, I Repent – President Museveni, Thursday 18 October 2012.

The New Vision (2012c). Parliament Kicks Off Jubilee Activities with Prayers, Monday 24 September 2012.

Uganda Bureau of Statistics (2008). Statistics Abstracts. Republic of Uganda, Kampala.

Vision 2025 (1999).Working Draft, Main Document, A Strategic Framework for National Development, Volume One, Republic of Uganda.

Wamimbi, R.N. (2010). Religious Tolerance and the State in Uganda. A paper presented to UTAH, USA, October 2010.

Wuthnow, R. (1994a). *Producing the Sacred: An Essay on Public Religion*. University of Illinois Press: Urbana.

Chapter 8

Rethinking Religious Diversity Management in Schools: Experience From Tanzania

GABRIEL EZEKIA NDUYE

Introduction

As the world becomes diversified, living and working together in the context of plurality of identity is becoming the reality of life. Being one of the major characteristics of African continent in general, and Tanzania in particular, religious diversity is a phenomenon to be studied and well understood, thus harnessing its potential for enriching life in all its aspects. Although Tanzania is the only country in East Africa that since its independence has remained stable in terms of peace, unity and solidarity, recently signs of religious intolerance have become apparent in numerous ways. This calls for intensification of religious diversity management in various areas of everyday life, including in the workplace. Based on literature study and guided by a theory of human dignity, this contribution attempts to address the question: 'What can be done to ensure proper management of religious diversity in the workplace, especially in the secondary schools in Tanzania?' By way of introduction, this chapter provides a short background of Tanzania and its nature of religious diversity, arguing in the light of human dignity from the African Christian theological point of view. Thereafter the chapter tracks measures taken by Tanzania throughout its history to ensure that religious diversity and other aspects of diversity are properly managed and used for the common good of all. A third section explores the significance of managing religious diversity in the workplace with special focus on secondary schools. Finally, ways are articulated through which religious diversity in schools can be properly managed especially in the context of pluralistic society.

Tanzania: Background

As it is the case in many formerly colonized countries, Tanzania's borders were created by colonial powers. The country first fell under German colonial rule from 1890 until the First World War when it was placed under British mandate (Gahnstrom, 2012). Unlike most African countries, Gahnstrom argues (2012), 'Tanganyika's (now Tanzania) road to independence was peaceful and the nationalist independence movement, known as TANU (Tanganyika African National Union) with its leader Julius Nyerere rose to head the newly established government enjoying universal support.' Tanzania, as it is known today, is the result of the union between Tanganyika and Zanzibar which took place in 1964. In 1967, the young nation of Tanzania embarked on its first development strategy. It was announced in the Arusha Declaration that the nation was determined to take a path of 'self-reliance and Ujamaa–African Socialism' (Gahnstrom, 2012). The central purpose of this strategy was to 'ensure an equitable economic development' aimed at promoting peace, justice and equality for all. In order to achieve this objective, all means of production were nationalized, especially those that were at the time privately owned (Gahnstrom, 2012). It is widely acknowledged that most countries in East and Central Africa such as Rwanda, Kenya, Uganda, the Democratic Republic of Congo (DRC) and Burundi have been suffering violent ethnic conflict and civil wars for the entire past half century. Erickson (2012) points out that only one State has, post-independence, remained peaceful and stable. Diversified as it is in terms of religion, ethnic groups, economic inequalities, unequal gender power relations and so on, and despite its limited economic success, Tanzania has 'managed to maintain a peaceful, stable state' through managing diversity in a manner that avoids ethnic-related politics (Erickson, 2012). As will be discussed later in this chapter, the sustained stability of Tanzania is the result of the creation of a common vision with regard to justice, equality and unity, as well as determination and a commitment to such goals (Erickson, 2012).

Religious Diversity in Tanzania

Given that religion means different things to different people, it can be conceptualized in many ways. According to Kilaini (2010), a Tanzanian Roman Catholic theologian, religion refers to the inner conviction or belief that humankind's worth goes beyond its existence here on earth and that there is life after this life. It is this belief which inspires humankind to strive to live a better life on earth. Advancing the same point further, Gahnstrom (2012) argues that religion has to do with a belief in the existence of an invisible world which has substantial influence on and power over the material or visible world. Such beliefs are directed to God who is conceived as the source of all things including humankind. The meaning of life and the destiny of humankind are seen as residing in God. On the basis of this understanding the Society for Human Resource Management (SHRM) (2008) points out that religion cannot be limited to traditional organized religions alone, but that, rather, it includes a range of religious beliefs to various degrees practised by people who are not part of formal church sects. These practices range from attending worship services, praying, using religious symbols, displaying religious objects, adhering to dietary rules, preaching, refraining from certain activities and many other forms of religious expression (SHRM, 2008).

Diversity, on the other hand, is a concept that reflects all the characteristics which make each human being unique and different from others. This is regardless of whether characteristics are individual or social, in other words associated with the human participation in social groups such as national, religion or age groups (Victorian Multicultural Commission, 2008). Furthermore, diversity can also be understood as reflecting the plurality in groups of one and the same identity inhabiting a particular geographical space. In this regard, diversity is engraved in the uniqueness of plurality of the identity of groups and societies that make up humankind (Atta-Asamoah, 2011). In the light of this, it is evident that diversity is a major characteristic of Africans.

Atta-Asamoah (2011) has this to say: 'Africa is a home of multiple ethnic, cultural, racial, religious, socio-economic, gender, political and biological markers that define the plurality of identities which distinguishes individuals and groups from each other.' Furthermore, contends Atta-Asamoah, the plurality of identities which distinguishes people from one another can either be ascribed or constructed. Ascribed identities involve those that are inherited and involve a certain quality expectation. These identities include traits such as gender, kinship, ethnicity, language, race and region. They tend to be exclusive and they cannot easily be transformed thus restricting individuals in a particular identity. Occasionally, they can be inclusive especially when there is room for inclusion of different identities (Atta-Asamoah, 2011). The concept of constructed identities refers to acquired characteristics such as shared values, beliefs, concerns and experiences. These tend to exist across different identity groups allowing for modification, based on changing circumstances, beliefs and experiences (Atta-Asamoah, 2011).

Diversity in Africa manifests itself in various contexts. There is firstly cultural diversity, which implies the most important attributes of social groups in Africa. It is culture which embodies or characterizes all aspects of African life and African worldview. It is culture which defines the way human beings are meant to live and behave (Atta-Asamoah, 2011). A second category of diversity is associated with the formal institutions and systems of the modern State. This diversity is evident in Uganda and Ghana where traditional structures continue to function parallel to State structures commanding the enormous respect and loyalty of sections of the citizenry (Atta-Asamoah, 2011).

The third category is related to gender and provides another form of diversity on the African continent. The gender aspect is associated with such issues as gender roles and sexual orientation. There is no doubt that the male–female divide exists at both the biological level and also in relation to access to power, allocation of positions and resources as well as cultural stratification. As a result there are traditional cultural identities whose practices conflict with the modern norm of equality of the sexes and gender roles. An example is that in some cultures women are treated as if they were owned by their husbands (Atta-Asamoah, 2011).

Generational diversity represents the fourth form of diversity, namely the diversity of children (below 15), youths (15–35), the middle aged (35–65) and older people (above 65). The fifth category is religious diversity. African is a multi-religious continent with a number of religious identities, although Christianity and Islam dominate with approximately between 400 and 500 million adherents each (Atta-Asamoah, 2011).

A sixth type of diversity in Africa has to do with the variety of nationalities and with migrants, and ultimately with race. In a way, this type of diversity has fostered cultural diversity thus promoting development in a number of ways. In countries such as South Africa, racial issues have been seen as a major source of contention. Finally, the seventh category of diversity on the African continent is linked to models of production and sources of livelihood ranging from peasantry at the grassroots, active as agriculturists and pastoralists, through the middle class dominated by small and medium enterprises, to sophisticated capital-intensive business and mechanized means of production. This forms a basis for socio-economic stratification as a result of differences in income (Atta-Asamoah, 2011).

According to Kilaini (2010), Islam is the oldest religion and has been active in Africa for more than 1,000 years. In some African countries, it is becoming an indigenous religion while in other countries it is registering constant growth. Christianity is the newest religion on the continent. With the exclusion of

North Africa, Ethiopia and Egypt, most of the African continent was effectively evangelized less than 200 years ago (Kilaini, 2010).

Apart from Islam and Christianity, there are also African Tradition Religions (ATRs), which are the oldest of all but unorganized compared to Islam and Christianity. Both Islam and Christianity try to find new followers among the adherents of ATRs which are therefore in decline (Kilaini, 2010). Because ATRs form part and parcel of everyday life in most African communities, argues Kilaini (2010) it has been argued that, unlike the West, Africa has a deep-rooted sense of the sacred. It is this sense of the sacred which unites people rather than dividing them. Although there are other religions on the continent, their following constitutes less than 3 per cent of the African population. Pope John Paul II, cited by Kilaini (2010), expressed this when he said: 'Africans have a profound religious sense, a sense of sacred, of the existence of God the creator and of a spiritual world. The reality of sin in its individual and social forms is very much present in the consciousness of these people as also the need for rites of purification and expiation.'

While this is the case on the African continent in general, it is also true for Tanzania that has been described as 'a deeply religious country with the vast majority of people committed to Christian or Islam faith' as well as traditional beliefs (Health Policy Initiative (HPI), 2013). Hence, as elsewhere in Africa, there are three dominant religions in Tanzania, namely Christianity, Islam and ATRs. A history of Islam shows that it began to take root in Tanzania in the ninth and tenth centuries. A history of Christianity, on the other hand, shows that most Christian denominations started their actual missionary work only in the nineteenth century. Although there are few exclusive practitioners of ATRs, their influence in almost all spheres of life cannot be underestimated (Gahnstrom, 2012, p. 115). Affirming this, Gahnstrom (2012, p. 116) argues that, although most Tanzanians today consider themselves to be either Christians or Muslims, ATR practices continue to be widespread in various areas including where issues related to the workplace are concerned. Apart from the contention that exists regarding religious statics, the International Religious Report (2011) based on a Pew Forum Survey conducted in Tanzania in 2010, has suggested that an aggregate of 60 per cent of the population are Christians whereas Muslims record 36 per cent while the remaining 4 per cent involves people of other faiths. However, these statistics are the subject of discussion.

Delivering a speech on 'High level dialogue on interreligious and intercultural understanding and cooperation for peace', the then Tanzanian Deputy Minister for Foreign Affairs and International Cooperation stated:

'Tanzania is home to difference races, over one hundred ethnic groups and several religions which co-exist in harmony with full freedom to express their cultural and religious diversities' (United Republic of Tanzania (URT), 2007). Such has been the situation since independence when the founding fathers of the 'independence movement deliberately focused on national unity' as a critical asset for managing great diversity in order to be able to harness its richness for socio-economic development of the people and of their nation at large (URT, 2007).

Based on this, Gahnstrom (2012) points out that religion in Tanzania has attained a culturally significant position, in the sense that it plays an important role in the everyday lives of believers. It also has social significance in that it contributes to social identification and interaction. Although in the early days there was tension between Christianity and Islam, the relationship between the two religions has remained cordial for a number of years. This harmonious co-existence has been evident when Muslims and Christians attend each other's festivals and funerals, as they commonly do, as well as in occurrences of intermarriage (Gahnstrom, 2012). This shows that, when managed in an appropriate manner as will be discussed later in this chapter, religious diversity can be a rich resource for nation building and for enhancing communal life.

Within the Christian sphere itself, there is a considerable amount of diversity as well in Tanzania. Gahnstrom (2012) records that Tanzanians are mainly 'Roman Catholics, Protestants, Anglicans, Moravians, Seventh Day Adventists and Pentecostals'. While Roman Catholics are the majority, constituting about two-thirds of all Christians, followed by Lutherans who constitute one-third, the Anglican, Moravian, Adventists, African Inland Churches, Independent Churches and Pentecostal Churches have recently registered a rapid growth (Fahlbusch, 2008: 310–313). Diversity is evident in Islam as well. However, it is commonly held that up to three-quarters of the Muslim population in Tanzania are Sufis, suggesting that they are the majority. Shia groups exist but are mainly Asians and Agha Khan Ishmaelites (Gahnstrom, 2012). As has been argued earlier, despite its vast religious diversity, Tanzania has remained stable, united and peaceful for many years, contrary to many other Sub-Saharan African countries in general, and East and Central Africa in particular, where violence and conflicts have been common occurrences. Why has Tanzania been different? The next section of this chapter will turn to this question.

Tanzanian Experience of Managing Religious Diversity

A sustained conflict on the African continent is a sign that management of diversity in its various forms is a critical challenge. According to the United Nations Economic Commission for Africa (UNECA) (2011), there are a number of reasons why managing diversity continues to be a persistent challenge, especially on the African continent. In the first place, the failure to manage diversity emphasizes that there are poor relations between diverse groups implying a governance deficit. Secondly, in this context the State's ability to address various problems by dispensing equitable citizenship rights and equitable access to resources for development is questioned. Atta-Asamoah (2011) adds that the destabilizing effect of unmanaged diversity in Africa can be traced back to the continent's immediate post-independence period. This is partly because many leaders were not aware of the negative effect of not properly managing diversity. This may be the reality of the situation on the continent, but it is evident that African countries have taken different measures to combat the challenges of managing religious diversity in its various forms. One of the countries that have somehow succeeded to a greater extent in managing diversity is Tanzania.

Tanzania's success in managing diversity is the result of deliberate and conscious policy choices, intended to build a common vision on the common good rather than on individual profiles. Such policy choices date back to the immediate post-independence period when the first government, led by the late Mwalimu (teacher) Julius Kambarage Nyerere, who is honoured today as the father of the nation, embarked on a conscious effort to construct a nation out of the states of Tanzania (Atta-Asamoah, 2011). The following are some of the most important diversity management initiatives behind the success story. Firstly, it was seen that in order to manage diversity properly, language had to be considered. Therefore, deliberate efforts were made to ensure that Kiswahili was adopted as a universal language to be used across the country. Erickson (2012) argues that the nationalization of Kiswahili was meant to connect people from different regions, ethnicities and backgrounds across the country. Much effort went into this strategy and it was not until 1967 that Kiswahili became the required language for all businesses to do with government and national institutions and by that time over 97 per cent of the population spoke Kiswahili well. Some commentators, such as Mbah and Igariwey (2008) have pointed out that this strategy tends to suppress ethnic identities. But in reality these ethnic identities are still in existence today while there exists at the same time the common vision of being part of a united nation. The nation cherishes these identities by annually celebrating cultural day and respecting traditional chiefs (kings) where they still exist.

Secondly, in order to form a nation that is united, all inhabitants needed to feel that they were Tanzanians before anything else. To allow for this to happen, the mainstreaming of pan-Tanzanian history into the education system was undertaken. The emphasis was placed on matters that united Tanzanians and this approach gradually reduced the relevance of existing differences (Atta-Asamoah, 2011). Thirdly, given that, in order to rule and colonize easily, part of the colonial methodology was to divide and rule, it became necessary for a young nation like Tanzania to make deliberate efforts to eliminate all divisive elements in the decision-making processes that could potentially enhance the concept of otherness. This included elimination of enmity among the tribes, chiefs and kings through a reconciliation process (Atta-Asamoah, 2011).

A fourth approach adopted by the Tanzanian Government was the formation of Ujamaa villages as part of its rural development policy. The formation of villages was necessary due to the fact that until then people lived scattered all over the land or located themselves according to kinship ties. Although this initiative was criticized because it involved forced displacement of people, it was based on the desire to create a community with a sense of belonging together that would co-exist harmoniously in all their diversity (Erickson, 2012). In the fifth place the concept and philosophy of Ujamaa policy were adopted soon after independence with the aim of integrating Western ideas and traditional African values such as family-hood and communalism. It became a useful tool for managing diversity in Tanzania based on its three key attributes: freedom, equality and unity. Each of these contributes in its own way to helping people co-exist beyond their differences. For example, equality leads to cooperation. It means that, when people have a sense of being equal they willingly cooperate with each other. Unity leads to peace, security and well being of all (Equality Authority, 2004).

Another strategy was to promote equal access to education. This came about as a result of the realization that most schools during the colonial and post-independence periods were owned by faith-based organizations, especially Christian Churches. If this was allowed to continue, it would imply that more Christians would have access to education than Muslims or people of other faiths and this would weaken the vision of building a nation with unity and cohesion. The imbalanced access to education was seen as dangerous for the future of Tanzania. It was clear that, in order to promote equal opportunities in all matters of employment and participation in national affairs, equity in education had to be achieved. Thereto legislation was proposed and passed in Parliament in 1962, which stipulated that all missionary schools, with the exclusion of seminaries, must enrol students from all faiths. Furthermore in 1969, all private schools, the majority of which belonged to the Christian mission, were nationalized for all to have access to education. One of the schools which were owned by the Southern Diocese of the Evangelical Lutheran Church in Tanzania known as Njombe Secondary (NJOSS) was nationalized in this process and is a public school till today.

Political messages were also used in various public places and in the media to promote national unity and to de-emphasize differences among people on the basis of ethnicity, religion or race and cultural background. Another initiative was putting in place a constitutional provision regarding religious matters. This involved the prohibition of organizations or practices that foment and amplify division in the country. As per political parties law 1992 for example, no political party formed on the basis of religion, race, sect, tribal or region is accredited or registered. Moreover, the national constitution defines Tanzania as a secular State, but also underscores the rights of all citizens to exercise freedom of worship or to join any religion of their choice (URT, 2006). Hence, freedom of worship and protection of religious freedom are integral to the guaranteed human rights in Tanzania.

A final strategy had to do with openness to religious and interfaith dialogue. The Government has always encouraged and assisted the establishment of interfaith dialogue. A good example is the formation of the joint commission for peace, development and reconciliation in 2000, a forum which brought together various religious leaders to discuss issues of national concern. To ensure the support of the Government for these initiatives, a Minister in the President's office has been appointed who is tasked with promoting political and social understanding and harmony among political parties, religious groups and, in general, people of Tanzania. In the light of all this, it is evident that religious diversity is not always an inevitable source of conflict or destabilization. Whenever such conflict occurs, it implies that something has gone wrong. It is not about diversity being a negative factor, but it is about how diversity is managed.

Incidents of Religious Tension in Tanzania

Of all the measures that have been taken countrywide to manage diversity in Tanzania, those concerning religion are of great interest to Tanzanians.

An International Religious Freedom Report (2011) affirms this as it points out: 'Religion is an important part of daily life' across the country. The report concurs with Halloran (2013) who underlines religion as an important aspect of daily life in Tanzania. Although the Government has taken a neutral position in its treatment of religious matters, generally, the people have positioned religion prominently in their private and public life.

This reality is manifested in a number of ways, including women wearing hijabs and other forms of covering, men putting on taqiyahs both in public and in the workplace. Furthermore, it is usual in Tanzania to see processions for weddings and funerals with musical accompaniment. These are a public manifestation of religious diversity but have not, for many years, fostered any division or tension. Rather they seem to enhance understanding and acceptance of one another (Akiri, 2013). While this can be seen as the norm, recently there have been some incidences which amount to abuse of the religious freedom that has been nurtured since independence. In this regard, Akiri (2013) contends that, although the country as a whole has maintained its peaceful, unified and tranquil nature, there have been a few extremists from both Christian and Islamic backgrounds who have challenged harmonious co-existence in Tanzania, leading to a rethinking of religious diversity management in contemporary situations. It is not intended to provide a detailed discussion of these incidences in this chapter, but it suffices to offer few examples.

Firstly, there are public debates held by both Christians and Muslims regarding the question of which religion is the true one as well as about the credibility of Jesus and the Prophet Muhammad as messengers of God. These debates were frequently held in the 1980s and 90s and occasionally they take place even today in some areas. The danger of these debates has always been the potential to lead to clashes, especially when one group feels that its religion has been undermined, despised, downplayed or even insulted. For instance, Christians, in cities such as Dar es Salaam, Tanzania, have conducted a debate that was titled '*Yesu ni Jibu*' [literally: 'Jesus is the answer']. This debate was seen as uncompromisingly and fiercely attacking Islam and its teachings.

A second example is the incident of Mwembechai which occurred in 1993. At this point in time, Muslim extremists attacked and destroyed 'pork stores', shops that sell pork meat, in Dar es Salaam (Akiri, 2013). The third example has to do with the destruction and the burning of churches. This incident demonstrated that religious tension in Tanzania was moving to a different level altogether. It occurred in Zanzibar where, in May 2012, six Christian church buildings were burnt down. The same thing happened in the suburbs of Dar es

Salaam in October 2012 where seven more church buildings were burned to the ground. It has been reported that here too a Muslim group was involved, after Friday prayers (Akiri, 2013).

Another example is the targeting of church leaders. Text messages, leaflets, CDs and DVDs propagating the intention of Muslims to kill church leaders all over the country have been spread among individuals and groups. Initially, this was not taken seriously but soon things began to happen. The first incident occurred in December 2012 when a Roman Catholic priest, Fr. Ambrose Mkenda, was gunned down late in the evening when he arrived home from the church. Though he survived he was badly injured. In February 2013 another Roman Catholic priest, Fr. Evarist Mushi, was gunned to death early in the morning as he was approaching the church to lead a mass. In November 2012 another incident of a similar nature was reported. This time it was a private secretary of the Head of the Muslim Council in Zanzibar, known as Sheikh Suleiman Soroga, who had acid thrown in his face. With severe injuries he was transferred to India for treatment (Akiri, 2013).

A fifth example of religious tension is the current demand for equal rights in slaughtering animals for butcheries. For many years, Muslim clerics have exclusively enjoyed certain rights and privileges so that all meat sold are Halal and they are paid for their services. In 2012, a group of radical Christians and church leaders emerged, calling for an end to this tradition or privilege. Behind this demand is the argument that the Muslim slaughtering of animals is part of Muslim worship, thus implicitly forcing non-Muslims to participate in their worship, especially those who buy beef (Akiri, 2013). These few examples of religious tension in Tanzania call for the need to rethink proper management of religious diversity in various places including at the workplace to which the discussion now turns. This means that every sector and organization, including faith-based organizations, must contribute to efforts aimed at improving the management of religious diversity and at harnessing its potential richness to minimize conflicts and enhance service delivery.

Managing Religious Diversity in the Workplace

According to Tanzania's Act No. 6 'Employment and Labour Relations Act', no discrimination in the workplace on the basis of, inter alia, religious ground is permitted (URT, 2004). Such legal provision implies the management of religious diversity in the workplace and the promotion of equal opportunities for all. As indicated in the Act, proper handling of religious aspects in the workplace can potentially lead to the promotion of 'economic development through economic proficiency, productivity and social justice' (URT, 2004). This becomes an important issue, particularly in the context of globalization and multicultural workplace settings. Hence, Alnamlah (2011) suggests that employers have no option except to properly manage varied cultures in the workplace. This is especially important as religion occupies a prominent place in the daily lives of the majority of Tanzanians.

TOWARDS A PROPER RELIGIOUS DIVERSITY MANAGEMENT

Insufficient management of religious diversity is a major cause of conflict and of low productivity in any organization or community. Recognizing this reality, Khudori (2012) calls on the nation-state, civil society, organizations and religious authorities to take seriously the management of religious diversity in the workplace and elsewhere, particularly in schools. On the basis of incidents discussed above, which demonstrate the need for enhancing harmony between religiously diverse groups in Tanzania, the following framework is recommended for actions which can potentially lead to the development of an effective religious diversity management in schools.

The framework involves as a first stage the creation of a common vision of life. Schools consist of diverse groups of teachers and students working towards a common goal. Therefore, recognizing their religious diversity and learning about it, is likely to lead to more harmonious and peaceful co-existence of the school population (Kollar, 2009). Students and staff must realize that human beings are meant to be with others and that they belong to each other in spite of all their differences. In most cases diversity offers a variety of survival possibilities, whereas exclusion or homogeneity contains the seeds of destruction of the entire society. Farming experience provides a clear understanding of diversity being a blessing rather than a curse. A farmer who sows only one type of seed creates a situation in which a single threat – disease, weather or a plague of insects – stands a good chance of destroying the entire crop. On the other hand, growing diverse types of crops together increases the chance of at least having something to harvest. Hence, 'diversity increases probability for survival and [that] sameness increases the probability for death' (Kollar, 2009).

When staff and students at a school develop a common vision of life, a sense of caring, purpose and concern for one another will emerge. This can potentially lead to mutual respect, to trust and truthfulness, to commitment, interdependence and sharing, all of which are important values in a safe environment of co-existence (Kollar, 2009). Thus tolerance and the willingness to learn from each other will increase and enhance peaceful co-existence.

The second stage in managing religious diversity in the workplace and at schools involves building an inclusive society. This has to do with embracing diversity in schools in an effort to create inclusive and harmonious conditions (National Integration Working Group for Workplace (NIWGW), 2009). A situation has to be created that allows for positive interaction between students and staff, leading to a better understanding of each other. Organizing formal and informal activities that foster interaction between employees of diverse backgrounds, setting up employees' or students' mentorship systems, recognizing role model students whose behaviour and values encourage inclusiveness and so on may lead towards the desired result (NIWGW, 2009). Creating an inclusive society as a way of managing religious diversity requires effective discussion among the employees at a workplace and among staff and students at schools, so that the importance of inclusiveness and harmony may be properly communicated.

The benefits of an inclusive community must be made explicitly clear to all and the role of each and every one in creating such a society must be highlighted (NIWGW, 2009). In this process, religion should be treated as an important tool for 'intercultural communication, peace and tolerance' in schools or organizations (Waisse, 2003). Moreover, peace and living together in harmony are likely to be guaranteed only when all social groups are treated equally and with respect. Mutual acceptance of and respect for each other is difficult in situations where religious diversity is not honoured, respected and appreciated. It is important to learn that religious diversity does not necessarily lead to discrimination. Rather, it should be seen as something that can bring mutual understanding of 'different backgrounds' which may lead to a 'clearer formulation of one's own position and promote' peaceful co-existence (Waisse, 2003).

A third aspect that has to be taken into account in managing religious diversity is the need to respect differences. According to Tanzania Council of Social Services (TasCOSS) (2012), a good organizational culture tends to respect all diversities in terms of 'skills, perspectives and backgrounds'. Such respect creates a situation where, instead of apparent discrimination and harassment, enshrined principles of equal employment opportunities, social justice, access to resources and equity will prevail. It is from a diverse workforce, the members of which respect each other, that an institution can harness a wide range of ideas and insights which are potentially useful in decision-making processes

(TasCOSS, 2012). Respecting religious diversity in the workplace does not only improve human relationships but can lead to better retention of employees and students, improve school attendance, reduce stress experienced by students and staff, and reduce staff turnover (TasCOSS, 2012). Even in areas where Christianity appears to dominate, followers of other faiths and those with no religious beliefs are to be respected and fairly treated.

Jesus Christ, the founder of the Christian faith, demonstrated his sensitivity towards religious diversity. An example is the narrative in the gospel according to Mark 7:24–30, where Jesus treats the little daughter of a non-Jewish religious Syrophoenician on the same basis as he treated Jews. Similarly, Christians are called to be sensitive, not only to their own beliefs but, more importantly, to the beliefs of others. Providing prayer breaks, accommodating dietary needs, and other religious observances, and setting aside quiet places and prayer rooms is one way in which religious diversity in schools can be appropriately managed for the benefit of both institution and students/employees. In most cases, religious diversity is in danger of becoming a critical issue if it is not properly managed. This is the case especially when one group is dominant over others because such a situation tends to encourage religious stereotyping whereby the stronger group considers itself superior, thus promoting religious tension within institutions.

A fourth requirement for the successful management of religious diversity in schools, and in the workplace in general, is a deliberate focus on the common good. The principle of the common good requires that people pay attention to common rather than individual concerns. It is based on the fact that human beings are both sacred and social beings and that they flourish better when co-existing harmoniously as a community where all have equal value and equal opportunity. It means that the good in an individual is linked to the good in the broader society. Therefore, concern for the common good entails concern for the welfare of the whole society, respect for equality and human dignity and relating to every level of life (Chartered Management Institute, 2008). An important lesson in this regard can be drawn from post-apartheid South Africa, argues Baker (2012) where, in order to avoid a continued segregated society, an approach was chosen that promoted civic nationalism as a mechanism broadly unifying all of society, as opposed to the existing narrow perceptions of identity that maintained segregation. Proper management of religious diversity is 'indispensable for socioeconomic' development of all kinds. It is a pre-requisite for nation building. It created a nation that is unified as well as peaceful (UNECA, 2011).

In the bringing about of effective management of religious diversity, awareness of human dignity also plays a role. Human dignity results from the fact that all human beings are the carriers of God's image. Although the concept of human dignity has occupied a prominent position in discussions about justice and human rights, it still poses a serious challenge which goes, however, largely unnoticed in the workplace discourse (Van Dun, 2001). The Universal Declaration of Human Rights (UDHR) states that human beings are born with dignity and equal rights. They are endowed with 'reason and conscience' which require from them to treat each other in the spirit of brotherhood in all areas of life including the workplace (Van Dun, 2001). Explaining this further, Valdes (2009) argues that dignity is not a descriptive term, but rather an ascriptive term triggered by the fact that one is a member of the human species whatever one's condition, age, ethnicity, race or religious background. Human dignity speaks about the quality of worthiness of the human being in all spheres of life, based on the simple fact that she or he is a human being without any other added status or background orientation (McCrudden, 2008; Donnelly, 2009). This makes human dignity into a foundational concept implying the worldwide human rights for all humankind (Donnelly, 2009).

Another aspect of religious diversity management in schools has to do with the policies that inform various practices at schools. According to Schreiner (2006), awareness of and sensitivity to religious diversity touches on various aspects of society. Key aspects include internal policies, social security systems, systems of relationships within the community, and ways to organize day-to-day life, all of which need to take religious diversity into account. In order to effectively manage religious diversity in schools as well as in other organizations, there has to be a constant building of students' or employees' capacity in life skills such as tolerance, respect for each other, reciprocity thinking, personal reflection and moderation in the public expression of one's own identity by keeping in mind that all of humankind is entitled to human dignity. These skills are critically important because religious convictions influence and shape both the personal and the collective understanding of such concepts as beauty, justice, right and wrong, as well as perceptions of past and future.

There are numerous approaches that can potentially lead to the achievement of the aforesaid objectives. From a phenomenological viewpoint, in order to advance peaceful co-existence in the context of religious diversity, no attempt should be made to promote a particular religious or non-religious view. Rather, much effort should be put into promoting knowledge and understanding of each other's religious orientation. Furthermore, anything that appears to try and impose one's own views and attitudes on others must be avoided.

Instead, empathy with persons of a different religious background or way of life must be enhanced (Jackson, 2006a).

From an interpretive approach, in order to manage religious diversity appropriately, religious tradition should not be presented as homogenous and a bound system. Rather religions must be understood in terms of their uniqueness and their potential to enrich each other, thus encouraging an open mind and the willingness to learn from others (Jackson, 2006b). From a dialogical approach, students can be taught that dialogue is an instrument to avoid conflict and promote peace, be it religious peace or otherwise. The focus of such dialogue should be on discovering the horizons, values and beliefs of others. Also, it has to focus on a better understanding of the self through comparison and interaction with others. In that way one may acquire skills of empathy and of practical cooperation with persons of different faiths, leading to the development of an identity that does not deny unity in diversity.

Contextual approach is another method that can be used to achieve an appropriate religious diversity management in schools as well other organizations. This approach takes into account the reality that every person looks at life through a different lens or from a different viewpoint and that there is no single view that is superior to others or that is common to all humankinds (Leganger–Krogstad, 2006). The contextual approach involves using a specific context or common features as a basis for inter-religious or inter-faith interaction. It includes an understanding that each particular religion has some 'features, history, artefacts, rituals, festivals, celebrations' that are enriching, as well as some aspects that are challenging and problematic (2006). Therefore, the important thing is to learn from each other instead of competing since no single religion is perfect.

Conclusion

The purpose of this contribution has been to explore ways of managing religious diversity, particularly in schools in Tanzania. Although Tanzania is diverse in terms of religion, race, tribes, cultures and so on, the country has maintained a significant level of peace and tranquility since its independence. This is the product of the fact that, soon after attaining independence, Tanzania took deliberate measures to manage its diversities. These measures included the adoption of Kiswahili as national language without affecting traditional languages, mainstreaming Tanzanian history in the education system, the elimination of divisive elements including tribal chiefs, and the formation of ujamaa villages as a strategy for rural development. Ujamaa policies which sought to integrate Western ideas and African worldviews for the sake of national development were consolidated, equal access to education for all was promoted, national unity was advanced, and constitutional provisions were made to ensure open religious and inter-faith dialogue.

However, recently there have been some incidents that indicate the existence of religious intolerance in various areas of Tanzania which could potentially affect the conditions in schools and in the general workplace. Such incidents include public debates held by Christians and Muslims justifying their positions, the destruction of workplaces (pork stores), the burning of churches and so on. These incidents call for a rethinking of religious diversity management in schools as well as in other organizations. This chapter proposes that appropriate management of religious diversity in Tanzania must begin with the creation of a common vision and an inclusive society. There needs to be respect for others and an appreciation of differences, a promotion of the common good, and an advancing of human dignity and of policies that respect diversity. The realization of these aims can be promoted by approaching religious diversity in a variety of particular ways, namely from a phenomenological, interpretive, dialogical and contextual viewpoint.

Bibliography

Akiri, M.J. (2013). *Religious Intolerance in Tanzania*. Dar es Salaam, Tanzania: Printing House.

Alnamlah, Y. (2011). 'A Suggested Model to Manage Religious Employees', *International Conference on Sociality and Economic Development*, 10, 469–73.

Atta-Asamoah, A. (2011). Overview of the Nature and Management of Diversity in Africa. Institute for Security Studies. Retrieved on April 23, from http//www.un.org/africa.

Baker, P.H. (2012). Getting Along: Managing Diversity for Atrocity Prevention in Socially Divided Societies. Retrieved on 20 October 2013 from http://www.report.stanleyfoundation.org.

Chartered Management Institute (2012). Embracing Diversity: Guidance for Managers. Retrieved on 12 November 2013 from http://www.managers.org.uk.

Centre of Concern (2008). The Principle of the Common Good. Retrieved on 29 December 2013 from http://www.educationforjustice.org.

Donnelly, J. (2009). Human Dignity and Human Rights. Retrieved on 11 October 2013 from http/www.udh1260.ch.

Equality Authority (2004). Building an Inclusive Workplace. Retrieved on 9 October 2013 from http://equality.ie.

Erickson, A. (2012). 'Peace in Tanzania: An Island of Stability in Sub-Saharan Africa', *Jackson School Journal of International Studies*, 3(1): 18–31.

Fahlbusch, E. (2008). *The Encyclopedia of Christianity Vol 5*. Gottingen, Eerdmann, Brill, pp 310–13.

Gahnstrom, C.S.L. (2012). Ethnicity, Religion and Politics in Tanzania: The 2010 General elections and Mwanza Region. Master's Thesis: Helsinki University.

Halloran, D. (2013). Are Religious Tensions Ripping Tanzania Apart? Retrieved on 21 May 2014 from http://www.persecition.org.

Health Policy Initiatives (HPI) 2013. Engaging Religious Leaders in the Response to HIV and AIDS in Tanzania. Retrieved on 9 October 2013 from http://wwwhealthpolictinitiatives.com.

International Religious Freedom Report (2011). Enhancing Religious Freedom at Workplace. Retrieved on 12 November 2013 from http://www.freedomreligious.au.

International Religious Freedom Report (2011). Tanzania: Executive Summary. Retrieved on 25 November 2013 from http:www.state.gov/document/organisation/192979.pdf.

Jackson, R. (2006a). The Interpretive Approach. In Keat, J. (ed.). *Religious Diversity and Intercultural Education: A Reference Book for Schools*. Council of Europe, Strasbourg, 52–6.

Jackson, R. (2006b). The Phenomenological Approach. In Keat, J. (ed.). *Religious Diversity and Intercultural Education: A Reference Book for Schools*. Council of Europe, Strasbourg, pp. 48–9.

Khudori, D. (2012). Religious Diversity in Africa and Asia: Conditions, Motor, Obstacles or Goal of Sustainable Development. Bundung, Asia–African Conference.

Kilaini, M. (2010). The Church in Africa and Tanzania in Particular. Retrieved on 23 November 2013 from http://www.africaworld.net.

Kollar, N.R. (2009). *Defending Religious Diversity in Public Schools: A Practical Guide for Building our Democracy and Deepening Our Education*. Greenwood Publishing Group, Santa Barbara.

Leganger–Krogstad, H. (2006). The Contextual Approach. In Keat, J. (ed.) *Religious Diversity and Intercultural Education: A Reference Book for Schools*. Council of Europe, Strasbourg, pp. 66–72.

Mbah, S. and Igariwey, I.E. (2008). African Socialism: An Anarchist Critique. Retrieved on May 18, 2014 from http://www.struggle.ws/africa.

McCrudden, C. (2008). International Law and Justice Working Paper. University Press, Oxford. Retrieved on 23 December 2013 from http://www.ilj.org.

National Integration Working Group for Workplace (NIWGW) (2003). Managing Workplace Diversity: A Toolkit for Organisation.

Schreiner, P. (2006). Educational Conditions and Methodological Approaches to Dealing with Religious Diversity. In Keat, J. (ed.). *Religious Diversity and Intercultural Education: A Reference Book for Schools*. Council of Europe, Strasbourg, 31–3.

Society for Human Resource Management (SHRM) (2008). Religion and Corporate Culture: Accommodating Religious Diversity in the Workplace. Retrieved on 22 October 2013 from http://www.shrm.org.

TasCOSS (2012). *Work Place Diversity Toolkit*. Department of Health and Human Services, Tasmania.

United Nations Economic Commission for Africa (UNECA) (2011). *Diversity Management in Africa: Findings from the African Peer Review Mechanism and a Framework for Analysis and Policy Making*. Addis Ababa, Ethiopia: UNECA: Governance and Public Administration Division.

United Republic of Tanzania (URT) (2007). The High Level Dialogue on Interreligious and Intercultural Understanding and Cooperation for Peace. Retrieved on 11 January 2014 from http://www.tanzania.org.

Valdes, E.G. (2009). 'Dignity, Human Rights and Democracy'. *Perspectives in Moral Science*. Retrieved from http://www.rmm-journal.de, 253–65.

Van Dun, F. (2001). 'Human Dignity: Reason or Desire? Natural Rights versus Human Rights', *Journal of Liberation Studies*, 15(4): 1–28.

Victorian Multicultural Commission (2008). Harnessing Diversity: Addressing Racial and Religious Discrimination in Employment. Retrieved on 21 December 2013 from http://www.humanrightscommission.vic.gov.au.

Waisse, W. (2003). Difference without Discrimination: Religious Education as a Field of Learning for Social Understanding. In Jackson, R. (ed.). *International Perspectives on Citizenship, Education and Religious Diversity*, New York and London: Routledge Falmer Taylor and Francis Group, 170–84.

Chapter 9

Are There Paths towards a New Social Pact during the Month of Ramadan? The Specific Case of Algerian Companies

ASSYA KHIAT, NATHALIE MONTARGOT AND FARID MOUKKES

Introduction

Are there possible paths towards a new social pact during the sacred month of Ramadan, when the Muslim religion prescribes the observance of ritual fasting? This is the core question we are asking. The month of Ramadan, one of the 12 lunar months in the Islamic calendar, is in particular marked by 'the privation of anything that might enter the body from sunrise to sundown (abstaining from food or drink, tobacco or sexual intercourse) and must be accompanied by an inner conversation, the reading of the Koran, donations to the poor … In the evening, dinner is an occasion for community gatherings and repasts to "break the fast"' (Coureau, 2013, our translation). However, is this sacred month in phase with a model of good practices in matters of HRM and behaviour in the workplace?

The hypothesis that we aim to test concerns the actual existence of organizational changes during the month of Ramadan and, if such is the case, their impact on productivity and the behaviour of people at work. To explore this question, we employed a dual methodological approach which led us to use Algerian companies as our research field.

One of the approaches is qualitative and required the processing of textual data with the help of the *Alceste 2010* software, using the transcriptions of 11 recorded interviews with HR directors in seven public and four private companies. The second is quantitative and is based on a survey involving 53 public and 45 private companies. The questionnaire used highlighted 21 items relating to specific HR practices and employee behaviours during the month of Ramadan.

This study, which is singular in its very theme, revolved around the question of paths towards a new social pact and the adaptation or lack thereof of Algerian companies in this particular context. The results of our dual field analysis suggest how prevalent ambiguity is, between the wish to demonstrate solidarity in this sacred month and its negatives consequences, both on an economic and social level. Conflicts, laxity and tensions are indeed among the many elements that impede a social pact.

The Paths towards a New Social Pact in the Workplace

A company, within this perspective of fundamental change, is a societal matter (Sainsaulieu, 1992). It must crystallize the aspirations and the commitment of the various stakeholders, above all those of a human nature, with the aim of paving the way for a new path, for the future of humanity (Morin, 2011).

A company is therefore a form of collective project with an extended social purpose, which breaks with the anonymization and the atomization of people (Hatchuel and Segrestin, 2012) who, much to the contrary, need to be supported in their cultural, social, sexual, political and religious diversity. In the end, the idea is to call upon another approach in the management of HR, beyond the instrumental model (Brabet, 1993). This requires the integration of the spirit of two criticisms made against the capitalist system: artistic criticism, based on freedom and individual initiatives, and social criticism, based on ethics and social justice – two criticisms that should constitute the basis for a new spirit of capitalism (Boltanski and Chiapello, 1999).

The path towards a future for humanity (Morin, 2011), which the new social pact in the workplace envisions, aims to demythologize the principles that have long governed companies under the influence of the ideology of shareholders' values – principles considered, incidentally, as unfounded, unfair and unproductive (Hatchuel and Segrestin, 2012). Unfounded, in that the maximization of profit constitutes a sort of 'economic messianism' par excellence, which shapes organizational behaviours, with senior executives in pursuit of this primal truth, thus reinforcing their own dependence upon shareholders. Unfair, in that the power to control and coerce is the prerogative of the shareholders, who then transfer the demand for profitability on to the employees, is of itself a denial of democracy and ethics. Unproductive, and this is a consequence of the above-mentioned democratic denial, in that the senior executives are unable to implement any other strategies aside from those aiming to deliver short-term productivity, even in contexts of high uncertainty.

Four paths can therefore be taken, albeit with difficulty, to restore the conception of a company faithful to its historical foundations and its initial and original missions. In the same vein as presented by Hatchuel and Segrestin in 2012, such paths are as follows:

THE COMPANY'S INVENTIVE AND INNOVATIVE MISSION

This path enhances the 'artistic and creative dimension' of the company. In this respect, invention, and innovation (which is the appropriate, contextualized use of this progress) do not mechanically result from a combination of production factors but from the significant enhancement and the necessary mobilization of potentials for action.

THE SENIOR EXECUTIVES' MANAGEMENT AUTHORITY

This path addresses the notion of leadership or 'political legitimacy' of the company's leaders, under the influence of the shareholders' values. This legitimacy is both split and contested because of two inconsistent, not to say contradictory, positions. On one hand, that of an autocrat, vis-à-vis the employees, and on the other, that of a clerk without autonomy, vis-à-vis shareholders. Restoring the leaders' political legitimacy and re-establishing the foundation of their management authority requires going back to their initial and original mission, which is to organize a neutral and creative compromise – a difficult, not to say impossible one – between the aspirations of the stakeholders, in order to consolidate the company's psychological contract.

COLLECTIVE COMMITMENT

This path gives to the inventive and innovative mission of the company its 'global and societal dimension', as it does to the leader's political legitimacy. To this effect, a reform of managerial thought is called for in order to embrace with all its complexity the relation between the company and its stakeholders, whether internal or external. The thought reform is in fact translated into responsible innovations that may be defined as 'the voluntary and proactive integration of environmental and social concerns in strategies, behaviours and processes, thus producing new, higher performance solutions through the development and productive use of resources and resulting in the creation of "societal" (economic, social and/or environmental) value' (Ingham, 2011, our translation).

SOLIDARITY OF COLLECTIVE ACTION

In a company aiming for collective progress, this path leads to the 'ethical dimension'. The consolidation of the new social pact in the workplace entails granting greater consideration to two kinds of solidarity, which are also to some extent civilization and life reforms (Morin, 2011). On one hand, this means extending the sharing of profits among all the members of the company for greater equity in incomes, and on the other, the support of commitment through the protection of each individual's potential to take action to enhance the quality of life in the workplace. The diversity of responsible players and functioning dimensions in companies are a 'non-distorting' prism of the companies' new social pact. This highlights the need for an overarching vision in corporate governance. In the same vein, the idea is to propose consistent cross-disciplinary readings on the political foundations, historical evolution and economic performance of capitalist companies to clarify and address questions that recent corporate history and liberal political philosophy have been raising: in the name of what is one granted the right to lead a company? What orientation can collective action be given when it is founded on a profound attachment to individual autonomy? (Gomez and Korine, 2009). And how can individual liberties be guaranteed while also promoting a good social climate? Finally, in Algerian companies, how do the companies' owners and the top management envision these issues in the transition towards a free-market economy?

The Algerian Company in View of a New Social Pact

Although reforms, often imposed and contested, have been made in the name of efficacy, efficiency and competitiveness, the fact remains that the organization and institutional configuration, which was supposed to reflect the new managerial spirit, hasn't changed and hasn't proved consistent. This inconsistency is justified by the country's political and economic history, which has defined the centres of power and the asymmetry in the balance of power.

Certain socio-anthropological considerations do not facilitate the use of the technical reform apparatus and surely do not legitimize them, hence the methodological problem lying in the schism between the conception and use of reforms, and the epistemological problem lying in their prescriptive vision – two problems that reify the notion of diversity and obstruct the paths towards the future for humanity discussed above.

AN AMBIVALENT TRANSITION

The conditions to lay the foundations of a new social pact in the workplace based on diversity, ethics and legitimacy are not really fulfilled because of the inconsistency and reductionism from which the dominant management system has been 'suffering' in Algerian companies. This makes any transition or evolution towards a diverse and responsible functioning ambivalent and meaningless. This lack of meaning, however, calls for answers to three fundamental questions (Boutenfnouchet, 2004) which are still unresolved:

1. The question of the awareness of the utility of the method. Indeed, it seems that attempts to lay new foundations for the functioning of Algerian companies have come with a severe lack of methodical pedagogy, although it was needed. This lack has been adroitly sustained, whether consciously or not, by spontaneity, a cultural and psychological element deeply rooted in Algerian society, but also by Algeria's recent history, which has been profoundly shaped by the hybrid socialist system in which the citizens lived on government benefits and the top management, as demands a one-party system, only did its thinking with the authorization of the powers-that-be and the party's local cell.

2. The question of the awareness of the value of information, which can be assessed in view of two problems laid down in a general manner: a data collection problem and an information problem – these are not without consequences on the relevance of analysis and the perspectivist reading of management situations. Such a configuration denotes shortcomings in the training of managers and their quasi-natural resistance to the circulation of information. Aggravating fact: some managers have a natural propensity for establishing themselves as an autonomous republic and tend to consider their area of intervention as a private hunting ground over which they have all rights and privileges.

3. The question of the awareness of integrated analysis. By integrated analysis, we mean the consistent combination of quantitative and qualitative analysis. Quantitative analysis usually dominates

since the expression of information through figures constitutes a reassuring comfort zone concealing all the information that would be doing managers a disservice. This quantitative analysis, however, loses its objectivity, given its partial and biased nature. Furthermore, it can conceal qualitative information that would be doing managers a disservice although it aims to reveal real political and social dynamics that are obvious obstacles in the company's sphere of activity.

CAN THIS AMBIVALENCE BE TRANSCENDED THROUGH RELIGIOUS SPIRITUALITY?

The domestication of scientific thought discussed above has potentially been brought about through religious reasoning, which is consubstantial with the Algerian society. In spite of the fact that the religion itself, in its exegetical texts, highlights the pressing need to rely on science in the construction of societies, the fact remains that this imperative had been reduced to the 'strict minimum' by the excessive religiosity cultivated by self-righteous minds, who transform any form of critical thinking into unanimistic totalitarian thought. Such thought accentuates the traditional divides between tradition and modernity, young and old, men and women, and conservatives and progressives. In that sense, we hardly see how religious spirituality, in any case in its fundamental version, which is in fact deeply rooted in Algerian society and in Algerian companies, could compromise with the new paths towards a future for humanity, notably in moments of spirituality (for instance the month of Ramadan, profoundly integrated in the standard functioning of companies, which legally alters work patterns). This period is conducive to moments of 'spiritual updating' reminding everyone of the importance of tolerance, solidarity and confidence in a religious practice which, because of confused and unchannelled interpretations, otherwise alleviate the reserve of consistency, methodology, criticism and innovation.

We wished to look into the particular period of Ramadan and its specificities in terms of business management. In order to find the answer to our research queries, we conducted a qualitative study and then a quantitative survey, which we are presenting below.

Analysis of Human Resource Management During the Period of Ramadan: The Qualitative Approach

In order to describe and analyse the views of HR managers during the period of Ramadan, we carried out a qualitative analysis that we processed statistically.

METHODOLOGY

We chose a qualitative approach, in that it allows for new discoveries by exploring further than the boundaries of a conceptual framework and (quantitativistic) process that consist in verifying pre-established hypotheses. Qualitative research does not require a preset framework and therefore allows for a greater degree of freedom for the researcher (Wacheux, 1996). We conducted the interviews around 21 items, themselves revolving around three main themes: HRM during the Ramadan month, behaviours at work and deviations during the Ramadan month.

Study sample

The corpus (complete set of textual date) comprises 11 interviews with HR directors and managers from various sectors of the economy. In order to preserve their anonymity, we identified the companies by labelling them E1, E2, E3 ... through E11. Seven of these companies belong to the public sector; the remaining four are in the private sector.

Processing of textual data

We chose to use a hierarchical descending classification, which has the advantage of being a method of processing the text through successive segmentation. It spots the strongest oppositions between terms in the text and then extracts classes of representative wordings. We chose to process the corpus with the help of the software *Alceste 2010* (for its analysis of co-occurring lexemes in a set of text segments).

We chose to use the software *Alceste 2010* to analyse the corpus (Lebart and Salem, 1994) and spot the strongest oppositions between terms in the text, because Alceste 'sets out to grasp the dynamics of verbal production through its "conflicting" nature, a principle that should not be ignored when interpreting the lexical classes thus obtained' (Kalampalikis, 2003, our translation). We were thus able to uncover essential information allowing us to identify several semantic universes.

As a tool, *Alceste 2010* seemed to us quite well suited for the task, because of the relevance of its processing representation and the reliability of its results (Kalampalikis, 2003). Indeed, it does not require the prior identification of partition variables to interpret the corpus. In this way, it guarantees the objectivity of a purely algorithmic method whose 'data are processed without a priori assumptions regarding the classes to be discovered' (Fallery and Rhodain, 2007). It thus appears well adapted to our exploratory approach (Duyck, 2001, 2002; Helme-Guizon and Gavard-Perret, 2004).

The statistical processing of speech by *Alceste 2010* segments the corpus, breaks it down and ranks it through a method of hierarchical descending classification. Table 9.1 shows the lexicometric characteristics of the analysed corpus before and after lemmatization, which consists in bringing the lemma to its root form.

Table 9.1   Lexicometric characteristics of the corpus analysed by *Alceste 2010*

	Corpus
Vocabulary Analysis	
Number of initial context units (i.c.u.)	11
Total number of forms contained in the corpus	120,691
Number of distinct forms	12,146
Average frequency by form	10
Number of hapaxes (forms present only once in the corpus)	1,085
Vocabulary Analysis after Lemmatization	
Number of reduced forms	1,097
Number of additional forms (articles, pronouns, and so on)	357
Number of elementary context units (e.c.u.)	1,056
Percentage of vocabulary richness	96.46

Source: Data from *Alceste 2010* detailed report.

RESULTS OF THE STATISTICAL ANALYSIS OF THE CORPUS

Alceste proposes a classification into four semantic universes applying to 69 per cent of the elementary context units (e.c.u.). The representativeness is good and does not show any anomalies as defined by Zipf's law.[1] Figure 9.6 allows us to visualize the classes thus reflecting the views of the HR professionals. We interpreted each class by studying its most representative forms and noticed that the e.c.u. were not evenly distributed, then we named and interpreted each semantic universe.

The different semantic universes present

Two main classes can be identified. They concern 'HR procedures at the time of the Ramadan' (class 2, 40 per cent of the e.c.u.) and the 'adaptation in the payment of salaries and wages' (class 3, 14 per cent of the e.c.u.). Class 3 is itself subdivided into two classes, that of 'individual difficulties in adaptation' (class 4, 12 per cent of the e.c.u.) and that of 'religious practices and improper individual behaviour' (class 1, 34 per cent). The classification tree resulting from the processing with the software *Alceste* is presented in Figure 9.6.

We will now reveal the semantic universes relating to each class and present the most representative forms, with the Chi-squared results between parentheses indicating the coefficient of association of a lexical form with a given class.

Class 1: Religious practices and improper individual behaviours (34 per cent)
The first class groups together lemmas belonging to the semantic universe of religious practices and the behaviours of co-workers, which in some cases are subject to sanctions. The vocabulary used refers to woman (21), prayer (22), man (14), time (30) and sanction (11). We can observe that the form 'woman' is connected to temporality and family-related tasks while the form 'prayer' is connected to temporality, place, adjustment and flexibility.

Class 2: Human resources procedures at the time of the Ramadan (40 per cent)
The second class groups together lemmas belonging to the semantic universe of HR procedures. The vocabulary used refers to management (30), training (30), human (28) and career (19).

Class 3: Adaptation in the payment of salaries and wages (14 per cent)
The third class groups together lemmas belonging to the semantic universe of the company's adaptation in terms of wages and salaries. The vocabulary used refers to Eid (14), action (12), buying (7), spending (10), salary (14) and

---

1   When classifying the words of a text by decreasing frequency, we may observe that the frequency of any word is inversely proportional to its rank in the frequency table.

expensive (6). We can observe that the form 'Eid' is connected with 'Fitr',[2] with expenses to be made and with fate.

Class 4: Individual difficulties in adaptation and decrease in productivity (12 per cent)
The fourth class groups together lemmas belonging to the semantic universe of individual difficulties in adaptation impacting productivity. The vocabulary used refers to young (14), Algeria (7), decrease (7), change (7), physical (9) and rhythm (6).

Interpretations of the results

The processing of the corpus allowed us to study in depth the HR directors' views and draw there from two main themes that we are now going to expound.

First theme: Managing the intensification of religious practices within the workplace
During the month of Ramadan, religious fervour is usually higher than normal. The HR directors therefore have to take into consideration this intensification of religious practices, since the employees 'are a little more disposed to observe prayer times' (Human Resources Director (HRD) 9).

The question of where such prayer times can take place thus arises. In one company, a spirituality space was planned all year round and it witnessed a rise in attendance since 'there are many people who pray during Salat Edohr' (HRD 6). In others, arrangements are made. They can be in the form of a room 'where they can go say their prayers on time with a certain flexibility at work to let people fully put their spirituality into practice for that month' (HRD9), or there can be a space in the employee's own office (HRD 2) or, when working on a construction site, a mosalla[3] (HRD 7). The length of prayer time increases, 'usually a prayer takes about ten minutes, but generally, during the Ramadan, it takes over a half hour. And therefore, he takes 15 minutes to wash up, 15 minutes to prepare his prayer' (HRD 2). Yet, in spite of the increase in prayer time, this ought not to be done 'at the expense of productivity' (HRD 8).

The main changes observed are related to 'productivity, schedules, and a certain tension' (HRD 9). It is therefore best to adjust schedules and take into account the strenuousness of work during this period, while promoting safety and the effectiveness of work.

---

2   Muslim celebration marking the end of Ramadan.
3   A dedicated open-air area.

In fact, there seems to be a need to 'reduce the pace so that the employees can at least bear the workload' (HRD 6). 'Productivity decreases and this can be explained by the fasting, which diminishes the intellectual and physical capacities and slows down the previously established rhythm. Some tasks or meetings that require a great deal of concentration or physical effort are scheduled after the Tarawih prayer' (HRD 9).

A possible strategy consists in taking into account 'very difficult tasks, in order to "place the worker on leave without consultation …, for instance, everything that involved welding, water or airproofing and woodworking. These tasks are considered difficult because they involve a level of risk, of danger' (HRD7). Fatigue accumulates during the sacred month. The state of weakness of the participants is all the more severe when Ramadan takes place in the summer. This can lead to schedule adjustments, especially during the first week, because of the adaptation to 'work conditions on tired bodies, without intake of food or drink' (HRD 9).

The last week is also considered particularly critical for women 'who bake cakes and have to stay up more or less late … this has repercussions on their physical condition and availability to work the next day … we make a small effort toward women to allow them to leave work earlier in relation to their increased housework load' (HRD 9). In some companies, we observe gender differences. 'Work hours are from 9am to 4pm for men and 9am to 3pm for women' (HRD 6)

Fatigue is also taken into consideration and some meetings are postponed or shortened in order to avoid conflict and tension. In fact, the risk of potential clashes or conflicts between employees seems to be feared by HR managers. 'We avoid meeting people, we avoid work meetings and committees, we avoid everything during the month of Ramadan … People are edgy; in a project it's truly difficult to work with this kind of person, so we just choose avoidance instead and that's all' (HRD 1). A specific population seems to represent a problem for HR directors because of their repeated lateness and conflicting relationship with their managers, 'with today's young people, strictness towards non-complying behaviours is indicated' (HRD 2).

A tolerance margin considering behaviours at work is, however, also expressed, yet the general consensus is that

> *any deviation going beyond a 'reasonable' framework should be subject to sanctions … If the deviation is considered serious or if the behaviour leaves much to be desired, the person can be brought to a disciplinary*

commission that will in turn judge the seriousness of the deviation and
the required sanctions (HRD 9).

Modification of practices and efforts on the company's part concerning salaries
The main functions of HR are impacted by the period of Ramadan; training, notably. 'the training service simply shuts down; we organize no training sessions during the month of Ramadan' (HRD 2). While recruiting is frozen during that month in companies that are organized 'through an annual plan, in the general framework of HRM' (HRD 9) and in which 'we do not recruit except if there is an actual, real emergency, otherwise we do not recruit during Ramadan' (HRD 6), other companies have no particular rules 'a few people … might be recruited' (HRD 2).

Concerning salaries, a financial effort is made on the company's part in order to anticipate the payment of employees. Indeed, Ramadan is a festive period during which prices go up while consumption increases. There are different organizational strategies. For some companies, within the framework of Ramadan, 'we do not pay advances on salaries or wages but on the occasion of Eid, we bring the payment date forward' (HRD 2). For others, bonuses might be distributed so as to 'maintain the personnel' (HRD 1). Special actions are also proposed: 'after Aïd Es Seghir, we share, for one hour, a light meal destined for the ritual pardon embraces' (HRD 9) and the Committee in charge of social actions, during this period, organizes 'the purchase of foodstuffs to then sell them at a lower price and thus lighten the burden of expenses that the employees have to bear during that month' (HRD 11).

Analysis of Human Resources Management during the Period of Ramadan: The Quantitative Approach

METHODOLOGY

We conducted a survey with a questionnaire involving nearly 100 public and private companies of the Oran region (53 per cent were public, 45 per cent private – see Figure 9.7). Our questionnaire included 21 items revolving around three themes: HRM during the month of Ramadan, behaviour at work during the month of Ramadan, and repeated deviations. See Figure 9.7.

The study took place from March to April 2013. The data were processed with the help of the software *Ethnos 4*. The direct results are shown in Figure 9.7. We further gave priority to some specifically cross-processed data, not only to corroborate our hypothesis but also to find out whether it was possible to correlate the results with our qualitative analysis.

RESULTS AND DISCUSSIONS

Ramadan and productivity

Q10: During the Ramadan, is productivity: lower/average/higher?
Q12: During which week is fatigue the greatest?

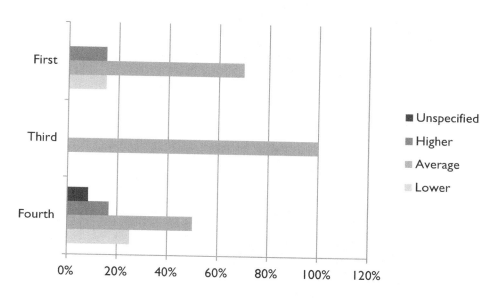

Figure 9.1   **Lexicometric characteristics of the analysed corpus before and after lemmatization**

During Ramadan, fatigue impacts productivity with the lowest productivity being recorded during the first and fourth week, although much more markedly the first week. These results confirm the findings in Lahbari's work (1995).

Ramadan and salaries

In another analysis, the crossed data processed the following questions: status of the company (Q18) with 'Do you process payroll during Ramadan within the same timeframe as other months?'

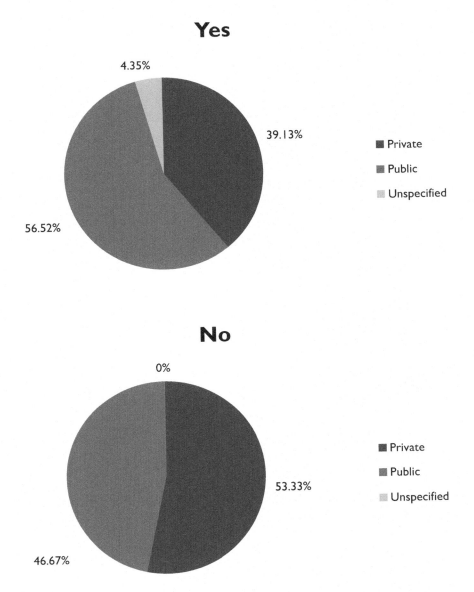

Figure 9.2   Payroll timeframe during Ramadan according to the type of organizations

Our findings show that 56.52 per cent of public companies and 39.13 per cent of private companies process payroll during Ramadan within the same timeframe as the other months (see Figure 9.2). A total of 46.67 per cent of public companies and 53.33 per cent of private companies do not process payroll during Ramadan within the same timeframe as the other months. Generally speaking, the public sector processes payroll in the same conditions as any other month, whereas the private sector, for obvious reasons of autonomy, processes payroll differently than for other months. This result corroborates our qualitative study.

Ramadan: flexibility in work hours

For a specific analysis, the crossed data processed the following questions: 'Do you implement flexibility in work hours?' (Q8) with 'if so, which one?' (Q9) and the results obtained can be synthesized as follows (see Figure 9.3).

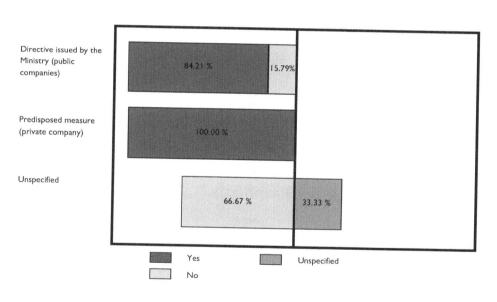

Figure 9.3 **Flexible scheduling during Ramadan**

All told, 84.21 per cent of public companies implement work hours, due to a directive issued by the public supervising authority (Ministry), 100 per cent of the companies implement it as a predisposed measure.

Ramadan: behavioural deviations and sanctions

Two pertinent questions were cross-processed here:

Q17: Is men's and women's lack of diligence subject to the same sanctions?

Q21: What is the nature of the deviations?

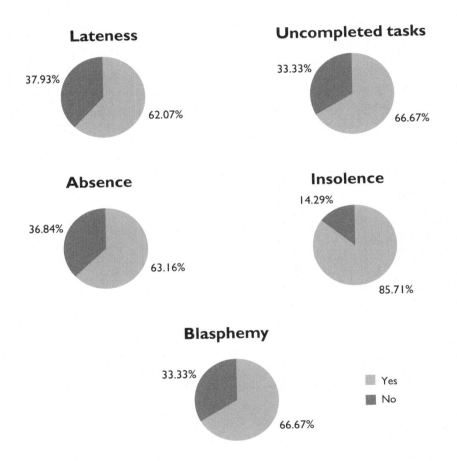

Figure 9.4   Ramadan and deviant behaviours

Figure 9.4 shows five light and dark circles, each representing a specific deviation. The positive answers are represented by the dark colour, with light indicating a negative answer to the questions of different deviations and the equality of sanctions between men and women.

Repeated lateness, uncompleted tasks, absences, insolence and blasphemy are the behavioural deviations observed at work on a daily basis during the month of Ramadan, up to 60 per cent or at times even 80 per cent. The results support the results recorded in the qualitative approach, which reported absences, conflicts, tensions and so on.

For 'Is men's and women's lack of diligence subject to the same sanctions?' the results are well above 50 per cent. However, men and women aren't subject to the same sanctions concerning lateness and absences.

When employees are late, 72.41 per cent receive warnings, 3.45 per cent have their salaries levied, 17.24 per cent are subject to no sanctions, 3.45 per cent are subject to other sanctions and finally 3.45 per cent are suspended, the severity of the sanction depending on the seriousness of the deviation.

When employees do not accomplish their work, 83.33 per cent receive warnings, 8.33 per cent have their salaries levied and finally 8.33 per cent are suspended, the severity of the sanction depending on the seriousness of the deviation.

When employees are absent from work, 75 per cent receive warnings, 10 per cent have their salaries levied, 10 per cent are subject to no sanctions, and finally 5 per cent are suspended, the severity of the sanction depending on the seriousness of the deviation.

When employees are insolent, 85.71 per cent receive warnings, and 14.29 per cent are subject to no sanctions (see Figure 9.5). Concerning blasphemy, an affront to divinity and religion, 100 per cent receive warnings.

Between warnings and impunity, tolerance is the watchword. Does this constitute the basis on which to build a social pact?

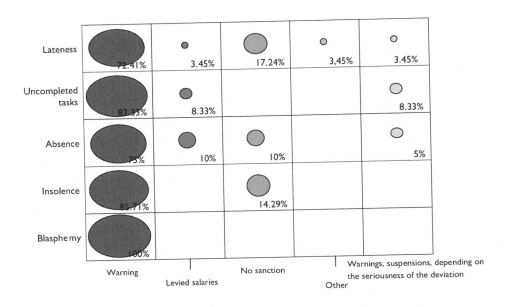

	Warning	Levied salaries	No sanction	Other	Warnings, suspensions, depending on the seriousness of the deviation
Lateness	72.41%	3.45%	17.24%	3.45%	3.45%
Uncompleted tasks	83.33%	8.33%			8.33%
Absence	75%	10%	10%		5%
Insolence	85.71%		14.29%		
Blasphemy	100%				

Figure 9.5   Ramadan and sanctions

Ramadan-related human resources specificities

About 75 per cent of companies do not recruit before and during the month of Ramadan; the others hire, for the most part, because of leaves taken by their employees during that month. The contracts issued then are therefore mainly short-term contracts (63 per cent).

About 76 per cent of the companies do not organize meetings after *Salat Ettarawi*, while 19 per cent do, since the personnel is available, and the energy levels are back to normal.

About 63 per cent of the companies put a place dedicated to spirituality at their employees' disposal, and 74 per cent claim that the highest attendance rate is for the Dohr prayer; however, the time spent in these places does not exceed 10 minutes for 57 per cent of the interviewees.

About 27 per cent of the companies interviewed declared they organize charitable actions for the benefit of their employees for Eid; while for Ramadan baskets, bonuses and circumcision, opinions are divided, with 32 per cent considering that all the employees benefit from them.

Conclusion

We started from a hypothesis, which consisted of seeing whether there were organizational changes during the month of Ramadan, and if so, what their impact on productivity and the behaviours of people at work would be. Our field results show the extent to which the qualitative approach corroborates the quantitative approach. While HRM dispositions are implemented during the month of Ramadan, there are strong repercussions on the companies' productivity and social life, and the Algerian economy experiences, during the month of Ramadan, a true decrease in economic activity and a strong increase in consumption (Belkacem, 2013), along with an observed rise in aggressiveness.

> *According to a study conducted just a few years ago by the Arab World Institute for Social Studies in Cairo regarding social behaviours during the Ramadan, productivity decreases by 73.3 per cent in Arab countries (and we are one, aren't we!), while consumer goods prices record an average increase of 35 per cent while some diseases (related to cholesterol, tension, diabetes) increase by 27.56 per cent divorces by 35 per cent while...' (Belkacem, 2013). We are, however, perplexed by the spiritual message borne by this sacred month. It would seem that the daily behaviour at work during the month of Ramadan is far from corresponding with the religious precepts teaching that work and the quality of one's behaviour are the product of a certain rapport with society. We are therefore faced with a dilemma as to how, in a month of solidarity, can conflicts, tensions and lower productivity thus endure? This phenomenon could be expressed through the term 'Tramdena' – someone 'mramden' being an enraged and uncontrollable person ('Tramdena' or 'mramden', a Ramadan phenomenon).[4]*
> *'Fasting is not merely refraining from taking food or drink, indeed fasting is refraining from futility and obscenity, thus if someone insults you or behaves with you with manifest ignorance, then you shall say: I am fasting, indeed, I am fasting' (Reported by Ibn Khouzeima and authentified by Cheikh Albani in Sahih Targhib, no. 1082).*

---

4   The potential noxious effects of Ramadan, 9 July 2013. Retrieved from http://brisonslemythe. canalblog.com/archives/2013/07/09/27354387.html.

References

Belkacem, A.D. (2013). Ramadhan: le grand dodo! *Quotidien d'Oran*, 18 July, p. 6.

Boltanski, L. and Chiapello, E. (1999). *Le nouvel esprit du capitalisme*. Paris: Edition Gallimard.

Boutefnouchet, M. (2004). *La société algérienne en transition*. Alger: Edition OPU.

Brabet, J. (1993). *Repenser la GRH*, Paris: Economica.

Coureau, T.M. (2013). Entreprises et diversité religieuse. Un management par le dialogue, Paris, AFMD-Association française des managers de la diversité. Retrieved from http://www.afmd.fr/IMG/pdf_AFMD-DIVERSITE-RELIGIEUSE-web.pdf.

Duyck, J.Y. (2001). 'Des lettres et des chiffres, vers la « troisième génération » du qualitatif en sciences de gestion', *Revue Sciences de Gestion*, 30: 179–206.

Duyck, J.Y. (2002). 'Crise économique et discours: quelques réflexions autour du mot du Président', *Revue Gestion 2000*, 6: 111–129.

Fallery, B. and Rodhain, F. (2007). Quatre approches pour l'analyse de données textuelles: lexicale, linguistique, cognitive, thématique, *16ème Conférence Internationale de Management Stratégique, Montréal*, 6–9 June 2007.

Gomez, P.Y and Korine, H. (2009). *L'entreprise dans la démocratie. Une théorie politique du gouvernement des entreprises*. Brussels: Edition De Boeck.

Hadj Nacer, A. (2011). *La martingale algérienne. Réflexions sur une crise*. Alger: Edition Barzakh.

Helme-Guizon, A. and Gavard-Perret, M.H. (2004). 'L'analyse automatisée de données textuelles en marketing: Comparaison de trois logiciels', *Décisions marketing*, 36: 75–90.

Hatchuel, A. and Segrestin, B. (2012). *Refonder l'entreprise*. Paris: Edition Seuil.

Ingham, M. (2011). *Vers une innovation responsable: pour une vraie responsabilité sociétale*. Brussels: Edition De Boeck.

Kalampalikis, N. (2003). L'apport de la méthode Alceste dans l'analyse des représentations sociales. In Abric, J.C. *Méthodes d'étude des représentations sociales*. Ramonville Saint-Agne: Erès: 147–63.

Lahbari, B. (1995). 'Sur le ramadan et le rendement: la baisse est imputée aux habitudes nocturnes', éditions l'Economiste, 167.

Lebart, L. and Salem, A. (1994). *Statistique textuelle*, Paris: Dunod.

Morin, E. (2011). *La voie: pour l'avenir de l'humanité*. Paris: Edition Pluriel.

Sainsaulieu, R. (1990). *L'entreprise: une affaire de société*. Edition PUF.

http://www.popuvox.com/musulmans-ramadan-s720988.htm.

Wacheux, F. (1996). *Méthodes qualitatives et recherche en gestion*. Paris: Economica.

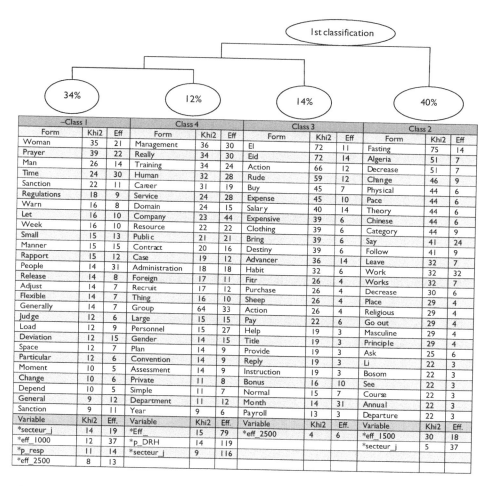

1st classification

| 34% | 12% | 14% | 40% |

–Class I

Form	Khi2	Eff
Woman	35	21
Prayer	39	22
Man	26	14
Time	24	30
Sanction	22	11
Regulations	18	9
Warn	16	8
Let	16	10
Week	16	10
Small	15	13
Manner	15	15
Rapport	15	12
People	14	31
Release	14	8
Adjust	14	7
Flexible	14	7
Generally	14	7
Judge	12	6
Load	12	9
Deviation	12	15
Space	12	7
Particular	12	6
Moment	10	5
Change	10	6
Depend	10	5
General	9	12
Sanction	9	11
Variable	Khi2	Eff.
*secteur_j	14	19
*eff_1000	12	37
*p_resp	11	14
*eff_2500	8	13

Class 4

Form	Khi2	Eff
Management	36	30
Really	34	30
Training	34	24
Human	32	28
Career	31	19
Service	24	28
Domain	24	15
Company	23	44
Resource	22	22
Public	21	21
Contract	20	16
Case	19	12
Administration	18	18
Foreign	17	11
Recruit	17	12
Thing	16	10
Group	64	33
Large	15	15
Personnel	15	27
Gender	14	15
Plan	14	9
Convention	14	9
Assessment	14	9
Private	11	8
Simple	11	7
Department	11	12
Year	9	6
Variable	Khi2	Eff.
*Eff_	15	79
*p_DRH	14	119
*secteur_j	9	116

Class 3

Form	Khi2	Eff
El	72	11
Eid	72	14
Action	66	12
Rude	59	12
Buy	45	7
Expense	45	10
Salary	40	14
Expensive	39	6
Clothing	39	6
Bring	39	6
Destiny	39	6
Advancer	36	14
Habit	32	6
Fitr	26	4
Purchase	26	4
Sheep	26	4
Action	26	4
Pay	22	6
Help	19	3
Title	19	3
Provide	19	3
Reply	19	3
Instruction	19	3
Bonus	16	10
Normal	15	7
Month	14	31
Payroll	13	3
Variable	Khi2	Eff.
*eff_2500	4	6

Class 2

Form	Khi2	Eff
Fasting	75	14
Algeria	51	7
Decrease	51	7
Change	46	9
Physical	44	6
Pace	44	6
Theory	44	6
Chinese	44	6
Category	44	9
Say	41	24
Follow	41	9
Leave	32	7
Work	32	32
Works	32	7
Decrease	30	6
Place	29	4
Religious	29	4
Go out	29	4
Masculine	29	4
Principle	29	4
Ask	25	6
Li	22	3
Bosom	22	3
See	22	3
Course	22	3
Annual	22	3
Departure	22	3
Variable	Khi2	Eff.
*eff_1500	30	18
*secteur_j	5	37

Figure 9.6   The extracted classes of meanings

Q1: Company status?

Q3: Workforce gender?

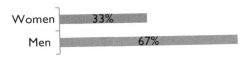

Q4: Do you hire before and during the month of Ramadan?

Q5: If the answer is yes, what is the reason for hiring?

Q9: Do you establish flexible work hours?

Q10: If the answer is yes, what kind?

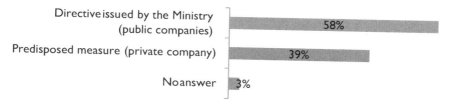

Q11: During Ramadan, is productivity:

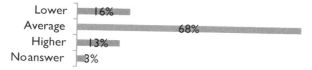

Q12: Is the impact of fatigue on the personnel:

Q13: During which week is fatigue the greatest?

Q14: Is there a specific space dedicated to prayer?

Q15: What is the attendance rate of the praticing Muslims during the month of Ramadan?

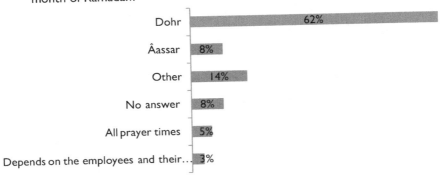

Q16: How much time is spent in the space dedicated to spiritual practice?

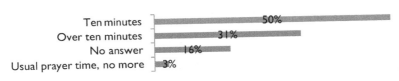

Q17: Is men's and women's lack of diligence subject to the same sanctions?

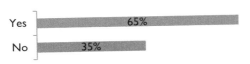

Q18: Do you process payroll earlier?

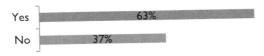

Q19: If the answer is yes, by how many days?

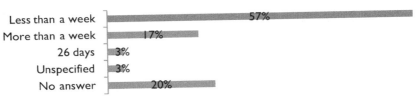

Q20: What sanctions are behavioural deviations subject to?

Q21: What are the main behavioural deviations?

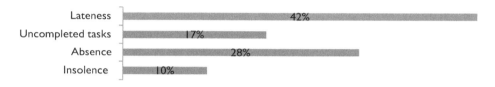

Figure 9.7   The survey questionnaire including 21 items

PART III
Middle East and Asia

Chapter 10

Women in Islamic Banks in the United Arab Emirates: Tradition and Modernity

CELIA DE ANCA

Introduction: Women in Financial Services and in Islam – Perceptions and Stereotypes

Perceptions exist whether or not we are conscious of them. Let us imagine three different head pictures at the top of a resume. The first is a German man, the second a Venezuelan woman and the third a Saudi woman, veiled. Now ask: 'Which one is the Financial Director of the Treasury Department of a leading international bank?'

If not guided by the title of this chapter, most people would not pick the veiled Saudi woman as the Financial Director, and not many would pick the Venezuelan woman either. In our common unconscious, financial services do not match with women in general and even less with Muslim women. By my experience of the past 15 years teaching women in leadership, I have noticed two common stereotypes underline the idea of Muslim women in financial services:

1.   The stereotype that a woman, regardless of her cultural background, is not very much inclined to work in financial services.

2.   The stereotype that Muslim women, if following Shariah (Islamic law), could not work in the financial industry and would not have independence in managing their own money.

The aim of this chapter is to analyse religion in banking via the concrete experience of Muslim women in the Emirates working in banking. However before going to the concrete case, I would like to clarify these two common perceptions that will help us in the second section of the chapter: what Islamic banks are and the role of Muslim women in the Islamic banking industry.

Demystifying Myths

WOMEN IN FINANCIAL SERVICES – A GLOBAL PERSPECTIVE

The financial industry is probably the most 'masculinized' industry in today's business world, which is particularly relevant since, as stated by Sheila Wellington, Catalyst President, 'few industries evoke more images of power and prestige than the financial services industry' (Bhagat, 2003).

Traditionally in Western countries, women were excluded from financial activities as we can see, for example, in the case of Spain where women were allowed to open a bank account without the signature of their husbands only as recently as 1976 (Molinero, 1998). Before then, women also needed to have the signature of their husbands in order to receive their father's inheritance or travel abroad, and single women would need the signature of their fathers or legal guardians. Spain was not the only case; in the late nineteenth century, as reflected in Jane Austen's books, as for example *Sense and Sensibility* (1811), English women could lose their inherited property to any male family member if they were not married.

Things fortunately have changed, but it is not a coincidence that banks did not target women as primary clients, since the perception was that women, while they did play a strong role in controlling household spending and in influencing family financial decisions, were not the account holders, and that men made the decisions on which banks to take a loan from, where to invest the family's assets and so on. When looking at the figures of women in the financial industry, we can see that these perceptions still prevail, as evidenced by the following examples:

- In US financial companies, women constitute only 16.8 per cent of executive officers and only 2.5 per cent of chief executives (Stock, 2010).

- In the insurance industry women are represented as follows: 18.1 per cent of executive managers, 16.8 per cent of board of directors members, fewer than 20 per cent of career agents in top insurance companies (Sweetser, 2004, p. 14).

According to data compiled by the recruitment firm Egon Zehnder International, Europe is not too different. Women make up about 19 per cent of European bank boards, compared with 33 per cent in the household-products industry, which has the highest level of female representation on boards (Chouldhury and Martinuzzi, 2013).

Based on these data, we must ask the following question – do the stereotypes applied to women limit those who want to pursue a career in financial services? The lack of women as financial agents also limits the capacity of the industry to create financial products adapted to the needs of women, as depositors, investors or credit applicants.

Some banks have recently understood that women as clients can be a lucrative market segment and have consequently developed products tailored for women. In March 2006, as a result of studies conducted by Emotion Banking that targeted differences in the preferences of women and men for banking, Raiffeissen opened the first Austrian bank for women in the ski resort of Gastein. The bank redesigned its space to accommodate the needs of women and even provided a play area to keep children occupied. Women employees serve customers to identify women's needs and clarify the bank's specific products for their clients.[1]

As stated in Financial Services ACCA (ACCA Position Paper, September 2009, p. 11), there is a need for a holistic approach to the demand and supply requirements of women in the financial industry, as an important and effective approach to developing women's enterprises. Recent examples illustrate that women are willing to hold, and are capable of holding, key positions in the financial services industry. For example, Fiona Woolf, a partner in the law firm CMS Cameron McKenna LLP was named in October 2013 as the 686th Lord Mayor of London, only the second woman chosen to head the financial district's municipal government in 800 years (Choudhury and Martinuzzi, 2013).

There is no longer a question of social justice in allowing women to occupy financial positions. Today, it is only a question of logic since, if more women filled positions in the financial industry, the end products of the industry would tap into the financial resources of many women around the world. At the same

---

1   http://www.moreinspiration.com/article/3631/banking-on-women?p=experience&t=financial, http://www.gastein.raiffeisen.at/eBusiness/01_template1/0,7572,79332371255048901-79339777926154319_291968977124448901-291968977124448901-NA-30-NA,00.html;jsessionid=4C56756533451DF58A6F35B652F7B61F.rpublic_a2p05, retrieved on 2 January 2014.

time, on the credit side, new credit products would be adapted to help women in developing their businesses (de Anca and Vazquez, 2007).

WOMEN IN BUSINESS AND ISLAM

According to a Forte Consultancy report (2012), women in the Middle East region control around USD 246 billion, which for many is a surprise since the stereotype of Muslim women describes them as individuals deprived of many social and economic rights.

Contrary to the common perception, women in Islam have been granted economic rights since the beginning of their civilization. In Islam, social rights are often separate from economic rights, and women have traditionally had full control over their own money and resources – a right that is guaranteed in Islamic tradition and jurisprudence (de Anca, 2004).

All Muslims recognize the leading role of the first women in Islam, especially Khadijah, the first wife of the Prophet Muhammed, who was a wealthy businesswoman who hired the Prophet Muhammed as her agent and partner to manage her business affairs in Arabia.

As a member of the Arab tribe of Quraish, Khadijah was born in the sixth century CE, the daughter of Khuwaylid and Fatimah Banu Hashim. Her father was a wealthy merchant, a caravan trader of goods between al Hijaz and other regions in Arabia such as Yemen and the Mediterranean coastlands of Syria. Khadijah successfully managed her inheritance and became the owner of some of the largest caravans in Arabia. She was well known for hiring talented people and compensating them well for their services. Therefore, she was very well respected in her community. Khadijah hired her agents on a Mudaraba basis, meaning that she contributed to the business (the caravan) by providing the capital, but she shared the profits with her agents/business partners who contributed their labour. Once the caravan had returned, profits would be calculated and shared according to pre-arranged percentages agreed upon between her and her agents (Iliasu and de Anca, 2011).

The tradition also mentions that Khadijah hired Muhammed because he was an exemplary person renowned for his honesty, She had also heard many good things about him from her family and from other merchants, and because of his reputation, she sent him a message asking him to bring some of her merchandise to Syria. Muhammed accepted, and that was the beginning of their commercial relationship (Lings, 1989).

Khadijah was 40 years old and the Prophet Muhammed was 25 when they got married. She was the mother of all his children except one, and the first to accept and believe in Islam, thus becoming the first convert to Islam. Muslims described her as the 'financier of Islam'. She remains a powerful role model, and also constitutes a symbol of the financial independence of women in Islam.

The example of Khadija is strong in the Islamic tradition and consequently Islamic Jurisprudence is clear on the rights of women to hold and manage their own money. Sheikh Osaid Kailani, the Global Head of Shari'ah and Executive Vice President of the Shari'ah Division of the Abu Dhabi Islamic Bank, stated (Iliasu and de Anca, 2011):

> *Islamic jurisprudence clearly forbids mixing the wealth of the husband with that of the wife. It is the man's duty to bear all financial expenses of the family, and even if he is poor he is never allowed to take the woman's wealth. Women thus enjoy full freedom to manage their finances independently.*

In fact, there are many recorded cases throughout Islamic history of women resorting to the protection of the law and to judges to enforce their right to manage their own wealth without any interference – not even from their husbands or family members, as recorded by Marin (2000) when talking about the women in Al-Andalus.[2] These women had an important role in economic matters of Al-Andalus both as workers and as investors or property owners. The documents on women in Al-Andalus recall examples of women working in different disciplines, including commerce, science and education. In addition to receiving remuneration for their work, women had full rights over their inheritances, and that granted them an important role in key family affairs and clan decisions. Occasionally, masculine members of a family tried to acquire women's inheritance rights to preserve the family's legacy, and on those occasions male members offered the women significant amounts of money in exchange for renouncing their legacy rights. Thus, women's wealth was relevant and enabled them to invest in real estate, to take part in commerce, or to act as financers in family businesses, as illustrated by a number of documents in which men appear as debtors to women family members. These studies illustrate the reality of life for Muslim women in Al-Andalus and in general in medieval Muslim societies in which women benefit from economic rights and their independent use of them under the protection of the Islamic law (Marin, 2000).

---

2   Name used to refer to Medieval Islamic Iberia.

Both Islamic jurisprudence and Islamic tradition support the idea that Muslim women today benefit from economic rights not so much as a result of Western influences but more because of their own tradition of women as independent economic agents.

Women in Islamic Banks: The Case of United Arab Emirates

ISLAMIC BANKING: A FINANCIAL OPTION FOR TODAY'S FINANCIAL NEEDS

The market for Islamic finance represents today a solid niche complementing conventional banking in Muslim countries. Today, 2 per cent of global banking assets are Shariah compliant, with an impressive annual growth of more than 30 per cent (ECB, 2013).

Conventional banking as we understand it today had its origins in the Western world in the seventeenth century, offering a well-organized channel from people's deposits to people's financial needs. The percentage of people using the banking system has grown steadily ever since, reaching more than 90 per cent in countries such as the US and the UK (2014 Global Findex). However, the penetration of the banking system is much lower in Muslim countries. According to the Global Financial Inclusion database (2014 Global Findex), the Middle East in general is the region where bank account penetration (for example, the percentage of the adult population with an account in a formal financial institution) is the lowest at 18 per cent, as compared with, for example, Sub-Saharan Africa (24 per cent), South Asia (33 per cent), Latin America (39 per cent), Europe and Central Asia (45 per cent), East Asia Pacific (55 per cent) and high-income countries in general (89 per cent).[3]

Although one explanation may be the level of development of some of the countries with lower percentages of bank account penetration, religion is one of the factors, according to the World Bank, that justifies the fact that many Muslim-headed households and micro, small and medium enterprises (MSMEs) may voluntarily exclude themselves from formal financial markets because Muslims believe that charging interest is forbidden (Mohseini-Cheraghlou, 2013).

---

3   Source: Global Fidex database. Retrieved on 15 January 2014 from http://econ.worldbank.org/ WBSITE/EXTERNAL/EXTDEC/EXTRESEARCH/EXTPROGRAMS/EXTFINRES/EXTGLOBALF IN/0,,contentMDK:23147627~pagePK:64168176~piPK:64168140~theSitePK:8519639,00.html.

Despite the voluntary exclusion from conventional finance of some wealthy members of the Muslim community, the majority of banks in Muslim countries are still conventional. The reason for this is historical, since although the traditional modes of Islamic finance have existed since the beginning of Islamic times, the financial industry in most Islamic countries originated in the 19th century, during the time of the European colonization and its commercial expansion. Thus the actual financial system in most of these countries is conventional similar to that of the Western world. However, since traditional times many Muslims have tried to live their financial lives according to Shariah principles and refuse to accept interest on deposits and refuse to finance things forbidden by Shariah such as pork or alcohol (Wilson, 1997).

The Islamic banking industry as a modern industry developed in the 1970s, (although some timid initiatives began in the 1950s and 1960s in Pakistan and Egypt). After 1973, triggered by the increase of wealth in the region due to soaring oil prices, the first major Islamic banks were created, and these included the Dubai Islamic Bank, which was established in 1975. Saeed Bin Ahmed Al-Lootah (Saaed Al-Lootah) founded the bank because of his belief in developing an economy without usury and speculation (de Anca, 2010).

According to Al-Lootah, 'In Islam, profits are only acceptable if they either come from work or from ideas – anything else should not be rewarded. This is why interest and all speculative practices are forbidden in Islam.' Therefore, an Islamic bank becomes either an agent or a partner in any commercial transaction (de Anca, 2012, pp. 100–101).

Now in his nineties, Al-Lootah has gone back to the simplicity of life in the desert. He remembers his youth at sea; where he spent four to six months a year searching for pearls with his father, Husain Ibn Naser Al-Lootah, who was a merchant and a poet. Then, in 1956, taking advantage of the opportunities offered by the new oil wealth in his country, he established the first construction company in Dubai, which soon became one of the UAE's most important holdings. After founding the first Islamic bank, he also founded in the 1980s and 1990s a number of Islamic foundations and training and educational centres. He firmly advocates for the need to heal the most urgent problems of society through the true application of Islamic economics and finance (de Anca, 2012, p. 101).

Islamic finance is a mode of finance based on Shariah principles. In essence, the Muslim believer's view of economics is based on man's obligation to organize his affairs in accordance with the will of God. Shariah is not against making money, but it emphasizes ethical arguments and economic justice as more important than the non-ethical profit return in the economic process. Islam recognizes private property as well as the legitimate profit resulting from economic transactions. Capital as well as labour and land are considered as constituent elements of the economic process, and as such it is legitimate for capital to obtain a profit as long as it is a justifiable reward, the goal being not equality but the avoidance of gross inequality (de Anca, 2010).

In Islam, money has no intrinsic utility but is seen as only a medium of exchange. Each unit of money is 100 per cent equal to another unit of the same denomination, and therefore there is no room for making profit through the exchange of these units *inter se* (for example, between or among themselves). Profit is generated when something having intrinsic utility is sold for money or when different currencies are exchanged.

The Shariah financial system is based on investment, and thus their ideal instruments of financing in Shariah are based on profit-sharing arrangements Musharaka and Mudarabah.[4] When a financier contributes money on the basis of these two instruments, it is bound to be converted into assets having intrinsic utility. However, Islam recognizes that in addition to investment, financing a loan is a basic need in any financial system, and thus financing a mortgage or the State Public Debt cannot be adjusted into a profit-sharing mechanism. Therefore, the Islamic financial system does accept that debt is necessary, although debt should be used for concrete consumption purposes and not for any non–productive speculation (Voguel, 2010).

Due to the prohibition of interest taking (Riba) in Islamic financial instruments, the financing condition is structured in such a way that the provider of capital still obtains some profit without interest taking. The most current structures are Murabaha, Salam, Istisna or Ijara.[5]

---

4   *Mudarabah:* A contract by which the money holder invests capital, while the receiver invests labour (or management) in a common project. The result coming from operation is then split between parties according to the pre-agreed arrangement.
      Musharaka: A contract that slightly differs from the Mudarabah system, by which the two entities (the money holder and the receiver) jointly contribute resources to a common project and the result of the operation are split according to a pre-determined agreement.

5   *Murabaha:* A contract by which the receiver pays for the goods or services to the capital holder with a mark-up profit.
      Salam: A contract by which the money holder pays at the spot where the delivery of the goods will occur at a future date.
      Istisna: A contract similar to the Salam, but which is normally applied to manufacturing.
      Ijara: A contract in which the money holder leases the asset to the client.

These instruments form the contract base on which the modern Islamic financial institutions are built. Today, 716 institutions in more than 80 countries are Shariah compliant, including 511 institutions that only provide financial products and 205 conventional institutions that offer financial products through Islamic Windows (The Banker, 2012). In the majority of countries – with some exceptions such as Iran, which has Islamized its financial system entirely – Islamic banks operate beside conventional banks, allowing customers to choose a conventional or Islamic financial institution to cover their financial needs, as is the case in the UAE.

Saeed–Lootah's bank, the Dubai Islamic Bank, was one of the world's pioneers in modern Islamic banking, and in his country, the UAE, it was the only Islamic bank until the incorporation of the Abu Dhabi Islamic Bank in 1997. Since 2000, new Islamic banks have been created in the UAE through conversion from conventional to Islamic or through incorporation of new banks. In 2010 there were a total of eight Islamic banks in the UAE, representing 15.8 per cent of total loans and advances of the banking system (USD 43.3 billion). It should be noted that the UAE banking system is made up of 53 banks, including 23 national banks, 22 foreign banks, and six banks from the Gulf regions.[6]

WOMEN IN THE ISLAMIC BANKING INDUSTRY: THE CASE OF UAE

The Middle East is a region that is experiencing significant challenges with respect to women's equality. The World Economic Forum (WEF) Global Gender Gap report, which monitors the inequality gap between women and men, reports that the region scored the lowest in 2013 with 59 per cent (100 per cent would mean total equality). This score compares with Sub-Saharan Africa (66 per cent), Asia Pacific (67 per cent), Europe and Central Asia (67 per cent). North America scored the highest at 74 per cent (Global Gender Gap Report, 2013).

However, the report also signals improvement and achievements, particularly in the area of women's education, with countries such as the UAE, Qatar, Bahrain, Kuwait, Algeria, Oman, Israel, Jordan, Lebanon and Saudi Arabia, having enrolment rates for women in tertiary education even higher than those for men. In addition to education, the region is the financial untapped resource in the high-net-worth feminine segment. Some figures can give us a picture of the potential of Gulf women for the financial industry, both as clients and employees.

---

6   UAE Central Bank. Retrieved on 15 January 2014 from www.centralbank.ae.

- 15,000 businesses in Saudi Arabia are in women's hands (4 per cent), with a total value of USD10,000 million (Bakhurji, 2003).

- Seventy per cent of total bank deposits in Saudi Arabia are in women's hands (The Economist Intelligence Unit, 2000, p. 4).

- In Bahrain, 1,491 women hold top-level positions in banks and accounting firms (Al-Khalifa, 2003).

Particularly in the UAE, women have achieved remarkable status in the political and economic spheres. Women occupy 18 per cent of the UAE cabinet seats and hold more than 22 per cent of the seats in the Federal National Council. Women constitute 10 per cent of the members of the diplomatic corps, and 30 per cent occupy decision-making leadership positions, and 66 per cent hold jobs in the government sector. The number of businesswomen in the UAE exceeds 11,000 with an estimated net worth of over USD 14 billon Dirham. Businesswomen in the UAE manage about 14 per cent of the local investments and own 33 per cent of the vital projects in the country. As for penetration in the banking industry, UAE women own about 25 per cent of the private wealth in the country, including approximately 30 per cent of bank deposits, with a total volume of savings of USD 100 billion (Iliasu and De Anca, 2011).

The current Minister of Foreign Trade, Sheikha Lubna al Qassimi has represented for years a role model for other businesswomen, and she has helped to remove existing career barriers for UAE women. She often encourages women to find the inner strength to fulfil their dreams and overcome their inner reluctance to pursue professional careers.[7]

As the number of businesswomen grows in the UAE, and the wealth of women is increasingly untapped by traditional saving schemes, the financial sector offers great potential for women, in both its conventional and Islamic forms. Women in the UAE work in mixed banking branches and women-only sections in both conventional and Islamic Banks. Women-only banking is now a regular practice in banks in the UAE, particularly in the Islamic banking sector, but also increasingly in conventional commercial banks (Iliasu and de Anca, 2011).

---

7   'Leveling the Playing Field, Upgrading the Wealth Management Experience for Women'. Boston Consulting Group, 2010. See also key points about women in the UAE (United Arab Emirates Ministry of Foreign Trade. www.moft.gov.ae).

The majority of Islamic banks operate with women-only sections. Some Islamic banks have given the women's section separate names. Examples include Johara in the Dubai Islamic Bank, DANA in the Abu Dhabi Islamic Bank, Al Reem in the Emirates Islamic Bank and Amirah in the Dubai Bank. The founder of the first Islamic bank in the UAE, Saeed-Lootha, explains that women have a relevant place in banking as workers as well as clients (de Anca, 2012, pp. 101–2):

> *There is no difference between the role of women and the role of men in Islamic economics, finance and … banking. In fact, I would love to see a bank totally managed by women to prove that there is no difference in their minds and to challenge those who do not believe it. From the very beginning, when we founded the first Islamic bank in 1975, we opened a section for women clients, run by women employees, separated from men and fulfilling the Islamic precepts – separate but not different.*

The UAE offers both conventional and Islamic financial services, a fact that gives some Muslim women a choice to work in an industry that might feel close to their religious values. Looking further at the opportunity of women to choose Islamic banks both as clients and as workers was the motivation behind a recent case study this author developed with Fatimah Iliasu of the women's section of the Abu Dhabi Islamic Bank, DANA (Iliasu and de Anca, 2011).

The Abu Dhabi Islamic Bank (ADIB) was established in May 1997, was listed on the Abu Dhabi Stock Exchange in November 2000 and has a presence in the UAE, Egypt, Iraq and Bosnia-Herzegovina. As a leading firm in the banking in the UAE, ADIB was given the Best Islamic Bank award in 2010 at the Banker Middle East Industry Awards. In 2011, ADIB had 1,568 employees, 576 of which are women, and as of April 2011 the total number of ADIB/DANA female customers was 162,610. In 2011, ADIB had a total of 60 branches, 23 of which were women-only branches. For many of the employees, living according to their Islamic values was an important incentive to work for DANA. As mentioned Salha Omer, DANA Bateen Branch Manager says (Iliasu and de Anca, 2011, p. 2):

> *Muslim women are often perceived wrongly. DANA illustrates that Muslim women can be anything they want to be, that they can work, can become directors, or anything they want, and show that they can be equal at work with men.*

Rula Atallah, ADIB Vice President of Central Operations, says (Iliasu and de Anca, 2011, p. 6):

> I had always dreamed of working in an Islamic bank. I had finalized my familial obligations at the time and could afford a lower income that would allow me to learn about Islamic banking and fulfil my professional dreams.' Being the only woman in a senior position, she is a role model for others. 'Now there are four female members in the management team, and increasingly our participation in the bank is widely recognized.

For some employees, working in an Islamic Bank in its women's division facilitates the possibility of working outside the home. Alia Ahmed Alali, Relationship Manager with ADIB DANA Priority Banking, states (Iliasu and de Anca, 2011, p. 6):

> I feel I am in an Islamic environment by working in a women-only division. I had offers from other banks with higher salaries, but I refused to accept those offers because doing so would have meant that I would not be able to send a part of my salary to my mother as I do now. She would refuse to accept it because if I worked in a conventional bank my income would not be lawful. I feel proud that I can help my mother, and she is proud that I am working in ADIB since in Islam we believe it is good for women to work because it helps strengthen the character.

Operating through separate women windows is also the reason why some clients prefer to work with them. According to Futoon Riyad Al Masri, an ADIB DANA high-net-worth client DANA (Iliasu and de Anca, 2011, p. 6), 'The reason I chose a women-only bank is that due to my beliefs I prefer to be in a women only environment separated from men. I also bank with ADIB because it is an Islamic bank.'

In addition, some clients feel confident enough to ask about financial matters, knowing that it is an Islamic bank and that any queries will be reviewed by the Islamic Board to assure performance correctly in an Islamic Manner. Sheikha Al Qubaisi, another Relationship Manager for ADIB DANA Priority Banking, says (Iliasu and de Anca, 2011, p. 9):

> Our customers feel they can trust us not only to take care of their finances but also to make sure that they practice their religious beliefs in their financial life. For example, by using our Islamic-covered cards, customers

feel they are adhering to Islamic principles and thus are protecting their families from Riba (interest)-based financing. They know that anything financed by ADIB is according to Islamic principles. For instance, customers feel it is safe to have a covered card account because it will not work in places where alcohol or pornography are sold.

Product Innovation

Both employees and clients feel they are a part of the women's Muslim community, and working in such an environment, whether in the supply or demand side, allows the creation of products tailored to the clients' needs. Thus, product innovation at ADIB arises naturally. An interesting innovation in the case of DANA was the Banun account. Banun is a special savings account for children which allows divorced women to open a savings account for their children without requiring the signature of the father of the children. The story of how this product was developed illustrates how community finance operates. Nawal Bayari, Vice President and Business Head, Women's Banking at ADIB, led a team that conducted focus groups and research to understand what improvements could be made in the women's banking segment of ADIB. In these different groups some new services were introduced, among which was the possibility of having a product such as the Banun account.

Women employees have for some time realized the need of their clients, particularly their divorced clients, to open accounts in the name of their children without the signature of their husbands, as required by the law. Once the need was acknowledged, the managers consulted with the Shariah division, which asked the Shariah Board for advice, and after some discussions they agreed to create a special product called Banun. Banun, which is only offered at DANA in the UAE, is a first example but others can follows, in the belief of clients and managers in new Shariah-compliant products and services targeted specifically to meet the needs of women.

Conclusions

This chapter first attempted to demystify two general assumptions regarding Muslim women and finances. The first was the common belief that women are not the main actors in the financial industry, and the second was the stereotype that Muslim women, regardless of their wealth, do not have a personal say in financial matters.

Once these two common beliefs were clarified, the chapter illustrated how values and business can work hand in hand. Community identification and belonging is one of the most crucial elements for today's business success. Religious identity is emerging as a key personal characteristic with relevance for business and organizations.

In the case of Muslim women working in a Muslim Bank, the religious identity has relevance in the different roles, of women as employees, of women as investors (depositors) as well as women as credit demanders.

Being women employees in a women-only Islamic bank makes them feel that they can pursue a career and at the same time be close to their traditions and values. Clients, on the other hand, feel they can mobilize their savings and fulfil their financial needs according to their religion values. As a result, a close, value-based community is created that grows in terms of human relations, which in turn makes them grow in a business sense as well, as illustrated in Figure 10.1.

Women leaders in the financial industry can transform the landscape for women in terms of investment through product innovation to match client's investments to client's capital demands.

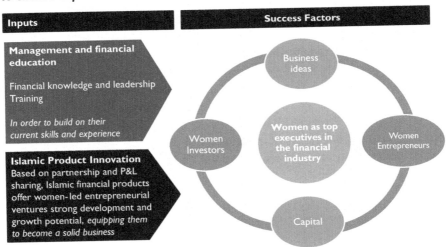

Figure 10.1   Women in Islamic finance

As investors, women can choose to deposit their savings in Islamic banks, since they feel the financial saving schemes offered relate closely with their religious beliefs.

As employees, women might choose a career in Islamic finance without having to break with their traditions and beliefs.

As entrepreneurs, women in the Middle East are increasingly starting their own companies, and Islamic contracts such as *musharaka* and *mudaraba* can offer great potential for business development.

A community of Muslim women working in Islamic banks to service a group of Muslim women clients offer a very good example of community finance, understood as a form of cash-flow that channels the financial resources of the savers of a community into the well-being of that community via economic activities, which members of the community believe should be undertaken and therefore willingly supports with their savings (De Anca, 2013). The community bonding, provided in this case for the religious identity, combined with sophisticate IT technologies, is key to understand business practices in the years to come.

References

ACCA Position Paper (2009). Equality: Women in Financial Services: The Association of Chartered Certified Accountants, (ACCA). September, p, 11. Retrieved from www.accaglobal.com.

Al-Khalifa, Y. (2003). 'Challenges and Business Opportunities in the Global Economy: The Business Women in the Kingdom of Bahrain'. Unpublished communication given at the conference, *Arab Women in the XXI Century: A Business Opportunity.* IE Business School Madrid, 30 June–1 July.

Austen, J. (1811) *Sense and Sensibility,* Thomas Egerton, Whitehall, London.

Bakhurji, N.H. (2003). 'The Challenges and Business Opportunities of Women in the Gulf Region, with Special Enphasis on Saudi Arabia'. Unpublished communication given at the conference, *Arab Women in the XXI Century: A Business Opportunity.* IE Business School Madrid, 30 June–1 July.

Bhagat, R. (2003). Where the Male Continues to Rule. *The Hindu Business Line,* December 29, Retrieved from http://www.thehindubusinessline.in/life/2003/12/29/stories/2003122900160400.htm.

Chouldhury, A. and Martinuzzi, E. (2013). Executive Women. *Financial Post* 3 October 2013. Retrieved from http://business.financialpost.com/2013/10/03/

credit-suisses-most-senior-female-investment-banker-says-it-will-be-years-before-women-make-up-a-greater-share-of-senior-positions-in-banking/.

de Anca, C. (2004). Mujer Arabe y empresa: Tradición y modernidad. In Vidal, F. (ed.) *La Deuda Olvidada De Occidente. Aportaciones del Islam a la Civilización Occidental.* Fundación Ramón Areces, Madrid, pp. 291–308.

de Anca, Celia. (2010). Investing with values: Ethical investment vs. Islamic Investment. In Fahim Khan, M. and Porzio, M. (eds) *Islamic Banking and Finance in the European Union.* Edward Elgar Publishing Limited, Cheltenham.

de Anca, C. (2012). *Beyond Tribalism, Managing Identities in a Diverse World.* Palgrave Macmillan, London.

de Anca, C. (2013). The End of Banks as We Know Them? *Harvard Business Review*, blog HBR.org. Retrieved from http://blogs.hbr.org/2013/09/the-end-of-banks-as-we-know-th/.

de Anca, C. and Vázquez, A. (2007). *Managing Diversity in the Global Organization.* London, Palgrave Macmillan.

European Central Bank (ECB) (2013). 'Islamic Finance in Europe', European Central Bank, Occasional paper series, no.146, June.

Forte Consultancy (2012). The Under Tapped Banking Consumer Segment of the World; Ladies. Retrieved from http://forteconsultancy.wordpress.com/2010/08/12/the-under-tapped-banking-consumer-segments-of-the-world-percentE2percent80percent93-ladies/.

Global Financial Inclusion (Global Findex) Database, World Bank. Retrieved on January 15, 2014 from http://go.worldbank.org/1F2V9ZK8C0.

Global Gender Gap Report (GGGR) (2013). World Economic Forum. Retrieved from http://www.weforum.org/issues/global-gender-gap.

Iliasu, F and De Anca, C. (2011). Dana: In the Footsteps of Khadija al-Kubra. *IE Case Study* DF1- 185-I. IE Business Publishing Madrid.

Lings, M. (1989). *Muhammad: su vida basada en las Fuentes más antiguas.* Hiperón, Madrid.

Marin, M. (2000). *Mujeres en al-Andalus. C.S.I.C*, Madrid.

Mohseini, C. (2013). Islamic Finance and Financial Inclusion: A Case for Poverty Reduction in the Middle East and North Africa. Retrieved from http://menablog.worldbank.org/islamic-finance-and-poverty-reduction.

Molinero, C. (1998). Mujer, franquismo, fascismo. La clausura forzada en un 'mundo pequeño', *Historia Social*, 30: 97–117.

Stock, K. (2010). Number of Women in US Finance Shrinks. *The Wall Street Journal*, September 21. Retrieved from http://online.wsj.com/news/articles/SB40001424052748704858304575498071732136704.

Sweetser, S. (2004). 'Women in Financial Services – An Ideal Match'. National Underwriter/Life & Health Financial Services, 108(2): 14.

The Banker (2012). Top Islamic Financial Institutions Ranking. Retrieved from www.thebanker.com.

The Economist Intelligence Unit. 2000. Business Middle East. p. 4.

Voguel, F. (2010) 'E. Islamic Finance: Personal and Enterprise Banking'. In En Fahim Khan, M. and Porzio, M. (eds) *Islamic Banking and Finance in the European Union*. Edward Elgar Publishing Limited, Cheltenham.

Wilson, R. (1997). *Islamic Finance*. Financial Times Financial Publishing, London.

Chapter 11

Management of Religious Diversity by Organizations in India

RADHA R. SHARMA AND RUPALI PARDASANI

Introduction

The word 'religion' has its origin in a Latin word 'ligare' implying to join or to link (Hinnells, 1997) which is used for people to connect with the powers that control their destiny (Johnson, 1997). Religion, as a subject, focuses on the search for the sacred within formal institutions (Hill et al., 2000; Roof, 2003). Although it is defined as an institutional construct, beliefs in one's own religion may be so deep rooted that it may make one intolerant of other religions (Harris, 2004). Just as all societies have their unique language, they have a unique religion as well (Bloom, 2007). An individual does not inherit religion but learns through social interactions and develops through the influence of culture in which one lives (Bloom, 2007). In all societies, religion is considered to be pertaining to an organized system of beliefs with common behaviours and rituals, endorsed by a group, making it more extrinsic and institutionalized (Hodder, 2007; Pargament, 1997). The discussions on religion and its effects have entered the modern business organizations (Cash et al., 2000). Management scholars and practitioners are evincing considerable interest in understanding the influence of religion in the workplace and on its members as religious diversity has been increasing in business organizations. The concern is timely due to rapid metamorphosis in the form of economic liberalization, increasing foreign investment, mergers and acquisitions, globalization, increasing number of expatriates, influx of multinationals in various countries affecting people and business performance.

This chapter introduces the concept of religious diversity in the workplace and discusses strategies for religious tolerance and implications for HR professionals for enabling people to practice their religion/faith. Section one introduces the concept of religious diversity in workplaces in India; followed by section two on strategies adopted by the organizations to manage religious diversity at the Indian workplaces. Section three throws light on external factors which have contributed to religious tolerance in the workplace and the final section provides implications for organizations and HR professionals.

THE CONTEXT: RELIGIOUS DIVERSITY IN INDIA

India is the birthplace of several world religions including Hinduism, Buddhism, Jainism and Sikhism and home, for thousands of years, to Jewish, Zoroastrian, Muslim and Christian communities (Rao, 2012). Though the Government of India does not promote any particular religion, religion has all along occupied a central place in the country. India has experienced both religious conflicts and assimilation of various religions that came with traders, invaders and settlers such as the Aryans, Greeks, Mongols, Arabs, Persians, Mughals and the Europeans during different periods of its history (Rao, 2012). Considering India's long history and multiplicity of religions and religious practices, this chapter does not provide scope for detailed coverage of religious diversity in India, however, the following paragraph presents a glimpse of its religious diversity.

India is a Sovereign Socialist Secular republic and the Constitution of India protects the religious freedom for all the citizens of the country through various articles: 'Article 15 of the constitution prohibits discrimination on grounds of religion. Article 16 provides equal opportunity for employment to all the citizens of India irrespective of the religion one follows and Article 25 provides its citizen the freedom to practice and propagate any religion' (The Constitution of India). According to the 2001 Indian census, Hindus are 80.5 per cent of the total population, whereas Muslims, Christians and Sikhs constitute 13.4 per cent, 2.3 per cent and 1.9 per cent respectively. Buddhists, Janis, Zoroastrians, Jews and Bahais constitute less than 1 per cent of the population each (India International Religious Freedom Report, 2012). Considering the magnitude of religious diversity in India, one can presume that the similar trend will be observed in workplaces too.

RELIGIOUS DIVERSITY IN THE WORKPLACE

Diversity has been defined as the 'set of conscious practices that involve understanding and appreciating interdependence of humanity, cultures and the natural environment; practising mutual respect for qualities and experiences that are different from our own' (Patrick and Kumar, 2012). People may experience diversity along various demographic and ideological dimensions such as gender, race, socio-economic status, religious beliefs, political beliefs and so on. In fact the concept of diversity is based on the principle of accepting, respecting and embracing these differences.

The term 'workplace diversity' originated in the US; but with the changing work environment it is becoming a workplace reality across the globe. The term broadly refers to the dissimilarity among the members of an organization in one or more attributes (Harrison and Klein, 2007; Williams and O'Reilly, 1998). Increasing globalization, advancements in technology, changing lifestyle and multinational collaborative work environment are widening the parameters of diversity in the workplace.

The much ignored parameter of religion, often considered as a controversial issue, is now emerging as an important parameter of classification of the workforce into different groups. While some countries have accepted religion at the workplace as a legal mandate; a few have considered religion to be relevant and influential factor in the workplace. A study by Rao (2012) on Indian managers reveals that 100 per cent of the sample felt that religion had an impact on the workplace. Over the last few decades, it is not uncommon to find people freely expressing their views about religion and looking for accommodation of their religious belief in the workplace (Morgan, 2004; Lips-Wiersma and Mills, 2002; Miller, 2007). This has posed a set of challenges for the employers who do not keep track of religious affiliations of their employees and some employers are not willing to openly discuss this sensitive issue (Rao, 2012). Research suggests that accommodation of employee's religious expression in the organization has a positive and significant impact on employee's job satisfaction (King and Williamson, 2005). From this perspective it would be important to allow religious expression at the workplace; but it appears that due to preconceived notions management literature has largely ignored this dimension of diversity. A study by Pitts and Wise (2010), indicates that during 2001–8 only four articles have addressed religion in the workplace. King (2008) has described research dealing with aspects of religion in workplace as 'light, sporadic, and mostly outside the mainstream of the field; lacking in theoretical grounding; and not programmatic in nature' (p. 215).

TOLERANCE OF RELIGIOUS DIVERSITY IN THE WORKPLACE

Organizations, in recent years, have been striving to manage a variety of diversity including religious diversity through diversity management programmes, training and workshops (Ellis, 1994). The purpose behind this is to help the employees appreciate, accept and respect the differences that may exist among a group of employees and not shared by everyone in the organization. Such initiatives aim at helping individuals protect their sense of self and at the same time accept characteristics/attributes different from theirs (King and Williamson, 2005). Also, employees are educated to refrain from having prejudice against the differences and to accept the diverse work environment. Management of diversity of all kinds requires time, energy and effort on the part of HR professionals, organizational leaders and top management teams (Jayne and Dipboye, 2004). It is essential to maintain a positive work environment free from biases against dissimilar groups so that all the employees can contribute to achieving the organization's goals effectively. With increasing religious diversity, it is imperative to reinforce and strengthen the value of tolerance. The following section presents strategies adopted by organizations in India to accommodate and manage religious diversity in the workplace.

Strategies for Managing Religious Diversity in India

EQUAL EMPLOYMENT OPPORTUNITY

Equal employment opportunity is rooted in the Indian constitutional provisions. The Article 16 of the Constitution of India, 1949 envisages 'Equality of opportunity in matters of public employment'. The law clearly prohibits discrimination based on any kind of religious ground. This provision in law creates a legal mandate for the employers and the organizations. For example, Aon Hewitt, India prohibits any discrimination based on one's religion and ensures that 'equal opportunity is given to all qualified individuals in terms of recruitment, hiring, training and development, promotion, compensation practices and other employment opportunities'.[1] Godrej Group, India, positions itself as 'Equal Opportunities Employer' and has explicitly articulated in its code of ethics and business conduct policy that 'the Company shall provide equal opportunities to all its employees and all qualified applicants for employment without regard to their race, caste, religion, colour, ancestry, marital status, gender, sexual orientation, age, nationality, ethnic origin or disability'.[2]

---

1   Retrieved on 8 January 2014 from http://www.aonhewittcareers.com/eeoc.html.
2   Retrieved on 8 January 2014 from http://www.godrejandboyce.com/godrej/godrejandboyce/pdf/CodeofEthics.pdf.

HOLIDAYS ON ALL MAJOR FESTIVALS OF ALL THE MAJOR RELIGIONS

The first Prime Minister of India, Pandit Jawahar Lal Nehru, described India as the land of multiple cultures and religions where all Indians celebrate festivals of different religions without any discrimination (Nehru, 2004). India, a melting pot for diverse religions, observes various festivals. In order to accommodate all the religions in the workplace, Indian organizations gather knowledge of diverse religions and their beliefs. One way to do so is to design policies for holidays and celebrations. To raise cultural awareness among the employees, many organizations accommodate diversity by celebrating festivals of different religions. For example, at Apollo Munich Insurance the HR department even communicates greetings with the details of the festival (its origin, why and how it is celebrated) and its significance to all the employees and professional contacts. Such initiatives enhance inclusion efforts of the organization for managing religious diversity in the workplace. Idea Cellular, a telecom brand in India, promoted the spirit of celebrations and togetherness through series of advertisements on television – 'it is a good idea to celebrate all festivals, no matter what faith one may follow'.[3] It is important to understand the diverse religious beliefs from a business perspective as well. To facilitate this, important meetings and work-related deadlines are avoided during festival season, marketing departments position their products in the market during the season, for example, Cadbury targets their products on major Indian festivals such as Diwali (festival of lights) and RakshaBandhan (a festival of love between brother and sister).[4]

ACCEPTANCE OF RELIGIOUS DRESSING

Wearing religious symbols is an important expression of an individual's religious belief and defines one's religious identity. This characterizes their faith and loyalty to a particular religion and thus demonstrates their avouchment to a particular religion (Dolgin, 1987). To find people freely wearing such religious accessories or dresses is not uncommon at workplaces and is a clear indication of symbol of diversity at workplace (Cash and Gray, 2000). In Indian settings, this form of diversity of symbols, artefacts and dresses can be observed at many workplaces. Sikhs in the workplace are usually found wearing turbans, many married Hindu women wear Sindoor (vermilion) and Mangalsutra (necklace with black beads); Christians wear the cross, among others. Firms accept and

---

3   Retrieved on 8 January 2014 from http://www.ideacellular.com/wps/wcm/connect/foryou/
idea/cellular_news/An%20Idea%20to%20celebrate%20all%20festivals.
4   Retrieved on 8 January 2014 from http://www.cadburyindia.com/in/en/brands/chocolate/
pages/cadburycelebrations.aspx.

allow employees to freely exhibit their religious artefacts which foster religious diversity. In fact, organizations are even relaxing the employer dress code to accommodate religious dressing. At Deloitte, there are employees from diverse religions and it is not uncommon to find people dressed in their religious outfits such as the hijab (veil) for women and kippah for men.[5]

DISPLAY OF RELIGIOUS MATERIALS IN THE WORKPLACE

Workplaces in India are melting pots of religious diversity. Individuals from different religions can freely keep religious symbols and materials with them at their workplace especially in one's office or cubical (Rao, 2012). It is very common for even an outsider to observe different people keeping different artefacts of their specific religion in their personal space. Employees keep idols, pictures of god and goddesses in the form of calendars, desktop screen savers and the like, and organizations also accommodate the desire of employees for religious decoration. An excellent example of accommodating all major religions under one roof is that of Narayana Hriduyalaya (a heart hospital in Bangalore, India) where people pray for the early recovery of their near and dear ones. At its entrance it has a place of worship which has four sides. 'One side has a Hindu temple, the other is a Christian prayer-room, the third a mosque and the fourth, a Sikh Gurudwara, all separated by common walls'.[6] Family members and friends of patients are seen praying together in their respective places of worship oblivious of their religious differences.

RELIGIOUS OBSERVANCE

Indian organizations encourage employees to strike a balance between their work and personal life. Some religions require its members to observe religious prayers at specific hours of the day. This may directly contrast with the working hours of an employee. But organizations in India are mostly found to accommodate religious observance requested by employees of different religions. This is achieved through providing flexible scheduling, allowing swapping of shifts, personal days off, compressed work weeks and other scheduling arrangements (Cash et al., 2000). For instance, IBM takes a number of initiatives to help employees achieve work–life balance. It provides flexibility and control in terms of working schedule to its employees to meet

---

5   Retrieved on 8 January 2014 from http://managementconsulted.com/consulting-firm-profiles/10-reasons-to-work-for-deloitte-consulting-and-6-reasons-not-to/.
6   Retrieved on 10 January 2014 from http://www.daijiworld.com/chan/exclusive_arch.asp?ex_id=214.

the needs of their personal life.[7] Also, employers are granted paid religious holidays; such arrangements provide flexibility to the employees for practising their religion/faith. Organizations in India have been explicitly articulating policies regarding religious holidays and time off. For example, allowing a Muslim employee who is required to attend Friday prayers may compensate for that time on other weekdays. Organizations cater to the needs of employees of a specific religion also by creating space for prayers in their premises and making it a part of the physical architecture of the company (Henle and Hogler, 2004). Allowing members of the organization to use organizational facilities for prayers and meditation is a recent trend adopted by firms like KPMG who provide facilities to its employees to 'engage in prayer and quiet contemplation during the working day and cultural/religious leave'.[8]

AVAILABILITY OF DIVERSE FOOD IN THE CAFETERIA

Employees following diverse religions may be sensitive to their dietary requirements in terms of what their religion allows or does not allow. Since employees spend most of their time in the organizational premises, organizations need to be attentive to the dietary restrictions of the diverse religious groups. This is accommodated by providing diverse menus in the cafeteria. Special attention is given to the dietary needs in official events or functions as well. Many organizations in India offer both vegetarian and non-vegetarian menus during lunch hours and some organizations offer a South Indian breakfast on the menu to cater to employees belonging to a specific region of the country.

TRAINING EMPLOYEES ABOUT DIVERSE RELIGIONS

Workplaces are embracing religious differences in the organization by generating awareness through training. The trend is towards building a culture of inclusion where all the employees feel valued and a part of the group. IBM offers a variety of learning in the field of diversity in the form of online courses, lectures and learning labs. Some of the areas are 'Diversity and Inclusive Leadership, Culture and Business, Culture and Globalization, Culture Shock: Working Internationally, Going Global, Networking, People with Disabilities, Remote and Mobile Management and Sexual Harassment and Valuing Diversity'.[9]

---

7 Retrieved on 10 January 2014 from https://www-07.ibm.com/in/isl/diversity/diversity_wfb.html.
8 Retrieved on 10 January 2014 from http://www.kpmg.com/au/en/about/diversity/pages/religion-and-ethnicity.aspx.
9 Retrieved on 10 January 2014 from http://www-07.ibm.com/in/isl/diversity/diversity_caa.html.

Factors Contributing to Religious Tolerance

The section above presented some of the internal strategies adopted by organizations and employers for managing religious diversity in the workplace. Besides, various societal and external factors contribute to promoting religious tolerance by the people in the society. These factors have directly or indirectly helped in changing the mindset and attitude of the society towards various religions. Some of these are elaborated below:

CONSTITUTIONAL PROVISIONS

As mentioned earlier, the Constitution of India provides freedom to practice one's own religion and promotes tolerance for diverse religions. The word 'secular' did not first appear in the Preamble of the Constitution, however, in view of its importance the Preamble was amended by the *42nd Constitution Amendment Act* of 1976. Since then 'India is a sovereign, socialist, secular, democratic republic'. The organizations operating in India are required to abide by the law of the land and thus cannot discriminate employees on the grounds of caste, colour, creed, religion or gender.

INFLUX OF MULTINATIONALS

The entry of multinationals in India has changed the composition of the workforce in terms of ethnicity, language, age, gender and other parameters. The multinational companies observe a variety of diversity in India and leverage these with the globally diverse workforce. These firms not only accommodate the religious beliefs of their employees, but also promote a secular culture. The secular culture promotes respect and tolerance for each other and prevents discrimination of any kind. Also, these multinationals bind the people together through the goals and objectives of the company which are shared with the employees in terms of the vision and mission of the organization. Thus all the people work in an organization for the common goal and are united to achieve a common goal. The increase in multinational firms and the culture they promote has affected the lifestyle and mindset of people (Hofstede, 1994). Society as a whole has become more open to interacting and building relationships with people from other religions.

COMPANY POLICIES

Diversity management is no longer an optional activity for organizations in India. Most of the organizations realize that diversity is the reality of the day and hence needs to be addressed in an effective manner. The organizations in India are accounting for management of diversity in their policy documents such as business code of conduct or rule of ethics. Thus the concept of diversity management is positioned as a strategic issue. For example, the policy and guidelines document of ITC Ltd. includes Human Right Consideration, which prohibits the company to engage or support directly or indirectly any kind of discrimination based on religion, caste and so on in its Significant Investments Policy. The divisional chief executives/strategic business unit (SBU) head of the concerned businesses are custodians of this policy and ensure its implementation.[10] The report released by Deloitte Global Human Capital Trends (2014)[11] highlights that most of the participating organizations are promoting diversity, building inclusive workplaces, 'enabling them to transform diversity programs from a compliance obligation to a business strategy' (p. 83).

HUMAN RESOURCE DEPARTMENT INITIATIVES

The HR department has been at the forefront of Indian organizations when it comes to managing diversity in the workplace. Since diversity management is largely an issue of dealing with people in the organization, the HRM function can handle it effectively. Human resource management seeks to leverage diversity in the workplace and thus contributes to the business strategy. Along with the organizational focus, HRM formulates people-centric policies to ensure people's well-being and satisfaction (Truss et al., 1997). HRM uses a variety of tools in managing diversity in the workplace such as hiring, recruitment, selection, performance appraisal, career development, compensation and so on (Dobbs, 1996).

LEADERSHIP COMMITMENT

The leaders and the top management teams take initiatives to make organizations more tolerant of diverse religions. By addressing the issues of sensitivity towards different religions they influence people to accept differences in the organization. In this regard, they act as the change agents in the diversity management process (Cox, 1993; Morrison, 1992). Along with this role of catalyst, top leaders ensure that the organizational structure or policies

---

10 Retrieved on 23 June 2014 from http://www.itcportal.com/about-itc/policies/policy-on-human-rights.aspx.
11 Retrieved on 23 June 2014 from http://www.deloitte.com/assets/Dcom-Namibia/Global HumanCapitalTrends2014_030714.pdf.

do not promote discrimination on grounds of religion (Hicks, 2002). Also, top management teams and organizational leaders formulate strategies to leverage diversity in the workplace for building competitive advantage for the team and the whole firm (Kearney, Gebert and Voelpel, 2009).

GROWING CONCEPT OF SPIRITUALITY AT WORKPLACES

There has been a marked increase in theory and research on the influence of spirituality in the workplace (Mitroff and Denton, 1999). Today, employees in the workplace look beyond performance and efficiency. They are inclined towards deriving meaning in their life and work and subsequently transcendence of self (Kinjerski and Skrypnek, 2008). For this many Indians prefer to take the route of spirituality and adopt the principle of secular spirituality as advanced by Swami Vivekananda, a noted philosopher, reformer and a spiritual leader whose thoughts and work had considerable impact nationally and internationally. In the face of such quest for transcendence, humanity, values and interconnectedness are finding their way which, in turn, helps to bypass the differences in terms of religion among the people in the workplace.

EDUCATION

'Education' plays an important role in developing people who enable organizations to set their own culture of secularism. The promotion of secularism in textbooks and writings is changing the mindset of the people. It is helping them develop a broader outlook and value humanity, peace and harmony over discrimination and religious conflicts. The National Council for Educational Research and Training takes care of it while preparing the curriculum and textbooks for the school level which are the foundation years for developing religious tolerance.[12] Higher educational institutions, in particular business schools strongly promote religious tolerance and a secular outlook to work in a globalized world.

ROLE OF MEDIA

In recent years, audio-visual and social media have gained considerable importance. With the advent of information technology and satellite communication there are global telecasts. Besides print media, radio and television have penetrated the whole length and breadth of the country. In the knowledge era, media plays the role of disseminator of information, facilitator

---

12   Retrieved on 23 June 2014 from http://www.ncert.nic.in/departments/nie/depfe/Final.pdf.

of development and an agent of change, thus media is considered the fourth pillar of the State. Also, the entertainment industry promotes religious diversity through films, documentaries and programmes. Jodha Akbar, a historical film, shows marriage between a Muslim emperor and a Hindu princess and promotes interreligion tolerance; there are several modern films too on interreligion marriages. The celebrities of the entertainment industry propagate messages of intercaste and interreligion networks, marriages both in real and reel life, and portray a positive image in terms of religious oneness.

Discussion

It is with certainty that one can claim that diversity in the workplace has increased dramatically (Ragins and Gonzalez, 2003). Since organizations have become a melting pot for people from various nationalities, religions, age, gender and so on, diversity management is no longer a fad or management jargon adopted by a handful of organizations. Most organizations, consultants and practitioners are seeking ways and tools to manage and leverage diversity and build a diversity friendly climate in the organization. Religion, which was once thought to be outside the realm of business and the dynamics of workplace, has turned out to be a major source of diversity. With employees of different religions, languages, geographic origins, personal beliefs and ideologies, no organization can consider religion to be irrelevant for the business. To remain competitive, organizations need to integrate the diverse mix and align these with the common organizational goals.

Academically, diversity research is witnessing a paradigm shift in its conceptualization. At present diversity is viewed from a positive lens, a source of competitive edge and an opportunity as against the old paradigms of victimization and discrimination. The growing literature on the subject has examined the effect of religion in the workplace in a variety of ways (Kriger and Seng, 2005; Niles, 1999; Vinten, 2000). Research results show that religion plays an important role in the process of decision making (Kuzma et al., 2009; Vasconcelos, 2009) and suggest that religion is deeply connected with the work values of an individual. For example, religion has been found to be connected to work attitudes, motivation and satisfaction of a person (Harpaz, 1998). It also provides ethical and moral guidelines for the followers (Beekun, 1996) and provides societal norms and the importance of work goals in one's life (Harpaz, 1998).

Accommodating religious diversity can be beneficial to both the organization and its people. Research suggests that allowing the employee to express his/her religious identity at work is positively related to the outcomes such as increased organizational commitment, enhanced citizenship behaviours, reduced burnout and enhanced job satisfaction (Kutcher et al., 2010). Awareness and acceptance of different religions helps in creating better understanding between people in the organization and leads to better interpersonal relationships. The benefits extend to reduced turnover and attrition (Cox and Blake, 1991). Effective and strategic management of diversity may help the company to achieve competitive edge. Organizations are seeking ways to improve management of religious diversity as there are legal and societal mandates for companies to accommodate religious beliefs in the workplace (Cash and Gray, 2000) as well as the undeniable fact that religion and work are indeed interrelated (Harpaz, 1998).

Conclusions

India has emerged as a global player facing the challenge of diversity in the society. Indian society consists of people from different religions, languages, regions and cultures which are reflected in all its aspects including workplaces. Religion has played an important role in all the societies and will continue to shape the identity of the people in the world. Religion extends to the workplace settings and all efforts to separate the two will not prove to be beneficial as it deeply impacts an individual's values, attitudes and behaviours (Rao, 2012). Thus, it is imperative for the organizations in India to be mindful of these complex socio-cultural factors. The leaders and top management teams need to understand the nuances of this diversity and determine its impact on business and the employees.

One may not come across religion-based conflicts in the workplace that often in India (Rao, 2012); this is due to the acculturation process whereby Indians are taught not just to be tolerant of other religions but also to respect them. Swami Vivekananda, in his speech at the World's Parliament of Religions (1893) in Chicago, mentioned that 'he was proud to belong to a religion which had taught the world both tolerance and universal acceptance' (Ziolkowski, 1993). He further added that Hinduism not just tolerates and accepts other religions, but also considers all religions to be true (McRae, 1991). However, globally we do observe incidences of religious rivalries, differences, intolerance and conflicts that can gradually enter the workplace. The policy makers and HR professionals are required to proactively use the power of religious diversity to promote tolerance, create amity and synergy. This chapter is an endeavour to present how organizations in India manage and leverage religious diversity in the workplace for religious tolerance, greater understanding and respect for other religions and business growth symbolizing 'Unity in Diversity' as advocated by the Indian society.

References

Bassett-Jones, N. (2005). 'The Paradox of Diversity Management, Creativity and Innovation', *Creativity and Innovation Management*, 14 (2): 169–75.

Beekun, R.I. (1996). Islamic Business Ethics. IIIT Institute, Herndon, VA.

Bloom, P. (2007). 'Religion is Natural', *Developmental Science*, 10(1): 147–51.

Cash, K.C. and Gray, G.R. (2000). 'A Framework for Accommodating Religion and Spirituality in the Workplace', *The Academy of Management Executive*, 14(3): 124–33.

Cash, K.C., Grey, G.R. and Rood, S.A. (2000). 'A Framework for Accommodating Religion and Spirituality in the Workplace/Executive Commentary', *Academy of Management Executive*, 14(3): 124–34.

Childs Jr, J.T. (2005). 'Managing Workforce Diversity at IBM: A Global HR Topic That Has Arrived', *Human Resource Management*, 44(1): 73–7.

Cox, T. (1993). *Cultural Diversity in Organizations: Theory, Research and Practice*. San Francisco: Berrett-Koehler Store.

Cox, T.H. and Blake, S. (1991). 'Managing Cultural Diversity: Implications for Organizational Competitiveness', *The Executive*, 45–56.

Dobbs, M.F. (1996). 'Managing Diversity: Lessons from the Private Sector', *Public Personnel Management*, 25(3): 351–67.

Dolgin, J.L. (1987). 'Religious Symbols and the Establishment of a National Religion', *Mercer Law Review*, 39: 495.

Ellis, C. (1994). 'Diverse Approaches to Managing Diversity', *Human Resource Management*, 33(1): 79–109.

Harpaz, I. (1998). 'Cross–national Comparison of Religious Conviction and the Meaning of Work', *Cross–Cultural Research*, 32(2): 143–70.

Harris, S. (2004). *The End of Faith: Religion, Terror and the Future of Reason*. Norton, New York.

Harrison, D.A. and Klein, K.J. (2007). 'What's the Difference? Diversity Constructs as Separation, Variety, or Disparity in Organizations', *Academy of Management Review*, 32 (4): 1199–228.

Hicks, D.A. (2002). *Religion and the Workplace: Pluralism, Spirituality, Leadership*. Cambridge, Cambridge University Press.

Henle, C.A. and Hogler, R. (2004). 'The Duty of Accommodation and the Workplace Religious Freedom Act of 2003: From Bad Policy to Worse Law', *Labor Law Journal*, 55(3): 155–65.

Hill, P.C., Pargament, K.I., Hood, R.W., McCullough Jr, M.E., Swyers, J.P., Larson, D.B. and Zinnbauer, B.J. (2000). 'Conceptualizing Religion and Spirituality: Points of Commonality, Points of Departure', *Journal for the Theory of Social Behaviour*, 30(1): 51–77.

Hinnells, J.R. (1997). *A New Handbook of Living Religions*. Penguin, New York.

Hodder, J. (2007). 'Young People and Spirituality: The Need for a Spiritual Foundation for Australian Schooling', *International Journal of Children's Spirituality*, 12(2): 179–90.

Hofstede, G. (1994). 'The Business of International Business is Culture', *International Business Review*, 3(1): 1–14.

International Religious Freedom Report for 2012 (2012). United States Department of State Bureau of Democracy, Human Rights and Labor. Retrieved from http://www.state.gov/documents/organization/208640.pdf.

Jack, E. and Dobbin, F. (2005). 'How Affirmative Action became Diversity Management: Employer Response to Anti-discrimination Law, 1961–1996', *American Behavioral Scientist*, 41(7): 960–84.

Jayne, M.E. and Dipboye, R.L. (2004). 'Leveraging Diversity to Improve Business Performance: Research Findings and Recommendations for Organizations'. *Human Resource Management*, 43(4): 409–24.

Johnson, P.G. (1997). *God and World Religions: Basic Beliefs and Themes*. Ragged Edge Press, Shippensburg.

Kearney, E., Gebert, D. and Voelpel, S.C. (2009). 'When and How Diversity Benefits Teams: The Importance of Team Members' Need for Cognition', *Academy of Management Journal*, 52(3): 581–98.

King, J.E. (2008). '(Dis) Missing the Obvious Will Mainstream Management Research Ever Take Religion Seriously?' *Journal of Management Inquiry*, 17(3): 214–24.

King, J.E., and Williamson, I. (2005). 'Workplace Religious Expression, Religiosity and Job Satisfaction: Clarifying a Relationship', *Journal of Management, Spirituality and Religion*, 2: 173–98.

Kinjerski, V. & Skrypnek, B.J. (2008). 'The Promise of Spirit at Work: Increasing Job Satisfaction and Organizational Commitment and Reducing Turnover and Absenteeism in Long-term Care', *Journal of Gerontological Nursing*, 34(10): 17–25.

Kriger, M. and Seng, Y. (2005). 'Leadership with Inner Meaning: A Contingency Theory of Leadership Based on the Worldviews of Five Religions', *The Leadership Quarterly*, 16(5): 771–806.

Kutcher, E.J., Bragger, J.D., Rodriguez–Srednicki, O. and Masco, J.L. (2010). 'The Role of Religiosity in Stress, Job Attitudes, and Organizational Citizenship Behavior', *Journal of Business Ethics*, 95(2): 319–37.

Kuzma, A., Kuzma, A. and Kuzma, J. (2009). 'How Religion Has Embraced Marketing and the Implications for Business', *Journal of Management and Marketing Research*, 2: 1–10.

Lips-Wiersma M. and Mills C. (2002). 'Coming out of the Closet: Negotiating Spiritual Expression in the Workplace', *Journal of Managerial Psychology* 17(3): 183–202.

McRae, J.R. (1991). 'Oriental Verities on the American Frontier: The 1893 World's Parliament of Religions and the Thought of Masao Abe', *Buddhist–Christian Studies*, 11: 7–36.

Miller D.W. (2007). *God at Work: The History and Promise of the Faith at Work Movement*. Oxford University Press, Oxford.

Mitroff, I.I., and Denton, E.A. (1999). *A Spiritual Audit of Corporate America: A Hard Look at Spirituality, Religion, and Values in the Workplace* (Vol. 140). Jossey-Bass, San Francisco.

Morgan, J. (2004). 'How Should Business Respond to a More Religious Workplace?' *SAM Advanced Management Journal*, 69(4): 11–19.

Morrison, A.M. (1992). *The New Leaders: Guidelines on Leadership Diversity in America*. Jossey-Bass Management Series. Jossey-Bass, Inc., Publishers, San Francisco, CA.

Nehru, J. (2004). *The Discovery of India*. Penguin Books, India.

Niles, F.S. (1999). Toward a Cross-cultural Understanding of Work-related Beliefs', *Human Relations*, 52(7): 855–67.

Pargament, K.I. (1997). *The Psychology of Religion and Coping: Theory, Research, Practice*. Guilford Publications, New York.

Patrick, H.A. and Kumar, V.R. (2012). *Managing Workplace Diversity Issues and Challenges*. Sage Open, 2 (2).

Pitts, D.W. and Wise, L.R. (2010). 'Workforce Diversity in the New Millennium: Prospects for Research', *Review of Public Personnel Administration*, 30(1): 44–69.

Ragins, B.R. and Gonzalez, J.A. (2003). 'Understanding Diversity in Organizations: Getting a Grip on a Slippery Construct', *Organizational Behavior: The State of the Science*, 2: 125–64.

Rao, A. (2012). 'Managing Diversity: Impact of Religion in the Indian Workplace', *Journal of World Business*, 47(2): 232–9.

Richard, O.C. (2000). 'Racial Diversity, Business Strategy, and Firm Performance: A Resource-based View', *Academy of Management Journal*, 43(2): 164–77.

Roof, W.C. (2003). Religion and Spirituality. Handbook of the Sociology of Religion, in M. Dillon (ed.), *Handbook of the Sociology of Religion*, Cambridge University Press, Cambridge, 137–48.

Sharma, O.P. and Haub, C. (2009). Change Comes Slowly for Religious Diversity in India. Population Reference Bureau. Retrieved from http://www.prb.org/Publications/Articles/2009/indiareligions.aspx.

The Constitution of India, Government of India Ministry of Law and Justice. Retrieved from http://lawmin.nic.in/coi/coiason29july08.pdf.

Truss, C., Gratton, L., Hope-Hailey, V., McGovern, P. and Stiles, P. (1997). 'Soft and Hard Models of Human Resource Management: A Reappraisal', *Journal of Management Studies*, 34(1): 53–73.

Vasconcelos, A.F. (2009). 'Intuition, Prayer, and Managerial Decision-making Processes: A Religion-based Framework', *Management Decision*, 47(6): 930–49.

Vinten, G. (2000). 'Business Theology', *Management Decision*, 38(3): 209–15.

Williams, K.Y. and O'Reilly, C.A. (1998). 'Demography and Diversity in Organizations: A Review of 40 Years of Research', *Research in Organizational Behavior*, 20: 77–140.

Williams, R.B. (1998). 'Asian Indian and Pakistani Religions in the United States', *The Annals of the American Academy of Political and Social Science*, 558(1): 178–95.

Ziolkowski, E.J. (1993). *A Museum of Faiths – Histories and Legacies of the 1893 World's Parliament of Religions*, Scholars Press, Atlanta.

Chapter 12

Managing Workplace Diversity of Religious Expressions in the Philippines

VIVIEN T. SUPANGCO

Introduction

Globalization and technological innovations have facilitated the movement not only of goods but also of people engaging in education and employment. A more recent development in the Association of Southeast Asian Nations (ASEAN) region is its economic integration, which is expected to take place in 2015. This will increase even more the movement of people within the region and will definitely increase the diversity of the workforce in organizations located in the Philippines, particularly in terms of ethnicity and religion. Increased mobility has indeed been found to increase diversity of religions brought about by migration (Warner, 1998). The integration will also increase the number of foreign companies that will do business in the Philippines. Thus there is more pressure on organizations in the Philippines to be prepared in addressing the needs of a more diverse workforce. The pressure comes from at least two fronts: from the workforce themselves in terms of religious accommodation (Borstoff, 2011) and from the increasing influence of practices of foreign companies locating in the Philippines.

As international mobility increases, workforce diversity also increases (Gebert et al., 2011). This includes religious diversity. A country's ability to accommodate the demands of a religiously diverse workforce is one area that has recently been considered in analysing country risk. Religion as an element of a country's political and social environment influences one's perception of country risk. As such, religious freedom affects investors' strategic positions (Alon and Spitzer, 2003). Religious freedom is negatively related to country risk measures used by international lending institutions.

Several researchers have put forward different definitions of religion. It is often construed as man's relationship with a transcendent being within a framework of principles and doctrines (King, 2007; Greenfield et al., 2009), standardized teachings and rituals (Emmons, 1999), prescribed practices (Lips-Wiersma and Mills, 2002; Cash and Gray, 2000), as well as sanctions (Howard, 2002). Religious expression is often organized and communal (Mitroff and Denton, 1999). Individuals are not only influenced by the teachings of their religions; their behaviours are affected by the fact that some religions specify the modes of conduct of members even beyond their places of worship (Cash and Gray, 2000).

Religion is a basic human right, and as such is universally acknowledged and supported through the Universal Declaration of Human Rights (UDHR) and the International Convention on Civil and Political Rights (ICCPR) (Sta. Lucia, 2011). To some individuals, it is important to express their religious beliefs in the workplace. Studies find that while most employees regard religious expression as inappropriate in the workplace, they still aspire that they are able to find expression of their complete self at work (Mitroff and Denton, 1999). It is reported that employees in organizations who score high in organizational workplace acceptance of religious expression (OWARE) are able to exchange more information about one's religion with co-workers (Moore, 2010). When employees feel safe about expressing themselves religiously and spiritually in the workplace, they are more open in their religious expression. Negative reactions on one's religious and spiritual expressions result in minimizing or regulating such expressions (Lips-Wiersma and Mills, 2002). In addition, the degree to which an individual finds comfort in expressing religious beliefs in the workplace relies on the openness of the organization to such religious expressions through endorsement by top management of values associated with religious expressions or are expressed by lower-level managers themselves (Duchon and Plowman, 2005).

Religion influences individual as well as social identities (Bailey and Autry, 2013). Individuals first learn values in the family. As a child grows older, other institutions, such as religion, play a part in moulding the character of the person. It provides guidelines in discerning the difference of right from wrong or good from bad. Beyond these, religion also promises salvation (Wellman and Tokuno, 2004). Different religions, however, specify different paths to salvation. This includes prayers, proselytizing, and observance of holy days and other practices. In addition, religion also influences how individuals define career success, which further influences how one approaches and prepares for it

(Dries, 2011). The influence of religion on the way individuals view the world and the workplace contributes to diversity.

Moreover, individuals categorize themselves and others on the basis of their membership in a religion (Jehn et al., 1999). Sharing the same religious practices and traditions is likely to influence their attitudes and values. Similarity of attitudes enhances their attraction to each other to the extent that it affirms their self-concepts, reduces uncertainty of being in groups, and provides reinforcement on how to fit in the group and the larger workplace (Ashforth and Mael, 1989; Hogg and Terry, 2000).

This chapter explores the ways organizations in the Philippines manage diversity of religious expressions. It identifies areas where organizations have consciously addressed religious diversity issues through policies, and whether or not multinational companies differed from local companies in these areas. It also looks into the various forms of religious expressions.

This study is important for several reasons. As globalization and the concomitant movement of people increase, workforce diversity, including religious diversity, increases. As religious freedom finds support more and more through the UDHR and the ICCPR (Sta. Lucia, 2011), individuals have asserted religious expression as a matter of right, as a manner to express themselves, or simply to find peace and comfort.

Organizations manage diversity for moral, legal and practical reasons (Gilbert and Ivancevich, 2000). Several studies have shown that religion influences several organizational outcomes. Religious differences affect how individuals relate to one another, which may be influenced by how accepting an organization is of religious expression (Moore, 2010). However, it is not religious diversity per se that leads to conflict but rather the degree of religious intolerance, which indirectly affects performance (Gebert et al., 2011). Religious participation also impacts on psychological well-being (Greenfield et al., 2009).

This chapter thus enables potential companies wishing to do business in the Philippines and those already operating in the Philippines that want to understand better religious expression to take a peek at the degree to which companies provide an environment that is open to religious expression and where employees feel empowered to do so.

Religions in the Philippines

The Philippines is a predominantly Christian country. With a total population of 92.1 million in 2010 (NSCB, 2012), about 80.6 per cent were Catholics, 2.7 per cent were Protestants, 1.1 per cent were Aglipayans (members of the Philippine Independent Church), and 2.4 per cent were members of Iglesia ni Cristo (Church of Christ). Muslims, the largest non-Christian religious group, constituted 5.7 per cent. In terms of growth rate of membership in these top religious groups, Islam grew the fastest at 32.74 per cent growth between 2000 and 2010. This was followed by Iglesia ni Cristo which grew at 27.74 per cent and Catholic which grew at 20.0 per cent. Aglipayans registered the biggest decline in membership at 30.07 per cent between 2000 and 2010. The number of Protestants also declined by 3.87 per cent. Higher growth rates of Islam and the Iglesia ni Cristo resulted in a slight increase in the percentage of Islam and Igelsia ni Cristo relative to the total Philippine population in 2010 compared to 2000 and a slight decrease in the percentage of Catholics in 2010 relative to 2000.

Geographically, Christianity is spread all over the country, except for a few provinces in Mindanao due to the Muslims' resistance to Spanish domination for more than 300 years. As a result, Christianity has failed to penetrate some provinces in Mindanao, making Islam the dominant religion in these areas (Francia, 2010).

Religious freedom exists in the Philippines and is guaranteed by the Philippine Constitution. Religious freedom is considered violated when a person is 'prevented from or punished for externalizing his religious belief or is forced to do something contrary to his religious belief' (Bernas, 2013). Inasmuch as the Philippines was under US colonial rule from 1898 to 1946, much of its laws on religious freedom is taken from American laws (Pangalangan, 2010; Sta. Lucia, 2011). For example, the Philippines adheres to the tenet of a separation of Church and State, taking as its model similar US law on the establishment and free exercise of religion (Pangalangan, 2010; Sta. Lucia, 2011). In addition, it is not surprising that cases on religious freedom are interpreted applying American laws (Sta. Lucia, 2011). The Philippines also does not identify any preferred religion. However, the Government made political and geographic concessions in response to the Islamic rebellion by creating the Autonomous Region in Muslim Mindanao (ARMM) and the Cordillera Autonomous Region (CAR). Moreover, the Philippine Constitution of 1987 defines the exceptions to neutrality to religion by recognizing the Shariah laws and the Shariah courts based on religion. On the other hand, the law is silent on public display of religious symbols (Pangalangan, 2010).

The Filipino people enjoy the right to employment regardless of creed (Ricafrente, 1994). Laws governing employment relations are contained in the Labor Code of the Philippines. Some religious teachings may present challenges in managing religious diversity, but the Labor Code takes into account the importance of religious freedom. While the Philippine Labor Code specifies that the weekly rest days of employees are determined and scheduled by their employer, the latter is required to respect the employee's preference as regards weekly rest day, especially when such is based on religious considerations. The Seventh Day Adventist Church considers Saturday its Sabbath Day; thus, its members are expected to take a rest from work on this day and participate in its religious activities (Sta. Lucia, 2011). In addition, worship services of the Iglesia ni Cristo are on Thursdays; thus, its members do not want to take overtime work on that day to be able to attend worship services after office hours. Inasmuch as they also do not celebrate the Christmas holiday, they also wish to be respected in this regard by not forcing them to attend Christmas parties. Another challenge to work scheduling related to religious beliefs is the practice of Muslims to pray five times a day, two occasions of which fall within office hours. Some accommodations have already been made in some sectors. For example, to enable Muslim employees in the different courts in Mindanao to attend to religious observances on Fridays between 10am and 2pm, they are allowed to adopt a flexible schedule to complete a 40-hour workweek during the month of Ramadan (A.M. No. 02-2-10-SC, 2005). Some government agencies also provide prayer rooms for Muslims and some facilities to clean themselves before praying. In terms of accommodating food choices, Muslim employees wish halal foods were served in office canteens.

Moreover, the Labor Code states that employees have a right to self-organization, and that this right shall not be abridged (DOLE, 1974); this, however, is rendered a less preferred position compared to religious freedom (Ricafrente, 1974). Thus several court cases involving members of the Iglesia ni Cristo, who are not allowed by their religion to join unions but were sanctioned by the union by virtue of the union security clause in their collective bargaining agreement, were decided in favour of the individual's freedom of religion (*Basa* v. *FOITAF*, 1974; *Anuncension* v. *National Labor Union*, 1977). Inasmuch as members of the Iglesia ni Critsto are not allowed to join unions, several organizations consider them an attractive source of applicants to their organizations (Managahas and Olarte, 2002).

By virtue of the structure of religious affiliation, which is predominantly Christianity, the Government grants holidays that allow the faithful to participate in religious celebrations such as Maundy Thursday, Good Friday, Black Saturday, All Saints' Day, All Souls' Day and Christmas. In addition to the aforementioned Christian holidays, the observance of Eid'l Fitr was first declared as a holiday in 2002 while Eidul Adha, which was proclaimed as a regional holiday in ARMM, has been celebrated as a national holiday since 2010. Chinese New Year has also recently been declared a non-working holiday in the Philippines.

Methodology

To address the objectives of this study, a snowball sampling scheme was used. An email containing the link to the questionnaire was sent to HR managers who belonged to the People Management Association of the Philippines. They were encouraged to forward the link to HR managers from other organizations. The same email was also sent to other HR managers who were also encouraged to forward the link to other HR managers. A total of 111 organizations responded to the survey conducted between December 2012 and October 2013. To describe the data, mean and mode are computed. To further look into the differences of practices between multinational and local organizations, and whether or not an organization is unionized, chi square tests were conducted.

Specific areas of interest in this study include the following: religious accommodation, religious harassment and differential treatment of employees based on religion. In addition, the state of practice of certain religious expressions was also examined (Borstorff et al., 2012). However, this study differs from that of Borstorff, Cunningham and Clark (2012) in terms of level of analysis. This study is an organizational-level analysis while the former is an individual-level analysis.

Results

A majority (64 per cent) of the organizations in the sample are local companies. They have been in existence for about 29.75 years on average, employing an average of 2,196 employees, 81.74 per cent of which are Catholics. A majority (77.3 per cent) of these companies are also not unionized.

Although the Constitution guarantees religious freedom and the right to employment regardless of creed, organizations in the Philippines have not reinforced these in terms of formalizing their stand on religious issues. For instance, 90.7 per cent of the organizations do not have a policy on religious accommodation, 94.4 do not have a policy on religious harassment and 94.4 per cent do not have a policy on preferential treatment due to religion.

In addition, in terms of state of practice, the following religious expressions, which were also examined by Borstorff et al. (2012), are examined: 'decoration of office space for holidays', 'display of religious materials in the work area', 'time off for religious observances', consideration of different religions in planning holiday-related activities, consideration of 'religious needs … when providing food/meals', allowing 'religious practices in the workplace (prayers, meditations and so on)', 'formation of on-site religious-based affinity groups', 'religious practices regarding dress/personal appearance code (for example, facial hair, head coverings and so on)', provision of 'space for religious observance (chapel, prayer room)', 'job transfer for religious reasons', wearing of 'religious messages on clothing (crucifix necklace, pro-life button and so on)' and scheduling changes, shift swaps for religious observances.

Most organizations in the sample have not formalized their stand regarding specific religious expressions; however, they have allowed their employees to practice them, especially if the religious expressions do not entail additional costs or undue difficulty on the part of the organization.

In general, no policies on the following religious expressions exist, but these are nonetheless practiced in most organizations in the sample (Table 12.1): 'decoration of office space for holidays', 'display of religious materials in the work area', 'time off for religious observances', consideration of different religions in planning holiday-related activities, consideration of 'religious needs … when providing food/meals', allowing 'religious practices in the workplace (prayers, meditations and so on)' and wearing of 'religious messages on clothing (crucifix necklace, pro-life button and so on)'.

There are also generally no policies on the following forms of religious expressions and they are not practiced by most organizations in the sample (Table 12.1): For example, 'formation of on-site religious-based affinity groups', 'religious practices regarding dress/personal appearance code (for example, facial hair, head coverings and so on)', provision of 'space for religious observance (chapel, prayer room)', 'job transfer for religious reasons' and scheduling changes, shift swaps for religious observances.

Table 12.1   State of practice of various religious expressions

Practices	With Policy and Practised	Without Policy but Practised	With Policy but Not Practised	Without Policy and Not Practised	N
Decorating office space for holidays	6.4	82.7	0	10.9	110
Time off for religious observances	8.1	72.1	.9	18.2	110
Display of religious materials in work area	.9	65.1	.9	33	109
Consideration of religious needs in providing food/meals	4.5	54.5	0	40.9	110
Consideration of different religions in planning holiday-related activities	10	53.6	.9	35.5	110
Wearing of religious messages on clothing (crucifix necklace, pro-life button and so on)	1.8	49.5	1.8	46.8	109
Job transfer for religious reasons	.9	12.8	.9	85.3	109
Religious practices regarding dress/personal appearance code (for example, facial hair, head coverings and so on)	3.7	29.4	0	67.0	109
Provision of space for religious observance (chapel, prayer room)	4.5	32.7	0	62.7	110
Formation of on-site religious-based affinity groups	2.8	35.8	0	61.5	109
Scheduling changes, shift swaps for religious observance	3.6	35.5	.9	60.0	110

Source: Author's analysis of survey data.

In order to further explore some patterns in the data, chi square tests were conducted to determine if the state of practice is independent of whether or not the organization is multinational or unionized.

Table 12.2   **Chi square tests of independence between practices and type of organization**

Practices	Multinational Status	N	Union Status	N
Decorating office space for holidays	.09	110	.64	109
Display of religious materials in work area	.15	109	.58	108
Time off for religious observances	.09	110	.42	109
Consideration of different religions in planning holiday-related activities	.55	110	.50	109
Consideration of religious needs in providing food/meals	.18	110	.88	109
Allowing of religious practices in the workplace (prayers, meditations and so on)	.81	110	.75	109
Formation of on-site religious-based affinity groups	.29	109	.17	108
Religious practices regarding dress/personal appearance code (for example, facial hair, head coverings and so on)	.01	109	.55	108
Provision of space for religious observance (chapel, prayer room)	.20	110	.04	109
Job transfer for religious reasons	.71	109	.66	108
Wearing of religious messages on clothing (crucifix necklace, pro-life button and so on)	.99	109	.28	108
Scheduling changes, shift swaps for religious observance	.58	110	.03	109
Policy on religious diversity	.66	107	.32	106
Policy on religious harassment	.01	107	.17	106
Policy on differential treatment based on religion	.11	107	.17	106

Source: Author's analysis of survey data.

Table 12.2 indicates that the exercise of religious expression is independent of multinational status except in the aspect of dress and personal appearance code (for example, facial hair, head coverings and so on) and in providing a policy on religious harassment. In addition, exercise of religious expression is also independent of unionization status except in the areas of providing space for religious observance and changing schedules for religious observance.

Conclusion, Limitation and Directions for Future Research

The results of this study provide us a description of the state of religious accommodation and expression in organizations in the Philippines. In general, Philippine organizations do not have policies on religious accommodation, religious harassment and preferential treatment based on religion. In addition, most organizations also do not have any policy on specific forms of religious expression. However, religious expressions that are individual in nature and which require no investment from the organization are practised in most Philippine organizations. There are forms of religious expressions that are not usually practised and these involve investment and work scheduling issues. In general, religious expressions are practised across all types of organizations, whether or not they are multinational organizations and whether or not they are unionized.

With the impeding ASEAN economic integration in 2015, organizations in the Philippines may want to consider its implications on labour mobility and the concomitant diversity of labour and religion. Currently, respondents have not encountered any challenges with respect to religious diversity. This is reflected in the fact that a majority of the organizations in the sample still do not have written policies on issues relevant to religious accommodation and harassment. However, as a proactive approach to managing religious diversity, there is need to reconsider this stance because as religious diversity increases, demand for religious expression also increases. While organizations in the sample have allowed religious expressions, the absence of policies introduces the risk of creating an environment that may be considered hostile to others and may also not be sustainable in the long run.

Inasmuch as the sampling employed was non-probabilistic, the results of this study should, strictly speaking, apply only to the organizations that participated in the survey. Notwithstanding this limitation, the results give us a description of what forms of religious expressions are practiced in most organizations and which are not.

Very little research has been done on managing diversity in the Philippines. As an exploratory study, this chapter provides a preview of the state of managing religious diversity in the Philippines. The results also point to more research questions on managing diversity in the Philippines. In addition, more theorizing is in order to understand why such practices are obtaining in the country. The apparent homogeneity of practices of religious expressions in Philippine organizations and the independence of religious expressions and type of organizations lead us to look into other factors that may help us explain these observations better. Does the result showing religious expression occur when employees have high religious tolerance or is it due to the fact that a majority of the employees in the sample are Christians? What are the consequences of managing religious diversity? Does it lead to higher profits or less conflicts? Answers to these questions allow us to develop a stronger theoretical base for understanding and managing religious diversity.

References

Alon, I. and Spitzer, J. (2003). 'Does Religious Freedom Affect Country Risk Assessment?' *Journal of International and Area Studies*, 10(2): 51–62.

A.M. No. 02210-SC (2005). Retrieved from http://sc.judiciary.gov.ph/jurisprudence/2005/dec2005/am_02_2_10_sc.

Anucension v. *National Labor Union*, G.R. No. L-26097 29 November 1977. Retrieved from http://www.lawphil.net/judjuris/juri1977/nov1977/gr_26097_1977.htm.

Ashforth, B. and Mael, F. (1989). 'Social Identity Theory and the Organization', *Academy of Management Review*, 14(1): 20–39.

Bailey, B. and Autry, J.Z. (2013). 'Religious Freedom Research and the Future of Asian Studies: An Introduction to the Summer 2013 Issue', *The Review of Faith & International Affairs*, 11: 1–5.

Basa v. *FOITAF*, G.R. No. L-27113 November 19, 1974. Retrieved from http://www.lawphil.net/judjuris/juri1974/nov1974/gr_l_27113_1974.html.

Bernas, J.S.J. (2013). 'Of Padre Damaso and Other Things'. *Philippine Daily Inquirer*. Retrieved from http://opinion.inquirer.net/46209/of-padre-damaso-and-other-things.

Borstoff, P. (2011). 'Protecting Religion in the Workplace? What Employees Think', *Journal of Legal, Ethical and Regulatory Issues*, 14(1): 59–70.

Borstorff, P., Cunningham, B. and Clark, L. (2012). 'The Communication and Practice of Religious Accommodation: Employee Perceptions', *Journal of Applied Management and Entrepreneurship*, 17(4): 24–36.

Cash K.C. and Gray, G. (2000). 'A Framework for Accommodating Religion and Spirituality in the Workplace: Executive Commentary. *The Academy of Management Executive*, 14(3): 124–34.

Department of Labor and Employment (DOLE) (1974). Labor Code of the Philippines. Retrieved from http://www.dole.gov.ph/labor_codes.

Dries, N. (2011). 'The Meaning of Career Success: Avoiding Reification through a Closer Inspection of Historical, Cultural, and Ideological Contexts', *Career Development International*, 16(4): 364–84.

Duchon, D. and Plowman, D.A. (2005). 'Nurturing the Spirit at Work: Impact on Work Unit Performance', *The Leadership Quarterly*, 16(5): 807–33.

Emmons, R.A. (1999). 'Religion in the Psychology of Personality: An Introduction', *Journal of Personality*, 67(6): 873–88.

Francia, L.H. (2010). *A History of the Philippines from Indios Bravos to Filipinos*. The Overlook Press, New York.

Gebert, D., Boerner, S. and Chatterjee, D. (2011). 'Do Religious Differences Matter? An Analysis in India', *Team Performance Management*, 17(3/4): 224–40.

Gilbert, J.A. and Ivancevich, J.M. (2000). 'Valuing Diversity: A Tale of Two Organizations', *Academy of Management Executive*, 14(1): 93–105.

Greenfield, E.A., Vaillant, G.E. and Marks, N.E. (2009). 'Do Formal Religious Participation and Spiritual Perceptions Have Independent Linkages Diverse Dimensions of Psychological Well-being', *Journal of Health and Social Behavior*, 50(2): 196–212.

Hogg, M.A. and Terry, D. J. (2000). 'Social Identity and Self-categorization Processes in Organizational Contexts', *Academy of Management Review*, 25(1): 121–40.

Howard, S. (2002). 'A Spiritual Perspective on Learning in the Workplace', *Journal of Managerial Psychology*, 17(3): 230–42.

Jehn, K.E., Northcraft, G.B. and Neale, M.A. (1999). 'Why Differences make a Difference: A Field Study of Diversity, Conflict, and Performance in Workgroups', *Administrative Science Quarterly*, 44(4): 741–63.

King, S.M. (2007). 'Religion, Spirituality, and the Workplace: Challenges for Public Administration', *Public Administration Review*, 67: 1103–14.

Lips-Wiersma, M. and Mills, C. (2002). 'Coming Out of the Closet: Negotiating Spiritual Expression in the Workplace', *Journal of Managerial Psychology*, 17(3): 183–202.

Mangahas, M. and Olarte, A.M. (2002). Iglesia ni Cristo: A Most Powerful Union. Philippine Center for Investigative Journalism. Retrieved from http://pcij.org/stories/2002/inc2.html.

Mitroff, I.I. and Denton, E.A. (1999). 'A Study of Spirituality in the Workplace', *Sloan Management Review*, 40(4): 83–92.

Moore, T.W. (2010). 'You Believe in What? An Examination of Religious Differences in the Workplace', *Journal of Applied Management and Entrepreneurship*, 15(2): 43–63.

National Statistical Coordination Board (NSCB) (2012). *2012 Philippine Statistical Yearbook*. National Statistical Coordination Board, Makati.

Pangalangan, R. (2010). Religion and the Secular State: National Report for the Philippines. In Durham, W.C. and Torron, J.M. (eds) *Religion and Secular State: National Reports*, 559–71.

Ricafrente, C. (1994). 'The Labor Code Rules through a Magnifying Glass', *Philippine Law Journal*, 49(5): 607–31.

Sta. Lucia, R.C. (2011). 'The Constitutional Foundation of the Sabbath: A Discourse on the Imperative for Religious Liberty', *Philippine Law Journal*, 85(3): 700–756.

Warner, R.S. (1998). 'Approaching Religious Diversity: Barriers, Byways, and Beginnings', *Sociology of Religion*, 59(3): 193–215.

Wellman, J.K. and Tokuno, K. (2004). 'Is Religious Violence Inevitable?' *Journal for the Scientific Study of Religion*, 43(3): 291–6.

Chapter 13

Work-based Religiosity Support in Indonesia

TRI WULIDA AFRIANTY, THEODORA ISSA AND JOHN BURGESS

Introduction

Indonesia is a very diverse country with a total population of about 250 million (Melisa and Muhammad, 2013) and is the largest Muslim country globally. The archipelago of Indonesia comprises 13,466 islands with five major islands namely Sumatra, Java, Kalimantan (Borneo), Sulawesi (Celebes) and Irian Jaya (Menkokesra, 2012). The majority of the Indonesian population are concentrated on Java, which is only 6.60 per cent of the total inhabited area of Indonesia (Suryadinata et al., 2003). Bahasa Indonesia is the national language. However, there are 250 other regional languages and dialects in Indonesia (Bennington and Habir, 2003). There are more than 1,000 ethnic/sub-ethnic groups with only five considered to be significant numerically: Javanese (41.7 per cent), Sundanese (15.41 per cent), Malay (3.45 per cent), Madurese (3.37 per cent) and Batak (3.02 per cent). The ethnic Chinese represent less than 2 per cent of the population yet are acclaimed as the engine behind Indonesia's economic growth (Suryadinata et al., 2003). Additionally, the Javanese, the largest ethnic group in Indonesia are politically dominant (Brown, 2012). Five of six Indonesia's Presidents since the independence have been Javanese while the higher echelons of the Indonesian National Armed Forces (that is, *Tentara Nasional Indonesia* or TNI) are dominated by Javanese (Brown, 2012).

The purpose of this chapter is to set out and evaluate work-based religiosity support in the context of Indonesia. Religiosity support in the workplace in Indonesia is essential because religion is fundamental to people's lives and contributes greatly to the way people see things in Indonesia. The rights of employees in religion-related matters are governed by special laws and regulations. Six religions are officially recognized in the Indonesian Constitution and in the regulations to support religious observance in the workplace.

The different forms of workplace support for religious observance are outlined. This chapter also provides empirical evidence of the relationship between religiosity support usage and employees' work attitudes and behaviours in Indonesian higher education institutions. Religiosity support investigated in the study includes longer breaks or days off to do religious rituals and religious holiday allowances. This religiosity support is very specific to the Indonesian context and has never been subject to systematic evaluation regarding its impact. A total of 159 subordinates (that is, 109 academic and 50 non-academic staff) and 100 supervisors (that is, 77 academic and 23 non-academic staff) from 30 higher education institutions across Indonesia completed the 159 matched surveys. To test the hypothesis, a hierarchical regression analysis was conducted. Findings demonstrate that the suggestion that the use of work-based religiosity support leads to positive work outcomes could hardly be supported in the Indonesian context. Analysis of the findings, limitations of the study and future research directions are discussed.

In the following sections the structure and composition of the Indonesian workforce is outlined. The six religions recognized by the constitution are listed, as are the official forms of support for religious observance in the context of employment. Then follows the details and analysis of a study of the impact of religious support programmes on employee commitment and performance within one sector of the workforce. The conclusions consider the findings and follow-up analysis of the study.

Indonesian Population

In terms of employment in Indonesia, the informal sector has been the main source of job creation in Indonesia (Manning and Sumarto, 2011). Out of 110,808,154 Indonesia's workforce (those who are 15 years of age and over), 39.86 per cent work in formal sector, while the rest of them (that is, 60.14 per cent) work in the informal sector (BPS-RI, 2012a). Table 13.1 and Table 13.2 list the number of Indonesian workers employed in both formal and informal sectors. Since the end of the Soeharto regime in 1997 there is a growing recognition at the policy level in addressing employees' interests in Indonesia (Bamber and Legget, 2001).

Table 13.1 Indonesian population 15 years of age and over by main employment status in 2012

No.	Main Employment Status	People	August 2012 People	%
	Formal Sector			
1	Employer with permanent workers	3,873,041		
2	Employee	40,291,583		
	Total		*44,164,624*	*39.86*
	Informal Sector			
3	Self-employed	18,440,722		
4	Self-employed assisted by family member/temp. help	18,761,405		
5	Casual employee in agriculture	5,339,998		
6	Casual employee not in agriculture	6,202,093		
7	Unpaid worker	17,899,312		
	Total		*66,643,530*	*60.14*
Total			**110,808,154**	**100.00**

Source: Adapted from BPS-RI (2012a).

Table 13.2 Indonesian population 15 years of age and over who worked by main industries in 2012

No.	Main Industry	August 2012 People	%
1	Agriculture, Forestry, Hunting and Fishery	38,882,134	35.09
2	Mining and Quarrying	1,601,019	1.44
3	Manufacturing Industry	15,367,242	13.87
4	Electricity, Gas, and Water	248,927	0.22
5	Construction	6,791,662	6.13
6	Wholesale Trade, Retail Trade, Restaurants and Hotels	23,155,798	20.90
7	Transportation, Storage, and Communications	4,998,260	4.51
8	Financing, Insurance, Real Estate and Business Services	2,662,216	2.40
9	Other Services	17,100,896	15.43
Total		**110,808,154**	**100.00**

Source: Adapted from BPS-RI (2012b).

Indonesia has experienced significant growth in female participation in the workforce (Bennington and Habir, 2003; Muntamah, 2012; Ridho and Al Raysid, 2010; Yakub, 2013; Yustrianthe, 2008). According to the World Bank (2013), women make up more than half of the Indonesian workforce and their roles have become more important in many Indonesian sectors. For example, Indonesian women account for 6 per cent of positions on corporate boards (The World Bank, 2013; UN Women, 2012), 18 per cent of the positions in Indonesia's national Parliament are held by women (UN Women, 2012) and at least 20 per cent of high positions in the Indonesian higher education sector are held by women (Yakub, 2013). The rise of female participation in the Indonesian workforce is one of the consequences of Indonesia's major achievements for women in reaching gender equality in education at the primary, secondary and tertiary levels (UN Women, 2012). With the significant growth in female participation in the Indonesian workforce, the number of dual-income earning households has also increased (Ridho and Al Raysid, 2010; Yustrianthe, 2008).

In addition, Indonesia has been acknowledged as being one of the most religious countries in the world. Any religiosity related issues are very sensitive in the Indonesian context (Colbran, 2010) and the provision of religiosity support is governed by Indonesian Laws and regulations (see the next section of the chapter). This issue contributes significantly to the understanding of the way organizations do business in Indonesia. Since Indonesia is categorized as one of the next generation of emerging industrialized countries, understanding how the way organizations do business in Indonesia is related to religiosity issues is important. This chapter discusses religiosity support in the workplace in the context of Indonesia. It highlights that in a religious country like Indonesia, where religion is fundamental to people's lives and contributes greatly to the way people see things, religiosity support in the workplace is essential. The right of employees related to religion-related matters are governed by special laws and regulations. This chapter also provides empirical evidence of the relationship between religiosity support usage and employees' work attitudes and behaviours in Indonesian higher education institutions.

Six Legally Acknowledged Religions in Indonesia

Indonesia is a multi-religious society. Currently, there are six legally acknowledged religions in Indonesia, (these are Islam/Muslim, Christianity–Catholic, Christianity–Protestant, Hindu, Buddhism and Kong Hu Cu). These religions are legally acknowledged in Indonesia under Presidential Decree Number 6 of 2000 (Presiden-RI, 2000) and Government Regulation

Number 55 of 2007 (Presiden-RI, 2007). It is worthwhile to note here that the religions categorization is quite different than that in other countries, whereas in other countries both Protestant and Catholic are considered as denominations under Christianity, in Indonesia this is different. The Government of Indonesia officially recognizes the two main Christian divisions in Indonesia, Protestant and Catholic, as two separate religions. Every Indonesian citizen is required to be registered member of one of those legally acknowledged religions which will be recorded on their national identity card (that is, Kartu Tanda Penduduk or KTP) (Hoon, 2011; Permatasari, 2013). In addition, it is a national policy to include religion as one of the compulsory subjects taught in elementary school in Indonesia (Rizal, 2012). Following is a brief discussion of the six legally acknowledged religions in Indonesia.

MUSLIM (ISLAM)

Indonesia has the largest Muslim population in the world (Colbran, 2010; Gupta et al., 2002), with over 85 per cent of the Indonesian population being Muslim (Bennington and Habir, 2003; BPS-RI, 2010). Muslim are spread throughout Indonesia, however the largest number of Muslim (that is, about 63 per cent of total Muslim) live in Java (BPS-RI, 2010), perhaps due to Java is the most populated area in Indonesia. The dominance of Muslim in Indonesia has a great impact on the way people lives and doing things (including businesses) in Indonesia. For example, in banking sector, several bank institutions (both public and private banks) apply Syariah Islam (Islam law) as their guidance in doing day-to-day operations. These banks are referred to as Syariah Banks. The main feature of these banks which differentiate them from non-syariah banks is that the relationship between the customer and the bank institution is considered as a partnership between investor and their fund manager, instead of between debtor and creditor (Maharani et al., 2013). The influences of Islam in the workplace in Indonesia will also be discussed in the religiosity support section of this chapter. In addition, in Aceh, a province in the west part of Indonesia, the local law and regulation applied are based on *Syariah Islam*. Aceh, priding itself as Serambi Mekkah (the Verandah of Mecca), has always been more devoutly Islamic compared to the rest of Indonesia (Milallos, 2007).

CHRISTIAN–PROTESTANT

Protestantism was brought to Indonesia in the sixteenth century during the Dutch East India Company (VOC) colonization (Reformed Online, 2002). Currently 6.96 per cent of Indonesian population are Christian–Protestants (BPS-RI, 2010). The largest number of Christian–Protestants (that is, about

23 per cent of total Christian–Protestants) live in North Sumatra, with the majority of them being ethnic Batak (BPS-RI, 2010). Chinese Indonesians also make up a significant part of the Protestant population (Reformed Online, 2002).

CHRISTIAN–CATHOLIC

Catholicism was initially brought to Indonesia by the Portuguese during spice trading in 1534. Currently 2.91 per cent of Indonesian population are Christian–Catholics, about 37 per cent of which live in the South East Nusa (Nusa Tenggara Timur/NTT) province (BPS-RI, 2010). Likewise Christianity–Protestant, Christianity–Catholic also spread among the Indonesian Chinese (Reformed Online, 2002).

HINDU

Hindus make up 1.69 per cent of the Indonesian population (BPS-RI, 2010). Although making up only a small percentage of Indonesia's 250 million population, Hinduism's influence can be seen throughout Indonesia (for example, Ganesha, one of Hindu gods, is imprinted on the Indonesian rupiah and several Indonesian institution nomenclatures are in Sanskrit). This is not surprising given the fact that Hinduism is a part of Indonesia's main history. Hindu influences reached the Indonesian Archipelago as early as first century. Several major kingdoms on the major Indonesian islands of Sumatra, Java, Bali and Kalimantan were highly influenced by Hinduism. The most influential Hindu kingdom was the Majapahit Empire on the island of Java, which reached its peak in the fourteenth century. However, during the fifteenth and sixteenth centuries, when the Majapahit Empire was conquered by Muslim sultanates, Hinduism lost its status as the main religion in the Indonesian archipelago. As the kingdom disintegrated, many of its leaders and influential people moved to Bali (McDaniel, 2010). The majority of Hindus (that is, about 81 per cent of the total Indonesian Hindus) are now concentrated on the island of Bali (BPS-RI, 2010). This makes Bali unique among the many islands of Indonesia. For example, on Nyepi, a Hindu day of silence or Hindu New Year in the Balinese Saka calendar, one of the Hindus' main religious celebrations, for 24 hours, no individual is allowed to do any activity outside the house. No light can be turned on and no noise (that can be obviously seen/heard from outside) is permitted in the house during Nyepi. Those who disobey these rules will be arrested and fined by Pecalang (a traditional security/authority in Bali who patrol the streets to ensure the prohibitions are being followed). The only exception is for hospitals and emergency matters (that is, life-threatening situations and women about to give birth). On Nyepi, all entrances to the island of Bali, including airports and seaports, are closed for 24 hours. All television and radio stations stop broadcasting in Bali during Nyepi (Atmodjo, 2014). In addition, tourists who are in Bali on Nyepi are also obligated to obey the rules and they have to stay within the hotel complexes and avoid doing outdoor activities (Atmodjo, 2014; Suara Pembaharuan, 2012). This of course would have an impact on business in Bali. For example, it has been reported that Nyepi has boosted business in the hospitality industry; hotels and villas in particular (Atmodjo, 2014). This is mainly because a tradition of fire war (perang api) and local parades the night before Nyepi of giant effigies (ogoh-ogoh) have become tourist attractions (Atmodjo, 2014; Republika Online, 2012). In addition, many hotels and villas offer special *Nyepi* packages for visitors in Bali, however they are not allowed to facilitate check in and check out for customers during this time (Atmodjo, 2014). Other than the hospitality industry, all business have to close for 24 hours during Nyepi (Atmodjo, 2014; Disparda Pemprov Bali, 2013; Suara Pembaharuan 2012).

BUDDHIST

Buddhist is the second oldest religion in Indonesia, arriving around the sixth century, just after Hindu (BDEA, 2008). Buddhist make up 0.72 per cent of the Indonesian population (BPS-RI, 2010). The largest number of Buddhist (that is, about 19 per cent of total Buddhist) are found in Jakarta (BPS-RI, 2010). However, some scholars consider Buddhism either as an ideology, philosophy or education rather than as a religion due to its non-theistic approach that does not focus on 'the question of the origin of the world or the sense of existence' (Masel et al., 2012, p. 308), Buddhism is considered a religion in Indonesia. Support from scholars (for example, Deneulin and Rakodi, 2011; Diener et al., 2011; von der Mehden, 1987) for considering Buddhism as a religion is also found. In addition, the world's largest Buddhist monument, Borobudur, is found in Magelang, Central Java Province. The monument was built in the eight and ninth century, by the Kingdom of Sailendra (UNESCO, 1991).

KONG HU CU

Kong Hu Cu (or Confucianism) was initially brought by Chinese merchants and immigrants to Indonesia in the third century. However, Kong Hu Cu has just been acknowledged as one of official religions in Indonesia in 2000 in the era of Abdurrahman Wahid, the fourth President of Indonesia, with the Presidential Decree 2000 (BBC, 2011; Presiden-RI, 2000). Currently, 0.05 per cent of Indonesian population are Kong Hu Cu, with 34 per cent of them living on the island of Bangka Belitung (BPS-RI, 2010). The majority of Kong Hu Cu in Indonesia are of Chinese ethnic background (BBC, 2011).

Religiosity Support across the Workforce

Any religiosity related issues are very sensitive in the Indonesian context (Colbran, 2010) and the provision of religiosity support is governed by the Indonesian Laws and regulations. Since the majority of Indonesians are Muslim, almost all organizations in Indonesia provide a longer break for their Muslim employees on Friday afternoon to do their compulsory prayers (that is, *sholat Jumat*). Under the Indonesian Labour Law, number 13 of 2003, article 80 of the law states that the employer must provide enough time for their employees to do compulsory religious rituals without any pay reduction. In practice, most organizations in Indonesia, especially public organizations, have an official break for about one hour on Friday afternoons so that their Muslim employees can do their compulsory prayers. For some organizations in private sector, the break is only for Muslim male employees because only males are obligated to do compulsory prayers on Friday (Pasca, 2013). Apart from the Friday prayer, in relation to the right of employees to do their religious prayer/ritual, under the Indonesian Labour Law organizations are also required to provide an appropriate place to perform such activities so that employees can do their daily prayer at the workplace. In addition, in the Muslim fasting month Ramadan, working hours are reduced by one hour each day for the whole month for employees (especially those who work for the Government departments and at all levels of employment). This results in working hours starting one hour later or finishing one hour earlier and this has become the national policy (Johara, 2012).

To support employees and their families in celebrating religious holidays, under Indonesian Minister of Manpower Regulation Number PER-04/MEN/1994, it is mandatory for employers to pay a religious holiday allowance (Tunjangan Hari Raya or THR) in cash and/or other forms at least a week before their employees' religious holiday celebrations (Menaker-RI, 1994). Religious holidays in Indonesia that are acknowledged and receive an allowance are Eid al-Fitr for Muslims, Christmas for Christians, Nyepi for Hindus, Waisak (Vesak) for Buddhists and Imlek for Kong Hu Cu. Those who are eligible for the allowance are employees who have a continuous tenure of at least three months. This allowance is to be paid once in a year with a minimum amount of one month's salary for those who have worked for at least 12 months, whereas employees with tenure of three months on a continuous basis, but less than

12 months, are entitled to the allowance of one month's salary in proportion to the period of employment (Menaker-RI, 1994). In practice, the allowance is given once a year close to Eid al-Fitr to all eligible employees regardless of their religion.

The Indonesian laws and regulations on employment related to religiosity support discussed in this chapter are meant to protect Indonesian workers in all levels and sectors of employment (both formal and informal sectors) (Presiden-RI, 2003). However, the majority of the articles on those laws and regulations only cover Indonesian workers in the formal sector (Ady, 2012). The majority of the Indonesian workers in the informal sector are not represented by trade unions and they operate outside of official employment regulations (Manning and Roesad, 2007).

Empirical Evidence Related to the Impact of Religiosity Support on Employee Performance

Empirical evidence that is presented here is based on a study on the effects of work-based support (that is, work–life balance policies) on work attitudes and behaviours of Indonesian university employees. The Indonesian context is chosen since there has been limited research that has examined the impact or work–life balance support in the workplace on employees in Indonesia. In addition, as mentioned, Indonesia is categorized as one of the future emerging industrialized countries and there is a growing recognition at the policy level to address employees' interest in Indonesia in 1997 after the fall of the Soeharto military regime (Bamber and Legget, 2001).

The work-based support investigated includes religiosity support which is the focus of the analysis presented in this chapter. This religiosity support is very specific to the Indonesian context and has never been subject to systematic evaluation regarding its impact. It is proposed in this chapter that the use of religiosity support (that is, longer breaks or days off to do religious rituals and religious holiday allowances) should have a positive impact on employees' work attitudes and behaviours. We use social exchange theory (Blau, 1964) to develop this hypothesis. The theory highlights that when individuals benefit from other people, or other entities, they are most likely feel obligated to reciprocate (Lambert, 2000). Based on this relationship, we suggest that individuals who valued and gained benefit from the use of work-based support (including religiosity support) provided by their organizations would be inclined to behave in a positive way for the benefit of the organizations.

Since religiosity plays significant roles in almost every aspects of Indonesian society (Colbran, 2010), providing work-based religiosity support would be most likely valued by Indonesian employees. In addition, in a religious country, religiosity is associated with greater social support, feeling respected and meaning in life (Diener et al., 2011). Thus, being able to use and gain benefit from the work-based religiosity support provided by the organizations would encourage the employees to give return in the form of good work attitudes and behaviours. This is also in line with the claim that the use of formal work-based support should have positive correlation with employees' work attitudes and behaviours (Beauregard and Henry, 2009; Butts et al., 2013; Galinsky et al., 2008; Muse and Pichler, 2011).

Work attitudes and behaviours that are examined in the study include organizational citizenship behaviours (OCB), in-role performance, organizational commitment and job satisfaction. These kinds of employee attitudes and behaviours are chosen to be tested in the study because it is generally claimed by employers that adopting formal organizational support on work and family (life) issues (including religiosity support) could increase these attitudes and behaviours, which then will benefit the organizations (Galinsky et al., 2008). However, very limited research has examined the impact of the support on employee's OCB and in-role performance (Beauregard and Henry, 2009; Butts et al., 2013; Muse and Pichler, 2011) despite the claim that the support could potentially increase employees' performance (for example, OCB and in-role performance) (Beauregard and Henry, 2009; Muse and Pichler, 2011). OCB is defined as 'individual behaviour that is discretionally, not directly or explicitly recognized by the formal reward system, and that, in the aggregate, promotes the effective functioning of the organisation' (Organ, 1988, p. 4). In contrast to OCB, in-role performance refers to employee behaviours related to the job requirements that are recognized by a formal reward system (Williams and Anderson, 1991). Organizational commitment is considered to be the individual attachment to the organization (Mathieu and Zajac, 1990). Job satisfaction refers to positive or negative emotional feelings related to one's job and job experiences (Locke, 1976). It is a 'temporal orientation toward the past and present rather than toward the future' (Brown and Peterson, 1993, p. 63). Spector (1997) suggests that there are two different approaches in studying job satisfaction. The first approach deals with specific facets of the job, and the other approach deals with general aspects of the job. Job satisfaction as one of the dependent variables in the study is viewed from the general approach. The study examined the impact of work-based support (including religiosity support) on the general emotional state of employees about their job.

As mentioned, social exchange theory (Blau, 1964) is used to develop the rationale behind the relationship between the use of work-based support (including religiosity support) and employees' work attitudes and behaviours proposed in the study. Social exchange theory posits that all human relationships are formed by the use of a subjective cost–benefit analysis and the comparison of alternatives (Blau, 1964). Social exchanges involve trust, not legal obligations (Stanford, 2008) and are built on a reciprocity principle (Lambert, 2000; Wang et al., 2011). The theory highlights the conditions under which individuals feel obligated to reciprocate when they benefit from other people, or other entities (Lambert, 2000). The basic principle underlying social exchange theory is that an individual who provides rewarding services to another creates a sense of obligation to the latter person. In return, the latter person must give benefits to the person who supplies the services. This exchange will continue if both parties value what they receive from the other (Blau, 1964). Thus, the application of social exchange theory suggests that employees will have a sense of obligation to exert positive attitudes or behaviours to their organizations if they are treated favourably and if they gain benefits from them (Lambert, 2000; Wang et al., 2011) through cooperation, OCB, commitment and goodwill at work (Allen, 2001; Aryee et al., 2005; Beauregard and Henry, 2009; Lambert, 2000; Scheibl and Dex, 1998; Wang and Walumbwa, 2007). Considering religiosity support as an indicator of favourable treatment (Grover and Crooker, 1995), employees who benefited from those treatment (by using the treatment) will respond to the organization in terms of positive work attitudes and behaviours. According to Butts et al. (2013), the use of work-based support should result in positive work attitudes and behaviours among employees because of the direct benefits gained from the employer-provided benefits.

Indonesian society places a high value on religiosity and religion is considered as a part of individual identity among Indonesians (Colbran, 2010), and as such it is suggested in the study that use of workplace support related to religiosity (longer breaks or days off to do religious rituals and religious holiday allowances) would lead to positive employees' work attitudes and behaviours (OCB, in-role performance, organizational commitment and job satisfaction). Research related to religiosity in the field of work and family (life) is very scarce (Green and Elliott, 2010), and there has been no empirical evidence found to support the proposed link between religiosity support use and employees' attitudes and behaviour. However, like any other types of work-based support, this proposition is also drawn from the social exchange theory (Blau, 1964). Having religiosity support from a workplace that is in line with employees' personal values (beyond work-related values) and gaining benefit from that support, may result in positive feelings about their workplace which in turn create a sense of obligation to give a 'better return' in the form of positive work attitudes and behaviours. Thus, the following hypothesis is proposed: *Religiosity support will have a positive impact on employee (a) OCB, (b) in-role performance, (c) organizational commitment and (d) job satisfaction.*

To test this hypothesis, a survey of 30 higher education institutions in Indonesia was undertaken. The questionnaires were developed in matched-pairs formats, with academic and non-academic staff and their supervisors participating in the research. The survey was conducted in 2012. Details of the 30 Indonesian higher education institutions who participated in the study are summarized in Table 13.3.

Table 13.3   **Details of higher education institutions who participated in the study**

Features	Number	%
Category of Institution		
Public	23	76.67
Private	7	23.33
Total	**30**	**100**
Type of Institution		
University	28	93.34
Polytechnic	1	3.33
Institute	1	3.33
Total	**30**	**100**
Geographic Regions		
Java	11	36.67
Sumatera	9	30
Kalimantan	4	13.33
Sulawesi	1	3.33
Bali	2	6.67
Lombok	2	6.67
Ambon	1	3.33
Total	**30**	**100**

Source: Afrianty (2014).

The original questionnaires for the study were developed in English. They were translated into Indonesian and then back-translated into English to ensure cross-linguistic comparability of the scale-item contents (Brislin, 1980). Multi-sources data (that is, self-rating data from subordinates and supervisor-rating data) were utilized to minimize a common method bias. The use of multiple sources of data in the study has been a call from scholars in this field (for example, Casper et al., 2007; Greenhaus et al., 2011; Kelly et al., 2008; Lyness and Judiesch, 2008). University staff members answered the questions regarding the use of work-based support, organizational commitment and job satisfaction. Supervisors were asked to rate their subordinates on the measures of OCB and in-role performance to reduce the self-report bias (Donaldson and Grant-Vallone, 2002; Greenhaus et al., 2011; Podsakoff et al., 2003; Tharenou et al., 2007).

In relation to work-based support (including religiosity support), respondents were asked to indicate support that they currently use or had used in the past. Supports that were not used were coded as 0 while supports that were used were coded as 1. A total of supports used (for each category score) was computed by summing the number of supports used, checked by the respondents, so that higher scores refer to a greater number of support used. This scoring scheme is adapted from Allen (2001) and Parker and Allen (2001). Several past studies (for example, O'Driscoll et al., 2003; Thompson et al., 1999) have also used this scoring scheme. Three of the five OCB dimensions (that is, altruism, conscientiousness and sportsmanship) developed by Podsakoff et al. (1990) were used in the study. These three dimensions of OCB were chosen because they have been found to be the most relevant to the Asian context (Chen, Hui, and Sego, 1998). Moreover, altruism and conscientiousness have been central categories of OCB (Chen et al., 1998). The items were assessed on a five-point Likert-type scale ranging from 1 = strongly disagree to 5 = strongly agree. Supervisors were asked to rate the extent to which they agreed or disagreed with each item related to their subordinates being assessed. Higher scores indicated higher employee OCB. Seven items from the in-role behaviours (IRBs) subscale of the performance scale (Williams and Anderson, 1991) were used to measure employees' in-role performance. Supervisors were asked to indicate their responses on a five-point scale (1 = never; 5 = very often) on each item related to their subordinates being assessed. Higher scores indicated higher employee in-role performance. Six items from Meyer et al.'s (1993) affective commitment scale were used to measure employee organizational commitment. This scale has also been used to measure organizational commitment in several past studies (for example, Allen, 2001; Aryee et al., 2005; Odle-Dusseau et al., 2012).

Affective commitment items measure employees' level of commitment as an affective attachment to the organizations. The items were assessed on a five-point Likert-type scale ranging from 1 = strongly disagree to 5 = strongly agree. Participants in the study were asked to rate the extent to which they agreed or disagreed with each item. The six items were summed to create a total score. Higher scores indicated a greater employee organizational commitment. Job satisfaction is measured with the three-item Overall Job Satisfaction scale from the Michigan Organisational Assessment Questionnaire (Cammann et al., 1983). The items were assessed on a five-point Likert-type scale ranging from 1 = strongly disagree to 5 = strongly agree. Individuals were asked to rate the extent to which they agreed or disagreed with each item. Higher scores indicated greater employee job satisfaction. Several variables that were believed to have a possible influence on the relationships between the independent and dependent variables were treated as control variables in the study. This was to ensure the unique impact added by the independent variables could be determined without being contaminated by other variables (Sekaran and Bougie, 2013; Tharenou, et al., 2007). The control variables of the study were gender, marital status, age, number of children, religion, the presence of paid help, job category and higher education category.

The mode of data collection was through mailed questionnaires. According to Sekaran and Bougie (2013), in order to be considered acceptable, a minimum response rate of 30 per cent is required for mail questionnaires. Of the 400 pairs of questionnaires distributed, 171 surveys were returned, for a response rate of 43 per cent. The response rate was considered as satisfactory considering that the data came from different sources that needed to be linked together. A total of 159 subordinates (for example, 109 academic and 50 non-academic staff) and 100 supervisors (for example, 77 academic and 23 non-academic staff) completed the 159 matched surveys. The proportions of male and female subordinates and supervisors who participated in this research are quite balanced at 59.12 per cent: 40.88 per cent and 55 per cent: 45 per cent respectively. Demographic information about the participants is shown in Table 13.4. To test the hypotheses, a hierarchical regression analysis was conducted using SPSS version 21. Prior to the hypothesis testing, preliminary analyses which include validity, reliability, regression assumption and the fitness of the model assessments were performed.

Table 13.4   Demographic information on survey participants

Remarks	Subordinate		Supervisor	
	N	%	N	%
Gender				
Male	94	59.12	55	55.00
Female	65	40.88	45	45.00
Total	**159**		**100**	
Age				
<30	68	42.77	7	7.00
30–40	50	31.45	40	40.00
41–50	25	15.72	30	30.00
51–60	15	9.43	21	21.00
above 60	1	0.63	2	2.00
Total	**159**		**100**	
Religion				
Islam (Muslim)	130	81.76	82	82.00
Catholic	2	1.26	0	0.00
Christian	9	5.66	7	7.00
Hindu	17	10.69	11	11.00
Buddhism	1	0.63	0	0.00
Kong Hu Cu	0	0.00	0	0.00
Total	**159**		**100**	
Marital Status				
Single	29	18.24	14	14.00
Married	128	80.50	83	83.00
Divorce/Widow	2	1.26	3	3.00
Total	**159**		**100**	
Children				
Have children	112	70.44	84	84.00
One child	49		14	
Two children	38		32	
Three children	18		30	
More than three children	7		8	
Do not have children	47	29.56	16	16.00
Total	**159**		**100**	

Table 13.4   *continued*

Remarks	Subordinate		Supervisor	
	N	**%**	**N**	**%**
Paid Help				
Have paid help	32	20.13	31	31.00
Do not have paid help	127	79.87	69	69.00
Total	**159**		**100**	
Job Category				
Lecturer (academic staff)	76	47.80	0	0.00
Lecturer who also hold administrative position (this group is also considered as academic staff)	33	20.75	77	77.00
Non-academic staff	50	31.45	23	23.00
Total	**159**		**100**	
Higher Education Institution Category				
Public	124	78	78	78
Private	35	22	22	22
Total	**159**		**100**	

Source: Afrianty (2014).

Findings

Findings from the study revealed that the use of religiosity support does not necessarily improve work attitudes and behaviours (OCB, in-role performance, organizational commitment and job satisfaction). It was found that the use of religiosity support was correlated significantly with employees' OCB ($\beta = -0.183$; $p < 0.05$) and in-role performance ($\beta = -0.235$; $p < 0.01$) but in a negative direction, contradictory to the research hypotheses.

It was revealed from the study that giving employees a longer break or days off to perform religious-related activities and giving religious allowances had a negative correlation with both employees' OCB and in-role performance. This may be because employees do not see work-based support that is specific, to support employees' religiosity concern, as an 'extra benefit' from the organization. It is more about policies that 'must' be provided by organizations in Indonesia as a religious country. Thus, it failed to encourage employees to perform 'extra'-role behaviours (that is, OCB). In fact, the religiosity support provided by the Indonesian organizations is mandated by Indonesian law.

As mentioned, under Indonesian Labour Law, number 13 of 2003, article 80 of the law states that the employer must provide enough time for their employees to perform compulsory religious rituals without any pay reduction. Under article 80 of the law, employees should be given opportunities to carry out their compulsory religious rituals and there should be no pay reduction for the employees related to this. Additionally, to support employees and their families to celebrate religious holidays, under Indonesian Minister of Manpower Regulation Number PER-04/MEN/1994, it is mandatory for employers to pay a religious holiday allowance (Tunjangan Hari Raya or THR) in cash and/or other forms at least a week before their employees' religious holiday celebrations (Menaker-RI, 1994).

In rationalizing the finding of the negative correlation between religiosity support usage and employees' performance specific to the job requirements (in-role performance), it may be because the utilization of these policies means sacrificing working hours and this may lead to reduced job performance. These are benefits that are not employer specific and employees do not feel bound to reciprocate given that they are receiving a legislated entitlement. As such there is no implied social exchange between the employee and the organization, as this is a State-based entitlement.

From a policy point of view, the issue related to religiosity support is very challenging. Organisations in Indonesia cannot simply terminate the religiosity support policies (even if they want to). As mentioned, any religiosity related issue is very sensitive in the Indonesian context (Colbran, 2010) and the provision of religiosity support is governed under the Indonesian Law and regulation. In a religious country, religiosity is related to greater social support, feeling respected, and meaning in life so that religious people in religious countries tend to have higher subjective well-being indicated by higher life satisfaction, more positive feelings and reduced negative feelings (Diener et al., 2011). The challenge here for organizations then is how to continuously manage religiosity support for employees while ensuring that employees successfully fulfil their expected job performances.

A relatively weak internal quality assurance mechanism which is also related to a weak employees' performance evaluation in the Indonesian higher education sector (Yuningsih, 2012) might also contribute to the contradictory finding related to the negative correlation between the use of religiosity support and employees' job-related performance (that is, in-role performance). As a result of the relatively weak performance evaluation, it seems that employees often take for granted their responsibilities to perform better after receiving the support benefits. As shown in Table 13.4, the majority of respondents in the study (for example, 78 per cent) work for a public university, thus they are acknowledged as pegawai negeri sipil (PNS) or public/civil servants. A performance evaluation for all Indonesian civil servants is conducted annually based on a performance evaluation measure called Daftar Penilaian Pelaksanaan Pekerjaan (DP-3) or List of Work Implementation Assessment which emphasizes the loyalty to Pancasila (that is, the official ideology of Republic of Indonesia) and the Constitution among other things (for example, job performance, responsibility, commitment, honesty, cooperation, initiative and leadership) (Azmi et al., 2012). This DP-3 is governed under the Indonesian Government Regulation number 10 of 1979 (Presiden-RI, 1979). The result of this performance evaluation is used as one of the determinants for employees' promotions. Since the current performance evaluation measure for employees (public/civil servants) is more focused on employees' personality rather than on job-related performance and the performance evaluation is often conducted as a process of 'formality' (that is, something that has to be done as usual) (Abizaid, 2012), it is most likely ineffective in encouraging high levels of job performance. In relation to this, the Indonesian Government has been working to improve the performance evaluation measures for employees. Government regulation number 46 of 2011, a new performance evaluation for civil servants, focuses more on job performance and will be implemented on 1 January 2014 (Presiden-RI, 2011). However, to what extent the performance evaluation measures in Indonesian public/civil services affect employees' performance has still to be tested.

It is important to note that data for the study were gathered only from one sector (that is, Indonesian higher education) and a set of occupations (that is, academic and non-academic staff). This research also applies only to the formal and regulated sector of the economy. Thus the results may be generalizable only to that population. More research is necessary involving respondents of various organizations from different sectors/industries to externally validate the research findings. However, although this research focused on only one sector and one set of occupations, this research involves 30 organizations representing both public and private institutions in quite dispersed regions (five main islands in Indonesia). Nonetheless, the sample size (n=159 matched survey) is appropriate for this research, allowing relationships between variables to be tested and examined.

Conclusion

Religiosity support in the workplace is an important issue to be addressed in the context of a religious country like Indonesia. In Indonesia, religion is fundamental to people's lives and contributes greatly to the way people see things, thus religiosity support in the workplace is essential. The findings of this study were that the usage of religiosity support did not relate to positive attitudes and behaviours in the workplace. The challenge for organizations in Indonesia is then how to continuously manage religiosity support for employees while ensuring that the intended organizational outcomes could be achieved. The rights available are not employer dependent in the formal sector and hence we would expect that the commitment would be towards the State, rather than the employer.

A qualitative study is needed to get an in-depth analysis on the religiosity support-related issues and its consequences on both employees and organizations in the Indonesian context. Considering that Indonesia has the largest Muslim population in the world, which tolerates other religions (Colbran, 2010; Gupta et al., 2002; Loh and Dahesihsari, 2013), it will be interesting to get a deeper understanding through a qualitative study on religiosity support and religious activities in the Indonesian workplace. In addition, research that examines religiosity/religion-related issues in the workplace was found to be lacking in the literature (Sprung et al., 2012), even in the context of a country which puts a great emphasis on religiosity/spirituality, such as Indonesia (Pekerti and Sendjaya, 2010). Considering the significant role that religiosity/spirituality plays in many individuals' lives and given the amount of time individuals spend at the workplace (Deneulin and Rakodi, 2011; Diener et al., 2011; Naimon et al., 2013; Sprung et al., 2012), it is consequently demanded that 'consideration of the subject of religion can no longer be avoided' (Deneulin and Rakodi, 2011, p. 45).

References

Abizaid, A. (2012). Aturan Baru, Pengganti DP3 PNS. Retrieved on 24 June 2013, from http://pa-maros.go.id/index.php?option=com_content&view=article&id=162:aturan-baru penganti-dp3-pns&catid=1:latest-news&Itemid=50.

Ady. (2012). Revisi UU ketenagakerjaan Penuh Polemik. Retrieved on 9 October 2013, from http://www.hukumonline.com/berita/baca/lt4fa7ebcbed481/revisi-uu-ketenagakerjaan-penuh-polemik.

Afrianty, T.W. (2013), Work Life Balance Polcies in the Indonesian Context. Unpublished PhD Thesis, Curtin University, Perth.

Allen, T.D. (2001). 'Family-supportive Work Environments: The Role of Organizational Perceptions', *Journal of Vocational Behavior*, 58(3): 414–35.

Aryee, S., Srinivas, E.S. and Tan, H.H. (2005). 'Rhythms of Life: Antecedents and Outcomes of Work–family Balance in Employed Parents', *Journal of Applied Psychology*, 90(1): 132–46.

Atmodjo, W. (2014). Tourists Enjoy Nyepi, Bali's Unique Celebration. Retrieved on March 19, 2014 from http://www.thejakartapost.com/news/2014/03/03/tourists-enjoy-nyepi-bali-s-unique-celebration.html.

Azmi, I.A.G., Ismail, S.H.S. and Basir, S.A. (2012). 'Women Career Advancement in Public Service: A Study in Indonesia', *Procedia-Social and Behavioral Sciences*, 58: 298–306.

Bamber, G.J. and Legget, C.J. (2001). 'Changing Employment Relations in the Asia–Pacific Region', *International Journal of Manpower*, 22(4): 300–317.

Beauregard, T.A. and Henry, L.C. (2009). Making the Link between Work-Life Balance Practices and Organizational Performance. *Human Resource Management Review*, 19: 9–22.

Bennington, L. and Habir, A.D. (2003). 'Human Resource Management in Indonesia', *Human Resource Management Review*, 13(3): 373–92.

Blau, P. (1964). *Exchange and Power in Social Life*. Wiley, New York.

BPS-RI. (2010). Penduduk Menurut Wilayah dan Agama yang Dianut. Retrieved from http://sp2010.bps.go.id/index.php/site/tabel?tid=321&wid=0.

BPS-RI. (2012a). Penduduk 15 Tahun Ke Atas Menurut Status Pekerjaan Utama 2004 – 2012. Retrieved on 5 April 2013 from http://www.bps.go.id/tab_sub/view.php?kat=1&tabel=1&daftar=1&id_subyek=06&notab=3.

BPS-RI. (2012b). Penduduk 15 Tahun Ke Atas yang Bekerja menurut Lapangan Pekerjaan Utama 2004–2012. Retrieved on April 5, 2013 from http://www.bps.go.id/tab_sub/view.php?kat=1&tabel=1&daftar=1&id_subyek=06&notab=2.

Brislin, R.W. (1980). Translation and Content Analysis of Oral and Written Material. In Triandis, H.C. and Berry, J.W. (eds) *Handbook of Cross-cultural Psychology* (Vol. 2). Allyn & Bacon, Boston, MA, pp. 389–444.

British Broadcasting Corporation (BBC). (2011). Pengakuan Negara atas Kong Hu Cu. Retrieved from http://www.bbc.co.uk/indonesia/laporan_khusus/2011/04/110407_agamakong.shtml.

Brown, G.K. (2012). 'Trade, Employment and Horizontal Inequalities in New Order Indonesia', *European Journal of Development Research*, 24(5): 735–52.

Brown, S.P. and Peterson, R.A. (1993). 'Antecedents and Consequences of Salesperson Job Satisfaction: Meta-analysis and Assessment of Causal Effects', *Journal of Marketing Research*, 30(1): 63–77.

Butts, M.M., Casper, W.J. and Yang, T.S. (2013). 'How Important are Work–family Support policies? A Meta-analytic Investigation of Their Effects on Employee Outcomes', *Journal of Applied Psychology*, 98(1): 1–25.

Cammann, C., Fichman, M., Jenkins, G.D. and Klesh, J.R. (1983). Assessing the Attitudes and Perceptions of Organizational Members. In S.E. Seashore, E.E. Lawler, P.E. Mirvis and C. Cammann (eds) *Assessing Organizational Change: A Guide to Methods, Measure, and Practices*. Wiley, New York.

Casper, W.J., Eby, L.T., Bordeaux, C. and Lockwood, A. (2007). 'A Review of Research Methods in IO/OB Work–Family Research', *Journal of Applied Psychology*, 92(1): 28–43.

Chen, X.-P., Hui, C. and Sego, D.J. (1998). 'The Role of Organizational Citizenship Behavior in Turnover: Conceptualization and Preliminary Test of Key Hypotheses', *Journal of Applied Psychology*, 83(6): 922–31.

Colbran, N. (2010). 'Realities and Challenges in Realising Freedom of Religion or Belief in Indonesia', *The International Journal of Human Rights*, 14(5): 678–704.

Deneulin, S. and Rakodi, C. (2011). 'Revisiting Religion: Development Studies Thirty Years On', *World Development*, 39(1): 45–54.

Diener, E., Tay, L. and Myers, D.G. (2011). 'The Religion Paradox: If Religion Makes People Happy, Why Are So Many Dropping Out?' *Journal of Personality and Social Psychology*, 101(6): 1278–90.

Disparda Pemprov Bali. (2013). Nyepi 2014 – seruan bersama majelis-majelis agama dan keagamaan provinsi Bali. Retrieved on 21 March 2014, from http://www.disparda.baliprov.go.id/id/NYEPI-2014---SERUAN-BERSAMA-MAJELIS-MAJELIS-AGAMA-DAN-KEAGAMAAN-PROVINSI-BALI.

Donaldson, S.I. and Grant-Vallone, E.J. (2002). 'Understanding Self-report Bias in Organizational Behavior Research', *Journal of Business and Psychology*, 17(2): 245–60.

Galinsky, E., Bond, J.T., Sakai, K., Kim, S.S. and Giuntoli, N. (2008). 2008 National Study of Employers. Retrieved from http://www.familiesandwork.org/site/research/reports/2008nse.pdf

Green, M. and Elliott, M. (2010). 'Religion, Health, and Psychological Well-being', *Journal of Religion and Health*, 49(2): 149–63.

Greenhaus, J.H., Ziegert, J.C. and Allen, T.D. (2011). 'When Family-supportive Supervision Matters: Relations between Multiple Sources of Support and Work–Family Balance', *Journal of Vocational Behavior*, 78(March): 1–9.

Grover, S.L. and Crooker, K.J. (1995). 'Who Appreciates Family-responsive Human Resource Policies: The Impact of Family-friendly Policies on the Organizational Attachment of Parents and Non-parents', *Personnel Psychology*, 48: 271–88.

Gupta, V., Surie, G., Javidan, M. and Chhokar, J. (2002). 'Southern Asia Cluster: Where the Old Meets the New? *Journal of World Business*, 37(1): 6–27.

Hoon, C.-Y. (2011). 'Mapping 'Chinese' Christian schools in Indonesia: Ethnicity, Class and Religion', *Asia Pacific Education Review*, 12(3): 403–11.

Johara. (2012). Selama puasa, jam Kerja pegawai dikurangi satu jam, *Pos Kota*. Retrieved from http://www.poskotanews.com/2012/07/19/selama-puasa-jam-kerja-pegawai-dikurangi-satu-jam/.

Kaplan, S., Bradley, J.C., Luchman, J.N. and Haynes, D. (2009). 'On the Role of Positive and Negative Affectivity in Job Performance: A Meta-analytic Investigation. *Journal of Applied Psychology*, 94(1): 162–76.

Kelly, E.L., Kossek, E.E., Hammer, L.B., Durham, M., Bray, J., Chermack, K. and Kaskubar, D. (2008). 'Getting There from Here: Research on the Effects of Work–Family Initiatives on Work–Family Conflict and Business Outcomes', *The Academy of Management Annals*, 2(1): 305–49.

Lambert, S.J. (2000). 'Added Benefits: The Link between Work–Life Benefits and Organizational Citizenship Behavior', *Academy of Management Journal*, 43(5): 801–15.

Locke, E. (1976). The Nature and Causes of Job Satisfaction. In Dunnette, M.D. (ed.) *Handbook of Industrial and Organizational Psychology (1297–1349)*. Rand McNally, Chicago, IL.

Loh, J.M.I. and Dahesihsari, R. (2013). 'Resilience and Economic Empowerment: A Qualitative Investigation of Entrepreneurial Indonesian Women', *Journal of Enterprising Culture*, 21(1): 107–21.

Lyness, K.S. and Judiesch, M.K. (2008). 'Can a Manager Have a Life and a Career? International and Multisource Perspectives on Work–Life Balance and Career Advancement Potential', *Journal of Applied Psychology*, 93(4): 789–805.

Maharani, V., Troena, E.A. and Noermijati, N. (2013). 'Organizational Citizenship Behavior Role in Mediating the Effect of Transformational Leadership, Job Satisfaction on Employee Performance: Studies in PT. Bank Syariah Mandiri Malang East Java', *International Journal of Business and Management*, 8(17): 1–12.

Manning, C. and Roesad, K. (2007). 'The Manpower Law of 2003 and its Implementing Regulations: Genesis, Key Articles and Potential Impact', *Bulletin of Indonesian Economic Studies*, 43(1): 59–86.

Manning, C. and Sumarto, S. (2011). Employment, Living Standards and Poverty: Trends, Policies and Interactions. In C. Manning and S. Sumarto (eds) *Employment, Living Standards and Poverty in Contemporary Indonesia*. Institute of Southeast Asian Studies, Singapore.

Masel, E.K., Schur, S. and Watzke, H.H. (2012). 'Life is Uncertain. Death is Certain. Buddhism and Palliative Care', *Journal of Pain and Symptom Management*, 44(2): 307–12.

Mathieu, J.E. and Zajac, D.M. (1990). 'A Review and Meta-analysis of the Antecedents, Correlates, and Consequences of Organizational Commitment', *Psychological Bulletin*, 108(2): 171–94.

McDaniel, J. (2010). 'Agama Hindu Dharma Indonesia as a New Religious Movement: Hinduism Recreated in the Image of Islam', *Nova Religio: The Journal of Alternative and Emergent Religions*, 14(1): 93–111.

Melisa, F. and Muhammad, D. (2013). 2013 Penduduk Indonesia Diperkirakan 250 Juta Jiwa. Retrieved on 14 September 2013 from http://www.republika. co.id/berita/nasional/umum/13/07/17/mq2oy6-2013-penduduk-indonesia-diperkirakan-250-juta-jiwa.

Menaker-RI (1994). Peraturan Menteri Tenga Kerja R.I NO.PER–04/MEN/1994 tentang Tunjangan Hari Raya Keagamaan Bagi Pekerja di Perusahaan, Jakarta: Kemnaker-RI. Retrieved from http://www.expat.or.id/info/ GovernmentPeraturan-1994-04-Tunjangan-Hari-Raya-Keagamaan.pdf.

Menkokesra. (2012). Di Indonesia ada 13.466 pulau, bukan 17.508 pulau. Retrieved from http://www.menkokesra.go.id/content/di-indonesia-ada-13-466-pulau-bukan-17508-pulau.

Meyer, J.P., Allen, N.J. and Smith, C.A. (1993). 'Commitment to Organizations and Occupations: Extension and Test of a Three-component Conceptualization', *Journal of Applied Psychology*, 78(4): 538–51.

Milallos, M.T.R. (2007). 'Muslim Veil as Politics: Political Autonomy, Women and Syariah Islam in Aceh', *Contemporary Islam*, 1(3): 289–301.

Muntamah. (2012). Ironi Wanita Pekerja, *Suara Merdeka*. Retrieved from http:// www.suaramerdeka.com/v1/index.php/read/cetak/2012/10/03/200818/Ironi-Wanita-Pekerja-.

Muse, L.A. and Pichler, S. (2011). A Comparison of Types of Support for Lower-skill Workers: Evidence for the Importance of Family Supportive Supervisors. *Journal of Vocational Behavior*, 79: 653–66.

Naimon, E.C., Mullins, M.E. and Osatuke, K. (2013). 'The Effects of Personality and Spirituality on Workplace Incivility Perceptions', *Journal of Management, Spirituality and Religion*, 10(1): 91–110.

Odle-Dusseau, H.N., Britt, T.W. and Greene-Shortridge, T.M. (2012). 'Organizational Work–Family Resources as Predictors of Job Performance and Attitudes: The Process of Work–Family Conflict and Enrichment', *Journal of Occupational Health Psychology*, 17(1): 28–40.

O'Driscoll, M.P., Poelmans, S., Spector, P.E., Kalliath, T., Allen, T.D., Cooper, C.L. and Sanchez, J.I. (2003). 'Family-responsive Interventions, Perceived Organizational and Supervisor Support, Work–Family Conflict, and Psychological Strain', *International Journal of Stress Management*, 10(4): 326–44.

Organ, D.W. (1988). *Organizational Citizenship Behavior: The Good Soldier Syndrome*. Lexington Books, Lexington, MA.

Parker, L. and Allen, T.D. (2001). 'Work/Family Benefits: Variables Related to Employees' Fairness Perceptions', *Journal of Vocational Behavior*, 58: 453–68.

Pasca, A.T. (2013). *Tinjauan hukum terhadap peraturan perusahaan atas pelarangan pekerjanya untuk melaksanakan sholat jumat ditinjau dari undang-undang nomor 13 tahun 2003 tentang ketenagakerjaan.* (Bachelor), Padjajaran, Bandung, Indonesia. Retrieved from http://fh.unpad.ac.id/repo/?p=3112.

Pekerti, A.A. and Sendjaya, S. (2010). 'Exploring Servant Leadership across Cultures: Comparative Study in Australia and Indonesia', *The International Journal of Human Resource Management*, 21(5), 754–80.

Peraturan Menteri Tenga Kerja R.I NO.PER–04/MEN/1994 tentang Tunjangan Hari Raya Keagamaan Bagi Pekerja di Perusahaan (1994).

Peraturan pemerintah republik Indonesia nomor 10 tahun 1979 tentang penilaian pelaksanaan pekerjaan pegawai negeri sipil (1979).

Peraturan Pemerintah Republik Indonesia Nomor 46 Tahun 2011 tentang Penilaian Prestasi Kerja Pegawai Negeri Sipil (2011).

Permatasari, P. (2013). Mendagri masih pikir–pikir soal penghapusan kolom agama di ktp. Retrieved from http://www.portalkbr.com/berita/nasional/3037429_4202.html.

Podsakoff, P.M., MacKenzie, S.B., Moorman, R.H. and Fetter, R. (1990). 'Transformational Leader Behaviors and Their Effects on Followers' Trust in Leader, Satisfaction, and Organizational Citizenship Behaviors', *Leadership Quarterly*, 1(2): 107–42.

Presiden–RI. (2000). *Keputusan Presiden Republik Indonesia Nomor 6 Tahun 2000 tentang Pencabutan Instruksi Presiden nomor 14 tahun 1967 tentang Agama, Kepercayaan, dan Adat Istiadat Cina.* Jakarta: DPR–RI. Retrieved from http://www.menkokesra.go.id/node/265.

Presiden-RI. (2007). *Peraturan Pemerintah Republik Indonesia Nomor 55 Tahun 2007 tentang Pendidikan Agama dan Pendidikan Keagamaan.* Jakarta: DPR-RI. Retrieved from http://sultra.kemenag.go.id/file/dokumen/PPNo.55Th.2007.pdf.

Reformed Online. (2002). Indonesia–(Asia). Retrieved from http://www.reformiert-online.net/weltweit/64_eng.php.

Republika Online. (2012). Parade Ogoh-ogoh Jadi Magnet Wisatawan Bali. Retrieved on 21 March 2014, from http://www.republika.co.id/berita/gaya-hidup/travelling/12/03/20/m16ac7-parade-ogohogoh-jadi-magnet-wisatawan-bali.

Ridho, S.L.Z. and Al Raysid, M.N. (2010). Partisipasi angkatan kerja perempuan dan rasio jenis kelamin: Studi kasus negara anggota ASEAN. Retrieved on 27 February 2013, from http://www.bappenas.go.id/blog/?p=297.

Rizal. (2012). Pada kurikulum 2013 hanya lima mata pelajaran wajib untuk tingkat SD. Retrieved from http://www.poskotanews.com/2012/11/14/hanya-lima-mata-pelajaran-wajib-untuk-tingkat-sd/.

Scheibl, F. and Dex, S. (1998). 'Should We Have More Family-Friendly Policies?' *European Management Journal*, 16(5): 586–99.

Sekaran, U. and Bougie, R. (2013). *Research Methods for Business: A Skill-building Approach* (6th edition). John Wiley and Sons Ltd, Chichester.

Spector, P.E. (1997). *Job Satisfaction: Applications, Assessment, Causes and Consequences*. Sage, Thousand Oaks, CA.

Sprung, J.M., Sliter, M.T. and Jex, S.M. (2012). 'Spirituality as a Moderator of the Relationship between Workplace Aggression and Employee Outcomes', *Personality and Individual Differences*, 53(7): 930–34.

Stanford, L. (2008). Social Exchange Theories. In L.A. Baxter and D.O. Braithwaite (eds), *Engaging Theories in Interpersonal Communication: Multiple Perspectives*, Sage, Thousand Oaks, CA, 377–89.

Suara Pembaharuan. (2012). Semua pintu masuk ke Bali ditutup selama perayaan Nyepi. from Suara Pembaharuan. Retrieved from http://www.suarapembaruan.com/home/semua-pintu-masuk-ke-bali-ditutup-selama-perayaan-nyepi/17658.

Suryadinata, L., Arifin, E.N. and Ananta, A. (2003). *Indonesia's Population: Ethnicity and Religion in a Changing Political Landscape*. Institute of Southeast Asian Studies, Singapore.

Tharenou, P., Donohue, R. and Cooper, B. (2007). *Management Research Methods*. Cambridge University Press, New York.

The World Bank. (2013). IFC Championing Women on Corporate Boards in Indonesia. Retrieved on August 15, 2013, from http://www.worldbank.org/en/news/feature/2013/07/31/ifc-championing-women-on-corporate-boards-in-indonesia.

Thompson, C.A., Beauvais, L.L. and Lyness, K.S. (1999). 'When Work–Family Benefits are Not Enough: The Influence of Work–Family Culture on Benefit Utilization, Organizational Attachment, and Work–Family Conflict. *Journal of Vocational Behavior*, 54: 392–415.

Undang–Undang Republik Indonesia Nomer 13 Tahun 2003 tentang Ketenagakerjaan, 13 C.F.R. (2003).

UN Women. (2012). Women are Integral Part of Indonesian Success. Retrieved on August 15, 2013, from http://www.unwomen.org/en/news/stories/2012/12/women-are-integral-part-of-indonesian-success.

United Nations Educational, Scientific and Cultural Organization (UNESCO). (1991). Borobudur Temple Compounds. Retrieved from http://whc.unesco.org/en/list/592.

von der Mehden, F.R. (1987). 'Religion in Asia as a Vehicle for Technological Change', *Bulletin of Science Technology and Society*, 7: 638–49.

Wang, P., Lawler, J.J. and Shi, K. (2011). 'Implementing Family-friendly Employment Practices in Banking Industry: Evidences from Some African and Asian countries', *Journal of Occupational and Organizational Psychology*, 84(3): 493–517.

Wang, P. and Walumbwa, F.O. (2007). 'Family-friendly Programs, Organizational Commitment, and Work Withdrawal: The Moderating Role of Transformational Leadership', *Personnel Psychology*, 60(2): 397–427.

Williams, L.J. and Anderson, S.E. (1991). 'Job Satisfaction and Organizational Commitment as Predictors of Organizational Citizenship and In-role Behaviors., *Journal of Management*, 17(3): 601–17.

World Bank (2013). IFC championing Women on Corporate Boards in Indonesia. Retrieved from http://www.worldbank.org/en/news/feature/2013/07/31/ifc-championing-women-on-corporate-boards-in-indonesia.

Yakub, E.M. (2013). Usaid latih 35 pimpinan perempuan ptn/pts. Retrieved on 16 August 2013, from http://www.antarajatim.com/lihat/berita/104972/usaid-latih-35-pimpinan-perempuan-ptnpts.

Yuningsih. (2012). *Multiple Performance Measures Use and Job-related Tension in the Indonesian Higher Education Sector: The Effect of Leadership Orientation Use and Organizational Culture.* (Doctor of Philosophy), Curtin University, Western Australia.

Yustrianthe, R.H. (2008). 'Pengaruh Flexible Work Arrangement therhadap rolr Conflict, Role Overload, Reduced Personal Accomplishment, Job Satisfaction and Intention to Stay', *Jurnal Bisnis dan Akuntansi*, 10(3): 127–38.

PART IV
Europe

Chapter 14

Religion and Spirituality – the Blind Spot of Business Schools? Empirical Snapshots and Theoretical Reflections

WOLFGANG MAYRHOFER AND MARTIN A. STEINBEREITHNER

Introduction – A Blind Spot

Our starting point is straightforward: religion and spirituality[1] have no established place in today's major business schools. More precisely, we posit that religion and spirituality constitute a blind spot for the goals and values of major business schools around the globe, in their daily routines and infrastructure, and in their leadership education curricula. To illustrate this assertion, three pieces of anecdotal evidence may suffice.

A cursory look at mission statements and core values of leading business schools reveals that religion and spirituality are, at best, only implicitly addressed. For example, Stanford's 'mission is to create ideas that deepen and advance our understanding of management and with those ideas to develop innovative, principled, and insightful leaders who change the world'. In order to do so, they urge their students to 'engage intellectually, strive for something great, respect others, act with integrity, and own your actions'.[2] HEC in Paris aims at 'training the global leaders of tomorrow, and taking an active part in the production of knowledge on management', building on three core values of selectivity in terms of attracting only the best individuals, international

---

1   We are well aware of the difference – and sometimes abyss – between spirituality and religion despite a number of commonalities (for a detailed discussion see, for example, Hill et al., 2000). For this chapter, we can safely include both viewpoints without differentiation – our argument holds up for both of them.

2   Retrieved on 27 February 2014 from www.gsb.stanford.edu/stanford-gsb-experience/leadership.

outreach, and a sense of initiative and social diversity.[3] Overall, in the eyes of a witty commentator this seems to reflect 'soul searching, not soul stirring' (Reisz, 2010).

In 2013, WU Vienna departed from its current location and moved all of its 24,000 students and operations to a new campus, consisting of six major sets of buildings on a lot of 90,000 square metres, larger than 12 soccer fields combined, and more than 100,000 square meters net usage area.[4] An overarching motto while designing the new campus was 'a place to live'. The only element explicitly addressing the religious and spiritual plane of this place to live is a so-called 'quiet room' of about 40 square metres which was the result of the lobbying efforts of a few members of the faculty, not integral to the project and not in usable condition six months after the opening.

Major textbooks on leadership show little, if any, regard for religious and spiritual matters. For example, an excellent textbook about teaching leadership (Snook et al., 2012) collects major voices in the field and takes a comprehensive view. Yet, links to the transcendental are hardly visible.

Assuming that this anecdotal evidence reflects a broader picture holding up under more rigorous empirical scrutiny, we first argue that these blind spots lead to substantial shortcomings with regard to the global impact of business schools, their educational imprint on students, and their effectiveness in terms of making the world a better place to live and work in. We will then show two brief examples of how two leading European business schools address the blind spot in substantially different ways. In a final step, and using various theoretical lenses, we will consider a broad spectrum of approaches how to handle this blind spot of business schools.

Of course, behind the assumed consequences and potential reactions we outline in this chapter lie a number of implicit basic assumptions about fundamental aspects of life. First, we assume that a transcendent plane exists in which individuals and their social and material context are embedded and which is important in order to understand individual and collective action. This differentiates us from people with a solely materialistic, atheistic and agnostic viewpoint. Second, we do subscribe to a monotheistic personal God who is both the beginning and the end of human history. Among others, this

---

3   Retrieved on 27 February 2014 from www.hec.edu/About-HEC/About-HEC-Paris/Mission-Values.
4   Retrieved on 27 February 2014 from www.campuswu.at/en/.

demarcates our perspective from views favouring an abstract supreme being or principle and a view of human development moving in birth–rebirth cycles. Third, we do acknowledge a Trinitarian God of Father, Son and Holy Spirit in the Christian traditions who, although still in struggle with the powers of darkness, has opened up the road to a bright future and eternal life through the death and resurrection of Jesus Christ. This perspective is as contested as it is unique within the array of monotheistic religions, most notably Judaism and Islam. From this vantage point, we first outline some consequences of aforementioned blind spot, most notably sacrificing international relevance, failing students by not providing perspectives which are now mainstream in the business world, and clinging to what deem an unreasonable bias. We then look at a couple of business schools' attempts to address this blind spot before closing with seven observations about the phenomenon at hand.

Consequences of the Blind Spot

Assigning spirituality and religion to constitute the blind spot of business schools has at least three major consequences: it reduces global impact and relevance of business schools; fails students by procrastinating the educational scope; and is at the brink of being unreasonable when trying to make the world a better place to live in. We will address these issues in turn.

SACRIFICING RELEVANCE

Religious and spiritual viewpoints arguably do play an enormous role in the work life of explicitly Islamic countries such as Pakistan or Saudi Arabia, in countries with a strong proportion of Hindu faith such as India or in regions with a strong Christian population, for example some states of the US such as Mississippi where 91 per cent of the population believe with absolute certainty in God (Pew Research Center, 2012). Not every country and region in the world assigns religion to the confines of church buildings (Norris and Inglehart, 2011). Anthropologists and students of cultural differences have long acknowledged that religion and its connected values need to be taken into consideration when working across cultural boundaries (Hofstede, 1980, 1991).

Similarly, even countries in the more secularized West acknowledge the contribution of faith-based organizations in the area of community building and service delivery (Jochum et al., 2007). Some governments dialogue with and actively encourage the participation of religious bodies in civic life, because of the benefit these organizations bring (Commission on Urban Life and Faith,

2006; Dinham et al., 2009; Putnam, 2000), even when such steps are looked at askance by some quarters.

A country like the UK, not particularly religious by most people's standards, still has 53 per cent of its population calling itself Christian and 7.6 million people attending church monthly (Ashwo and Farthing, 2007). Even just judging from the waning majority of Christians, religion is still important to many people in that country.

For all those reasons, blanking out issues of spirituality and religion from business education renders the taught concepts and their underlying assumptions vulnerable to the criticism of being incomplete, inaccurate and, consequently, less relevant than they could be (Crossman, 2003).

FAILING THE STUDENTS

Displaying a blind sport regarding spirituality and religion cripples business schools' educational efforts and mandate vis-à-vis their student body. Over the past decades, a substantial literature on management, religion and spirituality has emerged (see, for example, the overview about the relationship between spirituality and performance in organizations in Karakas, 2010). Likewise, its advocates have established themselves in prestigious professional associations such as the Academy of Management, for example through its MSR interest group, and founded respectable journals such as the *Journal of Management, Spirituality and Religion*. In spite of this, business schools seem to be reluctant to include this point of view into their goals and values, daily life, educational goals and curricula. Among others, as a consequence business schools turn out graduates, arguably a great proportion of which will climb a few, if not all, of the rungs of the corporate and societal career ladder, who are missing a holistic picture of individual and collective actors, their various contextual layers and their interplay which includes the religious and spiritual aspect. In this way they fall short of a comprehensive view which they offer their students.

The question whether one can reasonably claim to look at reality and then blank out all spiritual and religious issues shall be examined in the next section. For now, we simply want to consider whether a curriculum purged of any such allusions genuinely serves the needs of business students. If we judge by market demand, the answer must be negative. Even when frowned upon by some of the mainstream community, management and leadership consultants acknowledging and even using a religious framework are on the rise. Consider the success of books such as Covey's *Seven Habits of Highly*

Successful People (1989) or the Arbinger Institute's *Leadership and Self-Deception* (2010). Such books are no longer seen as lightweight fringe phenomena, as the acknowledgments of serious publications hardly suspicious of being friendly to religion and spirituality indicate.[5] While managers of Fortune 500 companies hire consultants who openly acknowledge the need of the spiritual as one dimension of human life and flourishing, such talk is noticeably absent from the various training institutions.

It has become commonplace to attribute the recent banking crisis and the subsequent economic meltdown to greed and lack of virtue (Sedlacek, 2011). But evidence that religious values impact ethical behaviour of managers pre-dates the crisis (Bennis and O'Toole, 2005; Cullen et al. , 2004; Georges, 2008; for a differentiated view see Leitner, 2013). In fact, until recently, it was considered common sense that one of the bases for morality was spirituality (Bennett, 1995), not only in the so-called 'Christian' West, but across the cultures and throughout the ages (Lewis, 2001).

It does not seem as overstated to posit that the lack of spirituality and religion in the business school curricula fails the very students they seem to educate. In addition, there is a more fundamental and epistemological reason to argue for religious and spiritual content, to which we now turn.

BEING UNREASONABLE

Blanking out religion and spirituality from regular theory and model building as well as teaching curtails its practical benefits. Removing such crucial parts from the picture inhibits, among others, the accuracy of theoretical reasoning and the effectiveness of leadership training. To be sure, management concepts in general and leadership theories and frameworks in particular do acknowledge the importance of 'soft' elements beyond classical competencies. These include, for example, values or ethical considerations, reflected in concepts such as value-based leadership (for example, Dahm and Waldhaim, 2011), servant leadership (Dierendonck and Patterson, 2010) or ethical leadership (for example, Millar and Poole, 2011). These discourses at least partly pay attention to the religious and spiritual element as whole.

However, universities following the US American type of division of Church and State consider any religious talk as belonging to the domain of churches and maybe of church-affiliated educational institutions. They maintain that

---

5   Retrieved on 25 February 2014 from www.economist.com/node/21559329.

their teaching deals with facts, and not with values or, even worse, deep-rooted religious and spiritual convictions. But it has been argued that such a distinction is hard to maintain (Sommerville, 2006). While secular universities often consider themselves progressive, some authors would hold that they are stuck in the post-modern era and need to adapt (Sommerville, 2009). Or, taking a broader historical perspective, that secular education which does not take into account religious questions, holds a bias which lacks intellectual integrity (Malik, 1982; Schaeffer, 1971). When John Henry Newman, a well-known religious figure in nineteenth century England and, among others, involved in the founding of University College Dublin's predecessor institution, set out what it would take to establish a university, he clearly considered moral and religious questions as part of the curriculum (Newman and Turner, 1996).

We could ask whether business discourse is even possible without any value reference. Macintyre has forcibly argued that such a path inevitably leads to universities' self-destruction (MacIntyre, 1985; MacIntyre and Bell, 1967; MacIntyre and Dunne, 2002). Human life and flourishing needs virtue, and virtue cannot be spoken about, let alone instilled, by means of Enlightenment ideas. It requires the reference to a higher being (MacIntyre, 1984). So far from needing to jettison all religious notions, universities need to reclaim lost ground if they seek to maintain intellectual integrity and relevance (MacIntyre, 2009).

Addressing the Blind Spot

In this section we take a brief exploratory look at two European business schools ranked among the top 20 in the *Financial Times* European Business School Rankings 2012: IESE in Barcelona, Spain; and Vlerick Business School, Leuven, Belgium. Based on existing documents and semi-structured interviews with faculty members of each institution, we analyse their goals for educating business school graduates, the core values they build on and the role of religion and spirituality in their daily routines.

EXAMPLE 1: IESE[6]

Founded in 1958, IESE is the graduate business school of the University of Navarra. It offers business leaders a holistic view of the firm and an emphasis

---

6   Unless stated otherwise, the text in this subsection builds on the information available at www. iese.edu/en (retrieved in March 2014), partially quoting verbatim, and on a semi-structured interview with a faculty member of IESE.

on the ethical and human aspects of business activities. IESE has its focus on people and their personal and professional development which it sees as a primary driver of positive change and impact on business and society. It is linked to the Opus Dei, a Personal Prelature – an institution where clergy and lay members carry out specific pastoral activities – of the Roman Catholic Church, which was founded in 2 October 1928 by Josemaria Escrivá de Balaguer.

Goals and values

For IESE, sustainable and long-term global prosperity can be achieved through a humanistic approach to business. This helps business leaders to influence companies and society positively, shaping the world for future generations. IESE strives to ensure that professionalism, integrity and a respect for others, are at the core of everything it does.

Daily routines and infrastructure

The Catholic–Christian heritage is visible both in the daily life and the organizational infrastructure. A few examples can illustrate this.

In terms of hardware, Christian symbols have a prominent place on campus. In every lecture room there is a statue of Mary, mother of Jesus. According to the teachings of the Opus Dei, sacred rooms such as churches or chapels should have a special place in the community. Consequently, the chapel has pride of place in the new campus.

In terms of daily routines, IESE seeks to take a holistic view of the life of its faculty members. New faculty get an invitation to a voluntary session on Opus Dei and its history. The family has a central role and is acknowledged through various means. This includes family days, that is events where the families of faculty members are invited, or a specific mass if a family member of one of the staff has passed away. IESE also offers support for the personal spiritual growth for faculty, students, and alumni based on Christian principles through the IESE Chaplaincy, staffed by Opus Dei priests. It is open to Christians and non-Christians alike and complements IESE's academic and professional programmes by providing the space and resources to allow those interested in the Christian faith to develop spiritually.

Teaching

In teaching, the transformative and ethical aspect of university education plays a visible role. The MBA semester starts with a Holy mass in a nearby church on a voluntary basis. There are specific faculty seminars where the new faculty learns about the mission of the school and the importance of ethical values. The ethical angle is also built as much as possible into all courses, a fact that is also part of the USP advertised to potential new students. This serves consequently as a kind of self-selection filter on the part of participants of the programme who choose this school because they are looking for this special perspective on the world.

In the MBA programme for example, the transformational impact of the programme is the major selling point. The brochure for the MBA programme emphasizes this,[7] In particular, it points out that 'a firm grasp of business ethics is becoming increasingly important for leading companies successfully and sustainably' and that 'ethics and the impact of business decisions on people inside and outside the company are interwoven into every IESE course'.

EXAMPLE 2: KU LEUVEN AND VLERICK BUSINESS SCHOOL[8]

Situated in the heart of Western Europe, KU Leuven has been a centre of learning for almost six centuries. Founded in 1425 by Pope Martin V, KU Leuven bears the dual honour of being the oldest extant Catholic university in the world and the oldest university in the Low Countries.

Vlerick Business School, as the management school of Belgium's two largest universities, Ghent University and KU Leuven, claims to be the oldest business and management school in Europe as it was founded in 1953 by the renowned academic, entrepreneur and politician, André Vlerick.[9] In 1999, there was a merger of the MBA programmes at De Vlerick School voor Management and KU Leuven and the foundation of Vlerick Leuven Gent Management School.

---

7   Retrieved on 5 March 2014 from www.iese.edu/en/mba/program-structure/.
8   Unless stated otherwise, the text in this subsection builds on the information available at www.kuleuven.be/english/ and www.vlerick.com/en (retrieved March 2014), partially quoting verbatim, and on two semi-structured interviews with a current and a former faculty member of KU Leuven/Vlerick Business School.
9   This claim might only be true if you strictly stick to the label 'business school' since *Handelshochschulen* in the German language area, for example in Leipzig, Vienna, or St. Gallen, were founded at the end of the nineteenth century and were very much like 'business schools' in the present sense.

Goals and values

In its identity and mission statement, KU Leuven describes the University's Catholic tradition, its identity, its value system, its role as a critical centre of thought in and for the Catholic community, and emphasizes its openness to all worldviews. At the same time, it emphasizes the University's autonomy as an essential condition for academic freedom. In recent decades, the University has taken care to protect its institutional autonomy and the Catholic Church has always respected that. The university wants to make its identity and autonomy explicit, both in its structure and in its pedagogical project. From this perspective, the University's course offerings include perspectives on religion and meaning, philosophy and ethics to include insights from diverse human perspectives and worldviews as well as from the natural and social sciences, cultural studies and the arts. The University seeks to further integrate openness, from a Christian perspective, in its staff policy, social engagement, diversity policy, social services for students, treatment of bioethical questions, mission and task of the university parish, development cooperation and humanitarian relief efforts, and so on.

Apart from focusing on its philosophical profile, the mission statement also emphasizes the University's international orientation, the intensity and inter-disciplinarity of its research, the quality of its education and the importance it attributes to serving society in diverse domains.

In terms of institutional structure, KU Leuven maintains a close association with the Catholic community but also emphasizes its full autonomy. 'KU Leuven' is the University's 'corporate' name. In an international context, the name may also be complemented when necessary or desired with the appended name 'Catholic University of Leuven', depending on the context or target group, or 'University of Leuven', as is already commonly done.

The mission statement contains, among others, the following:

- From its Christian view of the world and the human, KU Leuven endeavours to be a place for open discussion of social, philosophical and ethical issues and a critical centre of reflection in and for the Catholic community.

- KU Leuven offers its students an academic education based on high-level research, with the aim of preparing them to assume their social responsibilities.

- KU Leuven encourages personal initiative and critical reflection in a culture of idea exchange, cooperation, solidarity and academic freedom. It pursues a proactive diversity policy for its students and staff.

- KU Leuven aims to actively participate in public and cultural debate and in the advancement of a knowledge-based society. It puts its expertise to the service of society, with particular consideration for its most vulnerable members.

- From a basis of social responsibility and scientific expertise, KU Leuven provides high-quality, comprehensive health care, including specialized tertiary care, in its University Hospitals. In doing so it strives towards optimum accessibility and respect for all patients.

Vlerick Business School describes itself as offering fully-accredited, world-class education programmes combining a healthy mix of theoretical knowledge and practical insight leading to a solid, worldwide reputation as a leading, independent institution with a strong international focus and close ties to both the academic and corporate worlds. There are four major elements of the Vlerick spirit which sets this school apart from others: openness, vitality and a passion for innovation and enterprise. Beyond that, the school regards being international and being pragmatic as additional brand drivers.

Daily routines and infrastructure

Regarding daily routines, the spiritual and religious dimension hardly matters. There is no specific induction of new staff members. Among others, this means that new members do not systematically familiarize themselves with the history and value base of the University and business school. The primary principle of daily life is a blanking out of private activities and conditions: what you do in your private life is a private matter.

There are a few exceptions to the invisibility of the spirituality and religion dimension in daily life. For one, there is a church building linked to one building of the University which faculty can use for ceremonies such as marriage or funeral ceremonies. In addition, there is a University parish which welcomes people from various parts of the world; it strives to foster an open atmosphere where people from different backgrounds, cultures and countries, people of different age and walks of life, people affiliated with the University and people who have other affiliations can meet and share their faith. Its vision is to build a Christian community in a changing world.

Teaching

In teaching, business ethics and social responsibility are built into a variety of courses. In the curriculum, there are three mandatory courses – philosophy, ethics and religion – which you have to take whatever your chosen course of studies is. The European Credit Transfer System (ECTS) workload in these courses (three ECTS) is quite small compared to regular courses in the curriculum.

The inclusion of business ethics has at least two major roots. First, it is spurred by the various corporate scandals which have emerged over the past years and have brought the issue of 'right or wrong' more to the forefront. Second, the pressure towards accreditation by various agencies which often demand the inclusion of business ethics element into the curricula has contributed to the prominence of this subject, too.

Handling the Blind Spot: Seven Observations

Based on our basic assumptions and inspired by both our theoretical background in organizational theory and our exploratory empirical efforts we will in a next step formulate seven observations which address different aspects of the relationship between business schools and spirituality and religion.

PARASITIC PRACTICES

Business schools in WEIRD countries (Western, Educated, Industrialized, Rich, Democratic) face a situation where the explicit use of spirituality and religion in the public context is clearly regulated. Of course, this varies by degrees. In France, the ban of public prayer introduced by legislation in 2011 targets public expression of core faith-related activities. On the other hand, in the US, the First Amendment to the constitution provides a strong basis for the freedom of speech in many areas, making the US a country with one of the broadest views on this subject. In addition, there exists a certain tension between various forms of spirituality and religion on the one hand and the basic assumptions of science on the other, for example with regard to acceptable methodology or the role of transcendence.

Overall, this makes it difficult for business schools in these countries to directly address the spiritual and religious dimension of the society, economy and individual life. However, there are accepted ways of bringing these issues into the discourse. Arguably, the most prominent and accepted way is business ethics. Society, organizations and individuals do see the need to transcend pure instrumental rationality (*Zweckrationalität*) which is at the heart of the capitalist system of economy currently dominating the world and also include value/belief oriented rationality (*Wertrationalität*) related to the question of good or bad. Incidents such as Enron do make it hard to turn a blind eye to these issues. Business ethics promises at least a partial answer to this. It has become an accepted and respectable part of business school syllabi.

Therefore, it comes as little surprise that business school use business ethics and other accepted elements of the leadership discourse such as servant leadership or transformational leadership as an inroad, maybe even as a disguise for introducing some elements of spirituality and religion into an otherwise 'worldly' environment. For example, in the case of IESE, this is clearly visible. It has strong religious roots. While they are visible in various layers of the organizational culture, they are tellingly absent in the presentation of the school and programme to the outside world. At the same time, the inclusion of ethical issues and the recourse to ethics is a clear selling point for their programmes.

Theoretically speaking, business schools use parasitic practices (Serres, 1982). The respectability of business ethics and leadership discourse enables business schools to provide the 'host environment' if and when they decide to address spiritual and religious aspects. This leads to the following thesis:

> *Thesis 1: Business schools wanting to emphasize the spiritual and religious dimension use established leadership talk, buzzwords and concepts as a vehicle for bringing selected aspects of spirituality and religion into teachings.*

BEYOND THE POINT OF NO RETURN?

Enlightenment saw the break-up of the church's monopoly on education and the emancipation of many university institutions from religious patronage. This step was useful because it made possible research into previously taboo topics (see the Galileo controversy). Sciences, most notably the natural sciences, profited from such unshackling. But from seeking independence of ideological dominance the trend has moved to banning all religious speech at many institutions of higher learning.[10] Religious stances on particular moral issues are rarely tolerated, as in the case of France or the USA. One pretends that rational beings do have values, but such values are not allowed to be rooted in any religious beliefs. The Aspen Institute[11] is a co-founder of a business school initiative called 'Giving Voice to Values', seeking to help with developing value-based leadership, but nowhere in its materials does it state where one derives one's values, as if they suddenly appeared out of thin air. Conversely, very respected scholars such as Christensen get ridiculed when they out themselves and point concretely to their religious beliefs as the source of their values and mission (Christensen, 2010).

However, recent developments in the financial crisis have revealed that the so-called 'value-free' approach to business is not only fictitious, but dangerous, and business schools everywhere are scurrying to include the topic and ethics in their curricula. But often this amounts to 'castrating and then bidding the gelding to be fruitful' (Lewis, 2001). It would seem logical to consult experts, that is people who have dealt with ethical questions for a long time, and indeed this is what some people do, by inviting abbots, gurus and so on to speak on the subject. This leads to our second thesis:

> *Thesis 2: The 'laicite'[12] approach to modern education, while being useful when instituted, has outlived its purpose and now makes some forms of fruitful and efficiency-enhancing teaching impossible, or at least very difficult.*

LOCKING-IN EFFECTS

The division of religion and, arguably, spirituality on the one hand and modern universities on the other hand comes at a price. Being built into the institutional environment, for example legal regulations, as well as into the culture of existing organizations, it is an often not visible, but highly salient part of the daily life of business schools and their members. Accordingly, they have made decisions in line with these assumptions over time in the area of hiring, formulating strategies and mission, and making public announcements via their web pages, strategy papers and personal communications.

---

10 Retrieved on 3 March 2014 from http://news.bbc.co.uk/2/hi/6232869.stm.
11 Retrieved on 4 March 2014 from www.aspeninstitute.org/about/mission.
12 French technical term dating back to 1842 referring to the absence of religious symbols, topics or personalities in public life.

In line with the considerations of path dependence, this makes it difficult both for organizations and individuals to reintroduce explicit elements of spirituality and religion. Path dependence is 'a process that (1) is triggered by a critical event leading to a critical juncture; (2) is governed by a regime of positive, self-reinforcing feedback constituting a specific pattern of social practices, which gains more and more predominance against alternatives; and (3) leads, at least potentially, into an organizational lock-in, understood as a corridor of limited scope of action that is strategically inefficient' (Sydow et al., 2009). In our case, both at the macro-level of societal developments and at the micro-level of organizational history, such critical junctures can be identified. Be it the era of Enlightenment or, as with KU Leuven, the symbolic distancing by removing 'Catholic' from the name of the University: the path that business schools take makes it difficult for them to change direction even in case whole institutions or select individuals regard it as necessary to change course. From this, the following thesis emerges:

> *Thesis 3: The Western division public/private sphere of spirituality vs. teaching/research means that even 'religious' people and institutions find it hard to bridge that divide again – very much in contrast with Far or Near Eastern settings.*

AMBIVALENT PRACTICES

Modern business schools emphasize the secular angle. If at all, they use an accepted surrogate, business ethics, to address issues beyond the visible. Theoretically speaking, permanently favouring one pole – here: the secular angle – at the expense of an opposing pole – here: spirituality and religion – has several drawbacks for organizations. As Weick (1969) points out, keeping these poles and making use of discrediting is important. Discrediting has a number of facets. In the present context arguably the most important is that it in case of contradictory values, motives or goals, it is important to keep them alive in the organization and not destroy them by either focusing solely on one pole or trying to achieve a compromise which in the end destroys both potentials by taking middle ground. Ambivalence is the optimal compromise, as Weick (2000) suggests. This not only allows the organization to use existing potentials in a better way. It also strengthens the organization when coping with environmental changes and the required adaptations. Having greater internal variety allows organizations to cope with a broader variety of external developments and requirements.

Discrediting involves a specific handling of the contradicting poles. One approach is sequential use, that is to use them in a sequential way. Time is a differentiator here in the sense that at specific times, one pole has priority. For example, business schools priding themselves on being cutting-edge and modern do have times when they emphasize tradition and roots in the past, for example when designing award ceremonies and graduations. A second major way of keeping polarities alive is to institutionally segregate them. Here, the poles express themselves in different organizational arenas and activities. For example, making profits and being corporative socially responsible is partly contradictory. Building organizational units which represent these values and goals allows both of them to be present. In the case of business schools, they could, for example, build ambivalence into their position vis-à-vis spirituality and religion: being strictly neutral at the organizational level while, at the same time, allowing all kinds of activities at the grassroots-level of courses. This leads us to the following thesis:

> *Thesis 4: Business schools should not handle contradictory views about spirituality and religion by compromising or favouring one pole over the other in their syllabi and daily life, but by building ambivalence into their structures and processes.*

BASSO CONTINUO

It has often been argued that organizations have a life and culture of their own, almost or completely independently of its members and that culture is hardwired into the organization and thus remains even after all its members have moved on (see, for example, the debate on organizational culture (Frost, 1985; Schein, 1985) or views which regard social systems as fundamentally different from the individuals they are linked with, for example Luhmann, 1995). This phenomenon is actively encouraged and taken advantage of in the context of organizational learning (Argyris and Schön, 1978; Argote, 1999) which hopes to engrave certain routines and experiences into the organizational memory and thus not lose it when those who first discovered such knowledge exit the firm.

When one meets representatives of Catholic educational establishments, but also of so-called Catholic countries, one is often struck how little identification with Catholicism those people display. They are often indifferent, sometimes even openly critical of the historical heritage which their schools, universities or nations own. And still, that cultural Catholicism colours the teaching and life of those people. Examples for this include the existence and use of chapels linked to various religious traditions, the use of religious and/or spiritually loaded symbols such as advent wreaths, or the official acknowledgement of pastors being of service to students and faculty. This leads us to our next thesis:

> *Thesis 5: A historic organizational commitment to spiritual values impacts the teaching and life of an institution even if faculty members do not personally espouse those values – almost in spite of that fact.*

COMPETITIVE ADVANTAGE

We have argued above that avoiding the destruction of contradictory poles in the organization by discrediting and building in ambivalence into the organization strategically puts you into a better position to cope with changing environmental demands.

In the present day, there are a number of factors that call for a stronger presence of spirituality and religion in business schools' life and educational programmes. This includes a strong and in some regions, such as Central and Eastern Europe or Scandinavia, strongly increasing ethnic and spiritual diversity as indicated by a growing proportion of migrants permanently living in the country or by a diverse religious background. There is also a rediscovery of the spiritual and religious dimension of the economy:

> *The … crisis should warn us to fundamentally rethink the development of the moral framework and the regulatory mechanisms that underpin our economy, politics and global interconnectedness. It would be a wasted opportunity for all of us if we pretended that the crisis was simply a momentary hurdle. If we want to keep society together, then a sense of community and solidarity are more important now than ever before. The most fundamental question today is whether we can adopt a more communitarian spirit or whether we will fall back into old habits and excesses, thereby further undermining social peace.*

This view was not expressed by a spiritual or religious leader, but by Klaus Schwab, the World Economic Forum Founder and Chairman (World Economic Forum, 2011). In addition, calls for strengthening human rights and global justice are part of the global picture.

Business schools with a *modus operandi* including spirituality and religion have an additional resource to respond to these developments. Compared to their counterparts that exclude this dimension of societal, organizational and individual life, they are able to provide students and society with a greater variety and, we tend to argue, depth of answers. This leads to the following thesis:

Thesis 6: Openness to spirituality and religion and its inclusion into basic layers of the organizational culture provides a competitive advantage for business schools.

INOCULATION

Ever since Merton (1968), the idea of institutional anomy holds that as cultural values emphasizing achievement grow in societies, it becomes easier to justify the means via the ends, and thus social norms of ethical behaviour are being ignored. More recently this assertion of Merton's has been tested, both for nations (Messner and Rosenfeld, 1997) and for managers across different nations (Cullen et al., 2004). While the evidence is not completely conclusive, there seem to be grounds to believe that as values such as achievement orientation, materialism, universalism and individualism increase, so is the likelihood that people ignore what are considered universal norms of ethical behaviour.

Weber would have said that at least some of those values in question are actually the fruit of particular streams of Christianity (Weber, 1992). On the other hand, many religious traditions do emphasize such things as being over doing, detachment from material goods and seeking the common good over one's own. It would seem logical therefore that institutions which are steeped in some of those spiritual traditions would produce graduates less ready to engage in unethical behaviour. Hence our last thesis:

Thesis 7: Educational establishments which espouse the spiritual values of community, material detachment and humility produce graduates which are less likely to engage in unethical behaviour than their 'secular' equivalents.

Conclusion

The anecdotal empirical evidence suggests that there are three types of business schools as regards their approach to religion and spirituality. First, schools such as IESE exist, which are comparatively young, have explicitly religious roots and aims, and who seek to integrate actively spiritual elements into life and teaching. Second, business schools such as KU Leuven exist which have deep roots in religious institutions, but over the past 50 years or so they have very actively tried to shed any pious image and to appear modern, 'with the times' and free from any ideological affiliation. In this process they have potentially sacrificed what would be a competitive advantage as regards religion and spirituality. Third, and they arguably constitute the majority, there are schools without any religious affiliation or tradition. They come to the topic of spirituality from a virgin perspective, with little previous know-how or hang-ups.

Such a 'typology' potentially helps frame future research as one tries to isolate factors which hinder and others which encourage a fruitful use of spiritual content in business school teaching and practice. Our initial assertion was that ignoring religion and spirituality in business schools potentially harms universities as they interact with representatives from other cultural and national contexts such as the Middle and the Far East. It is clear that major regions of the world differ systematically when it comes to that issue, such as North America, Europe, Islamic countries and India. Theoretical sampling has yet to be fully worked out, but different related yet still distinct dimensions stand out, like the degree to which religion is a private matter, the division of 'Church and State', and the level of religiosity of the population. All those would be key considerations during theoretical sampling and before engaging in systematic comparative case studies. But we would expect such research efforts to be fruitful in helping to clarify the role of spirituality and religion in business schools and allowing them to learn from each other – for their own benefits and those of their students.

References

Arbinger Institute. (2010). *Leadership and Self-deception: Getting Out of the Box.* San Francisco: Berrett-Koehler Publishers.

Argote, L. (1999). *Organizational Learning: Creating, Retaining and Transferring Knowledge.* Kluwer Academic, Boston, MA.

Argyris, C. and Schön, D. (1978). *Organizational Learning: A Theory of Action Perspective.* Addison–Wesley, Reading, MA.

Ashwo, J. and Farthing, I. (2007). *Churchgoing in the UK. A research report from Tearfund on church attendance in the UK.* Tearfund, London.

Bennett, W. J. (1995). *Moral Compass: Stories for a Life's Journey.* New York: Simon & Schuster.

Bennis, W.G. and O'Toole, J. (2005). 'How Business Schools Lost Their Way', *Harvard Business Review*, 83(5): 96–104.

Christensen, C.M. (2010). 'How Will You Measure Your Life?' *Harvard Business Review*, 88(7–8): 46–51.

Commission on Urban Life and Faith. (2006). *Faithful Cities*. Church of England, London.

Covey, S. (1989). *The Seven Habits of Highly Successful People*. Fireside, New York.

Crossman, J. (2003). 'Secular Spiritual Development in Education from International and Global Perspectives', *Oxford Review of Education*, 29(4): 503–20.

Cullen, J.B., Parboteeah, K.P. and Hoegl, M. (2004). 'Crossnational Differences in Managers' Willingness to Justify Ethically Suspect Behaviors: A Test of Institutional Anomy Theory', *Academy of Management Journal*, 47(3): 411–21.

Dahm, M.H. and Waldhaim, M. (2011). *Value–based Leadership: Gaining Sustainable Competitive Advantages*. Shaker, Aachen.

Dierendonck, D.V. and Patterson, K. (2010). *Servant Leadership: Developments in Theory and Research*. Palgrave Macmillan, Basingstoke.

Dinham, A., Furbey, R. and Lowndes, V. (2009). *Faith in the Public Realm: Controversies, Policies and Practices*. Policy, Bristol.

Frost, P.J. (1985). *Organizational Culture*. Sage Publications, Beverley Hills, CA.

Georges, R.P. (Producer). (2008). Making Business Moral. First Things. Retrieved on 17 December 2014 from http://www.firstthings.com/article/2008/10/002-making-business-moral.

Hill, P.C., Pargament, K.I., Hood, R.W., Jr., M.E.M., Swyers, J.P., Larson, D.B. and Zinnbauer, B.J. (2000). 'Conceptualizing Religion and Spirituality: Points of Commonality, Points of Departure', *Journal for the Theory of Social Behaviour*, 30(1): 51–77.

Hofstede, G. (1980). *Culture's Consequence-International Differences in Work-Related Values*. Sage Publications, Newbury Park.

Hofstede, G. (1991). *Cultures and Organizations – Software of the Mind*. McGraw-Hill, London.

Jochum, V., Pratten, B. and Wilding, K. (eds.) (2007). Faith and Voluntary Action. An Overview of Current Evidence and Debates. NCVO, London.

Karakas, F. (2010). Spirituality and Performance in Organizations: A Literature Review *Journal of Business Ethics*, 94(1): 89–106.

Leitner, J. (2013). Religiosität als Prädiktor ethischer Urteile im Wirtschaftskontext – ein Beitrag zur Unternehmensethik als Individualethik. Doctoral Dissertation, WU Vienna, Vienna.

Lewis, C.S. (2001). *The Abolition of Man*. HarperOne, New York.

Luhmann, N. (1995). *Social Systems*. Stanford University Press, Stanford, CA.

MacIntyre, A. (1985). Relativism, Power and Philosophy. Paper presented at the Proceedings and addresses of the American Philosophical Association.

MacIntyre, A. 2009. *God, Philosophy, Universities – A History of the Catholic Philosophical Tradition*. Continuum, London.

MacIntyre, A. and Bell, D. (1967). 'Symposium: The Idea of a Social Science'. *Proceedings of the Aristotelian Society*, Supplementary Volumes, 41: 95–132.

MacIntyre, A. and Dunne, J. (2002). 'Alasdair MacIntyre on Education: In Dialogue with Joseph Dunne', *Journal of Philosophy of Education*, 36(1): 1–19.

MacIntyre, A.C. (1984). *After Virtue*. University of Notre Dame Press, Notre Dame, IN.

Malik, C.H. (1982). *A Christian Critique of the University*. InterVarsity Press, Downers Grove.

Merton, R.K. (1968). *Social Theory and Social Structure*. The Free Press, New York.

Messner, S.F. and Rosenfeld, R. (1997). 'Political Restraint of the Market and Levels of Criminal Homicide: A Cross-national Application of Institutional–Anomie Theory', *Social Forces*, 75(4): 1393–416.

Millar, C. and Poole, E. (2011). *Ethical Leadership: Global Challenges and Perspectives*. Palgrave Macmillan, New York.

Newman, J.H.C., & Turner, F.F.M. (1996). *The Idea of a University*. Yale University Press, New Haven & London.

Norris, P. and Inglehart, R. (2011). *Sacred and Secular: Politics and Religion Worldwide*. Cambridge University Press, Cambridge.

Pew Research Center (2012*). The Global Religious Landscape. A Report on the Size and Distribution of the World's Major Religious Groups as of 2010*. Pew Research Center's Forum on Religion & Public Life, Washington DC.

Putnam, R.D. (2000). *Bowling Alone – The Collapse and Revival of American Community*. Simon & Schuster, New York.

Reisz, M. (2010). 'Soul Searching, Not Soul Stirring', *Times Higher Education*, 20 May.

Schaeffer, F.A. (1971). *True Spirituality*. Tyndale House Publishers, Wheaton, IL.

Schein, E.H. (1985). *Organizational Culture and Leadership. A Dynamic View*. Jossey-Bass, San Francisco, CA.

Sedlacek, T. (2011). *Economics of Good and Evil: The Quest for Economic Meaning from Gilgamesh to Wall Street*. Oxford University Press, Oxford.

Serres, M. (1982). *The Parasite*. Johns Hopkins University Press, Baltimore, MD, London.

Snook, S., Nohira, N. and Khurana, R. (eds) (2012). *The Handbook for Teaching Leadership: Knowing, Doing, and Being*. Sage, Los Angeles, CA.

Sommerville, C. J. (2006). *The Decline of the Secular University*. Oxford University Press, Oxford.

Sommerville, C. J. (2009). *Religious Ideas for Secular Universities*. William B. Eerdmans, Grand Rapids, MI.

Sydow, J., Schreyögg, G. and Koch, J. (2009). 'Organizational Path Dependence: Opening the Black Box', *Academy of Management Review*, 34(4): 689–709.

Weber, M. (1992). *The Protestant Ethic and the Spirit of Capitalism* (T. Parsons, Trans.). Routledge, London and New York.

Weick, K.E. (1969). *Social Psychology of Organizing.* Addison-Wesley, Reading, MA.

Weick, K.E. (2000). *Making Sense of the Organization.* Blackwell, Malden, MA.

World Economic Forum (2011). *Faith and the Global Agenda: Values for the Post-Crisis Economy.* World Economic Forum, Geneva.

Chapter 15

Managing Muslim Employees and Islamic Practices at Work: Exploring Elements Shaping Policies on Religious Practices in Belgian Organizations

KOEN VAN LAER

Introduction

In recent years, Islam, the place of Islamic practices in the public sphere and the relations between Muslims and non-Muslims have become important, and often controversial and polarizing topics in societal and political discussions in Western countries. Fuelled by references to national and international incidents and conflicts, the rhetoric and arguments in these debates have over the years taken an increasingly negative turn and become infused by anti-Muslim sentiment and Islamophobia (Bousetta and Jacobs, 2006; Helbling, 2014; Spruyt and Elchardus, 2012). While these discourses and debates also permeate the boundaries of organizations (Siebers, 2010), the topic of Islam and the specific experiences of Muslim employees has so far received relatively little attention in organization studies (Essers and Benschop, 2009; Forstenlechner and Al-Waqfi, 2010; Van Laer and Janssens, 2011). Existing studies on these subjects have mainly explored the barriers and disadvantages Muslims are exposed to in organizations and in the labour market. In doing so, they have highlighted how these individuals are faced with interpersonal and career-related discrimination (for example, Forstenlechner and Al-Waqfi, 2010; Ghumman and Ryan, 2013; Van Laer and Janssens, 2011) and with organizational norms which tend to disadvantage them as they aim to gain acceptance and inclusion in organizations, especially if they make their religious identity visible (Syed and Pio, 2010; Van Laer and Janssens, 2014).

Less attention, however, has been paid to the way organizations, as part of their HR or diversity programmes, deal with, or manage, Islamic practices and Muslim employees.

The aim of this chapter is to advance the understanding of the way organizations in the West approach the management of Islam, Muslim employees and Islamic practices. Drawing inspiration from the literature on diversity (management) in organizations, and based on interviews in three organizations in Belgium, this chapter explores the policies organizations use to deal with Islamic practices at work, and examines the different material and discursive elements that shape, influence or constrain the adoption of policies regarding Islamic practices. This chapter first discusses the existing literature on Muslim employees and the relevant literature on workplace diversity. Then it describes the findings from the interviews and highlights the most important lessons which can be drawn from them.

The Specific Organizational and Career Experiences of Muslim Employees

In recent years, a small body of literature has explored the topic of Islam and the experiences of Muslim employees in organizations, particularly highlighting two themes. First, it has explored the discrimination Muslim employees experience on the labour market and in organizations. Such studies have highlighted that Muslims experience employment discrimination when trying to find work (for example Forstenlechner and Al-Waqfi, 2010; Ghumman and Ryan, 2013) and career-related and interpersonal discrimination once they are employed (for example, Syed and Pio, 2010; Van Laer and Janssens, 2011; 2014). These forms of discrimination are embedded in a long tradition of Western discourses constructing the Islamic world and Muslims as the West's essentially different, mysterious, backward and inherently menacing Other (Said, 1978; 1981), which are now often captured using the term 'Islamophobia' (Spruyt and Elchardus, 2013; Strabac and Listhaug, 2008). Dominant themes in these Islamophobic discourses are Islam as a force threatening Western security and world peace, as a religion undermining 'Western' or 'liberal' values such as the separation of Church and State, and as a tradition endangering the rights of women (Spruyt and Elchardus, 2013; Strabac and Listhaug, 2008). Seen as essentially determined by their faith, Muslims become constructed by these discourses as backwards and hostile fundamentalists and as potential terrorists, or, in the case of Muslim women, as docile, submissive and oppressed (Ghumman and Ryan, 2013; Syed and Pio, 2010).

A second important theme in the literature on Islam and Muslims in organizations is the issue of the expression of Islamic practices or identities at work. It has been argued that mainly three types of Islamic practices might become visible within the boundaries of organizations (Ball and Haque, 2003; Bouma et al., 2003). The first one involves the ritual prayer or Salat, which is to be performed at five specific moments during the day, some of which fall within traditional working hours. Normatively, this prayer is performed in a clean place, preceded by a ritual purification, and once a week, on Friday afternoon, in congregation. A second type of potentially visible practices involves dietary customs. Specifically, certain types of food tend to be identified as halal or permissible and others as haram or not permissible. The latter category includes for example alcohol, pork or meat from animals not slaughtered following specific prescriptions. Furthermore, fasting between dawn and sunset is prescribed during Ramadan, the ninth month of the Islamic calendar. A third set of practices which might make Islamic identities visible at work revolve around appearance and clothing. While the most well-known of such practices involve the different types of veils or headscarves worn by Islamic women, it can also refer to other forms of 'modesty' in clothing or to beards worn for religious reasons (Ball and Haque, 2003; Bouma et al., 2003).

As Western workplaces tend to be guided by secular and/or Christian norms (King et al., 2009), which are, for example, embedded in the organization of the working week, the types of food served in cafeterias, or the way employees are expected to dress, engaging in Islamic practices can be perceived as deviant behaviour, potentially fuelling individuals' exclusion and evoking discrimination. Because of this, Muslims might feel compelled to not express their religious identity, and rather assimilate to dominant workplace norms (Forstenlechner and Ali-Waqfi, 2010; Syed and Pio, 2010; Van Laer and Janssens, 2014), thereby suppressing a potentially important aspect of who they are. To better understand how organizations deal with visible and invisible differences among their workforce, we turn to the literature on diversity (management) in organizations.

Management Practices Dealing with Differences

Mainly focusing on issues of race and gender, the diversity literature has produced a broad array of insights into the way organizations manage diversity and deal with the disadvantages specific groups are faced with. Two dominant ways (Ghorashi and Sabelis, 2013; Hamde et al., 2011; Liff and Wajcmann, 1996) of managing diversity in organizations involve what Konrad and Linnehan (1995) have labelled 'identity-blind' and 'identity-conscious' approaches. Identity-blind or colour-blind approaches attempt to achieve workplace equality through formalized HRM practices, which 'level the playing field' by being blind to differences and treating everyone the same, regardless of their socio-demographic background (Ghorashi and Sabelis, 2013; Janssens and Zanoni, 2014; Konrad and Linnehan, 1995; Liff and Wajcmann, 1996). However, this approach has been criticized for maintaining the dominant (for example secular or Christian) norms of the organization, causing all employees to be judged based on norms which privilege the majority and forcing minority individuals to assimilate to the majority's idea of the 'ideal employee' (Ghorashi and Sabelis, 2013; Janssens and Zanoni, 2014).

By contrast, identity-conscious approaches acknowledge group differences and take them into account in policies and decision making (Hamde et al., 2011; Konrad and Linnehan, 1995; Liff and Wajcman, 1996). The underlying logic is that such an approach is needed as it is not possible for individuals to disregard 'identities', to suppress all biases or to erase the effects of years of oppression by a mere promise to treat everybody the same (Konrad and Linnehan, 1995; Prasad et al., 2006). Despite their possible positive effects on career opportunities of disadvantaged groups (Konrad and Linnehan, 1995), such approaches also have certain downsides. Not only are they often met with opposition and backlash from the dominant group, they also risk essentializing difference. Most importantly, like approaches based on sameness, they risk not resulting in fundamental changes in an organization's culture, structure and dominant ideas of the 'ideal employee', which can prevent them from really contributing to workplace equality (Ghorashi and Sabelis, 2013; Janssens and Zanoni, 2014).

The diversity literature has further shown how the diversity approach a specific organization adopts is strongly influenced by its organizational characteristics and by material and discursive organizational structures. For example, the construction and management of diversity is influenced by the way specific differences (are believed to) hamper or contribute to organizational functioning within a specific organization of labour (Janssens and Zanoni, 2005; Zanoni and Janssens, 2004; Zanoni, 2011). Diversity management approaches are further influenced by the broader legislative, political and social context in which an organization is embedded. For example, societal power relations and dominant public discourses affect the diversity issues and identities that become salient, the meanings attached to them, and the power relations between groups and individuals in organizations (Siebers, 2010; Syed and Özbilgin, 2009). Similarly, governmental actions and legislation play an important role in promoting diversity and anti-discrimination policies in organizations, while labour market demography will have an important impact on the labour pool organizations (can) recruit from (Brief et al., 2005; Pringle, 2009; Syed and Özbilgin, 2009).

Drawing inspiration from such insights, the aim of this chapter is to explore the management of Islamic practices and Muslim employees in organizations. The goal is to specifically examine the material and discursive elements that shape, influence or constrain the adoption of policies regarding Islamic practices, highlighting the different themes employers and employees draw on as they adopt, or argue for the adoption of, specific ways to deal with Islamic practices at work.

Method

This chapter draws on empirical material collected in three organizations in Belgium, which have all devised policies concerning Islamic practices at work. The first organization, called *Car*, is a large production plant that is part of a multinational organization in the automotive industry. In this organization, a person responsible for diversity management and four Muslim employees were interviewed. The second organization, called *Door*, is a smaller local production company. In this organization, a person responsible for diversity management and five Muslim employees were interviewed. The third organization, called *Translate*, offers mediation and translation services to organizations such as hospitals to improve their communication with clients of foreign descent. In this organization, which is part of a non-profit organization aimed at promoting equal opportunities and diversity in society, the manager, who is also responsible for diversity management, was interviewed, and eight Muslim employees participated in a focus group, which they preferred over individual interviews and to which three of them added some further comments during informal conversations.

The interviews with the three individuals responsible for diversity management focused on the organization's perspective on diversity, the way the organization deals with diversity in general and religion specifically, the reasons for doing so, and the way they believe these policies influence how employees experience the workplace. The focus group and individual interviews with employees focused on the way they experience the (diversity) policies in the organization, the way they feel in the organization, the expression of Islamic identities at work and the way their organizational experiences could be improved. These interviews were fully transcribed and analysed, looking for the way the organizations deal with Islamic practices, the material or discursive elements influencing the way they do so, and the way employees reflect on, and experience, these policies and the elements driving them.

Before proceeding to the findings, it is important to shortly introduce the Belgian context in which this research took place. While Belgian debates on the expression of religion in the public sphere are influenced by France's discourses on neutrality (Bousetta and Jacobs, 2006), Belgium's approach to religion is not characterized by the same strict ideas on the separation of Church and State. For example, Belgium officially recognizes and materially supports different religions, including Islam. Still, in contrast to one of its other neighbouring countries, the Netherlands, Belgium does not have a strong tradition of religious pluralism, as it has a predominantly Catholic history, and as Catholic organizations continue to maintain a central role in public life, and are involved in, for example, education, hospitals and caring facilities (Coene and Longman, 2008; Fadil, 2013).

The position of Islam in public life remains a very controversial issue in Belgium, which was, for example, one of the first countries to ban the face veil, and headscarves are banned in many schools and in many jobs with customer contact (Coene and Longman, 2008; Fadil, 2013). Similarly, the popular view in Belgium of Muslims and Islamic practices is, compared to other Western European countries, rather negative (Helbling, 2014; Strabac and Listhaug, 2008). This is also reflected in the opposition to the expression of Islamic practices in the workplace. A recent survey (2012) on religion at work with 2,481 respondents organized by the newspaper *Vacature* showed for example that about 80 per cent felt there is no place for religion at work, 78 per cent considered prayer rooms to be unacceptable, 75 per cent did not accept visible religious symbols at work, and about 45 per cent did not accept adapting meals at work to religious rules.

Elements Influencing the Management of Islamic Practices

GENERAL (DIVERSITY) MANAGEMENT APPROACHES

A first element that is important in shaping the way organizations deal with Islamic practices consists of their general approaches to, and perspectives on, HR and diversity. Specifically, each organization is guided by a different perspective on diversity, leading to different approaches to managing Islamic practices.

Car's diversity programme, which is inspired by its mother company, avoids practices that target specific groups, as it feels this is 'positive discrimination,' and rather aims to ensure that 'everybody can enjoy the policies' (Manager *Car*, 90–91). In line with this general approach, *Car* allows Muslim employees to pray, but only during the normal breaks. Moreover, to avoid backlash, the organization is very careful in what and how they communicate about their diversity policies. For example, it only informally communicates some of its policies to its team leaders, who are asked to implement them within their team. As a result of this approach, many employees do not seem to know that prayer is allowed by management, creating the feeling their team leader is doing them a favour by allowing it. One employee stated: 'I don't think managers know about that. It's the team bosses who do that. I don't think managers busy themselves with the fact that some employees pray in the factory' (Muslim employee 3 *Car*, 245–7).

Door started its diversity programme when they had trouble finding enough qualified workers, causing them to increase their efforts to attract and retain 'older' and ethnic minority workers. As they recruited their first ethnic minority workers, *Door* reflected proactively on potential problems and questions that might arise, aimed to create an organizational culture in which everyone feels at home and strongly communicated this vision throughout the organization. Reflecting these principles, the organization for example decided that Islamic employees should have priority to take the day off on religious holidays, openly defends employees' right to pray at work and sponsored an employee barbecue for Eid al-Adha (Feast of the Sacrifice) serving only halal food.

Finally at *Translate*, diversity is part of the core of the organization, not only because of its mission, but also because knowledge of foreign languages and cultures are core competencies for the organization. The overall diversity approach is based on an inclusive philosophy, on consultation between management and employees and on maximum freedom. Consequently, all employees are free to practise their religion in the organization, as long as they consult their colleagues and management if they are affected.

NEUTRALITY

As in the public sphere (Joppke, 2007; Kastoryano, 2004), a second main element that shapes the way organizations deal with Islam is their understanding of neutrality. Reflecting societal discourses and French discourses on *laïcité*, this notion can be used to argue against religious accommodations, as is done by the management of *Car*: 'We're not going to have a specific prayer room for

Muslims, because we also don't do that for Christians, and we also don't do that for Jews. We want to be neutral in that' (Manager *Car*, 224–6).

Employees of *Translate* encounter similar arguments regarding the headscarf in organizations where they are asked to mediate. For example, one employee was told the following in a hospital: 'We don't tolerate a crucifix, let alone a headscarf. We have fought for that for years, and now you're going to try to get in here with a headscarf' (Manager *Translate*, 189–91).

Countering this approach to neutrality, employees of *Translate* pointed to the fact that Belgian organizational life is not religiously neutral, highlighting how official holidays are very Catholic as they include Easter Monday, the Feast of the Ascension, Pentecost Monday, the Assumption Day, All Saints' Day and Christmas. In discussing this issue, the employees did not necessarily call for the abolition of such holidays, but rather reflected on the possibility of a more 'comprehensive' form of neutrality (Joppke, 2007), which embraces all religions equally. Similarly, rather than not having a prayer room because of neutrality, the following employee of *Car* would rather like to see a place of worship for all religions: 'If you only tolerate that Muslims get a Mosque, or a place to pray, that's going to have reverse effects. But if you say, we going to have a prayer room for everyone…' (Muslim employee 4 *Car*, 440–43).

SAFETY AND HEALTH CONCERNS

A third element that often returns in reflections on Islamic practices at work is a concern for safety or health. For example, the manager of *Translate* highlighted how she feels safety and health are justified reasons to not allow Islamic practices such as the headscarf: 'For me, it's all about the work. And I feel safety and health rules should always be considered … If a headscarf compromises health or safety, then you have the right, that's in the Quran, to temporarily remove that headscarf, or any religious symbol' (Manager *Translate*, 250–57).

Similarly, *Car* feels that 'safety is a priority' if employees want to pray in the factory, highlighting how they should not do so 'between the machines or in busy places where forklifts drive back and forth' (Manager *Car*, 348–50). However, because of the lack of a prayer room and the informal way in which diversity policies are organized, employees at *Car* are often unsure of where they are allowed to pray. As a result, they try to find quiet and clean places for themselves throughout the factory. However, as these are not always available in the vicinity of where they work, they often end up praying in ways and places which are potentially unsafe, for example taking their shoes off in places where this is normally not allowed: 'I don't know if it's allowed. Perhaps if the big bosses see it, if they see me without shoes … I don't know how they would react. Perhaps they would say: "he's not wearing his safety shoes, how's that possible?"' (Muslim employee 1 *Car*, 726–8).

Further reflecting on safety concerns linked to wearing a headscarf near machines, another *Car* employee highlighted how the idea of safety is used to ban Islamic practices, while other, equally unsafe behaviour, is not always scrutinized in the same way. He also feels that, in the end, safety depends on how careful an individual is:

> *The question is: 'what is safe?' That depends on yourself. A person can also cause an accident without a headscarf. If a woman has long hair and she doesn't tie it together, that's the same. It's just like … safety … what is safety? You have to make sure for yourself that you work safely (Muslim employee 2 Car, 171–4).*

EFFECTS ON EMPLOYEE RELATIONS

Reflecting debates on backlash to diversity initiatives (Linnehan and Konrad, 1999), a fourth important theme guiding decisions on policies on Islamic practices is the way they are perceived by other employees and potentially impact employee relations. First, there can be concerns, both among employers and Muslim employees themselves, about whether non-religious employees will perceive the policies as fair. For example, at *Translate*, one employee strongly stressed that she feels employees fasting during Ramadan should not get any special privileges.

Similarly, her supervisor makes sure that practices with regards to religion do not disadvantage co-workers: 'If I see that someone takes advantage of it, then I react quickly. In the end, that would be at the expense of their own co-workers' (Manager *Translate*, 498–9).

Considerations about perceptions of fairness, and hence, backlash, not only influence the way organizations implement policies, but also the way they communicate about them. While *Car* keeps most of its policies informal and low-profile and is careful in its communication to avoid criticism, the management of *Door* engages in attempts to convince majority members that their policies regarding religion are fair. They do so by communicating about how they approach all their employees in an individual way, taking each individual's personal situation into account:

> *Sometimes you get people making comments like: 'they're praying while we have to work,' or whatever. It all depends on how you react at that moment. If you start hiding that ... But if you say: 'you go smoking three times a day, while it's also only allowed once.' So it's always a give and take. And I think you have to sell it to people (Manager Door, 178–82).*

Second, both employers and employees are often concerned that allowing religious practices at work might lead to pressures on Muslim employees to adhere to specific religious norms. As employees from *Translate* described, the idea that it will put pressure on others to wear it is an argument often used by organizations to ban the headscarf: 'I can image this [pressure] is a fear they have. That's why they're so opposed to the headscarf' (Muslim employee *Translate* 1, 37–9).

Even the manager of *Translate*, who is of Turkish descent herself, has encountered such pressures within her own organization:

> *We once had a Chechen employee, a very religious woman. She was very open, so I didn't have a problem with that. But when we had lunch and put food on the table, she started checking the food additives on the labels to see whether something was halal or haram. I noticed that people were influenced by this, and even I started checking whether something was halal or haram. That just can't happen. It also goes too far if one employee tells another one that she has to wear longer sleeves ... I told her: 'I don't care if you walk around like that, but if it's your intention to influence someone else, then that's a problem' (Manager Translate, 433–42).*

Also employees noted that making religion too visible at work might create pressure among employees:

> *[At my previous employer] men didn't go and pray together, everyone went separately. In that way, there was no pressure on those not praying (30–32) ... Discretion is important so that there is no group pressure (71–2) ... It was Ramadan, and I had broken my fasting twice, because I couldn't focus anymore. So I drank a coffee because I couldn't take it anymore. And I felt less guilty because nobody was paying attention. Here, I would perhaps feel more guilty because others here are also fasting (46–51) (Muslim employee 3 Translate).*

PRODUCTION AND SERVICE NEEDS

Reflecting arguments in the diversity literature (Janssens and Zanoni, 2005; Zanoni and Janssens, 2004), a fifth element which often features in arguments to restrict the expression of religion at work are the constraints imposed by the production process or by customers. For example, the ability to provide religious accommodations at *Car* is strongly determined by the demands of the production process driven by a conveyor system, which puts strict pressures on the employees, and limits the time they have to take a break and pray. One employee said: 'It's very difficult … I don't go to the bathroom and don't get coffee. The only thing I do is purify myself, pray, quickly smoke, and then back to the line' (Muslim employee 1 *Car*, 498–500).

Similarly, the production process limits the amount of people who can take the day off on religious holidays, as explained by one employee: 'Us Muslims have two official Islamic holidays, and so you ask the boss: "Look, it's our holiday, we want to stay home." And the boss says: "I can only give the day off to five people, and there are already five people, so you have to work"' (Muslim employee 1 *Car*, 175–8).

By contrast, as they are not constraint by a production line, employees at *Door* have more freedom to pray, as the following employee described: 'For example, when it's time to pray, you have to look around. If there's not too much work, then you can go pray for five minutes. And done. The boss told us that's not a problem' (Muslim employee 1 *Door*, 110–12).

To further accommodate its employees, the organization changed its work schedule on Friday, allowing employees to go home earlier. This was not only positive for Muslim employees who want to go the Mosque but also benefitted non-religious employees: 'So we adapted our work schedule, which was good for ethnic minority employees, but also for others, who for example want to attend a sport event or something like that on Friday. Often you see that measures you consider for one group are also an advantage for another group' (Manager *Door*, 224–8).

Translate struggles with the concern of balancing their own policies with the possibility to offer language and mediation services. For example, while the organization allows individuals to stop working earlier during Ramadan, enough people are expected to be present to maintain their services. Similarly, the organization asks its employees to take their headscarves off if they have to provide services in an institution which prohibits wearing them. While the manager originally refused to ask this of her employees, she later felt this policy mainly hurt the group they are supposed to give assistance to:

> There was an institution where they did not have a Moroccan translator for two years because I only had one with a headscarf (118–99) ... Later I thought: 'Why did I not offer assistance to these patients for two years? Why did I take away their rights because of a headscarf?' (184–5) ... The most important thing is assistance to the patient. Now I tell employees when they are hired: 'You can wear a headscarf in our organization, but if you go to another institution you might have to take it off' (128–31) (Manager Translate).

RELIGIOUS AND LEGAL RULES

A sixth element that plays a role in the implementation of Islamic practices at work consists of legal and religious rules. While legislation can promote accommodations of religion at work (Ball and Haque, 2003; Cromwell, 1997), it can also limit the ability to implement specific policies. For example, when employees at *Translate* asked whether they could skip their lunch break during Ramadan, the manager found out that this was against labour regulations: 'I thought, I'll just allow them to keep working, but legally, that's not allowed. A collective bargaining agreement makes it mandatory to take a 40-minute lunch break. These are the kinds of things I look into' (Manager *Translate*, 465–7).

Furthermore, both employers and employees often draw on 'what Islam really says' to justify not accommodating religion, or justify why it is not problematic not to engage in specific practices at work. For example, the manager of *Door* actually studied Islam to understand his employees better. The manager of *Translate* further justifies her position on why it not a problem to take the headscarf off under certain conditions by referring to the Quran: 'The Quran also says that if you're a mother and you're the sole earner, and if your employer demands you to take off your headscarf, that you're obliged to take it off' (Manager *Translate*, 261–3).

Similarly, and while they ultimately decided to allow it informally during the breaks, the management of *Car* consulted religious experts to see whether it was really necessary to accommodate prayer at work: 'They gave us the advice that it's not necessary to have a space to pray for Muslims. They have time enough after work to pray, to go to the Mosque' (Manager *Car*, 229–31).

Discussion and Conclusions

Based on interviews in three organizations which – to some degree – allow the expression of Islamic practices at work, this chapter has explored the elements influencing the way organizations approach the management of such practices. Besides offering an insight in these different elements, the findings specifically highlight three important lessons concerning the management of Islamic practices at work. First, this chapter points to the political nature of the management of Islamic practices at work, as the implementation of policies regarding these practices are the outcome of political processes. Second, the findings show how the management of Islamic practices can both reproduce and challenge the organizational status-quo, the way work is organized and the existing norms on accepted organizational behaviour and the 'ideal employee'. Finally, the findings highlight the crucial, yet ambiguous role of communication in the management of Islamic practices at work.

MANAGING ISLAMIC PRACTICES AT WORK AS A POLITICAL AND AMBIGUOUS PROCESS

This study shows that managing religion in general and Islamic practices specifically does not entail a simple choice between banning or not banning religion or specific practices at work. Rather, it involves a complex set of decisions on whether, how, when and under which conditions specific practices are permitted or forbidden. This chapter has identified six elements involved in shaping the way organizations deal with Islamic practices at work. First, three elements were identified which refer to organizational policies and practices, namely general (diversity) management approaches, notions of workplace safety and health, and production and service needs. Second, two elements have been identified which are linked to broader societal debates, namely approaches to neutrality, and religious and legal rules. And third, there is one element which captures relations between employees. While some of these elements reflect criteria previously identified for organizations to use when deciding on whether to allow the expression of religion (Cash et al., 2000), this study shows there are few 'universally applicable' principles or norms that can help management 'neutrally' or 'objectively' decide on policies concerning religious practices. Rather, these elements are embedded in specific relations of power and can be used, interpreted and constructed in different ways, with different power effects for different groups. On the one hand, these different discursive and material elements can – by themselves or combined – help maintain traditional relations of power and cause organizations to ban Islamic practices from the workplace or to allow them within the boundaries of existing organizational norms. On the other hand, organizations can approach these elements in a way that challenges traditional relations of power and more clearly embraces religious diversity on its own terms.

A first set of elements is related to current organizational policies and practices, which are embedded within a specific organization of work and specific labour relations (Janssens and Zanoni, 2005; Zanoni and Janssens, 2004). It is these structural and political dimensions of an organization, together with management philosophies, which determine employees' autonomy, freedom to express certain individual or group differences, and the degree to which such activities influence, and are allowed to influence, production and service. Similarly, what is perceived to be 'safe' or 'healthy' is tied to the organization of work within a particular work setting, and is the outcome of a negotiation over what kinds of danger and risks are tolerated at work (Turner and Gray, 2009). Together, these organizational policies and practices are the result of managerial choices and political negotiations between employers and different groups of employees, and therefore, always open to change (Adler et al., 2007; Alvesson and Deetz, 2000; Litvin, 2002).

The fact that organizational policies and practices – and hence the possible way policies on Islamic practices can be implemented – are outcomes of political decisions, is illustrated by the two opposite approaches adopted in *Car* and *Door*. Specifically, influenced by existing managerial choices, organizations can implement policies allowing Islamic practices in a way that does not fundamentally change the organization of work, and the construction of the 'norm employee' and of expected organizational behaviour. This is clearly visible in *Car*, where Islamic practices are allowed, as long as they fit into the traditional organization of work, the standard organizational rules, and the dominant idea of 'normal and correct' organizational behaviour. In other words, organizations can allow Islamic practices by fitting them into the norms reflecting the majority's traditional (non-religious) workplace behaviour, thereby seriously constraining employees' ability to practice their religion.

On the other hand, as they implement policies concerning Islamic practices, organizations can fundamentally rethink the organization's culture and work processes, thereby challenging the privileges of the dominant group (Ghorashi and Sabelis, 2013; Janssens and Zanoni, 2014). This is particularly visible in the case of *Door*, where religious practices are allowed to change the traditional organization of work, the standard organizational rules, and the dominant idea of 'normal and correct' organizational behaviour. This is not only visible in their implementation of more identity-conscious practices (Konrad and

Linnehan, 1995) such as an Islamic barbecue on an Islamic holiday, but mainly by their adoption of policies which, although accommodating the minority's religion, ultimately benefit all employees. Examples of this are the permission to take breaks for either smoking or praying, or the change in the work schedule creating work–life benefits for all employees. As others have argued (Janssens and Zanoni, 2014; Ghorashi and Sabelis, 2013) such approaches creating new norms might be the most effective in moving towards workplace equality, as they fundamentally rethink what is considered to be 'normal workplace behaviour'. In this way, organizations can accommodate religion without essentializing difference, as these altered norms allow the expression of multiple individual and group identities.

A second set of elements influencing the implementation of policies concerning Islamic practices consists of societal debates, which are tied to power relations between groups within that society. These societal relations of power are reflected in legislation, which cannot only provide support for religious accommodation (Cash et al., 2000; King et al., 2009) but also hamper it, as is the case in *Translate*. Furthermore, the implementation of policies on religious practices is embedded in debates on the place of religion, or a specific religion, in the public sphere. Whether organizations interpret the idea of neutrality in a more closed – banning all religions equally – or a more open – allowing all religions equally – way, is obviously strongly shaped by societal discourses on this issue. Still, organizations have the possibility to go against dominant discourses of neutrality, thereby maintaining control over the interpretation of neutrality guiding their policies. Similarly, the way religion can be practised within the organization can be embedded in the debates – and power relations – within a specific religious community. As Islam is a decentralized religion with different traditions and interpretations (Fadil, 2013; Sen, 2006), specific 'official' voices or readings can be used to argue for or against specific policies within the workplace, thereby institutionalizing one particular reading of that religion, and suppressing different religious voices and views.

A third element influencing decisions on Islamic practices are interpersonal and intergroup relations at work. First, as policies concerning Islamic practices might impact relations between the minority and the majority, it seems crucial to ensure they are perceived as fair to avoid backlash. Yet, as Linnehan and Konrad (1999) have argued, abandoning diversity efforts because of potential backlash is a sign of the same 'intergroup inequality that diversity programs should be trying to correct' (p. 408), as it means the majority ultimately decides which diversity practices are acceptable. In other words, the fairness of diversity practices cannot be understood outside of the relations of power between the minority and the majority within the workplace. Second, policies can also impact relations between individuals with (seemingly) similar religious identities. While this issue, which is related to the debate on (the perception of) proselytizing when allowing religion at work (Gebert et al., 2014), can too easily be used to suppress religious identities at work, it cannot simply be ignored. After all, policies concerning religion have to ensure that all employees, and not only those with the strictest religious views, benefit from them and feel more at home in the organization. This again highlights how policies regarding Islamic practices at work involve a negotiation of interests of different groups with different power at work.

Related to this issue, this study highlights the importance of communication in the implementation of policies on religious diversity. Communication is important, as employees' perceptions of organizational policies are not simply determined by the designed practices, but also by the way they are implemented, communicated about, and 'sold' or framed (Bowen and Ostroff, 2004; Kossek et al., 2006; Purcell and Hutchinson, 2007). This means that communication can impact the way employees perceive the fairness of specific policies relating to Islamic practices, and the backlash that might be caused by them. Consequently, others' reactions to, and perceptions of, specific practices are embedded within the way organizations communicate about these policies, making these elements again open to change. Still, clear communication about religious practices also harbours the risk of imposing visibility onto relatively invisible identities and practices, which can result in heightened scrutiny from other employees, in stigmatization of, and pressures on, religious identities.

Further adding to the complexities and politics involved in decisions on religion, the different elements guiding organizations' management of Islamic practices are not only inherently ambiguous and political by themselves; they can also come into conflict with each other. For example, not accommodating Islamic practices can reflect adherence to a specific form of neutrality, but can result in safety problems, while different, more open approaches to neutrality might result in an accommodation of Islamic practices, which in turn can affect production or other employees. This further points to the political nature of decisions on Islamic practices, as rather than purely technocratic decisions, they involve weighing different elements, values, interests and groups against each other, within the context of power inequalities.

CONCLUDING REMARKS

Exploring the relatively under-researched topic of the management of Islam, Islamic practices and Muslim employees, this chapter has shown the complexities involved. Given the societal evolutions in many Western countries, both in terms of demography and societal discourses, more attention from the organizational (diversity) literature for Islam in specific (Van Laer and Janssens, 2011), and for religious diversity in general (Gebert et al., 2014; King et al. 2009) continues to be needed. Following suggestions for the diversity literature in general (for example Pringle et al., 2006; Zanoni et al., 2010), it seems especially important for future research to pay specific attention to societal influences on workplace debates on this topic and to adopt methods that capture the contextualized organizational experiences of Muslim employees themselves. It is only by paying attention to this controversial, yet highly pressing diversity issue, and by listening to the too often unheard voices of minority employees that we might come closer to the ideal of organizations which are truly open to all identities, religious or otherwise.

References

Adler, P.S., Forbes, L.C. and Willmott, H. (2007). 'Critical Management Studies', *Academy of Management Annals*, 1(1): 119–79.

Alvesson, M. and Deetz, S. (2000). *Doing Critical Management Research*. Sage, London.

Ball, C. and Haque, A. (2003). 'Diversity in Religious Practice: Implications of Islamic Values in the Public Workplace', *Public Personnel Management*, 32(3): 315–30.

Bouma, G., Haidar, A., Nyland, C. and Smith, W. (2003). 'Work, Religious Diversity and Islam', *Asia Pacific Journal of Human Resources*, 41(1): 51–61.

Bousetta, H. and Jacobs, D. (2006). Multiculturalism, Citizenship and Islam in Problematic Encounters in Belgium. In Modood, T, Triandafyllidou, A. and Zapata–Barrero, R (eds) *Multiculturalism, Muslims and Citizenship, a European Approach*. Routledge, London, 23–36.

Bowen, D.E. and Ostroff, C. (2004). 'Understanding HRM-firm Performance Linkages: The Role of the "Strength" of the HRM System', *Academy of Management Review*, 29(2): 203–21.

Brief, A.P., Butz, R.M. and Deitch, E.A. (2005). Organizations as Reflections of their Environments: The Case of Race Composition. In Dipboye, R.L. and Colella, A. (eds) *Discrimination at Work. The Psychological and Organizational Bases*. Lawrence Erlbaum Associates, New Jersey, 119–48.

Cash, K.C., Gray, G.R. and Rood, S.A. (2000). 'A Framework for Accommodating Religion and Spirituality in the Workplace [and Executive Commentary]', *Academy of Management Executive*, 14(3): 124–34.

Coene, G. and Longman, C. (2008). 'Gendering the Diversification of Diversity. The Belgian Hijab (in) Question, *Ethnicities* 8(3): 302–21.

Cromwell, J.B. (1997). 'Cultural Discrimination: The Reasonable Accommodation of Religion in the Workplace', *Employee Responsibilities and Rights Journal*, 10(2): 155–72.

Essers, C. and Benschop, Y. (2009). 'Muslim Businesswomen Doing Boundary Work: The Negotiation of Islam, Gender and Ethnicity within Entrepreneurial Contexts', *Human Relations*, 62(3): 403–23.

Fadil, N. (2013). 'Performing the *Salat* [Islamic prayers] at Work: Secular and Pious Muslims Negotiating the Contours of the Public in Belgium', *Ethnicities* 13(6): 729–50.

Forstenlechner, I. and Al-Waqfi, M.A. (2010). '"A Job Interview for Mo, but None for Mohammed": Religious Discrimination against Immigrants in Austria and Germany', *Personnel Review*, 39(6): 767–84.

Gebert, D., Boerner, S., Kearney, E., King, J.E., Zhang, K. and Song, L.J. (2014). 'Expressing Religious Identities in the Workplace: Analyzing a Neglected Diversity Dimension', *Human Relations*, 67(5): 543–63.

Ghorashi, H. and Sabelis, I. (2013). 'Juggling Difference and Sameness: Rethinking Strategies for Diversity in Organizations', *Scandinavian Journal of Management*, 29(1): 78–86.

Ghumman, S. and Ryan, A.M. (2013). 'Not Welcome Here: Discrimination towards Women Who Wear the Muslim Headscarf', *Human Relations* 66(5): 671–98.

Hamde, K., Janssens, M., Van Laer, K., Wåhlin, N. and Zanoni, P. (2011). Diversity and Diversity Management in Business and Organization Studies. In Knotter, S, De Lobel, R, Tsipouri, L and Stenius, V (eds) *Diversity Research And Policy. A Multidisciplinary Exploration.* Pallas Publications – Amsterdam University Press, Amsterdam, 159–79.

Helbling, M. (2014). 'Opposing Muslims and the Muslim Headscarf in Western Europe', *European Sociological Review*, 30(2): 242–57.

Janssens, M. and Zanoni, P. (2005). 'Many Diversities for Many Services: Theorizing Diversity (Management) in Service Companies', *Human Relations*, 58(3): 311–40.

Janssens, M. and Zanoni, P. (2014). 'Alternative Diversity Management: Organizational Practices Fostering Ethnic Equality at Work', *Scandinavian Journal of Management*, 30(3): 317–31.

Joppke, C. (2007). 'State Neutrality and Islamic Headscarf Laws in France and Germany', *Theory and Society*, 36(4): 313–42.

Kastoryano, R. (2004). 'Religion and Incorporation: Islam in France and Germany', *International Migration Review*, 38(3): 1234–55.

King J. E., Bell, M. P. and Lawrence, E. (2009). 'Religion as an Aspect of Workplace Diversity: An Examination of the US Context and a Call for International Research', *Journal of Management, Spirituality and Religion*, 6(1): 43–57.

Konrad, A.M. and Linnehan, F. (1995). 'Formalized HRM Structures: Coordinating Equal Employment Opportunity or Concealing Organizational Practices?' *Academy of Management Journal*, 38(3): 787–820.

Kossek E.E., Lobel S.A. and Brown J. (2006). Human Resource Strategies to Manage Workforce Diversity. Examining the 'Business Case'. In Konrad, A.M., Prasad, P., and Pringle, J.K. (eds) *Handbook of Workplace Diversity*. Sage, London, 53–74.

Liff, S. and Wajcman, J. (1996). '"Sameness" and "Difference" Revisited: Which Way Forward for Equal Opportunity Initiatives?', *Journal of Management Studies*, 33(1): 79–94.

Linnehan, F. and Konrad, A.M. (1999). 'Diluting Diversity: Implications for Intergroup Inequality in Organizations', *Journal of Management Inquiry*, 8(4): 399–414.

Litvin, D.R. (2002). The Business Case for Diversity and the 'Iron Cage'. In Czarniawska, B. and Höpfl, H. (eds) *Casting the Other: The Production and Maintenance of Inequalities in Work Organizations*. Routledge, London, 160–84.

Prasad P., Pringle J.K. and Konrad A.M. (2006). Examining the Contours of Workplace Diversity: Concepts, Contexts and Challenges. In Konrad, A.M., Prasad, P. and Pringle, J.K. (eds) *Handbook of Workplace Diversity*. Sage, London, 1–22.

Pringle, J.K. (2009). Positioning Workplace Diversity: Critical Aspects for Theory. In Özbilgin, M.F. (ed.) *Equality, Diversity and Inclusion at Work. A Research Companion*. Edward Elgar, Cheltenham, 75–87.

Pringle J.K., Konrad A.M. and Prasad P. (2006). Conclusion: Reflections and Future Directions. In Konrad, A.M., Prasad, P. and Pringle, J.K. (eds) *Handbook of Workplace Diversity*. Sage, London, 531–9.

Purcell, J. and Hutchinson, S. (2007). 'Front-line Managers as Agents in the HRM-performance Causal Chain: Theory, Analysis and Evidence', *Human Resource Management Journal*, 17(1): 3–20.

Said E. (1978). *Orientalism*. Pantheon Books, New York.

Said E. (1981). *Covering Islam*. Pantheon Books, New York.

Sen A. (2006). *Identity and Violence: The Illusion of Destiny*. W.W. Norton and Company, New York.

Siebers, H. (2010). 'The Impact of Migrant-hostile Discourse in the Media and Politics on Racioethnic Closure in Career Development in the Netherlands', *International Sociology* 25(4): 475–500.

Spruyt, B. and Elchardus, M. (2012). 'Are Anti-Muslim Feelings More Widespread than Anti-foreigner Feelings? Evidence from Two Split-sample Experiments', *Ethnicities*, 12(6): 800–20.

Strabac, Z. and Listhaug, O. (2008). Anti-Muslim Prejudice in Europe: A Multilevel Analysis of Survey Data from 30 Countries. *Social Science Research*, 37(1): 268–86.

Syed, J. and Özbilgin, M. (2009). 'A Relational Framework for International Transfer of Diversity Management Practices', *The International Journal of Human Resource Management*, 20(12): 2435–53.

Syed, J. and Pio, E. (2010). 'Veiled Diversity? Workplace Experiences of Muslim Women in Australia', *Asia Pacific Journal of Management*, 27(1): 115–37.

Turner, N. and Gray, G.C. (2009). 'Socially Constructing Safety', *Human Relations*, 62(9): 1259–66.

Vacature. (2012). 78% tegen gebedsruimtes op de werkvloer, 7 April 2012, 4–7.

Van Laer, K. and Janssens, M. (2011). 'Ethnic Minority Professionals' Experiences with Subtle Discrimination in the Workplace. *Human Relations*, 64(9): 1203–27.

Van Laer, K. and Janssens, M. (2014). 'Between the Devil and the Deep Blue Sea: Exploring the Hybrid Identity Narratives of Ethnic Minority Professionals', *Scandinavian Journal of Management*, 30(2): 186–96.

Zanoni, P. (2011). 'Diversity in the Lean Automobile Factory: Doing Class through Gender, Disability and Age', *Organization*, 18(1): 105–27.

Zanoni, P. and Janssens, M. (2004). 'Deconstructing Difference: The Rhetoric of Human Resource Managers' Diversity Discourses', *Organization Studies*, 25(1): 55–74.

Zanoni, P., Janssens, M., Benschop, Y. and Nkomo, S. (2010). 'Unpacking Diversity, Grasping Inequality: Rethinking Difference Through Critical Perspectives', *Organization* 17(1): 9–29.

Chapter 16

Performing Religious Diversity: Atheist, Christian, Muslim and Hindu Interactions in Two German Research and Development Companies

JASMIN MAHADEVAN

Introduction

Nowadays, many organizations worldwide are characterized by increasing workforce diversity (Harzing and Pinnington, 2011). Depending on the specific economic, socio-political and cultural context, the prominent dimensions of such widespread workplace diversity might be age, ethnicity, gender, culture or many more (Prasad et al., 2006). Workplace diversity can be studied from either a subjectivist or an objectivist perspective (Prasad et al., 2006). This chapter is based on subjectivist thought which assumes that individuals make sense of the world through their social interactions. In short, they interpret reality. From this perspective, identity and belief are not individually fixed but fluid social concepts which emerge and are made stable through social interaction (Lawler, 2008). Research on workplace diversity might focus on the macro-societal, meso-organizational or micro-individual level; studies might have high or low power-awareness (Prasad et al., 2006). Often, HRM research has been critiqued for focusing solely on the individual level and for neglecting power (Al Ariss et al., 2014). For more inclusive perspectives, researchers should take multiple contexts into account and acknowledge imbalances of power, for example, the degree to which individuals are restricted in their agency by structural or institutional constraints (Al Ariss et al., 2014). Following this call, this chapter intends to link multiple levels of analysis when studying religious diversity and work and to reflect on imbalances of power, mainly the intersections between structure and agency in context. It does so by taking a performative perspective on religious practice and by linking it to wider contexts. Analysis is based on the case of two German research and development (R&D) companies whose workforce struggles with the meanings of religious practice. The contribution of this chapter lies in providing performativity as a new lens for analysing religious diversity and in suggesting the need to acknowledge intersections across multiple contexts for understanding the emic meanings of religious practice.

For doing so, this chapter proceeds as follows: first, the theoretical background is presented. Next, research design and method will be explained. Afterwards, the two cases will be highlighted, which leads to the presentation, analysis and discussion of findings. As a major implication, multilevel intersections with regard to managing religious conflict emerge.

Theoretical Background

Workplace diversity is a reality of many organizations (Harzing and Pinnington, 2011). Religion can be considered a feature of such diversity. Hence, it is a dimension which needs to be considered when designing strategies and tools for managing increasing cultural diversity at work. With regard to its implications for international HRM and cross-cultural management (CCM), religion has mainly been considered on the level of values (Parboteeah et al., 2009). In contrast, this chapter suggests studying religion at the level of practices and performances in order to truly grasp the meaning ascribed to religion by diverse groups of individuals in a specific organizational context. This meaning can then be related to larger discourses on religion, meaning the dominant way in which religion is perceived in a specific societal, political or economic context.

The more diverse a group of employees is, the higher the likelihood that individual and social identities might be endangered (Prasad et al., 2006, Rothman, 1997), for example by religious practice of another social group. Social identity refers to the fact that individuals categorize themselves and those surrounding them into groups of perceived 'We' and groups of perceived 'Other', thereby creating or formalizing difference between groups of people (Tajfel and Turner, 1986; Prasad et al., 2006). When doing so, 'in-group bias' might play a role: the own group is viewed as superior to the other, unfamiliar, group.

Social identity theory has been critiqued for neglecting the implications of contexts for how groups of perceived 'We' (social self) and 'Other' (social other) are constructed socially (see Prasad et al., 2006). Hence, this chapter understands 'social identity' in its original sociological/anthropological meaning as the interactive process of interpersonal interactions between social self and other through which culture is made and re-made within certain boundary conditions. From this viewpoint, interpretative processes and individual agency on the micro-level always need to be related back to wider social contexts and structure.

When speaking of 'culture', this chapter understands it in the broad anthropological sense as 'that complex whole which includes knowledge, belief, art, morals, law, custom, and any other capabilities and habits acquired by man as a member of society' (Tylor, 1920). Religion is part of this 'complex whole'. Culture – as based on this definition and religion as one aspect of the cultural 'complex whole' – is usually studied interpretatively. The interpretative perspective on culture intends to uncover sense-making from the actors' point of view and uses qualitative methods for doing so (Mahadevan, 2013). This perspective is based on social constructivism (Berger and Luckmann, 1966) and subjectivist thought; consecutively, it differentiates between inside (emic) and outside (etic) meanings (Mahadevan, 2013): the meaning which those acting give to their doings (emic perspective) is different from how these doings are perceived from the outside (etic perspective). Often, the etic perspective is negative, based on in-group bias (Tajfel and Turner, 1986). However, those acting most likely ascribe positive meanings to their doings. This implies that management needs to understand such emic meanings in order to design and implement measures for managing religious diversity which are *meaningful* to those concerned.

In summary, the interpretative perspective has the following advantages for gaining in-depth insights into workplace diversity. Firstly, it acknowledges the sense-making process of those involved: it cannot uncover the process of how social identities and perceived 'Otherness' are actually made through interpretation and interaction within specific boundary conditions. Secondly, it links several contexts, for example individual and macro-structural levels of analysis (see Prasad et al., 2006). Thirdly, it might enable other objectivist HRM practice to reflect upon its own assumptions and to gain a more holistic understanding of religious diversity at work (see Al Ariss et al., 2014).

When implementing the interpretative perspective, the researcher might choose from various options (Hatch and Yanow, 2003). The most prominent is the classic interpretative viewpoint which understands culture as a 'web of meanings' or a 'text' to be researched and read by the researcher (based on Geertz, 1973). However, for the study of religious practice, this perspective does not seem helpful: by focusing solely on abstract meaning, it neglects the bodily interaction, the process and the performance of *doing culture*. Yet, the often repetitive and ritualized performative dimension – *doing religion* – is a major part of most belief systems which might be neglected by a purely interpretative approach.

For overcoming the shortcomings of the purely interpretative approach, this chapter applies a performative perspective (*doing culture*) on religious diversity. *Doing culture* focuses on how individuals give meaning to the social fabric through their actions (Conquergood, 1989). It is based on ritual theory (Turner, 1986). The performative perspective has developed out of the study of spiritual and religious performances. This development has been labelled the 'performative turn' in anthropology, cultural studies and the social sciences (Conquergood, 1989); it can be considered a counter-movement against classic interpretative anthropology (based on Geertz, 1973) and has now entered management and organization studies (see Hatch and Yanow, 2003). A performative perspective on religion assumes that one knows the social world 'through the body', an experience which precedes and transcends conscious thought and rational knowledge (Csordas, 1990). From this viewpoint, religion is not 'understood' reflexively – it is experienced through *all* the bodily senses.

When studying religious diversity and religious conflict at work, the performative perspective is helpful due to the following reasons: firstly, it takes into account how identity is *done* on the micro- and macro-level, thereby uncovering how perceptions of religious diversity are *made* and which conflicts might arise in the process. Secondly, it takes the performative character of religious practice (*doing religion*) and its role for *making identities and organizations* into account. Following this perspective and the call for a more inclusive and power-aware HRM research, this chapter views religion as a category of practice in a specific context: it focuses on what people actually *do* when 'being religious' and links the meaning derived from these doings to larger structures, contexts and discourses on religion.

Research Design and Method

This chapter combines findings from two ethnographic research projects on two similar technical companies. Both companies are characterized by workforce diversity and organizational change. Hence, they were ideal fields for studying how individuals make sense of such difference and to uncover which categories of collective 'self' and 'other' are meaningful to them and in which context (Lawler, 2008). For doing so, longitudinal ethnographic methods employed were participant observation and qualitative interviews (Van Maanen, 1998). Company 1 was studied full time between 2004 and 2006. Company 2 was studied part time between 2008 and 2010.

In the case of Company 1, data was collected through initial interviews with 15 key actors and subsequent participant observation over two years. A field diary was kept and analysed on a regular basis. Besides that, the researcher fully participated in organizational life. Additionally, cultural documents such as internal information distributed by corporate communications, corporate press releases and information spread by media were analysed. In Company 2, data was collected through multiple methods such as participant observation, meeting observation, informal and formal interviews, and group discussion. Multiple methods over a longer period of time enable the researcher to trace organizational sense-making and change (Van Maanen, 1998).

Formal interviews were based on the narrative biographical approach (Flick, 2002). They were audio-recorded and transcribed verbatim using f4. All interviews lasted 60 to 120 minutes with an average time of 80 minutes; transcripts ranged from 6,400 to 15,100 words. Informal interviews were documented via memory protocol; experiences during participant observation were documented in a field diary which was reflected upon at regular intervals (Van Maanen, 1998). Field notes from memory protocols and the field diary were processed using Microsoft Word. Analysis was conducted in three steps and followed the principles of open ethnographic analysis (Spradley, 1979). Required coding was done manually.

Case Presentation

The presentation and analysis of these two cases is used to highlight potential dilemmas of managing religious diversity. Research outcome from both cases has been originally published in the *International Journal of Cross-Cultural Management* (Mahadevan, 2012a) and the *Journal of Organizational Change Management* (2012b), focusing on cross-cultural conflict and narrative diversity change, respectively. Selected aspects of these cases will now be presented with a new focus on managing religious diversity.

COMPANY 1

Company 1 is a technical company based in southern Germany. During the time of research (2004 to 2007), it employed approximately 8,000 people in Germany and 35,000 worldwide. A new offshore site in India, mainly for implementing new product specifications from corporate headquarters in Germany, was just being built up. As such, the offshore site in India was part of an internal research and development unit (to be called Unit 1 in this chapter). Its purpose was to develop a complex and interdependent technological system that was to be used by internal customers all over the globe for improvement of microchip design. Whereas specifications originated mainly from the German headquarters, the newly hired engineers at the Indian site needed to implement these specifications. During the time of research, the official corporate language was English, as was the language of those working together technically. Yet, the day-to-day language at the German headquarters was still German. Approximately 15 per cent of all Unit 1 employees at the German site were non-German nationals, mostly from Western Europe. No manager at the German site was a non-German. At the Indian site, all but one expatriate manager from France were ethnic Indian, some of them possessing an US–American or Canadian passport due to prior work experience abroad. All members of Unit 1 considered themselves to be 'engineers' in contrast to 'managers', meaning 'non-technical employees' (see Mahadevan, 2012a). Their shared task was to create and manage a complex technological system which was subjected to constant change through new customer requirements, system failures and overall interdependencies. From an individual and collective engineering perspective, such changes endanger the individual engineer's ability to perform. Hence, system failure or change is also a challenge to collective engineering identity as 'masters of technology' (Mahadevan, 2012a). In summary, the challenges for those working at Unit 1 were to manage organizational change and growth, to transfer knowledge offshore and across sites, and to continue excelling at technological performance (Mahadevan, 2012a).

COMPANY 2

Company 2 is a research company located in East Germany, in a region that was part of the former German Democratic Republic (GDR). During the time of research, the number of employees rose from approximately 150 to 240. All of these employees were engineers or researchers; virtually all of them were hired outside Germany. The reason given for this by corporate HR was that qualified German candidates were hard to come by, and furthermore, did not want to work in the provincial town in which Company 2 is located.

From an organizational perspective, this was a fairly recent and involuntary change which began in 2007. During the time of research, management and senior researchers were still exclusively German; their day-to-day language was German. In contrast, more than one-third of all researchers and more than half of all doctoral students (about one-third of all researchers) were non-German nationals. Many of the new non-German researchers from such diverse countries as India, Bangladesh, Turkey, China, Iran, Russia, Southeastern and Eastern Europe did not speak German; for them, English was the language of day-to-day interaction. All researchers considered English to be the language of their technological work, yet, for many German employees, especially those who had grown up in the former GDR, English was just a written and not a spoken language. In summary, the main challenge for Company 2 was to manage organizational change and increasing workforce diversity, to transfer knowledge to new members and to maintain technological excellence for its national and international customer base.

Findings: Doing Religion at Work

COMPANY 1

In Company 1, culture and religion were perceived as something outside daily work practice. Overall, there was a strong belief in being *one* global engineering community, regardless of societal cultural differences, language or country of origin, amongst engineers and engineering management of all sites (Mahadevan, 2012a).

Still, religious practice and local traditions were noted when employees travelled between sites. During coffee and lunch breaks, German and Indian employees frequently engaged in conversations on local traditions, such as Easter egg hunting and decorating a Christmas tree in Germany or visiting temple and performing religious prayers in India. At both sites, this was one of the main themes during first contact situations or initial small-talk interactions. When being asked about religion, most German employees categorized themselves as Christian, and most Indian employees categorized themselves as Hindu or Jain, the latter being an Indian religion that has originated from Hinduism. Christian and Hindu religious rituals and traditions were often talked about. Employees frequently visited temples, churches and monasteries, being guided by their local colleagues. Still, no importance was ascribed to these interactions; there was still the firm belief that this was a dimension of culture which took place solely outside engineering work.

However, one aspect of Indian behaviour was commented upon and perceived as negative by German employees (see Mahadevan, 2012a). It was called 'this vegetarianism at the Indian site' (in German: 'Dieses Vegetariertum am indischen Standort'). During shared lunch hours, either at the German or the Indian site, this practice by Indian employees was noted by German employees. Especially in the canteen at the German headquarters, this created insecurities about what to offer and what to eat. Questions were asked, and most Indian employees offered pragmatic and practical explanations as to why they adhered to a vegetarian diet. 'It tastes better', 'I am used to it' and 'it is healthier' were amongst the most common explanations (quoted from Mahadevan, 2012a). Still, this did not seem to satisfy German employees. Comments were made such as: 'Why is this so important to them?', and even: 'I am really annoyed by this vegetarianism at the Indian site' and 'Do they always have to force their vegetarianism on us?' (Mahadevan, 2012a).

Based on these comments, German employees did not seem to grasp how and why it was important to many Indian employees to adhere to a vegetarian diet. Furthermore, some of them even seemed to experience adhering to a vegetarian diet as something endangering or aggressive (Mahadevan, 2012a). This prompted the assumption that 'it must have something to do with Hindu religion'. The fact that no Indian engineer seemed to give a religious explanation to this practice even aggravated this feeling, for it must be a very deep aspect of religion if no one actually verbalizes it. At this point, some German employees also started searching for signs of religious practice elsewhere and found it in the fact that many employees had placed pictures or statues of gods and goddesses on their desk, and that many employees had adorned their forehead with ash marks or colourful dots when arriving at work, which surely was a religious symbol, too. Yet, the meaning of these practices remained unclear.

COMPANY 2

In company 2, religion has never been a part of organizational life, as it was common in the former GDR. Whereas celebrating an annual Christmas party, setting up a Christmas tree and sending out and emailing Christmas cards and greetings to colleagues all over the world was a common practice at Company 1, Company 2 adhered to the former East German tradition of celebrating an 'end of the year party' and sending out 'end of the year greetings' (in German: Jahresendzeitgrüße). A Christmas tree was not common in Company 2.

The category of religion only entered the company in 2008/2009 with the arrival of 13 Muslim employees who had been hired from Serbia, Turkey, Iran,

Bangladesh, India and Pakistan, some of whom started to perform religious prayers at work. Like all those employees hired from abroad, they were most commonly referred to as 'our foreign guests' by German management (Mahadevan, 2012b).

As is common in the former GDR, virtually all employees from former East Germany categorized themselves as atheist and reacted negatively to any question associated with religion. Only those originating from former West Germany categorized themselves as Christian. However, regardless of their personal belief, virtually all employees asserted that religion was a category that should remain firmly outside organizational life and outside work-practice. Only once did I observe an employee stating that his 'being Christian' actually made him perform better at work, a statement which other employees reacted against with vehement opposition (Mahadevan, 2012a).

Upon seeing Muslim employees pray at work, sometimes in open offices, more often in the corporate gymnastics room, German employees reacted with uncertainty and confusion. They asked questions such as: 'Why do they pray?', 'What does it mean?', and also wondered: 'Can I talk to them about religion?' and 'Is it okay to step over them if I really need to cross the office?' (Mahadevan, 2012a). At this point, those employees from such diverse countries as Serbia, Turkey, Iran, Bangladesh, India and Pakistan were solely perceived as 'Muslim', this being the dominant category of difference that was being projected upon them. When being asked about their religious practice (by me), most Muslim employees referred to it as 'tradition','something I just do' or 'a way to meditate' (quoted from Mahadevan, 2012a). To me, this seemed a similarity to how Indian engineers explained their adherence to a vegetarian diet at Company 1. However, in contrast to Company 1, religion was not talked about in Company 2. In fact, when I mentioned religion once in a group discussion, a German employee said: 'You cannot be serious: This is a private topic!' (Mahadevan, 2012a), a statement to which the other German employees present agreed.

Summary of Both Cases

In both cases, German employees in two different R&D companies in two different regions of Germany struggle with two specific phenomena of what they perceive as religious practice, namely adhering to a vegetarian diet and performing Muslim prayers. This is the specific micro-level interaction to be analysed. In both cases, those performing this practice do not actually perceive it as a religious act. It remains unclear whether this is due to a lack of awareness and reflexivity from the part of those engaging in this practice or whether others interpret too much of religions meaning into an otherwise profane act.

However, despite these similarities, the way which employees reacted to the display of religious performances is notably different: in Company 1, employees continued their exchange on religious topics. In Company 2, no exchange on religious topics took place at all. In Company 1, corporate HR and higher management were not concerned with managing religion; it was not a topic, management was even aware of. In Company 2, corporate HR and higher management struggled with the display of religious performances which they perceived as alien and endangering, yet, did not ask Muslim employees about their religious needs at all – the results were complete 'religious silence' and managerial inaction.

Case Analysis and Discussion

This section analyses and discusses the two cases in comparison and in relation to theory. Studies on various aspects of international Human Resource Management (HRM) such as migration, diversity or talent management have been critiqued for focusing solely on the individual (for example, Al Ariss et al., 2014) and for neglecting workforce complexities and the contexts and boundary conditions which influence and shape these complexities (McKenna and Richardson, 2007). Furthermore, the contextuality of diversity has been overlooked (Prasad et al., 2006). For example, a viewpoint that solely focuses on the intersections between individual abilities and organizational needs when identifying new 'talents' might neglect the fact that limiting boundary conditions might constrain an individual's ability to build up the social, human, economic and cultural capital that is required for being identified as 'talent' (Al Ariss et al., 2014). For overcoming this limitation, Al Ariss et al. (2014) suggest that researchers take the organizational, institutional, sectoral, national and international context of individual actions into account for understanding how to manage a diverse workforce. By linking religious performances in a specific context to wider contexts, this chapter does so in the following.

PROFESSIONAL IDENTITY AND SOCIO-RELIGIOUS BACKGROUND

The fact that employees in both companies do not ascribe their practice to religion might signify specific traits of the global engineering community which are often understood by its members as being a rational and culture-free community (Mahadevan, 2012a). This community is characterized by a shared habitus of expertise and the need to display this habitus in front of other members of the community (Mahadevan, 2012a). Hence, the *sectoral or professional context* suggests that members of engineering professions might downplay the impact of religion on their professional life or might not even perceive such an influence because such an interpretation would thwart the collective self-image of global R&D engineering: true engineers only perform the principles of their science. The fact that even a presumably 'harmless' practice such as adhering to a vegetarian diet might be perceived as endangering – as the quote 'Why do they always have to force their vegetarianism on us!' shows – might be interpreted in this light: namely as violating the emic professional social identity of R&D engineers as being rational and free-spirited problem-solvers who are not limited by non-technical influences or emotional attachments (see Mahadevan, 2012a). Hence, even those adhering to the ideal of purity in their actual performances might not be aware of doing so due to the importance of performing a rational and culture-free professional social identity of 'engineers' in front of other group members. The emic and etic interpretations of Muslim prayer in Company 2 might be viewed in this light as well.

However, further analysis of their *socio-religious background* is needed for deeper insights into religious performances beyond the actors' interpretative scope. Such an analysis suggests that the degree to which different religions might rely on bodily knowledge and bodily performances to put ideals into practice might vary. For example, Christian faith largely relies on verbal performances (*saying* prayers) and intellectual faith. In contrast, Muslim faith relies largely on the structuring principles of repetitive action, for example *performing* prayers. Hinduism is not even a formalized book religion but rather a philosophy that is ingrained into the practices of daily life.

An important ideal in Hinduism is the principle of purity and the need to 'stay pure' (see Dumont, 1970). The act of consuming food is often viewed as impure for it allows the (dirty) outer world to enter the (to be purified) inner body. Jainism, a religion that has developed from Hinduism, has taken over this belief. Hence, Hindu and Jain engineers adhering to a vegetarian diet can be understood as one way of performing this ideal of purity. From early childhood on, such behaviour might have become so ingrained into personal routines that it does not require conscious and reflexive thought. Hence, it is not consciously perceived as a specific religious performance. The ideal of performing Muslim prayer, as practiced in Company 2, is characterized by its focus on bodily routines requires visible and repetitive action as well. These performances might be meaningful to an individual through the body itself, without intellectual reflexivity, and might not require conscious religious purpose that can be put into words. Hence, in both cases, these practices might not even be perceived as a conscious religious act by those performing it. In both cases, the focus is on pre-verbal performances and bodily knowing and not on verbalized intellectual faith: in contrast, Christian religion – especially Protestant belief – is based on intellectual faith and thinking. Hence, religious performances might not be understood in their own right.

It is important to note that most German employees at the headquarters of Company 1, which are located in Southern Germany, were Catholic. They defined themselves either as 'Christian, but not very religious/not going to church' or 'Christian and practising religion'. This suggests a differentiation between personal belief and Church as a religious structure. In both cases, they were familiar with the elaborate ritual and bodily performance of Catholic belief and liturgy. At Company 2, however, which is located in the North-East of Germany, most employees from former West Germany categorized themselves as Protestant. Compared to Catholicism, Protestantism religion can be considered more focused on intellectual thought and less relying on ritual and performances. Moreover, virtually all employees from former East Germany (about 75 per cent of the German workforce) categorized themselves as Atheist and rejected religion altogether as being 'non-rational'. This suggests that religious ritual and performance might be perceived as more alien in Case 2, both being Protestant and Atheist employees.

WIDER CONTEXTS AND ORGANIZATIONAL LIFE

Furthermore, wider contexts, such as *political, economic, historical, local* and *societal contexts,* need to be considered when understanding the specific way in which an organization makes sense of religious performances.

For example, in Company 1, Christian religious practice is part of organizational life, for example via Christmas celebrations and wishing each other Merry Christmas. In contrast, religion is silenced at Company 2 as being 'non-rational', and most employees categorize themselves as 'Atheist'. In contrast to the former Federal Republic of Germany (FRG), the former GDR considered itself a non-religious State, and Church affiliation could, indeed, affect one's social and professional life negatively and thus was often kept private. One might conclude that this *historical context* impacts an individual's ability to perceive religious symbolism and related performances as a 'normal' part of organizational life. Hence, the symbolic significance of *any* religious performance in Company 2 might be perceived as much more severe than in

Company 1. The finding that even 'non-visible' and 'silent' Christian belief is opposed in Company 2 adds further proof.

Furthermore, the *local context* needs to be considered when analysing organizational sense-making in context. Whereas Company 1 is located in a major cosmopolitan German city in a highly affluent region of Germany, Company 2 is located in a provincial remote town at the Polish border that suffers from economic recession and high unemployment. Radical right-wing youth organizations are perceived as a major issue. Many German employees at Company 2 worry about the safety and security of those employees who look ethnically 'non-German', and many employees – both German and non-German – do not actually live in this town but commute on a daily or weekly basis. Hence, 'diversity' as a concept and as a way of life is much more alien to Company 2 than Company 1, and one can assume that even the highest reflexivity and good-will of corporate HRM will not overcome in-group biases, negative ascriptions of imbalances of power which are formed on wider societal level.

With regard to the *societal context*, it has to be noted that anti-Muslim discourse or at least the doubtful question to whether Islam is part of German culture and society is present in German media and politics. In a recent study on 'group-specific hostility' with more than 23,000 participants (Heitmeyer, 2012), 22.6 per cent of respondents agreed to the statement: 'Immigration to Germany should be prohibited for Muslims' and 30.2 per cent supported the viewpoint: 'Because of the many Muslims here, I sometimes feel like a stranger in my own country.' In contrast, there is no anti-Hindu or anti-Jain discourse in Germany. The same is true for members of the respective faiths: in comparison to Muslim communities in Germany, the Hindu faith is virtually non-present in Germany and the Jain religion might even be unheard of. Hence, the respective social 'Other' is not yet labelled with specific ascriptions and in-group biases are less likely to emerge in already predefined forms.

With regard to the wider *economic context*, there are notable differences as well: Company 1 is embedded into the history of a market economy (FRG) which has immersed itself in the European Union (EU) over time. At the German headquarters, about 10–15 per cent of the work force originate from other EU member states, and frequent travels to other corporate sites is a common feature of organizational life. Sometimes, employees also transfer from headquarters to other sites. In summary, the change towards increasing workforce diversity has been a slow and reciprocal one at Company 1 in Germany. This makes it less likely that employees are endangered by ethnic otherness – as long as other contexts, such as the professional or organizational context, are not perceived as disruptive, as might happen in times of downsizing or organizational redesign. In contrast, Company 2 has been embedded in the closed economic and political system of the former GDR. It used to be one of the major research companies in its field in the former GDR and the whole of Eastern Europe. After the fall of the Berlin wall, however, the company almost did not survive privatization and system change. Only the former R&D department survived; manufacturing was abandoned altogether. Consecutively, the overall workforce was downsized from about 3,000 to about 150 employees. It was only in 2008 that the company experienced moderate workforce growth again. However, at this point, the company was not one of the most sought after employers in the country anymore but a miniscule player in a remote region of Germany. Many German candidates were unwilling to relocate and work there – hence, the company needed to hire from abroad, and as it turned out, most qualified applicants originated from what were perceived as rather 'alien' countries in Asia, the Middle East and Southeastern and Eastern Europe. Hence, in contrast to Company 1, Company 2 experienced a sudden, profound and involuntary rise in workforce diversity which was linked to previous developments that threaten established social identities and even the organization as such. This makes it more likely that religious performances at work will be interpreted as yet another feature of disruptive organizational change and continuing identity endangerment.

Furthermore, diversity change at Company 2 was not reciprocal (as it was at Company 1): most German employees had never experienced living or working together with other nationalities of ethnicities before. Those hired were inferior in terms of organizational status (junior researchers) and in times of organizational security (most of them only had a fixed-term work contract), and German employees had never travelled for work purposes, let alone experienced living and working abroad themselves. This makes it more likely that imbalances of power will impact potentially integrative strategies to overcome difference.

This assumption is given further proof by the fact that non-German employees were referred to as 'our foreign guests' by German management and many German employees (see Mahadevan, 2012b). This metaphor can be related back to the history of the former GDR: foreign workers or students were invited there in order to be trained or educated; however, they were not allowed to engage in personal contact with German citizens or to settle in the GDR. They lived in separate compounds and were expected to leave the country again (Mahadevan, 2012b). Hence, the metaphor of *foreign guests* can be understood as a signifier of the temporality and inferiority which is ascribed to non-German employees in general. At the same time, it implies the obligation of German employees – the 'hosts' – to take care of the guests' needs: 'guests' are not asked for what they need – it is decided for them. This might explain the 'non-communication' on Muslim religious practice at Company 2. Yet, this strategy of 'religious silence' cannot be successful, for these performances are beyond the hosts' interpretative scope, and due to imbalances of power, those praying are not allowed the agency to speak for themselves.

Implications: Multi-Level Intersections and Managing Religious Conflict

As the previous analysis and discussion has shown, employee reactions towards religious performances can only be analysed in context. The intersections between these contexts provide insights into whether and how management should manage religious conflict at work. Such a conflict could emerge from religious performances by part of the workforce that are perceived as alienating by other parts of the workforce, as is the case in Companies 1 and 2.

Conflict in culturally diverse organizations often arises when social identities are endangered (Rothman, 1997; Dalton and Chrobot-Mason, 2007). Based on current theory (overview in Ma et al., 2007; Amason, 1996; Deutsch, 1973), conflicts can be analysed by differentiating between constructive or deconstructive (Deutsch, 1973), and functional or dysfunctional (Amason, 1996) conflicts. For management, this means: only potentially harming types of conflict (dysfunctional and deconstructive) require intervention. Potentially harmless types of conflict (functional and constructive) need not be managed: they actually help the organization change, adapt, grow and be innovative and can be left to be 'played out' (Goffman, 1959). When adapting this through to the study of religious diversity at work, this means: management needs to understand what a religious conflict *means* from the perspective of those involved in order to manage religious diversity.

In the given case, the following dimensions seem relevant to understand the meaning of religious conflict: at both Company 1 and 2, employees seem to share a professional identity of R&D engineers. This professional identity focuses on brainwork and requires rational thinking. Hence, it does not seem easily reconcilable with those religious beliefs which enact religious ideals via practice and performance – both from the perspective of those performing religion and from the perspective of those observing this practice. This discrepancy might be the root of a potential religious conflict.

However, the scope of conflict varies considerably between Company 1 and 2: at Company 1, it does not go beyond the professional context. Religion is a part of daily and organizational life, and all engineers continue their exchange on religious practices. The analysis of wider historical, socio-political and economic contexts suggests that increasing workforce diversity is reciprocal, and has developed over time and within supportive and stable boundary conditions. Hence, it seems likely that the interpretative gap at the intersection between professional identity and one performative aspect of Hindu and Jain religion – namely adhering to a vegetarian diet – will be overcome by other links. Hence, one can assume that this religious conflict at Company 1 is a functional and constructive one which can be left to be played out.

In contrast, religious conflict at Company 2 seems to be aggravated by wider contexts: the regional, economic and historical boundary conditions are not supportive; and corporate HR is impacted in their reflexive abilities by a dominant negative societal discourse on Islam. Furthermore, religious performances at work might be directly related to disruptive organizational change and threats to organizational and professional security. There is no sign that employees possess the interpretative ability to overcome the gap between social 'We' and 'Other': rather, there is silence on any matters religious. Hence, this conflict seems to bear a high potential of being disruptive and deconstructive, one which needs to be managed. As a first step, the breaking of 'religious silence' through team activities is recommended. For doing so, HRM needs to acquire higher reflexivity and become aware that they themselves are limited by dominant discourse on religion and Islam in their actions. Rather than 'speaking for' those who are called 'foreign guests', HRM should devise measures of 'speaking with' them.

Conclusion

This chapter has analysed two corporate cases with regard to the meanings of religious practice at work. The viewpoint taken was a *doing culture* perspective on religious performances. This approach suggests that religion should be studied on the level of actual practice and not on the level of values in order to understand what a religious conflict *means* to those interacting, even though they themselves might not be able to put this into words reflexively.

For analysing the in-depth meanings of religious performances at work, one needs to proceed from a social–constructivist viewpoint and employ interpretative and qualitative methods. Through this approach, the emic and etic meanings of *doing religion* and related dynamics of how social self and other are *perceived* in a specific context are made visible. In the given case, such analysis delivered insights into the interrelations between professional identity and perceptions on Christianity, Islam, Hinduism, Jainism and Atheism.

However, in order to design and implement HRM strategies and action, one needs to move beyond the specific context of actual interaction and reflect upon the impact of wider societal, economic, historical or political contexts on interpersonal and organizational sense-making and interaction. As a main point, the interrelations between structure and agency and potentially limiting boundary conditions which might disadvantage specific actors need to be considered. Such a wider analysis will enable HRM researchers and practitioners to reflect upon organizational and HRM structure, strategy and practice critically and to include previously neglected perspectives. In the given case, this analysis delivered insights into the character of religious conflict: the risk for religious conflict in Company 1 does not seem to go beyond the professional level and can therefore be left to be played out. In contrast, the risk for religious conflict at Company 2 emerges at the intersections of multiple levels and is directly linked to social identity threats and disruptive and negative organizational change. Hence, it should be managed through increased HRM reflexivity which aims at overcoming omnipresent 'religious silence'.

The research implications of these findings are: objectivist HRM research and practice might fail to become aware of its own limitations and assumptions when dealing with religious diversity at work. Hence, reflexive, qualitative and in-depth research – for example from an interpretative perspective – is required to overcome these limitations. The managerial implication suggests going beyond the individual or even the organizational level when designing HRM strategy and action. This requires a critical reflection on what might influence own and organizational perceptions on religious diversity. This calls for more reflexive and holistic HRM practice and also for a more pragmatic approach to religion at work. Rather than being considered on the level of values (which often cannot be put into words), it should be understood as a category of practice wherein values are actually *made* and *done* through religious performances.

This chapter has provided first insights into the intersections between multiple contexts, between social structure and the making of social identities in context, and between dominant discourses and individual agency. However, it can only provide a first glimpse of the meanings of religious performances at work and suggest an approach of how to analyse these in context. This includes: (1) the making of social self and other in context; (2) organizational strategy, structure and practice; (3) wider contexts and their inter-linkages with interpersonal and organizational practice; and (4) interrelations between power, structure and agency. Further qualitative and interpretative research should be undertaken in this area, focusing on *doing religion at work in context* and on increasing HRM reflexivity through such analysis.

References

Al Ariss, A. Cascio, W.F. and Paauwe, J. (2014). 'Talent Management: Current Research and Future Directions', *Journal of World Business*, 49(2): 173–9.

Amason, A. (1996). 'Distinguishing the Effects of Functional and Dysfunctional Conflict on Strategic Decision Making: Resolving a Paradox for Top Management Teams', *Academy of Management Journal*, 39(1): 123–48.

Berger, P. and Luckmann, T. (1966). *The Social Construction of Reality*. Doubleday, New York.

Conquergood, D. (1989). 'Poetics, Play, Process and Power: The Performative Turn in Anthropology', *Text and Performance Quarterly*, 9(1): 82–8.

Csordas, T.J. (1990). 'Embodiment as a Paradigm for Anthropology', *Ethos*, 18(1): 5–47.

Dalton, M. and Chrobot-Mason, D. (2007). 'A Theoretical Exploration of Manager and Employee Social Identity, Cultural Values and Identity Conflict Management', *International Journal of Cross-Cultural Management*, 7(2): 169–83.

Deutsch, M. (1973). *The Resolution of Conflict: Constructive and Destructive Processes*. Yale University Press, New Haven, CT.

Dumont, L. (1970). *Homo Hierarchicus: The Caste System and its Implications*. Chicago University Press, Chicago, IL.

Flick, U. (2002). *An Introduction to Qualitative Research*. Sage, London.

Geertz, C. (1973). Thick Description: Toward an Interpretive Theory of Culture. In Geertz, C. (ed.) *The Interpretation of Cultures: Selected Essays*. Basic Books, New York, 3–30.

Goffman, E. (1959). *The Presentation of Self in Everyday Life*. Doubleday, New York.

Hatch, M.Y. and Yanow, D. (2003). Organization Theory as an Interpretative Science. In Tsoukas, H. and Knudsen, C. (eds) *The Oxford Handbook of Organization Theory*. Oxford University Press, Oxford, 63–87.

Harzing, A.-W. and Pinnington, A. (eds) (2011). *International Human Resource Management*. Sage, London.

Heitmeyer, W. (ed.) (2012). *Deutsche Zustände* [German conditions] Vol. 10. Suhrkamp, Berlin.

Lawler, S. (2008). *Identity: Sociological Perspectives*. Polity, Cambridge.

Ma, Z., Lee, Y. and Yu, K.–H. (2007). 'Ten Years of Conflict Management Studies: Themes, Concepts and Relationships', *International Journal of Conflict Management,* 19(3): 234–48.

Mahadevan, J. (2012a). 'Are Engineers Religious? An Interpretative Approach to Cross-cultural Conflict and Collective Identities', *International Journal of Cross-Cultural Management,* 12(1): 133–49.

Mahadevan, J. (2012b). 'Utilizing Identity-based Resistance for Diversity Change: A Narrative Approach', *Journal of Organizational Change Management,* 25(6): 819–34.

Mahadevan, J. (2013). 'Performing Interplay through Intercultural Simulations: Insights on Tacit Culture in a Taiwanese-German Management Team, *International Journal of Cross-Cultural Management,* 13(3): 243–63.

McKenna, S. and Richardson, J. (2007). 'The Increasing Complexity of the Internationally Mobile Professional: Issues for Research and Practice', *Cross Cultural Management: An International Journal,* 14(4): 307–20.

Parboteeah, K.P., Paik, Y. and Cullen, J. (2009). 'Religious Groups and Work Values – A Focus on Buddhism, Christianity, Hinduism, and Islam', *International Journal of Cross Cultural Management,* 9(1): 51–67.

Prasad, P., Pringle, J.K. and Konrad, A.M. (2006). Examining the Contours of Workplace Diversity: Concepts, Contexts and Challenges. In Konrad, A.M., Prasad, P. and Pringle, J. (eds) *Handbook of Workplace Diversity.* Thousand Oaks, London, 1–22.

Rothman, J. (1997). *Resolving Identity-based Conflict in Nations, Organizations, and Communities.* Jossey–Bass, San Francisco, CA.

Spradley, J. (1979). *The Ethnographic Interview.* Wadsworth, Chicago, IL.

Tajfel, H. and Turner J. (1986). The Social Identity Theory of Intergroup Behaviour. In Worchel, S. and Austin, L.W. (eds) *Psychology of Intergroup Relations.* Nelson-Hall, Chicago, IL, 7–24.

Tylor, E.B. (1920) [1871]. *Primitive Culture, Volume 1* (6th ed.). J.P. Putnam's Sons, New York.

Turner, V. (1986). *The Anthropology of Performance.* PAJ Publications, New York.

Van Maanen, J. (1998). *Qualitative Studies of Organizations.* Sage, London.

Chapter 17

Conclusion:
Religious Stimuli in the Workplace and Individual Performance: The Role of Abstract Mindset

SHIVA TAGHAVI

Introduction

Beliefs and ideologies have always been recognized as possible drivers of individuals' behaviours. Thus, exploring the impact of religion as a potential antecedent of work attitude and behaviour would be beneficial to managers in religiously diverse environments in order to apply the appropriate practices. In this chapter, we will incorporate a social psychological approach in order to probe the effect of religious thoughts on work attitude and behaviour.

People internalize certain types of values based on their religious beliefs. These values when evoked, would impact attitudes and behaviours (Saroglou, 2010; Saroglou et al., 2004). Particularly, prior research has shown that religious values are significantly associated with psychological and behavioural outcomes. For instance, priming religious thoughts and values increases psychological well-being, prosocial behaviour, altruism and self-regulatory behaviour (Laurin et al., 2011; Norenzayan and Shariff, 2008).

It is not very clear yet whether religious beliefs could impact behaviours and attitudes regarding work. Considering the diverse work environment within the multicultural and multinational firms, individuals are encountering various religious cues that could, in turn, prime religious values and beliefs regarding work ethic. Moreover, the underlying mechanism is still elusive. A leading inquiry is to discover the fundamental channels that this process works through.

Thus, this research aims to shed light on the relationship between religious cues at the workplace and the individual's work behaviour. More specifically, it is expected that religious stimuli influence attitude towards work and eventually motivation and performance. Moreover, we will propose the underlying psychological variable that may account for this effect. In this regard, we investigate the effect of activated religious values on the construal-level, namely abstract (versus concrete) mindset. This research suggests that activated values trigger an abstract mindset that in turn results in an enhanced attitude towards work. The level of mental construal in which the concept of work is perceived mediates the link between religious values and work behaviour.

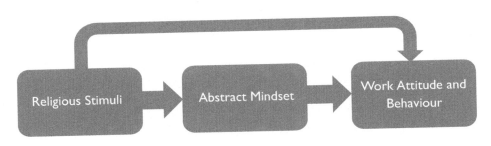

Figure 17.1   Mindset mediates the link between religious stimuli and work attitude and behaviour

Figure 17.1 exhibits the mediating effect of mindset on the relationship between religious stimuli and work attitude and behaviour. We begin with the implicit religious beliefs. It is essential to realize how implicit ideological beliefs could form our attitudes and regulate our behaviour. We argue that these beliefs, when activated, could guide individual's behaviour. Next, we establish the link between religious beliefs and work attitude based on the religious roots of work ethic. Finally, in order to shed light on the underlying mechanism, the role of construal level will be discussed. We argue that religious stimuli could activate abstract mindset in the sense that concepts would be construed in higher and more abstract level. This process ultimately results in perceiving work in more positive way.

Implicit Religious Thoughts and Work Attitude

Recently, research has tried to establish the causal effect of religious beliefs on individual's behaviour in controlled settings. For instance, explicitly and implicitly priming with religious ideas triggered higher levels of public self-awareness and led individuals to respond in a more socially desirable manner (Gervais and Norenzayan, 2011) and remembering God as a punishing agent decreased the cheating behaviour in an anonymous setting (Shariff and Norenzayan, 2011). Many studies exhibit that religious beliefs go beyond the consciously accessible cognitive domain and can act in a more implicit way (Boyer, 2003). Individuals who have been primed with concepts related to God behaved more prosocially by allocating more money to anonymous stranger (Shariff and Norenzayan, 2007). Laurin et al. (2011) argue that because God is considered as an omnipotent, controlling force, and at the same time an omniscient, all-knowing force, priming with God concepts affects self-regulatory behaviour, by increasing self-control and resistance of temptation but decreasing active goal pursuit.

Although many of these studies addressed the effect of reminding people of divine concepts and religious thoughts on prosocial and cooperative behaviour (Atran and Norenzayan, 2004; Norenzayan and Shariff, 2008; Randolph-Seng and Nielsen, 2007; Shariff and Norenzayan, 2007), very few explored the consequences of triggering religious thoughts on individuals' behaviour regarding work and profession. A recent study by Uhlmann et al. (2011) reveals that ideological and religious values can also be activated and operated unconsciously to influence work performance. Priming the divine concepts provides proof that the judgments and behaviours of contemporary Americans are implicitly influenced by traditional Puritan–Protestant values. Americans who were primed with words related to salvation and divinity performed significantly better on the task than Canadians (Uhlmann et al., 2011).

Although American culture has been known as having great respect for religious, and mainly Protestant values, the US is not the only country holding such characteristics. Moreover, even though Protestantism has been cherished as the religion of the greatest work ethic (Weber, 1905), many other ideologies such as Islam and Judaism have highly appreciated the 'hard work' as a core value (Sharabi, 2010). The fact that these ideologies have never been noticed and researched may be due to the political, economic or academic concerns. However, some other religions share the same core values regarding the centrality of work. More specifically, in both Islam and Judaism there is an immerse emphasis on hard work. However, these value systems differ from

Protestantism in taking a more collectivist and family-oriented attitude towards hard work in the form of providing for the family and promoting the society (Sharabi, 2010; Sidani and Thornberry, 2010). Thus, it would be of great value to explore the impact of religious beliefs and spirituality in general, on work attitude, among nations of different religions.

It should be noted that in many societies, practising religion is not part of everyday life however; religious values have been internalized due to tradition, rituals, family-oriented customs, educational systems and media. As a result, individuals in many countries are highly committed to a religious work ethic indicating a set of values associated to work in religious cultures (Ali, 1988; Ali, 1992; Ali and Al-Owaihan, 2008).

The results of studies on Islamic work ethic (Ali, 1988; Ali and Al-Owaihan, 2008; Moayedi, 2010; Yousef, 2000, 2001), for example, reveal that Islamic culture is extremely inspiring for people to be sincere and committed towards work. In another study, Muslim individuals who were subliminally primed with spirituality exhibited more a positive attitude towards work and performed significantly better on a task (Taghavi and Segalla, 2014). The fact that individual differences in the degree of religiosity and religious affiliation did not moderate the link between religious prime and work ethic indicates that religious cues would stimulate implicit religious thoughts and affect attitudes and behaviour.

In this vein, we can deduce that if these implicit values are chronically accessible they can be activated through situational cues to guide individuals' work attitude and performance. Activated religious thoughts lead individuals to connect with the religious values related to work attitude and behaviour. Consequently, we expect a more positive attitude towards work and a higher level of motivation among individuals for whom the religious thoughts have been activated.

SITUATIONAL RELIGIOUS CUES

Research on implicit cognition demonstrates that goals, motives, stereotypes and traits can become implicitly and unconsciously active in the presence of situational cues and eventually can drive behaviour (Bargh and Chartrand, 1999; Bargh et al., 1996; Chartrand and Bargh, 1996). More specifically, goals are associated with their attainment means, namely, environmental features such as settings, individuals and behaviours. Encountering these means will automatically evoke the goal. The strength of the goal–means association depends on the degree to which the means is perceived to facilitate goal pursuit (Shah, 2005). Thus, there will be an automatic association between goals and characteristics of the environment in which they are being frequently pursued. Once the goal is triggered, and during the time it remains active, it drives individual's behaviour like the consciously aroused goal, but without the individual's awareness, and thus unlikely to be controlled (Chartrand and Bargh, 2002).

With regard to this argument, in a series of studies, Bargh and his associates, unobtrusively primed participants with different specific goals such as the goal to remember information and the goal to form an impression of someone (Chartrand and Bargh, 1996), and achievement and cooperation goals (Bargh et al., 2001). Results demonstrate that the participants in the primed condition perform in line with the activated goal even in the absence of a conscious goal. The subconsciously primed goals can also interact with conscious ones and affect the performance.

Studies show that values can also invoke behaviours in the similar manner (Verplanken and Holland, 2002), though the effect was not found very strong and in fact, being moderated by variables such as self-centrality, interactions among social values, reasons supporting the importance of the values, and abstract versus concrete mindset (Darley and Batson, 1973; Maio et al., 2001; Torelli and Kaikati, 2009). Thus, cultural knowledge can be temporally accessible when being activated by the situational cues. However, in order to activate the cultural values, they need to be first, available by being internalized and extensively experienced by the individual. Second, the cultural knowledge elements have to be chronically accessible – widely shared, frequently used and cognitively accessible to members of the group. Finally, the cultural knowledge and values are to be applicable to that very situation (Hong et al., 2007).

Furthermore, research on implicit beliefs reveal that values and belief systems are associated with their environmental features such as settings, individuals and behaviours. Encountering these means will automatically evoke the value system. Thus, there will be an automatic association between value and characteristics of the environment in which they are being frequently pursued. Once the value system is triggered, and during the time it remains salient, it drives individual's behaviour without the individual's awareness, and is thus unlikely to be controlled (Chartrand and Bargh, 2002). Accordingly, one could argue that religious beliefs, when activated, are influential as far as they are in congruence with the environmental and cultural setting. In a comparative setting, Taghavi and Segalla (2014) activated religious thoughts for both Moroccan and French participants and measured their work attitude and behaviour. The results reveal that religious beliefs when activated would positively influence work attitude and behaviour for Moroccans but not for French participants. Thus, religious thoughts, if in line with the cultural setting, could impact work ethic, job involvement and eventually performance and a religiously diverse environment provides different religious cues that could result in stimulating religious beliefs.

In sum, we propose that religious thoughts could be triggered through the religious stimuli in a religiously diverse environment and affect attitudes and behaviours. Specifically, interacting with religious individuals could activate implicit religious thoughts. Religious thoughts, when triggered, would positively impact work attitude and motivation, only if the cultural setting incorporates religious values.

Religious Thoughts and Mental Construal

In the following section we argue that the ideological values derived from religious beliefs are more concerned about the abstract meanings. Moreover, these values are being perceived in a psychologically distant future. Therefore, they will impact work attitude and motivation in a positive way.

CONSTRUAL LEVEL THEORY

According to construal-level theory (Trope and Liberman, 2003), events and objects can be represented at different levels in individual's mind. More distal concepts that are more remote from direct experiences are understood on a higher level and involve more construal. This happens because, normally, we have less knowledge about the more distant future and past, the faraway places and people, and the less imaginable alternatives to reality. This lack of knowledge about the more remote events, places and alternatives results in a more abstract representation of them. More proximal entities, however, involve less construal and are represented in a more concrete way due to the more detailed knowledge in hand and more feasible experimentation.

A high-level construal results in an abstract conceptualization of information about the events and objects. A low-level construal, in contrast, entails creating concrete conceptualizations. Because abstract representations capture and highlight the superordinate central features of the objects and events, high-level construals are more concerned about the general meanings. These representations tend to be simpler, less ambiguous, more coherent and more schematic, because the irrelevant and inconsistent details have been omitted. Low-level construals, however, concentrate on the processes, procedures and exemplars by extracting the subordinate peripheral characteristics of the event or object. Thus, while concrete mindset is looking for the *how*, the abstract mindset seeks the *why*. In this regard, psychological distance is one of the core elements of the theory. The farther the event, the more likely is the perceiver to construe the situation on a high, abstract level (Fujita et al., 2006; Levin-Sagi, 2006; Trope and Liberman, 2003, 2010).

Religious values are very much related to ideological and spiritual beliefs such as salvation and divinity. These values are abstract and decontextualized in nature and 'are represented in memory at the most abstract level of an organized hierarchy' (Bargh and Chartrand, 1999, p. 469). Moreover, concepts such as 'afterlife' and 'heaven' are psychologically distant and remote from the direct everyday life experiences. In a series of four studies, Eyal et al. (2009) found a very strong link between activated values and temporally distant future. In this sense, values are more associated with actions and behaviour in the distant future mainly because they involve more construal and thus, trigger an abstract mindset.

Thus, according to construal-level theory, ideological concepts are construed on a higher level and involve more construals. Religious values essentially focus on the meanings, purposes and higher-level goals. Thus, activated values related to salvation and divinity indirectly portray a psychological distant situation and result in a more abstract conceptualization. Thus, religious thoughts, when triggered, would activate an abstract mindset. This abstract mindset would impact motivation and attitude in several ways.

Research on construal-level theory demonstrates that there is a positive and significant relationship between high-level construal mindset and self-control (Fujita et al., 2006; Haws, 2007; Levin-Sagi, 2006; Schmeichel et al., 2011). In this sense, when there is a conflict between two opposing motivations, for example tendency to take a coffee break every ten minutes and necessity to work hard to prepare the report on-time, it is actually challenging two levels of mental construals. A series of studies by Fujita et al. demonstrate that activating a higher-level construal mindset increases self-control (Fujita et al., 2006). Thus we can expect that religious thoughts, through activating abstract mindset, would increase self-control.

In a similar way religious thoughts that trigger an abstract mindset would increase the desirability of the action. Studies also show that there is an association between arguments in favour and against an action and the construal level. In a series of experiments, Eyal et al. (2004) posit that considerations in favour of an action (pros) are superordinate to considerations against the action. These studies exhibit that individuals in abstract mindset tend to generate more pros than cons for a given action. In another study, Herzog et al. (2007) show that when people perceive the action in the distant future and therefore in a higher construal level, it would be easier for them to generate ideas in favour of the action and more difficult to generate ideas against the action. While the action is being represented on a higher level of mental construal, the individual would automatically give more weight to long-term goals and desirability of the action, and it would be easier for him/her to generate thoughts and arguments in favour of the action.

In general, the abstract mindset boosts the effect of activated value on behaviour (Torelli and Kaikati, 2009). Torelli and Kaikati (2009) triggered the values and the abstract mindset simultaneously and observed an augmentation in value-congruent judgements and behaviours. The abstract mindset improves the effect of activated values on behaviour. We can expect the same effect while the abstract mindset is triggered through religious stimuli. Thus, a higher level of construal boosts the consistency between triggered religious values and work behaviour. In this sense, we expect individuals on a higher level of mental construal to have a more positive work attitude and abstract mindset to increase the effect of religious thoughts on motivation and performance.

In sum, religious stimuli would increase work attitude and motivation through triggering a higher level of mental construal. The abstract mindset increases self-control and desirability of the action and at the same time boosts the value-behaviour congruency.

Conclusion

This chapter seeks to shed light on the effect of activated religious values on work behaviour. Religious values have been recognized to have a solid influence on the members of the societies that embrace and cherish religion and spirituality. In these societies, individuals identify strongly with their religion even though they do not practice regularly.

However, the religious values related to work and business have remained relatively undiscovered. The goal of this research was to explore the consequences of activating the implicit values related to work regarding individuals' work attitude and behaviour. Furthermore, this work examines the cognitive consequences of activating religious beliefs. It demonstrates that religious thoughts are able to trigger higher levels of construal that can lead individuals to process information and make decisions in a more abstract way. According to construal-level theory, the abstract mindset leads individuals to focus more on the superordinate goal and behave in a more self-regulatory manner. Thus, it is proposed that the construal level will mediate the link between activated work values and work behaviour.

The main outcome of this research has both academic and practical implications. It contributes to the literature in work attitude and motivation by establishing the link between religious psychology and work values. From a practical perspective, the results might be extremely constructive in HR practices in religiously diverse environments. It would be important for practitioners to draw on this model to have a better understanding of the psychological impact of religious stimuli on employee's motivation in cultures that embrace religious values.

References

Ali, A. (1988). 'Scaling an Islamic Work Ethic', *The Journal of Social Psychology*, 128(5): 575–83.

Ali, A.J. (1992). 'The Islamic Work Ethic in Arabia', *Journal of Psychology: Interdisciplinary and Applied*, 126(5): 507–19.

Ali, A.J. and Al-Owaihan, A. (2008). 'Islamic Work Ethic: A Critical Review', *Cross Cultural Management: An International Journal*, 15(1): 5–19.

Atran, S. and Norenzayan, A. (2004). 'Religion's Evolutionary Landscape: Counterintuition, Commitment, Compassion, Communion', *Behavioral and Brain Sciences*, 27(6): 713–29.

Bargh, J.A. and Chartrand, T.L. (1999). 'The Unbearable Automaticity of Being', *American Psychologist*, 54(7): 462.

Bargh, J.A., Chen, M. and Burrows, L. (1996). 'Automaticity of Social Behavior: Direct Effects of Trait Construct and Stereotype Activation on Action', *Journal of Personality and Social Psychology*, 71(2): 230.

Bargh, J.A., Gollwitzer, P.M., Lee-Chai, A., Barndollar, K. and Trötschel, R. (2001). 'The Automated Will: Nonconscious Activation and Pursuit of Behavioral Goals', *Journal of Personality and Social Psychology*, 81(6): 1014.

Boyer, P. (2003). 'Religious Thought and Behaviour as By-products of Brain Function', *Trends in Cognitive Sciences*, 7(3): 119–24.

Chartrand, T.L. and Bargh, J.A. (1996). 'Automatic Activation of Impression Formation and Memorization Goals: Nonconscious Goal Priming Reproduces Effects of Explicit Task Instructions. *Journal of Personality and Social Psychology*, 71(3): 464.

Chartrand, T.L. and Bargh, J.A. (2002). Nonconscious Motivations: Their Activation, Operation, and Consequences. In Tesser, Abraham, Stapel, Diederik A. and Wood, Joanne V. (eds) *Self and Motivation: Emerging Psychological Perspectives B2 – Self and Motivation: Emerging Psychological Perspectives*. American Psychological Association, Washington, DC.

Darley, J.M. and Batson, C.D. (1973). 'From Jerusalem to Jericho': A Study of Situational and Dispositional Variables in Helping Behavior', *Journal of Personality and Social Psychology*, 27(1): 100–108.

Eyal, T., Liberman, N., Trope, Y. and Walther, E. (2004). 'The Pros and Cons of Temporally Near and Distant Action', *Journal of Personality and Social Psychology*, 86(6): 781.

Eyal, T., Sagristano, M.D., Trope, Y., Liberman, N. and Chaiken, S. (2009). 'When Values Matter: Expressing Values in Behavioral Intentions for the Near vs. Distant Future', *Journal of Experimental Social Psychology*, 45(1): 35–43.

Fujita, K., Trope, Y., Liberman, N. and Levin-Sagi, M. (2006). 'Construal Levels and Self-control', *Journal of Personality and Social Psychology*, 90(3): 351.

Gervais, W.M. and Norenzayan, A. (2011). 'Like a Camera in the Sky? Thinking about God Increases Public Self-awareness and Socially Desirable Responding', *Journal of Experimental Social Psychology*, 48(1): 298–302.

Haws, K. (2007). 'A Construal Level Theory Approach to Understanding Self-Control Strategies', *Advances in Consumer Research*, 34: 334–5.

Herzog, S.M., Hansen, J. and Wanke, M. (2007). 'Temporal Distance and Ease of Retrieval', *Journal of Experimental Social Psychology*, 43(3): 483–8.

Hong, Y., Wan, C., No, S. and Chiu, C. (2007). 'Multicultural Identities', *Handbook of Cultural Psychology*, 3: 323–45.

Laurin, K., Kay, A.C. and Fitzsimons, G.M. (2011). 'Divergent Effects of Activating Thoughts of God on Self-Regulation', *Journal of Personality and Social Psychology*, 102(1): 4–21.

Levin-Sagi, M. (2006). *Construal Level Theory and a Comprehensive Approach to Self-control.* Tel Aviv University, Tel Aviv.

Maio, G.R., Olson, J.M., Allen, L. and Bernard, M.M. (2001). 'Addressing Discrepancies between Values and Behavior: The Motivating Effect of Reasons* 1,* 2', *Journal of Experimental Social Psychology*, 37(2): 104–17.

Moayedi, N.N. (2010). *Islamic Work Ethic and Muslim Religious Beliefs Impact on Organizational Commitment in the Workplace.* University of Pheonix, Pheonix.

Norenzayan, A. and Shariff, A.F. (2008). 'The Origin and Evolution of Religious Prosociality', *Science*, 322(5898): 58.

Randolph-Seng, B. and Nielsen, M.E. (2007). 'Honesty: One Effect of Primed Religious Representations', *The International Journal for the Psychology of Religion*, 17(4): 303–15.

Saroglou, V. (2010). 'Religiousness as a Cultural Adaptation of Basic Traits: A Five-Factor Model Perspective', *Personality and Social Psychology Review*, 14(1): 108–25.

Saroglou, V., Delpierre, V. and Dernelle, R. (2004). 'Values and Religiosity: A Meta-analysis of Studies using Schwartz, Äôs Model', *Personality and Individual Differences*, 37(4): 721–34.

Schmeichel, B.J., Vohs, K.D. and Duke, S.C. (2011). 'Self-Control at High and Low Levels of Mental Construal', *Social Psychological and Personality Science*, 2(2): 182.

Shah, J.Y. (2005). 'The Automatic Pursuit and Management of Goals', *Current Directions in Psychological Science*, 14(1): 10.

Sharabi, M. (2010). 'Jewish and Arab Academic Graduates in Israel: Ethnicity, Education and Work Values', *International Journal of Intercultural Relations*, 34(1): 66–9.

Shariff, A.F. and Norenzayan, A. (2007). 'God is Watching You', *Psychological Science*, 18(9): 803.

Shariff, A.F. and Norenzayan, A. (2011). 'Mean Gods Make Good People: Different Views of God Predict Cheating Behavior', *The International Journal for the Psychology of Religion*, 21(2): 85–96.

Sidani, Y.M. and Thornberry, J. (2010). 'The Current Arab Work Ethic: Antecedents, Implications, and Potential Remedies', *Journal of Business Ethics*, 91(1): 35–49.

Taghavi, S. and Segalla, M. (2014). When Culture Advocates Spirituality: The Moderating Effect Culture on the Link between Spirituality and Work Ethic, *Working Paper*.

Torelli, C.J. and Kaikati, A.M. (2009). 'Values as Predictors of Judgments and Behaviors: The Role of Abstract and Concrete Mindsets', *Journal of Personality and Social Psychology*, 96(1): 231–47.

Trope, Y. and Liberman, N. (2003). 'Temporal Construal', *Psychological Review*, 110(3): 403.

Trope, Y. and Liberman, N. (2010). 'Construal-level Theory of Psychological Distance', *Psychological Review*, 117(2): 440.

Uhlmann, E.L., Poehlman, T.A, Tannenbaum, D. and Bargh, J.A. (2011). 'Implicit Puritanism in American Moral Cognition', *Journal of Experimental Social Psychology*, 47(2): 312–20.

Verplanken, B. and Holland, R.W. (2002). 'Motivated Decision Making: Effects of Activation and Self-centrality of Values on Choices and Behavior', *Journal of Personality and Social Psychology*, 82(3): 434.

Weber, M. (1905). *The Protestant Ethic and the Spirit of Capitalism*. Scribner's, New York. Originally published in 1958.

Yousef, D.A. (2000). 'The Islamic Work Ethic as a Mediator of the Relationship between Control, Role Conflict and Role Ambiguity – A Study in an Islamic Country Setting', *Journal of Managerial Psychology*, 15(4): 283–98.

Yousef, D.A. (2001). 'Islamic Work Ethic – A Moderator between Organizational Commitment and Job Satisfaction in a Cross-cultural Context', *Personnel Review*, 30(2): 152–69.

Index

Page numbers in **bold** refer to figures and tables.